Weslayen Methodist Missionary Society

The missionary controversy: discussion, evidence and report

Weslayen Methodist Missionary Society
The missionary controversy: discussion, evidence and report
ISBN/EAN: 9783743341999
Manufactured in Europe, USA, Canada, Australia, Japa
Cover: Foto ©ninafisch / pixelio.de

Manufactured and distributed by brebook publishing software (www.brebook.com)

Weslayen Methodist Missionary Society

The missionary controversy: discussion, evidence and report

THE MISSIONARY CONTROVERSY:

DISCUSSION,

EVIDENCE AND REPORT.

1890.

LONDON:
WESLEYAN METHODIST BOOK ROOM,
2, CASTLE STREET, CITY ROAD, E.C.,
AND
66, PATERNOSTER ROW, E.C.

1890.

CONTENTS.

	PAGE
A New Missionary Policy for India	1
Bangalore Report	15
Special Meeting of the Foreign Missionary Committee	39
The Proposed New Missionary Policy	81
Evidence	105
Report of Sub-committee on Indian Missions	237
Appendix A	245
Appendix B	349
Appendix C	351
Appendix D	353
Official Missionary Statistics relating to the American Methodist Episcopal Churches	361
Adjourned Meeting of General Committee	369

A NEW MISSIONARY POLICY FOR INDIA.

I.—Try Democratic Methods.

ON the 27th of May, 1830, Alexander Duff landed in Calcutta. In six short weeks this extraordinary man, then 24 years of age, had completed, to his own satisfaction, his investigations into existing missionary methods, and had concluded, as his biographer states, "that the method of his operations must be different from that of all his predecessors in India." On the 13th of July in the same year his college was opened—an institution which was destined to revolutionise missionary policy in the East, and to inaugurate that development of higher education which is so important a factor in the India of to-day. For half a century the policy of this great Scotsman has received an unquestioning approval from all the leading missionary societies. This policy was to substitute for the existing evangelistic work amongst the lower classes of Indian society an educational work amongst the Brahmins. It was maintained that in this way Hinduism would be attacked at its heart, that when once the influence of Western science and philosophy had been brought to bear upon the philosophy and pseudo-science of Hinduism, the whole system would crumble to the dust; and over and above all else, that as the Brahmins were the recognised leaders of Hindu life, their conversion would be speedily followed by the conversion of the whole nation. In urging the claims of his work upon the people of Scotland, Dr. Duff thus stated his expectations: "We shall, with the blessing of God, devote our time and strength to the preparing of a mine, and the setting of a train which shall one day explode and tear up the whole from its lowest depths."

Instead of the realisation of this vision, we see in India to-day a great effort ending in disastrous failure. Instead of an explosion within the citadel of Brahminism, as the result of missionary work, we witness the walls of that citadel crumbling beneath the influence of the "Zeit Geist," built up again in a new form and with a new strength by the young Brahmins educated in our missionary colleges. As the Madras *Hindu*, as recently as the 25th of last February, said, "The effect of the secular education which we have been receiving has been an attempt to re-model Hinduism on a strong, firm, popular basis, and this result is due, not to the exertions of our old Sastries (for they are to be found nowhere), but to the steady efforts of our young men from schools and colleges."

The missionary policy of the men who preceded Alexander Duff being based on Christ's rule, "To the poor the Gospel is preached," tended to the uplifting of the lower castes, and the creation of a powerful Indian Christian democracy. This policy of educating the Brahmins has enabled a haughty and exclusive caste to substitute an intellectual ascendancy for the spiritual supremacy possessed by their fathers. There is no greater danger to the National Movement in India, than that it should be dominated by a Brahminical caucus, and if that result ever does ensue it will be due to the carrying out of the policy of Alexander Duff.

The majority of Indian missionaries have little idea, the English religious public have no idea, how large a proportion of the missionary funds expended in higher education goes to the education of the Hindu aristocracy. I am indebted for the following important statistics to an admirable article entitled, "Shall we Educate the Brahmins?" by the Rev. F. W. Gostick, in the October number of *The Harvest Field*. Mr. Gostick states that whilst the native Christians constitute $2\frac{1}{4}$ per cent. of the total population of the Madras Presidency, and the Brahmins $3\frac{3}{4}$ per cent., or half as many more, the proportion of Brahmins who are being at present educated in the missionary colleges, is 67 per cent. of the total number of students, whilst the proportion of native Christians who are thus benefiting educationally from the existence of missionary colleges is only 7 per cent. The case is not quite so bad in the secondary schools, but even here there are thirty-seven Brahmins to every ten Christians. But this does not at all cover the whole case as formulated by Mr. Gostick against our present policy. Whilst the Brahmins are only $3\frac{3}{4}$ per cent. of the population, the Vaisyas and Sudras (middle classes) are $59\frac{1}{4}$ per cent., and "other Hindus" (lower classes) are $28\frac{1}{4}$ per cent., yet the missionary colleges only contain twenty-two students of the middle-classes, and six of the lower-classes, to every sixty-seven Brahmin students. The secondary schools contain forty-three students of the middle-classes, and two of the lower-classes, to every thirty-seven Brahmins. Mr. Gostick well observes, "There should surely be some overwhelming reason to account for the fact that missionary societies are spending 37 per cent. of the large sum which they annually spend on secondary education, and 67 per cent. of the amount spent on colleges, on this small class, and also for the fact that so many of the societies' most able men should be given to this work."

But unfortunately the arguments to be deduced from half-a-century's experience afford no such "overwhelming reason" for the present expenditure, but rather tell heavily against it. The record of actual conversions in the high schools and colleges which have been carried on by Dr. Duff and his successors is lamentably brief. A few names such as Ram Chandra Bose, of Lucknow, Kali Churn Bannerjee, of Calcutta, and N. Subramania Iyer, of Madras, stand prominently forward, the more prominently on account of their very rarity. But it may well be doubted whether the Mission high schools and colleges can show an average number of Brahmin conversions of one for each school and college for every five years of their existence. Meanwhile they have been diverting from evangelistic work the energies and talents of at least three-fourths of the ablest men sent out by all the Protestant Missionary societies. It is claimed for them that they have been leavening Indian thought with the ethics of Christanity. In this contention there is no doubt some force, but on the other hand it must be remembered that Christianity has no more pronounced foes in India to-day than many of the Brahmins who are indebted for their education to Christian liberality. The men who are organising Hindu tract societies, and endeavouring in every possible way to promote an anti-Christian renaissance of Hindu thought and feeling, have in numberless instances graduated from the missionary colleges. This very fact enables them to parody and travesty the history and teaching of our Scriptures in a fashion that would have been impossible to them, if young Duff's six weeks' investigations had led him to follow in the track of his predecessors.

It is unnecessary to point out to any who have given even a cursory study to the conditions of Indian life the close parallel which exists between the Pharisees of Judæa and the Brahmins of India. If Christ and His apostles had adopted the policy now pursued by so many Indian missionary societies, they would have attacked Judaism in its citadel by devoting all their energies to the conversion of the Pharisees. But we know that, whilst Christ uttered His scathing rebukes to the Pharisees, the glad tidings were ever proclaimed to the multitudes who "knew not the law" and were "cursed," to the Paraiahs of Palestine. And it is time that the missionary societies of England and America looked this question full in the face, acknowledged the failure of Duff's policy, and declared their determination to return to the simpler and more apostolic methods pursued by the earlier evangelists of India. If one-half of the men and the funds devoted to the education of the Brahmins had been employed in giving the same high education and training to our poor Indian converts, the native Protestant

Church in South India, if not in Bengal and Bombay, would have before now taken the foremost position in the Presidency, and native Christians would have occupied half the positions of honour and emolument. If the other half of the men and the money thus employed had been consecrated to the work of winning the masses of the people, the glorious history of the Tinnevelly Mission would have been repeated over and over again in all parts of India. Great as has been the loss of time and waste of money, it is not too late to remedy largely the errors into which our missionary pioneers have fallen. We are told "*Experientia docet.*" Let our great missionary societies now show that they have learned from the experience of the last fifty years. Let them devote the money now expended in higher education partly to primary schools for the masses of the people and partly to the development of native agencies. Let them send their best men to the work of preaching the Gospel. In a word, let them try democratic methods. The societies which have the courage thus to act will find themselves supported gladly and ungrudgingly by the great Christian democracies of England, Scotland, and America.

II.—The Evils of a False Position.

The direct result of the policy of Dr. Alexander Duff has been that the men engaged in educating and training the aristocracy of India have by a natural sequence of events taken a position in India and Anglo-Indian society far removed from that which would naturally be occupied by the evangelists of the masses. This position and style of living have provoked the vigorous attacks of Canon Taylor and others. Meanwhile the Salvation Army has been developing a work which is rapidly becoming a most powerful standing criticism on all previous methods of evangelisation. Under this fire of criticism the friends of our own society and of all similar Protestant societies, are being compelled to ask themselves the question, "Is the charge of luxury brought against our missionaries justifiable?" Nothing but careful consideration, a thorough knowledge of the facts, and an alternative policy to propose, could justify any one in asserting the truth of this charge. It is no light matter to take the pen in hand on such a question. The task is rendered the more difficult by the fact that any one who really knows the truth on this question must himself have enjoyed the luxury which he undertakes to prove. Nevertheless, the situation is becoming so grave, the necessity for a change in missionary policy *amongst all Protestant societies* so apparent, and the cry for help from heathen lands so loud, that the truth must be spoken at all hazards.

And the truth leaves no choice but to say that the charge of luxury, as our English middle-class people who support the missionary societies understand the word, is fully justified by the facts of the case, alike among Episcopalian, Presbyterian, London Missionary Society, and Methodist missionaries.

Every missionary immediately on landing in India finds himself at once received into "society." In Calcutta he is presented at Court, and makes his bow to the Viceroy. In the other Presidency towns he is always welcome at the public receptions at Government House. I am fully prepared to admit that missionary influence ought to be exerted in official circles. Cases arise from time to time, such, for instance, as that of the girl Luchmin, when it is a matter of the gravest importance that the decision of the Government should not depend solely upon the will of the official clique. In many questions of imperial policy, such as the C. D. Acts, the Abkari system, the Salt Tax, and the Opium question, the voice of the missionaries ought to influence powerfully the decisions of the legislative councils. But I hope to show later on that influence of this kind does not depend upon a certain expensive style of living, but depends solely on the personal character of the missionaries, and the influence they possess with the peoples of India.

It might certainly be desirable, under any circumstances, that the Chairmen of Districts, whose official relations bring them constantly in contact with members of the Government, should maintain their present style of living. But the Wesleyan Society is recognising, what all Protestant societies must soon be compelled to acknowledge, that the *number* of highly paid agents in India must be greatly lessened. Whilst admitting the necessity for the Chairmen to maintain what is practically an episcopal position in a style worthy of the Church to which they belong, I am fully convinced that the regular missionary gains very little, and loses much, by his official recognition in "Society." It places him at once in a wrong position. Most missionaries, the writer included, would have gone down grey-headed to their graves in England without ever seeing a "Drawing-Room." And this new social status entails a number of expenses following in natural sequence. Persons who go to Court must dress in a certain style, cannot go about in the towns in any less fashionable vehicle than a phæton, and must keep up a certain establishment. The result is, that men who left the London docks with the simplest ideas of life and duty, full of lofty purposes of self-denial and devotion, have scarcely trodden Indian soil a twelvemonth before they find themselves settled down to a mode and fashion of living from which a year ago they would have shrunk back in dismay.

This is no over-statement of facts. The missionary in India with £300 a-year and his bungalow—and this may be taken as a fair average of all the societies—is able, with ease and comfort, to mix in Anglo-Indian society in a style which he could not possibly do on less than £1,000 a-year in England. Any one who has tried to live in London, keeping a one-horse brougham, mixing in society, dining late, and everything else in harmony with these features, will know that this estimate is not very wide of the mark. But this does not by any means state the whole case. Viewed from the native standpoint, his social position is yet more "magnificent." The day labourer in India gets as wage from two annas to four annas (2d. to 4d.) a day. The English artisan gets as many shillings. It is therefore plain that the relation of the missionary's income to that of the masses whom he is sent out to evangelise is in the same ratio as that of an Anglican bishop to the day-labourers in his diocese. The missionary's income, at the present rate of exchange, is about 72,000 annas. The bishop's is about 80,000 shillings. Each, in fact, receives annually about 20,000 to 25,000 days' wages of the people over whom he is appointed overseer. Bishops may have their sphere, but no one would dream of attempting the evangelisation of England by bishops only. Is the evangelisation of India much more likely to be successful on the same lines? The answer is emphatically, No! The effect of this mode of living is inevitably to separate the missionary from the people, instead of bringing them into close contact with them. It is almost impossible for any man to occupy for years the position of a feudal lord without developing the feudal spirit. Men do successfully fight against it here and there, but it is not in human nature generally to wield almost absolute power, and receive abject reverence, without losing sight, more or less, of the great Christian principle of the brotherhood of all men.

The responsibility for the existing state of affairs does not rest upon the present generation of missionaries at all. It is well open to doubt whether there is a man now in the Indian mission field in any of the great missionary societies, who considered when he first offered his services to the Missionary Committee how much his pay would be, or how many or how few would be the comforts of his home life. Nine out of every ten missionaries in India landed on the "coral strand" without the vaguest conception that anything approaching luxury would ever be within their grasp so long as they remained in the mission field. And to-day there are many men at work in India, as the writer can testify from personal knowledge, who would welcome gladly and heartily a general and sweeping reduction in missionary stipends, which would compel a change in the style of living all round. In proof of this assertion it is only necessary to point out, with regard to South India alone, that during the last few months the Wesleyan missionaries in the Mysore District have voluntarily handed back to the Missionary Society a considerable percentage of their salary; the Madras missionaries offered a few weeks since to pay the salary of one of their number out of their own pockets if he could stay in India; and from the Negapatam and Trichinopoly Districts a letter has just come in which a missionary there offers to board and lodge any volunteer from England who will go out to help in the educational work of that district.

These facts show plainly that our own missionaries do not lack the spirit of self-sacrifice, but we have put them in a position where they have little opportunity of practising it. Compelled by the customs of the social world in which they move to live in a certain style, their usefulness is crippled, their influence is lessened, and the societies are financially embarrassed. The world of subscribers at home asks for stories of heroism and self-denial. These qualities are plentiful enough in our mission field to-day, but there is little room for their display under such circumstances as are described above. Between this extreme, on the one hand, and the Salvationist extreme, on the other hand, there is an untrodden "Via Media" which seems to be a more excellent way. What that pathway is, and the arguments in its favour must hold over till next week.

III.—The Untrodden "Via Media."

The able article on "Missions," by Sir W. G. Hunter, followed by the attack of Canon Taylor, and the still later letters of Mr. Caine, have directed English attention to a method, the absolute antithesis of that which we considered last week. Before proceeding to argue in favour of any middle course, it may be well to point out several strong objections to the ascetic method which has found so much favour with the critics just named. In the first place it has never been shown that asceticism as practised by European Christians does appeal specially to Hindus. Mr. Bowen, who in his later years was identified with the mission of the American Methodist Episcopal Church, lived for many years on a bare pittance in the native quarters of Bombay. As a devoted missionary he has never been surpassed, and missionaries everywhere have expressed their admiration of his zeal; but it is a striking fact that he did not succeed in making converts. Father O'Neill, in another part of India, submitted himself with heroism to self-denial and hardships, such as few Europeans would be physically equal to, but he scarcely baptised a single person. The Oxford missionaries in Calcutta are stated to have gained a position of considerable influence amongst educated natives, but they have as yet been very unsuccessful in the direct work of conversion. The Salvation Army, as the authorities themselves say in their Annual Report, is still on its trial in India. They have already had to record a terrible expenditure of life and health, and have been compelled, by the exigencies of the case, to modify their methods in many important respects. During the last twelve months they have abandoned vegetarianism, and have allowed their officers the use of sandals. With such changes as these taking place, the whole movement can only be regarded at present as tentative. The truth is that the Hindu Fakir can always beat the Christian pseudo-Fakir on his own ground. Christianity is not an ascetic religion. Hinduism, in some of its phases, is essentially so. Unnatural asceticism is anti-Christian, and these attempts have so far proved that Christianity cannot be propagated by non-Christian methods.

What, then, is the untrodden " Via Media "? In the India of to-day there are three totally distinct modes of living—the Anglo-Indian, the Eurasian, and the Native. The first of these is that adopted by the civilian and military classes and by the missionaries of the great Protestant missionary societies. The second is that adopted by the large town population of mixed descent and by the Roman Catholic priesthood. The third is that of the great mass of the people, which the Salvation Army has tried to adopt with such disastrous results. Last week I endeavoured to show that great evils arose from the adoption of the first by our missionaries. I now ask all true friends of missions, including the missionaries themselves, whether the time has not come when all those missionary societies who disbelieve in the principle of enforced celibacy should, for the first time, and unanimously, adopt the second of these styles of living. It would mean a considerable sacrifice for all concerned. It would involve the reduction of stipends from £300 to £150 per annum for married missionaries, and a corresponding reduction for single men. Instead of having, as now, butler and cook, the Eurasian plan of having one servant in the dual capacity would have to be adopted. Corresponding changes would have to be made in the rest of the staff of servants. The missionary bungalows would necessarily be houses of half the rental which is now paid. In Calcutta, where rentals vary from £150 to £200 a year, this would be a very important relief to the funds. In Madras, where rentals are scarcely half this rate, the reduction would, nevertheless, be a great gain. If once the majority of our missionaries resolutely adopted a style of living of this character, many expenses of all kinds which are necessary to maintain their present social position would speedily disappear.

If any such change as is here proposed should come within the range of practical missionary politics, it would be necessary at once to insist that such a change of life should be compulsory on no single missionary who has entered the work under the old *régime*. Due and tender regard should be had for the exceptional and temporary cases of the men now in the field, who have formed associations and made friendships which ought not to be ruthlessly imperilled or destroyed by any violent change. If any of the present staff voluntarily offered to the parent society with which they were identified to thus enter the "Via Media," the balance of their salary should be regarded as a subscription freely given and gratefully received.

The suggestion now made is that the men who are at present in missionary colleges, and those who may enter them in the future, shall be definitely informed, when they are accepted as missionary candidates for India, that they will be expected to live on the lines laid down above. I am fully convinced that there is not one man in a hundred of those who offer for mission work who would hesitate for one moment, if at the outset of his missionary career he were asked to enter the work on these conditions.

If any of the great societies should ultimately decide to adopt the policy here suggested, there are three items of expenditure which ought on no account to be reduced, but should rather be increased. The allowances for children in England ought to be on the most liberal scale. If missionaries are to spend their lives for India they have every right to demand that the Church at home shall see to it that their children are not handicapped in the race of life as compared with the children of ministers in English work. It is hard enough for parents to be separated from their children. The Church has a sacred duty to perform in this matter, and must do it ungrudingly. It is no part of the policy of the "Via Media" to let the children of the missionary suffer. Nor must there be any reduction in the allowances for sickness. Everything must be done that can be done to keep our workers in good health, and when their health fails the Church must take care of them. The present sanatoria on the hills must also be maintained unsparingly. On these three lines of expenditure there must be no attempt at saving.

It may possibly be argued that health will suffer seriously from such a change in the mode of living. There will always be a percentage of any given number of Europeans who will find themselves unable to bear the Indian climate. But it would be exceedingly difficult to prove that the health of non-commissioned officers in the Army, foremen in mills and places of business, and other Europeans who live in India on an income of £100 to £200 per annum, is worse in any way than that of civilians and commissioned officers in the army.

The advantages of the style of living which I have ventured to call the "Via Media" over ascetic methods, which have found so much favour of late, are manifold. There are very important advantages in the existence of one happy Christian *home* in a purely heathen Indian town. It is an object lesson of the blessings of Christianity which has more weight than hundreds of sermons. Many educated Hindus to-day watch with a scarcely-to-be-regretted envy the fellowship and sympathy which unite the English missionary and his wife. The missionary home is a powerful influence for the amelioration of the lot of Indian women and the regeneration of Indian society. On the lines of the Salvation Army this phase of missionary influence vanishes. This is only one of many advantages which the "Via Media" has over the methods of the ascetic school.

The gain which would result to the missionary societies from the substitution of this for their present policy would obviously be great. The immense distance which now separates the English padre from his Indian flock would be at least diminished by one-half. His own people would realise, what a great many of them certainly do not believe to-day, that his presence amongst them was due to love for them, and not to a desire to earn a livelihood. The manifest self-sacrifice and devotion involved in such a life would react upon the whole native Church. The mercenary spirit which now, alas! animates too many of our native ministers and catechists would be rebuked in the daily life of the missionary, and the whole tone of affairs within the Church would be purified and elevated. And how great would be the gain in the work amongst the heathen around! No longer would they regard the missionary, as they often do to-day, as only one member of the same family of which other members were the collectors, the engineers, the officers of the Army, and the heads of the Salt and Abkari departments. They would realise vividly that these men had come to India for love of Christ and for love of them, and such a conviction would mightily help in the work of winning India to Christ.

It is scarcely necessary to point out that the economies involved would enable the societies almost to double the number of their workers in every direction. Men whose hearts have been changed by the love of Christ would respond to the call for missionary workers the more readily because of the appeal to their self-sacrifice. The Churches, knowing that every penny contributed was spent with the truest economy, would fill the missionary treasury with their gifts and offerings. The word "Retrenchment" would disappear from the missionary vocabulary. The work now being carried on would be strengthened everywhere, and the number of workers greatly increased. The spirit of self-sacrifice would spread from the missionaries to their converts, and the whole Church of Christ in India would become what it ought everywhere to be, a great missionary army.

IV.—The Secret of Missionary Finance.

The committees of all the principal missionary societies in Great Britain are looking forward to their next subscription list with many anxious forebodings. They naturally fear lest the strong fire of criticism which they have had to pass through will thin the ranks of their supporters. Those societies will suffer most by the present trying ordeal who have kept their subscribers worst informed as to the nature of their operations and the success which has attended their efforts. No articles in *The Fortnightly Review* or letters from India to the Provincial Press would ever seriously affect the support given either to the China Inland Mission or to the Salvation Army. The reason why these two organisations are so completely fortified against criticism is that Mr. Hudson Taylor, on behalf of the one, and General Booth, on behalf of the other, have spared no pains or energy to record vividly the "Progress of the War" in India and China. The result is that the readers of *China's Millions* and of *All the World* give, "not grudgingly or of necessity," but intelligently and cheerfully. It is, perhaps, as well that those societies which have devoted their best men and large sums of money to the propping up of an effete and decaying aristocracy should have published the record of their work in pamphlets foredoomed to be destroyed unread There are obvious reasons why missionary organisations which employ large numbers of Brahmins still idolaters, still wearing idol marks upon their foreheads, to teach our sacred Scriptures to other Brahmins seeking education at our hands, but hating us in their hearts, should certainly not endeavour to issue popular and complete accounts of their work in foreign fields. But the missionary society which will adopt a policy commanding the approval of the masses of the English people, which will cease to buttress a caste ascendency condemned by the spirit of the age, as well as by the New Testament, which will devote itself to the education of its own converts and of the masses, and the evangelisation of the entire nation, and which will place its missionaries in a social position in harmony with such work, may boldly court the completest publicity in the full assurance that the more widely its work is known the longer will its subscription list become.

When once such a programme has been adopted in India no pains should be spared to familiarise the English public with the leading features of the policy and the manner in which it is being carried out. With the two exceptions already named, there is no Protestant missionary society the record of whose work is written *for the people.* The annual reports are generally ponderous volumes, got up in the most unattractive style, and full of details equally uninstructive and uninteresting. Mr. Hudson Taylor in his annual volume has shown that this can be remedied. The monthly magazine is too often manifestly a "scissors and paste" production. It ought to contain well-written articles discussing the great questions of missionary policy, and relating in a style worthy of the great missionary enterprise the current history of missionary work the world over. The *Harvest Field*, published by the Wesleyan missionaries in the Mysore District, shows what may be done to make monthly missionary literature interesting. If this can be done in one Indian district, what might not be done by an able and energetic editor in touch with work all over the world!

But the missionary society which really seeks to enlist the sympathies of the English people in the evangelisation of India ought not to stop at annual and monthly literature. There is ample room in England for a halfpenny missionary weekly, illustrated in a popular fashion, and recording the work from week to week with a freshness and accuracy emulating that with which the secular Press would record the progress of a great European war. The spiritual struggle in which Christianity is now engaged in the East, in its endeavour to overthrow Brahminism, Buddhism, and Confucianism, concerns the future of the whole human family infinitely more than the question whether General Boulanger shall sound "*La revanche*," and succeed in again wresting the provinces of the Rhine from the Empire of Germany. Yet the triumph of Boulangism, and the declaration of a war of revenge between these two nations, would send up the circulation of the great English dailies by some hundreds of thousands. The lesson of all this to the managing bodies of our missionary societies is that they have only to publish a vivid and faithful account of the great war of the creeds which is now being waged *à l'outrance* through the confines of Asia and Africa to obtain a wide circulation for a missionary weekly, and to rouse and maintain an interest in missionary endeavours which will secure them a strong and abiding support for the most vigorous policy that they may undertake to initiate.

But the very extent and duration of the war renders it necessary that some further means should be devised to keep constantly before its supporters at home the nature of the conflict and the needs of those who are carrying it on. In order that this may be done the interest must be localised. It is practically impossible for those whose life's work is not in some direct way connected with Foreign Missions to succeed in maintaining a deep interest in every branch of missionary work. The time has now arrived when the leading missionary societies should endeavour to allocate to certain districts in Great Britain the support of the missions in certain specified provinces in the mission field. The Wesleyan system of districts at home and abroad and the Anglican system of dioceses specially lend themselves to such an arrangement. The same object might be attained by the Presbyterian and Congregational societies by grouping together a number of churches at home and a number of missions abroad. If the division into districts proved the success which many supporters of missions believe it would, the policy might be further extended by making individual churches or circuits responsible for the support of individual mission stations. The Church Missionary Society has to some extent adopted this policy with the most admirable results. There are financial difficulties superficially apparent in such arrangement, but able and statesmanlike authorities in the mission-field have considered these difficulties, and have declared that they could be easily obviated.

It is almost unnecessary to point out the many and great advantages which would follow the adoption of such a policy as this. No longer would missionary deputations be content to make the work done in the South Seas fifty years since the one burden of their song, but they would be compelled by the expectations of the people and the necessities of the case thoroughly to study the work of God in at least one of our foreign districts, and to give a clear and instructive account of the progress of the work supported by the district to which they had been sent as deputation. The ministers of the home circuits would be brought into real touch and living sympathy with their brethren abroad. The monthly missionary prayer-meetings might be made the occasion for reading letters from the missionaries supported by the district. Above all else, the people would no longer subscribe their guineas annually to a great fund, the destination of which they but dimly comprehended, but would cheerfully contribute to the utmost of their power to help in a conflict of which they clearly understood the issues.

Such, in brief outline, is the home policy which would accord with, and secure support for, the foreign policy advocated in the preceding papers. It is only an outline, and is, therefore, capable of great modifications. Success may possibly be achieved by other methods. But those who have studied carefully and conscientiously the history of the youngest and most successful missionary societies of to-day must be convinced that such a home policy as is here advocated would win hearty support. The time has come when the people must be fully trusted alike with the history of our failures and the history of our successes. Happy will be that Church and prosperous will be that missionary society whose leaders will thus devote all their energies to gain the sympathy and confidence of the great masses of the Christian public.

BANGALORE REPORT.

ON the second day of the Conference, after considerable discussion, the following resolution was unanimously agreed to :—

That a Committee consisting of Messrs. Brown, Cobban, Cooling, Fentiman, Findlay, Haigh, Hocken, Little, Patterson, and Sawday, with Mr. Findlay, Convener, be appointed to prepare a statement dealing in detail with the charges preferred against Indian missionaries by the *Methodist Times* for communication to the Home Committee, and that the question whether we should request the Home Committee to appoint a Commission to investigate the evidence on which those charges are made be left over until the report of this Committee is received.

When on the fourth day of the Conference the Committee presented the Statement it had drawn up, the Conference unanimously agreed :—

(1) That the Statement now read be adopted by the Conference as expressing its mind on the subject.

(2) That the Committee be directed to add a paragraph to the Statement requesting the Home Committee to appoint a Commission to investigate the evidence on which the allegations objected to were made. At a later stage this additional paragraph was brought up and adopted by the Conference.

The following is the Statement :—

As this Conference affords the first opportunity which we, your Indian missionaries, have had of unitedly offering our opinion in regard to certain statements affecting our life and work made in the *Methodist Times* during the last six months, we desire to declare to you our unanimous and absolute repudiation of the description of us which those statements present, and our sense of the irreparable injury to our work which they have occasioned. The action of the British Conference in relation to them, and many private expressions of sympathy, assure us that we have not lost the confidence of our brethren in the ministry and of many among the laymen of our Church. It is impossible to doubt, however, that widespread distrust of us has been engendered and we feel that this distrust would be confirmed, and that we should deserve to incur the suspicion even of our friends, if we did not seize the first opportunity to deny statements which attribute to us a spirit and manner of life which we consider unworthy of missionaries of the Gospel, and to point out the gross misinformation and misconception on which those statements are based. The assertions to which we refer are contained in Articles II. and III. on "A New Missionary Policy for India," found in the issues of the *Methodist Times* of April 11th and 18th respectively; in several later references in that journal to the same subject, chiefly under the head of "Notes on Current Events," and in a speech made before the British Conference in its Pastoral Session by Dr. Lunn as reported in the *Methodist Times* and the *Methodist Recorder*. The description of Indian Missionary Life presented in these utterances is complete, consistent and graphic. The language used is so clear, precise and reiterated that we are shut up to one interpretation of it; and the alteration or withdrawal of particular words and phrases would not affect the definite and detailed presentation of us which the whole series of statements affords. Your missionaries are declared to fall within the scope of the delineation, and the fact that the author of it appeals to his own experience, which he gained in our circle, together with the fact that his assertions were published in a Methodist journal, forbids us to regard ourselves as unaffected by them. The writer acquits those whom he professes to describe of all moral blame in leading the life which he attributes to them, and we heartily acknowledge his innocence of all intention to impeach our character. We cannot for a moment, however, accept his moral estimate, and should regard missionaries such as he describes as base in the extreme, unfaithful to their calling and unworthy of the confidence of the Church that had sent them forth. We cannot therefore be content to allow the public either at home or in India to believe the truth of what we regard as a most damaging caricature of our life and spirits.

We declare with a good conscience before God and the Methodist Church that the description of Indian missionaries presented in those statements is wholly and radically false, whether of your missionaries generally or of any among them in particular; while the impression which such a description must inevitably make upon a public ignorant of India is even more utterly contrary to truth than that which we ourselves derive from it. We profess that our life and spirit are not only not such as are here portrayed, but do not even give colour or excuse to such a description of them. We make bold to maintain that, however many shortcomings there may be in our service to God and His Church, the most searching scrutiny would acquit us of these forms of imperfection.

We desire, in addition to this general repudiation, to exhibit in detail the errors contained in the statements under consideration. But we would point out first that, while a large number of passages professing to be statements of fact, are either untrue or grossly misleading, much of the misrepresentation is effected by the arrangement and connection of the statements, by the suggestions they contain and the impressions they create, by the omission of a multitude of facts which would have tended to correct them, and by the completeness of the delineation which they present when taken as a whole.

The chief charges that have been made against us are the following. We enumerate them that we may briefly indicate our attitude regarding each of them :—

I. We are accused of luxury. " The charge of luxury as our " English middle class people who support the Missionary " societies understand the word, is fully justified by the facts " of the case alike among . . . and Methodist missionaries." We affect, it is represented, a style and magnificence of life unbecoming to missionaries of the Cross and injurious to our work. The truth of this charge we indignantly deny both for ourselves and for all other missionaries with whom we are acquainted.

(A) In regard to our stipends, we are described as "Mission- " aries with £300 a year and a bungalow" (Article II.) ; it is said that "the worst paid missionaries in India are better paid than our Missionary Secretaries or best paid ministers at home" (Notes on Current Events, May 21st) ; and we are told of " Non-commissioned officers in the army, foremen in mills and places of business, and other Europeans who live in India on an income of £100 to £200 per annum " (Article III.). We need not point out to you the inexcusable confusion which is here made between the personal income of your missionaries and the total outlay required of the Society on their account ; but it is our place to inform you that such classes as foremen, &c., living on £100 to £200 per annum are a figment of the writer's imagination, and that, as a rule even artizans and engine-drivers coming to this country from England receive larger stipends than missionaries of the Gospel. We append to our minutes a financial statement carefully based on the prolonged experience of brethren from all the fields of our Indian work, which will enable you to

B

realize the necessities of our expenditure and to compare our position with that of our brethren in the home work.

(B) Criticising our circumstances in detail, Dr. Lunn specifies the following points in support of his charge of luxury :—

1. The houses in which we live are too large and costly. He refers especially to Calcutta and Madras and thinks that half the rent now paid might be saved. We entirely disagree with him. There would be no worse economy in our opinion than a reduction under this head. Airy rooms are an absolute necessity in a tropical climate ; and in number of rooms many of our houses are inconveniently small. It will be sufficient under this head if we remind you that the houses rented for missionaries are in all respects similar to those occupied by English bank clerks or mercantile assistants, who come to live in this country. In very few instances, moreover, is any rent at all paid on account of houses for us. Nearly all our missionaries live on mission premises, and in most cases these premises have by wise management been acquired at a cost nearly, if not quite, corresponding to such a rental as Dr. Lunn declares to be adequate.

2. The conveyances which we use are said to be too pretentious. A missionary, we are told, "cannot go about in any "any less fashionable vehicle than a phaeton." In his Conference speech, Dr. Lunn stated by implication that the ordinary conveyance of the missionary is superior to that commonly used by native judges or barristers. This is untrue, and all references made to this subject are misleading. The conveyances used by missionaries are everywhere modest and unpretentious. It is universally agreed that in a tropical climate a conveyance of some sort is necessary. Their employment is justified, and their style is regulated, not as Dr. Lunn's references to them imply, by considerations of social status, but solely with a view to the needs of our work. Public conveyances, other than hired vehicles, are absolutely non-existent, except in Calcutta and Bombay, and where our stations happen to lie on railway routes ; and it would be absolutely impossible for us to do our work without the vehicles that you have always permitted us to possess. They need no other defence than that which justifies the use of a circuit conveyance in England. And when we say that the sum granted for purchase of horse and carriage is only Rs. 300 (that is, at present rates, about £21) it will be seen that the most rigid economy is practised in regard to them.

3. We are told that the missionary landing in India finds himself posessed of a "new social status" entailing expenses of various

sorts in dress and what not. He is "received into society," and moves in a circle that in England he could not aspire to. We know nothing of all this and are compelled to denounce it as totally misleading. If missionaries entered into far more intimate association with the European residents in this country than they do, we should not consider it an evil; but the fact is, that such social intercourse as they do enjoy with Europeans outside the mission circle (and on many stations the absence of Christian Europeans makes such intercourse entirely impossible) is both more limited in its extent and more modest in its nature than that which falls to the lot of a minister in a town circuit at home. It is worth while pointing out in this connection that when Dr. Miller, in his recent article in the *Contemporary Review*, found fault with the tone of Anglo-Indian society, the response of the leading Madras newspaper was—Dr. Miller knows nothing of Indian society, he is not "in" it. And yet Dr. Miller is far more "in it" than the majority of missionaries.

We need not specify further particulars or enter at greater length into this distasteful subject. Let it suffice to say that we are unanimously of opinion that the life of every missionary is modest and simple, and that whatever may be our defects and shortcomings, in this respect at least we neither bring discredit on our profession nor impede the progress of the Gospel.

II. But no less serious and dishonouring to us is the further statement, which the assertions traversed above are used to support, that our style of life expresses and nourishes a spirit of alienation from the native population inimical to success in our work. In the nature of the case the only reply which such a statement admits of, is the emphatic and indignant contradiction which each man's consciousness of integrity enables him to give for himself. We know of no such alienation in sympathy from the native population as Dr. Lunn professes to have discovered, and watching over each other as we do with constant jealousy, we should have been quick to detect and condemn it. On behalf of ourselves and all our brethren, we repudiate the charge with indignation and abhorrence. We know of no missionary who does not sympathise more deeply with the lowest and most degraded of the people, than with those castes which Dr. Lunn speaks of as an "aristocracy." Their condition invites, and our convictions compel, our sympathy. Everywhere throughout our mission the right-hand of loving fellowship is held out equally to high and low, nor do we believe that, apart from those whose minds have been poisoned by the recent controversy, there is among the native population any doubt of our sympathy. We have seen no signs of any such doubt, nor are we aware that anyone else has.

In addition to our denial of the truth of the description of us presented in the *Methodist Times*, we feel it due to ourselves and to you that we should express our sense of the extreme gravity of the present situation created by its utterances both at home and abroad. A spirit of mistrust has been engendered amongst the supporters of missions which it will probably take years to allay. Of the popular feeling in England you will be better able to judge than we are, but it is manifest that there is on all hands a feeling of discontent and unrest. It is felt that statements have been made utterly destructive of the credit of missionaries and of their claim to sympathy and support; that these statements have been made by men of influence and authority, and have not yet been fully met and answered. It is felt, moreover, and properly felt, that if these statements are true then the present race of missionaries are unworthy of the support and confidence of the Church, and reforms amounting to the entire abolition of the present state of things are absolutely necessary. With this feeling we entirely sympathise; for we do not believe that any pure Church could accept Dr. Lunn's account of missionary life as true and at the same time refuse to face the necessity of an absolute revolution in its missionary methods and organization. No true missionary enthusiasm is possible unless the Church is assured of the devotion and purity of motive of its agents; and therefore, wherever the recent allegations are believed, the cause of missions must decline. If this is not already the case, it is because the public at home know that missionaries have not yet been heard in their own defence, and judgment is suspended until they have had a fair and impartial hearing. If we were now to remain silent judgment would inevitably go against us by default.

But serious as are the consequences of the controversy at home the effects which have been produced in India, and which are known only to us, are simply incalculable. We have here a strong and growing antagonism to everything English, and still more to everything Christian. Missions have always had to cope with determined and vigorous opposition, and that opposition is becoming stronger as the influence of missions is spreading. Young India is rousing itself to a vigorous defence of what it euphemistically calls the Aryan religion, and anything that will serve to discredit Christian missionaries is seized with avidity. The most objectionable portions of the articles published in the *Methodist Times* have been reproduced in the native newspapers and hailed with delight. And little wonder. "Here are missionaries," it is said, "exposed at last by one of themselves, their character and motives unveiled, their hypocrisy discovered, and their work set before the world in its true character. They have fattened on deceit, but at last their fraud is detected and the widows and orphans whose donations support them have discovered how vilely the fruits of their self-denial are prostituted to low and selfish ends. The support will soon cease, and missionaries will be withdrawn." We are guilty of no exaggeration in thus representing the tone of a large section of the vernacular press of India. There are Hindu papers it is true that rise to a higher conception of missionary motive and endeavour, but these are comparatively few ; and those that take the position we have enunciated influence the great bulk of the people among whom we work. As a specimen of the taunts to which we are now exposed we may mention that recently at the prize-giving of a native high school on one of our stations, with the editor of the *Hindu* in the chair, a dialogue called "The Missionary" was recited by two of the boys, and the staple of the dialogue was provided by Dr. Lunn's articles amplified and exaggerated.

Nor is the pernicious influence of the statements we are considering confined to the Hindu population. The Christian population, both native and European is, also affected. Those among the latter who had never much sympathy with mission work have now an excellent excuse for neglect or for contempt. Subscriptions to our funds and other marks of interest have in some places been withdrawn, and on many hands missions and missionaries are now completely discredited. The effect produced in some places upon the native Christians has been even more calamitous. Confidence in the unselfish devotion and purity of purpose of those who are their spiritual fathers and guides is rudely shaken, and the conviction is widely gaining ground amongst them that missionaries have become such because they can thus gain a more decent and comfortable living than they could get at home. It needs no argument to show that such a state of things is unendurable, and that unless it can be remedied missionaries everywhere will be robbed of their influence and their power for good. That influence depends very largely upon their credit for unselfishness and singleness of aim. However earnest and impassioned their appeals may be, if they are believed to be prompted by no higher motive than a desire for a comfortable living they will fall on deaf ears. Hitherto missionaries have been credited with higher motives and have had all the influence that such credit gives, but the recent discussions and so-called disclosures have done much everywhere to rob them of it.

The facts that we have here laid before the Committee afford, we believe, ample justification for the conviction which we strongly and unanimously hold, that the situation cannot be allowed to remain as it is, but that steps must yet be taken to remedy the evil that has been wrought. We have declared our repudiation of the charges and we trust you will make this declaration public. But we are painfully conscious that among those who regard us as placed on our trial by the assertions of the *Methodist Times*, our declaration will amount to little more than a vigorous plea of not guilty, and will lose even this value if it is not followed by some independent and decisive vindication of us. You have published your own judgment that we do not deserve the aspersions cast on us; but it is obvious that the General Committee of the Society so completely shares with us the responsibility for the present mode of missionary life and work that to those in whom distrust has been engendered its statements will be regarded as *ex parte* equally with ours.

The British Conference gave prolonged attention to some aspects of the controversy; and we are grateful for the unshaken confidence in us indicated in the tenor of its debates and declared in its resolutions. Amid widespread obloquy it is a strength and comfort to us to be assured that our brethren of the British Conference, ministerial and lay, needed no vindication of us from charges such as these, and were able without investigation to affirm their unabated trust in our integrity and zeal. We cannot feel however, nor do we think that the Conference itself considered, that its resolutions effected all that is necessary to be done towards redressing the injury which the work of God in this land and the interests of the Society generally have suffered. We hold this conviction on the following grounds :—

1. The form which the question assumed before the Conference was mainly as to the culpability or innocence of the authors of the statements alleged against us. On that question it reached a conclusion which we heartily accept : and in addition to this, it declared its own confidence in us. But it did not conduct or initiate an investigation into statements and the evidence on which they are declared to rest, such as could alone be satisfactory to those who had yielded to suspicions of us. The demand for formal investigation is one that would naturally and appropriately come from us, and we have had no opportunity before the present one of unitedly making such a demand.

2. General feeling in England, as indicated by the whole tone of the religious press, and universal opinion in this

country, as proved in our daily painful conduct with it, indicates a sense that no satisfactory issue has yet been reached, and that the grave aspersions cast upon missionary integrity and devotion have neither been rebutted nor withdrawn. It is universally felt that some further vindication of us is needed than judgments pronounced by a Committee implicated in the charge equally with ourselves, or expressions of confidence by a Conference antecedently attached to us by close ties of sympathy and trust. And indeed looking at the situation in its simplest issues, it appears to us obvious that when descriptions of us gravely damaging to our reputation and work have obtained wide currency and belief, nothing less than an independent and authoritative vindication, founded upon enquiry, can be expected to satisfy either us or those who have been led to entertain suspicions of us.

3. The declaration made to Conference by the authors of the statements, and accepted as the basis of its resolutions, expressed only the intentions of Messrs. Hughes and Lunn in writing the articles, and *their* judgment as to the bearing of the articles upon our reputation. It did not to any appreciable extent relieve us of the imputations which the *Methodist Times* appeared to us to contain; and indeed, since making the "declaration" the authors of it have reaffirmed as strongly as possible the correctness of their delineation of us. In his speech before Conference, made later than this "declaration," Dr. Lunn used expressions stronger and more damaging than those for the use of which he had expressed regret; and the *Methodist Times* published his speech under the heading "Dr. Lunn maintains his ground." This we submit took away all value from the admissions which he and Mr. Hughes had made, and rendered their "declaration" absolutely nugatory, except in its bearing on their own motives and sentiments. Moreover Mr. Hughes maintained at Conference that he had in reserve a body of evidence which would amply confirm his description of us. This profession of reserved evidence leaves us under a weight of undefined imputation upon which Conference has had no opportunity of pronouncing its judgment.

These considerations convince us that the action of the British Conference in the nature of the case could not be, was never intended to be, and has not generally been regarded as being a final and conclusive vindication of us. That vindication we, assembled here in Conference from all our Indian districts, now respectfully but imperatively claim.

Jealous maintenance of our honour we regard as a

sacred part of the duty laid upon us, equally vital to the support of the Society at home and the prosecution of its work in India. In presence of statements so destructive to our reputation and to the whole interests of the Society, as those made in the *Methodist Times*, circulated widely and under eminent authority in our Church, we feel that there is but one course for us to pursue—to deny in the most solemn manner the allegations made against us and to require, as an imperative necessity, that vindication from without, which any *ex parte* denial of the charges is unable to afford us. We have therefore by an unanimous resolution called upon you for the appointment of a Commission to enquire into the statements made in the *Methodist Times*, and by Dr. Lunn in Conference, and into the evidence on which they are based. We make no suggestions as to how the Commission should be constituted, since we are confident that no body of intelligent men having the facts of the case before them can fail to confirm our absolute repudiation of the description of us which has been presented. But we would very strongly emphasize the necessity that the Commission, though initiated by you on our demand, must be so independent of ourselves and of you as to be accepted as impartial by those to whom we and you alike have become objects of suspicion, so competent as to command universal respect, and that it must be empowered to adopt any means it may deem necessary for sifting the matter to the very bottom. We feel also the importance of the Commission being so constituted that Mr. Hughes himself shall admit its qualifications to pronounce authoritatively and finally on the questions at issue, and we trust that he may be induced to lay before it all the evidence which he has repeatedly declared he has in reserve. To facilitate this, we are willing that you should assure Messrs. Hughes and Lunn that we heartily accept their disclaimer of intentional moral imputation against us, and that we have no wish whatever to disturb the peace of the Connexion or to injure Mr. Hughes' position or influence by raising anew the personal controversy which was set at rest by the vote of Conference. Our sole concern is with statements which, so long as they are believed, will continue to cause lamentable injury to the work of God. We have appointed a Committee to consider and deal in our name with the matter in its further developments; and we request you to advise this Committee of the form of enquiry which you propose to institute before finally deciding upon it. We can scarcely think it necessary to contemplate the possibility of your refusal to secure for us that vindication which we have shown to be so imperatively essential; but in that eventuality also this Committee is authorised to take action in our behalf.

We pray that in this most momentous and difficult matter the General Committee may be abundantly endued with wisdom and grace from on high.

The following additional resolutions were unanimously agreed to :—

(1). The Conference being of opinion that this Statement will not answer its full purpose unless it is printed and laid before the Methodist public, expresses the hope that the Home Committee will authorise its publication, unless they desire to reserve it for publication with the findings of the Commission.

(2). That a Sub-committee, consisting of the Chairmen of the Southern Districts in consultation with the Chairmen of the other Indian Districts, be appointed to consider any reply which may be received from Home touching the Statement forwarded to the Committee on the *Methodist Times* Controversy, and to decide what further steps it may be advisable to take. The Sub-committee will have power to add to its number.

Finance.

The Conference receives and adopts the following Report of the Committee on Finance connected with European Agency.

This report is in three parts :—

Part I.—A statement showing the stipends, allowances and other ordinary expenses connected with European Agency as now paid in each District together with notes of explanation. Four recommendations dealing with minor points are added. The question of stipend and children's allowances is dealt with in Part III.

Part II.—A statement respecting certain special allowances and District expenses. The Committee has two recommendations under this head.

The object of the Committee's resolutions under Parts I. and II. is to make the allowances for certain purposes uniform in all the Districts.

Part III.—A statement respecting the cost of living in the different Districts, a comparison of District with District and with the cost of living in England, and certain recommendations for a re-adjustment of the present rate of stipends.

PART

Table shewing the stipends and ordinary allowances, Committee's Schedules, for the European

	Madras.	Negapatam.	Mysore.
Stipend (1)	Married £230. Single £125.	Married £230. Single £125.	Married £230. Single £125.
Children's allowances	£14 per child.	£14 per child.	£14 per child.
Education do.	£12 do.	£12 do.	£12 do.
Postage and Stationery (2)	£4-4-0.	£4-4-0.	£4-4-0.
Medicines and Medical attendance (3)	\multicolumn{3}{l}{In all the districts the}		
Wear and Tear of Furniture (4)	Rs. 80 with Rs. 20 additional if a young man resides in the house.	Rs. 80 with Rs. 20 additional if a young man resides in the house.	Rs. 50. Rs. 25 for an unmarried man when living apart.
New Furniture when authorised (5)	Rs. 1,000 for furnishing a house for a married man.	Rs. 1,000 for furnishing a house for a married man.	Rs. 1,000 for furnishing a house for a married man.
House Repairs, Mission property (6)	In all districts the actual cost is charged. The cost of charges for enlargements and for			
Rent and Taxes (7)	In most districts the houses in which the Missionaries house, water, lighting and other taxes are charged, also the actual amount			
Horse allowance or Travelling on circuit (8)	Rs. 360 a year with Rs. 300 for purchase.	Rs. 360 a year with Rs. 300 for purchase.	Rs. 380 a year, no allowance for purchase.
Travelling to & from District Meeting	No charge hitherto necessary.	Two 2nd class tickets and one third.	Two 2nd class tickets and one third.
Removals Pundits (9)	Rs. 120 a year as long as is necessary.	Rs. 120 a year as long as is necessary.	In all districts the Rs 120 a year for three years, afterwards Rs. 60 a year.

I.

&c., according to the headings in No. 4 of the Home, Missionaries in all the Indian Districts.

Hyderabad.	Calcutta.	Lucknow.	Burmah.
Married £230. Single £125. £14 per child.	Married £250. Single £150. £14 per child.	Married £250. Single £150. £14 per child.	Married £230. Single £125. £14 per child.
£12 do. £4-4-0.	£12 do. £4-4-0.	£12 do. £4-4-0.	£12 do. £4-4-0.
actual expenses are charged.			
Rs. 80 with Rs. 20 additional if a young man resides in the house.	Rs. 60.	Rs. 50 with Rs. 25 for single men.	Rs. 50.
Rs. 1,000 for furnishing a house for a married man	Actual expenditure.	Actual expenditure.	Actual expenditure.
ordinary small repairs varies from Rs. 50 to Rs. 100 a year, but extra special repairs have occasionally to be made.			
live are the property of the Mission and under this head only Municipal the Government land tax and premium. Where the brethren rent houses paid is charged.			
Rs. 360 a year with Rs. 300 for purchase.	Rs. 360 a year with Rs. 300 for purchase.	Rs. £350 a year. The horses and carriages are the property of the Mission and actual cost is charged.	Rs. 360 a year with over Rs. 250 for purchase.
Actual cost.	Two 2nd class tickets and one third.	Two 2nd class tickets and one third.	Actual cost of journey.
actual cost is charged.			
No fixed allowance. Actual cost charged, which is usually about Rs. 120 a year.	Rs. 120 a year which ordinarily terminates at the end of three years.	Rs. £120 a year as long as is necessary.	No fixed rate— actual cost hitherto charged.

NOTES.

(1.) £25 extra is allowed to an unmarried probationer in Madras, Negapatam, Hyderabad and Burmah when he has to maintain a separate establishment, but it has rarely been drawn.

(2.) The Chairmen of the Madras, Negapatam, and Mysore Districts receive a special allowance of Rs. 100 a year for postage and stationery. In the Hyderabad, Calcutta, Lucknow and Burmah Districts, the Chairmen charge the actual amount they expend.

(3.) In the Madras, Negapatam, Mysore, Hyderabad and Burmah Districts there is an allowance of Rs. 100 for each confinement. In the Calcutta and Lucknow Districts the allowance is Rs. 150.

(4.) The allowance for wear and tear of furniture is not a personal one, only so much of the allotment as is actually spent being entered in the Committee's Schedules.

(5.) In the Southern Districts no house or table-linen or articles of plate are provided out of the Committee's grant.

(6.) No expenditure on new buildings is allowed in any district without the previous sanction of the District Meeting or the Chairman. Sanction must also be similarly obtained for repairs of old buildings which exceed Rs. 100.

(7.) The income tax is not allowed under this head. The brethren residing in the Native States of Hyderabad and Mysore and in the Province of Upper Burmah are not liable to this tax, but all others are.

(8.) The allowance for horse and carriage does not include the cost of touring, nor of such journeys as cannot be performed by horse.

(9.) In all districts there are examinations in the vernacular which must be taken by every probationer who receives allowance for a pundit.

Recommendations of the Conference on the ordinary allowances to European Missionaries.

1. *Furniture.*—That the allowance in all Districts be Rs. 80 a year for a married man, with the understanding that no grants for new furniture be made except in very extraordinary cases, and that in no District shall plate and linen be supplied by the Mission. Carried *nem. con.*

2. *Taxes.*—Whereas in some Districts the Municipal Horse and Carriage tax is paid by the missionary and in others from mission funds, the Conference recommends that in the future those taxes in all Districts be paid by the mission. Carried by 11 to 6.

3. *Income Tax.*—That inasmuch as the Income tax falls very unequally upon the brethren, some not having to pay at all and some paying only a small amount, and inasmuch as it is desirable to equalise our financial arrangements, the Conference recommends that henceforward that tax where it has to be paid be a charge upon the Committee. Carried by 11 to 4.

4. *Horse and Carriage Allowance.* — That the allowances and arrangements in the Mysore and Lucknow Districts be assimilated to those in the other Districts, but that this shall

not have retrospective effect in the Lucknow and Benares District. Carried *nem. con.*

Part II.—Special allowances, District expenses and administration.

1. *Allowances for visits to Hill Stations on account of health.*—In all Districts permission to visit the Hills must first be obtained from the District Meeting or, if that cannot be done, from the Chairman. Those brethren who have obtained leave receive a grant to meet the expenses of travelling and of rent, or in cases where the brethren have to go to a boarding house an allowance in lieu of rent.

2. *Chairman's servant or messenger.*—In all the Districts, except Calcutta and Burmah, there is a charge varying from Rs. 60 to 100 a year for a servant or messenger, who is at the disposal of the Chairman for work connected with the District.

3. *Allowances for entertaining missionary visitors.*—The rule which was passed at the Indian Conference of 1877, viz., that a brother who is called upon frequently to entertain missionaries when passing through his station shall be entitled to charge the mission funds Rs. 2 a day for each person entertained is in force in all the Districts except Lucknow, with the exception that the charge made is only Rs. 1-8 a day for each person. In some districts, however, though in force, it has not been acted upon. In the Lucknow district the Chairman receives a special allowance of Rs. 250 for this purpose.

4. *Expenses of holding District Meetings.*—In Madras, Negapatam, Hyderabad and Calcutta Rs. 1-8 a day is charged for each missionary and his wife during their stay at the District Meeting In Mysore, Lucknow and Burmah the charge is Rs. 2 a day.

Recommendations of the Conference.

1. *Allowances for entertaining visitors.*—That with reference to the allowance for entertaining missionary visitors, the rule of the Indian Conference of 1877 apply to all districts. Carried *nem. con.*

2. This Conference regards with serious apprehension the necessity that has arisen in every District for the appropriation of a large part of the gain by exchange on the grant for Native work to the ordinary current expenses of that work instead of as directed by the Home Committee to a fund for the acquisition of property. This gain is at best a precarious source of income and no District can ever be in a thoroughly satisfactory financial condition so long as its ordinary work is not met by the grant from the Home Committee converted at par.

3. The question of the allowances of the Home Committee to missionaries on furlough in England was raised It appeared from statements made to the Conference that the practice of the Committee in recent years on this matter has been very diverse. Reference was made to a circular sent by the General Secretaries to the Chairmen of Districts in November, 1888, in which it was stated that henceforth missionaries at home on furlough would be paid direct from the Mission House at the Committee's furlough scale, and that the proportion of the grant on behalf of such brethren would be debited to each District. In order that the brethren may know what they will receive when they return home and that the districts may know how much their grants are to be debited with in such cases, we respectfully ask that the furlough rates determined upon by the Committee may be communicated to each Chairman.

Part III.

The Committee next proceeded to form an estimate of the cost of living for a European missionary (both single and married) in the different Indian districts. It took as the basis of its calculations the resolution of the last British Conference given in page 214 (*a*) of its *Minutes*:—

"That the missionaries should continue to be placed in a "financial position corresponding to that of ministers in com- "fortable circumstances at home."

The Committee heartly accepts this resolution as a statement of the financial position in which Indian missionaries should be placed, and believes that it correctly describes their present style of living.

The Committee obtained from the representatives of each district information as to the cost of firewood, lighting, and of each important article of food. They had before them lists of the servants necessary in each District, and of the wages which must be paid to each. These lists were carefully compared and scrutinised. The kind of clothing necessary in each District together with its cost was enquired into. The average expenditure of the brethren on house linen, plate, and other articles of furniture not supplied from mission funds was obtained. The amounts paid by the brethren as income tax, horse, carriage and other taxes, was ascertained. An estimate was also made as to the amount which each brother might be expected to spend upon books, newspapers and periodicals. We did not enquire into the amount spent by each brother in charities, but we assumed that a tenth of a man's income might reasonably be devoted to this purpose. We also assumed that every brother ought to make some provision for old age, or for his widow in case of death, other than the sum he or his widow will be entitled to from the Annuitant and Auxiliary Funds. We have therefore entered in our table the annual premium of an Endowment Assurance for £500 in the Star Life Assurance Society, commencing at 25 and payable at 60 years of age. In estimating the cost of assurance, however, we have not added anything for extra premium on account of Indian residence. This is, as a rule, 1½ per cent., and therefore a sum of £7 10s. would need to be added to every item under this head, and to the corresponding totals. We have also entered our annual payment to the Annuitant Society.

The following tables shew (No. I.) the expenditure of an unmarried probationer in the Southern Districts, (No. II.) of one in the Northern Districts, and (No. III.) of a married couple without children in each of the Districts separately.

Table I.—Expenditure of Unmarried probationer in Southern Districts, living with a family.

	£	s.	d.
Food	40	10	0
Servants	13	10	0
Clothing	18	0	0
House Linen	1	0	0
Charities	12	10	0
Books, &c.	5	0	0
Insurance	13	6	8
Income Tax	2	8	0
Annuitant Society	5	5	0
	£111	9	8

Table II.—Expenditure of Unmarried probationer in Calcutta and Lucknow districts, living with a family.

	£	s.	d.
Food	40	10	0
Servants	15	6	0
Clothing	18	0	0
House Linen	1	0	0
Charities	12	10	0
Books, &c.	5	0	0
Insurance	13	6	8
Income Tax	2	8	0
Annuitant Society	5	5	0
	£113	5	8

N.B.—In Burmah the average expenses of an Unmarried man would be about £123.

Table III.—Expenditure of a Married Missionary and Wife, without children.

	Madras.			Negapatam.			Mysore.			Hyderabad.			Calcutta.			Lucknow.			Burmah.		
	£	s.	d.	£	s.	d.	£	s.	d.	£	s.	d.	£	s.	d.	£	s.	d.	£	s.	d.
Food ...	81	0	0	81	0	0	81	0	0	81	0	0	81	0	0	81	0	0	90	0	0
Servants ...	49	10	0	40	10	0	46	16	0	54	0	0	64	16	0	60	6	0	72	18	0
Clothing ...	36	0	0	36	0	0	36	0	0	36	0	0	36	0	0	36	0	0	36	0	0
House Linen and Furniture *not supplied* by the Mission	6	0	0	6	0	0	6	0	0	6	0	0	6	0	0	6	0	0	6	0	0
Charities 10% ...	23	0	0	23	0	0	23	0	0	23	0	0	23	0	0	23	0	0	23	0	0
Books, &c. ...	8	0	0	8	0	0	8	0	0	8	0	0	8	0	0	8	0	0	8	0	0
Premium on £500 ...	13	6	8	13	6	8	13	6	8	13	6	8	13	6	8	13	6	8	13	6	8
Income and other taxes ...	6	7	6	5	10	0	0	18	0	—			3	10	0	4	17	6	—		
Annuity Society ...	6	0	0	6	0	0	6	0	0	6	0	0	6	0	0	6	0	0	6	0	0
Total ...	229	4	2	219	6	8	221	0	8	227	6	8	241	12	8	238	10	2	255	4	8

The items in these three tables which are paid in Indian currency have been calculated at the rate of 1s. 6d. per rupee. It is true that to-day the Missionary Society's 30 days' Bills of Exchange can be sold for 1s. 5d., but we do not think an estimate by which our salaries in the future are to be regulated should be made on so low a rate of exchange as that. If, however, it is wished to determine from these tables our exact financial position to-day, we may point out that this difference of a 1d. in the rupee on the items paid in Indian currency, viz., food and servants, will reduce the cost of these in the four southern districts by about £7, in the two northern districts by about £8, and in Burmah by £9.

It will be seen that we have estimated the cost of food, including firewood and lighting, to be the same in all districts with the exception of Burmah. There were differences in the price of articles of food between one district and another, and between the towns and country places of each district, but it was found that where in one district a particular article was costly others were correspondingly cheap, and if in country places articles produced on the spot were cheap as compared with towns, the extra cost of carriage of European stores about equalized the whole cost of food.

The brethren, from their peculiar position in this country, are called upon to show hospitality to a much greater extent than is the case with ordinary Wesleyan ministers at home. We have also included in our estimate the extra cost of food in times of sickness.

With regard to servants the districts differ. In Northern India a greater number of servants must be kept than in the South, and the average rate of pay is slightly higher. It is not that the brethren live in greater 'style' in the North than in the South, but that the division of labour among domestic servants has there been carried to a greater extent. It will be seen that there is a difference of £15 in this item between the average of the four Southern Districts and the average of the two Northern. Burmah in this matter, as in that of food, is abnormally high.

Under the head of clothing we have put down the same amount in each district. What difference there is in cost under this head is rather between those of our brethren who live in towns and those in country districts than between one part of India and another. It may appear to some that this amount—£36 a year for man and wife—is large, but it must be borne in mind that Englishmen living on the plains in India—and all our missionaries are on the plains—have to provide themselves with a double set of clothing, one for wear on the plains, and another for wear when they visit the colder

C

parts of this country or return to England on furlough. It may be said by those unacquainted with India that the wear of the warmer clothing is small, and therefore it must last long, but everyone in India knows that woollen clothing is destroyed in this country by insects as fast as it is destroyed by legitimate wear in England. With regard to under clothing and to thinner outer clothing the necessities of the climate require us to have a more frequent change and hence a larger number of articles than in England. Where *one* summer suit suffices there the brethen here need a *dozen*. We have also included under this head requisites for our work in touring, such as rugs, blankets, pillows, portmanteaux, &c.

We have entered in the Schedule an item under the head of house-linen, &c. It must be remembered that missionaries in India have to meet out of their stipends several items of expense that do not usually fall upon their brethren in English circuits. Not only must every article that is used by the wife to convert four bare walls into a home be paid out of his stipend, but such necessaries as forks and spoons, curtains, sheets, pillow-cases, towels, *et hoc genus omne*, must be provided—if at all—from the same source. When the extraordinary gift that the Indian washerman has for destroying such articles as these last is borne in mind, £6 a year will not be thought too large a sum for this purpose.

In explanation of the item "Books, &c., £8," we need only say that except in the Presidency towns there are no circulating libraries and that if a brother is to keep himself in touch with current thought in England or in India, or in both, he must spend something on newspapers and periodicals, and to do his work efficiently he must have a small library of books on India and Indian missions, whilst owing to the insects and the damp many of us have scarcely a book in good order upon our shelves.

It may be thought by some that the demands on the private charity of Indian missionaries is not as great as on their brethren at home. It is true they have not exactly the same privileges in this respect that Home ministers have, but they have many similar ones. In all appeals in connection with their churches they are expected to head the list, and when called upon to relieve the distressed, except in the case of those brethren who have charge of English churches, they have no funds to go to but their own private resources. Nor is there the opportunity of supplementing those resources by fees for marriages, funerals, or from special services which are enjoyed by many Wesleyan ministers in England.

We have not entered in our tables nor have we in these

remarks referred to the allowance for children, which in all districts is £14 a year for each child. This we consider equitable, though it is far from meeting the whole cost of children in this country: but when they have to be boarded and educated in England, whilst their parents are out here, the sum is regarded by all as inadequate. The education allowance is £12. The experience of all the brethren who now have children in England, is that the minimum cost for board and education is £40, or £14 a year more than the Committee's present allowances. This difficulty is felt especially in a missionary's second or third term of service when he probably has several children at school in England.

Comparing the estimates of expenditure which we have drawn up with the stipends now paid, we have for probationers :—

1. In Southern Districts, and living with a family :—
   Estimated expenses, £111; present salary, £125.
2. In Northern Districts, and living with a family :—
   Estimated expenses, £113; present salary, £150.

It is only right that we should add that in the Northern Districts it is customary for a probationer to live alone, and that it is admitted that when a young man has to keep up a separate establishment, and especially when he is alone upon a station, that his expenses are greater than when boarding with a mission family. Hence, in four of the Southern Districts the resolution of the Indian Conference of 1877 which grants an extra allowance of £25 a year to a probationer when keeping up a separate establishment has been in force though it has not often been acted upon. We have later on recommended that probationers in such circumstances shall have an extra £20 a year. If we add this extra £20 to the estimated expenses of a probationer in the North that will make his expenses £133 with a salary of £150.

Making a similar comparison for a missionary and wife without children, we have—

1. In the four Southern Districts :—
   Average estimated expenses, £224; present salary, £230.
2. In the two Northern Districts :—
   Average estimated expenses, £240; present salary, £250.
3. Burmah :—
   Estimated expenses, £255; present salary, £230.

With the exception of probationers living and boarding with a family, the margin between our estimated cost of living and the stipends received is small. In one District, Burmah, our estimate considerably exceeds the stipend paid, and Brother Winston assures us that exercising the most rigid economy and making no provision by insurance for old age he has not been able to live within his income.

Many of the brethren have not insured their lives as in our tables we assume they ought to do. Nor have all been able to enjoy the privilege of spending one-tenth of their income on charities. These two items amounting to £36 6s. 8d. together with the amounts our estimates are within our stipends have provided a margin out of which the brethren have met special expenses connected with marriages, or with prolonged sickness or such extraordinaries as loss of horse, and those men who have children have met that part of their cost not covered by the children's allowance. In some cases provision has to be made out of this margin for aged parents or other relatives.

On the other hand a few of the brethren may have some private income. Into this subject we have not made any inquiry. We refer to it now simply because it may be that a few extra comforts enjoyed by some brethren have been provided for out of private income and not, as critics may have assumed, from ordinary stipend.

The Committee gave long and careful consideration to the question whether we should suggest to the Home Committee any changes in our stipends. It is now 20 years since the present rates were fixed. Since then the relative value of English currency to Indian currency has undergone considerable change. The English sovereign to-day purchases more of the commodities of life than it did 15 or 20 years ago. Therefore in common with all our ministerial brethren in England— and indeed with all in any rank of life whose salaries are paid in gold and have remained the same—our stipends have a greater purchasing power to-day than they had when fixed 20 years ago. We have not, however reaped the same advantage from this appreciation of gold as ministers and others in England have done. A much smaller part of our income is spent in English commodities than of theirs. Moreover the purchasing power of silver in this country has greatly decreased. The number of measures of rice or of any of the other grains which form the staple food of the people which can be bought for a rupee is much less to-day than it was 20 years ago. Consequently all kinds of service are dearer. Servants' wages are higher; so is labour generally and so are all articles produced by labour. Whilst therefore on that part of our stipend which we spend in England we are better off now than formerly, it is not so with that portion which we spend out here.

On a review of the whole subject the Committee unanimously recommends to this Conference and to the Home

Committee the following scheme which shall apply to all Districts for a readjustment of the present rate of stipend. As the scheme is based upon the principle that the reductions which are made during the earlier years of a missionary's career shall be made up to him in his later years, the Conference presents this scheme to the Home Committee as a whole. It would not recommend the reductions in the earlier years, as they certainly involve hardships, were there not to be some compensation at a later period when the expense of maintaining and educating children in England has to be borne.

1. For a probationer when boarding with another missionary £120 a year, and, if the District Meeting should deem it necessary, when keeping up a separate establishment £140 a year.

2. For a married missionary until he has completed ten years in the ministry £220 year, and after he has completed ten years £230 a year.

3. For a missionary who remains unmarried after being received into full connexion an increase of £10 every year for five years.

N.B.—This recommendation is in harmony with the Committee's Circular of May 8th, 1889.

4. Married missionaries in the Calcutta, Lucknow and Burmah Districts shall receive an additional £15 to meet the extra cost of living in those Districts.

5. For children who are in England the educational allowance shall be, during their stay there, £18 instead of £14 as heretofore.

6. That should the preceding resolutions bear with hardship upon any particular case we ask the Home Committee to receive and favourably consider any such cases which the District Meetings may recommend to it.

If this scheme is approved by the Home Committee we calculate its effect will be to reduce the cost of the European agency throughout India by about £110 a year. Should, however, the average length of service in India rise above what it now is, and thus a larger number of children be in England for their education, the cost will be proportionately increased.

SPECIAL MEETING OF THE FOREIGN MISSIONARY COMMITTEE.

Indian Missionaries on their Defence.

THE PRESIDENT OF THE CONFERENCE occupied the chair. There was a large attendance.

Reporting.

The PRESIDENT said that several representatives of the Press had requested permission to report the proceedings of the Committee. He would like to know what answer should be returned to them.

After a brief conversation, it was decided by an almost unanimous vote that one of the ministers present, whose abilities as a reporter were well known, should be asked to send a full and impartial report of their proceedings to the *Methodist Recorder* and *Methodist Times,* and that professional reporters should not be admitted.

The Bangalore Report.

The Rev. M. HARTLEY read the minute of the Committee on the Bangalore Report, on the authority of which the special meeting had been called.

The Rev. WESLEY BRUNYATE asked by whose authority the Bangalore Report (which was a private document) had appeared in one of the public prints?

The Rev. G. W. OLVER, B.A., said that there was reason to believe that that document had not been obtained from any Methodist in England. (Hear, hear.)

Order of Procedure.

The PRESIDENT suggested that the two brethren from India (the Revs. Geo. Patterson and W. H. Findlay, M.A.) should now be heard.

The Rev. H. P. HUGHES, M.A., asked permission, first of all, to make a statement which was partly personal, but which also had an important bearing on the order of procedure. He might say that he had been strongly urged by some of his friends not to attend that meeting; but as a member of the Committee he had felt it to be his duty to be present—(hear, hear)—and he trusted that his presence there would assist in promoting peace and harmony and good understanding. It was in that spirit he was there that day. (Hear, hear.) Two distinct issues were before them—there was a question of policy, and a question that was personal. He was strongly of opinion that all those personal questions that were discussed at the last Conference should be passed by; to bring them up again would be like trying a man a second time. (Hear, hear.) He felt very strongly on that point, and he should not be able to take any part in the proceedings of that Committee if those personal issues were raised. But there were other personal issues which were not raised in the Conference, but which were of a very grievous character, and he would submit that they ought in the first instance to occupy the attention of the Committee. (Hear, hear.) He held in his hand a letter from Mr. Patterson to Dr. Lunn which, if true, so entirely discredited him (Dr. Lunn) as a witness as to put him out of court. He thought that the course which was followed by Dr. Rigg, some twelve months ago, in the Missionary Committee in relation to an analogous case, might well be taken as a precedent. On that occasion Dr. Lunn was accused of having written some letters which appeared in an Indian newspaper, and Dr. Rigg very properly said that if Dr. Lunn had been guilty of such disreputable behaviour they ought not to tolerate his presence amongst them. They all entirely agreed with Dr. Rigg, but a few questions elicited the fact that Dr. Lunn had not written the letters referred to, and he did not know who had written them. There were now some other charges, not so grave perhaps as those to which he had alluded, but sufficiently grave to destroy Dr. Lunn's credibility as a witness if they were substantiated, and his own strong conviction was that they would best promote the object they had in view by considering those personal questions at once. If Dr. Lunn was discredited, one very important element in their discussions would be eliminated; on the other hand, if Dr. Lunn succeeded in defending himself, they would all be able to rejoice with him, and all the more so because for some time past he had been under a cloud. He believed that by adopting this course they would remove misunderstanding, prevent wrong issues, facilitate progress, and promote peace. (Hear, hear.) There would be a certain unreality in all their discussions unless this were done, and he begged that these matters might be now considered with as much freedom from objectionable phraseology as God might permit. (Hear, hear.)

The Rev. Dr. RIGG said he was not surprised that Mr. Hughes should have made that suggestion, but he (Dr. Rigg) saw great difficulties about it. On full consideration he thought it would be better to keep all those things out of the way until the question remitted to them by the last Conference had been disposed of. Right or wrong, that was the conclusion he had arrived at, and he had come to that meeting to act dispassionately and impartially, as if there were no such things. He wanted them, without any ruffling of mind, just quietly to go through the business for which they were met—viz., to deal with the questions that were raised at the last Conference, but which had not been settled, and leave the other questions to be dealt with by-and-bye. Nevertheless he thought it was exceedingly natural that Mr. Hughes should take the view he had taken. But he had another difficulty: The questions raised were really and truly of the nature of disciplinary questions. If they were to discuss these questions they would not be able to do the work for which they had met. (Hear, hear.)

The Rev. M. RANDLES thought they should hear their brethren from India. Mr. Hughes and Dr. Lunn had been requested to re-state what they complained of, and he presumed that the representatives from India would have that re-statement in view in their reply. (Hear, hear.)

The Rev. H. P. HUGHES, M.A., very seriously protested against being compelled with his colleague to discuss the questions before them under the threat of a minor District Meeting from the Chairman of his own District. He was rather surprised that Dr. Rigg should wish to reserve that personal question for consideration elsewhere, when he did not think that to be an objection on the occasion when charges were brought against Dr. Lunn. When these charges were gone into it was proved that the brother in India who made these charges had made a mistake, and (he was glad to say) he sent an apology to Dr. Lunn, and that matter was settled. He thought they might in a very short time dispose of all those issues, which were very largely the result of misconception and misunderstanding, but if what Dr. Rigg had now suggested were acted upon—and they were to proceed to discuss other issues whilst Dr. Lunn and himself were to lie under the threat of a minor District Meeting—he was sure that the effect upon the public mind would be very serious indeed. He implored the Committee not to take such a step. Dr. Lunn appeared before them that day as a witness, but if there were moral charges against him—if he had been guilty of falsehood—how could he (Mr. Hughes) adduce him in evidence? He thought, as a matter of justice to him and of wise policy that they ought to be permitted to do now what Dr. Rigg himself did twelve months ago. (Hear, hear.)

Dr. RIGG: The last thing I should ever do would be to hold a minor District Meeting in which I, myself, was in a position of bringing a charge. I should do nothing of the kind. I never dreamed of calling a minor District Meeting. (Hear, hear.)

The Rev. H. P. HUGHES, M.A.: I believe that if the Committee had permitted Dr. Lunn to explain one or two points about it, we might have settled this issue before now. (Hear, hear.)

The Rev. JOHN BOND hoped they would not go farther in that direction. Dr. Lunn appeared amongst them as a credible witness—(hear, hear)—as credible as Dr. Rigg himself, and so he would be regarded until he was proved to be the opposite. It appeared to him that they ought to proceed on the basis of the two pamphlets that had been issued. There were three issues in the case. (1) As to policy. (2) As to finance—the allowances to brethren in India, &c. (3) As to the question of luxury, &c. (Hear, hear.)

The Rev. J. E. CLAPHAM rose to order. The personal issue had not yet been disposed of. He thought that the new charges against Dr. Lunn should be dealt with as the case to which Mr. Hughes referred had been dealt with twelve months ago. (Hear, hear.)

The PRESIDENT: There is this difference between the two cases. In the former instance the charge had relation to certain letters which had appeared in the newspapers—in the latter the charge has relation to a private letter. Dr. Lunn is here as an invited witness. He is invited because we believe him to be credible. If we thought that Dr. Lunn was a man likely to deal in untruths here we should not have invited him. My own private view is that it is not necessary to justify Dr. Lunn's character at all. If Professor Patterson or anyone else has a charge against Dr. Lunn, let him prefer it at the proper time and place, but no charge has been brought before this Committee, and I think that this fact materially alters the case. (Hear, hear.)

The Rev. J. E. CLAPHAM moved that the Committee should agree with the request of Mr. Hughes.

Mr. P. F. WOOD seconded the motion.

The Rev. H. O. RATTENBURY moved an amendment to the effect that the representatives from India be heard at once.

The Rev. JOHN BOND seconded the amendment, which, on being put to the vote, was carried—47 voting in favour, and 18 against.

Address by the Rev. George Patterson.

The Rev. GEORGE PATTERSON said: Mr. President, I feel myself placed this morning in a position of very considerable difficulty. That difficulty arises in part from the fact that we who have been in India have not been able to follow with sufficient minuteness the inquiry that the Committee has conducted in the past. Certain words that I have heard this morning have shown me that there are many members of this Committee who look upon the investigation which awaits us, and which we are sent home to urge and to assist, as being somewhat different from anything which our brethren in India desire, and which we this morning ask for. But before addressing myself to this point I should like to remove one or two causes of ill-feeling, and to say what I can to make our inquiry cordial and friendly. I wish to defend myself and my brethren in India from any charge of unfriendliness to Mr. Hughes. We have been pained exceedingly to find that any such motives were attributed to us. We should like to assure Mr. Hughes that nowhere in our Connexion has he had in the past a larger number of admirers—a larger number of sympathisers with him in the work he has been doing in London, than in the East—among men who have been endeavouring in various ways—in the pulpit, in the college and in the streets—to use with effect the very weapons of vigorous evangelism which he has wielded with such power in the West. We have been looking to Mr. Hughes with pride, and with love, and nothing could have been a more sincere grief to us than the estranged feelings that have arisen between Mr. Hughes and ourselves. Nothing could be a greater joy to us than to have those feelings entirely removed, and to be able again to join hands and hearts with Mr. Hughes. That is our earnest desire. We wish him God-speed in all his work, and everything we can do to assist him in that work we shall be willing to do. (Hear, hear.) I should like also to make a similar remark, with reference to another equally honoured and equally loved member of this Committee —I refer to Mr. Champness. Mr. Champness has all his life long been an earnest missionary, and he is now developing an organisation which, we trust, will be a very valuable and almost indispensable auxiliary to the work of this Society in India and elsewhere. We in India have always regarded Mr. Champness' work with hopefulness. We have received the men he has sent us with cordiality and affection, and have assisted them as far as it lay in our power. That being the case, you will understand that it has been with a feeling of extreme regret that we have learnt that our silence has given pain to Mr. Champness. We wish to assure Mr. Champness this morning, that the pain we have given him has been wholly unintentional. His men abroad have no reason to complain with regard to the affection and love with which they have been received, and if any silence of ours has anywhere been interpreted to mean a lack of sympathy, let me repudiate such an interpretation. (Hear, hear.) I should like at this point to read a single sentence from a letter which I have in my hand from the Chairman of the Mysore District and the President of the Indian Conference, Mr. Hudson. He says: "While I think that Mr. Champness is too sanguine with regard to the financial aspect of his scheme, I have faith in it, and I think it is well worth a trial. So far he has certainly sent us good men who are likely to be successful, and he has left me all the discretion I could desire." I have referred to these personal differences at the outset, because, in view of the grave issues that are before us we wish to do everything in our power to remove all causes of personal hostility. We in India have not lost love for anybody at home. We are not proud; we claim no infallibility; and we ask that we may be credited with the love that we feel, and that no personal feelings may be attributed to us which any brother would be ashamed to avow for himself. And now, Sir, having touched these personal questions, I must ask you to permit me to read to the Committee a paper of instructions which was put into our hands on the eve of our departure from India. These instructions, I may say, were drawn up by the Committee of Chairmen appointed by the Bangalore Conference. They specify and limit the work which in the interests of our brethren abroad we are sent here to do. "In selecting representatives for the special inquiry granted by the Home Committee, we have had to act upon instructions necessarily very brief, contained in the telegram from the Secretaries. Our object has been to appoint brethren who possess the fullest knowledge of all matters connected with the *Methodist Times* controversy. While we leave the general management of the case to Messrs. Patterson and Findlay, we think it well to give them the following explicit instructions: First, we presume that an inquiry will be instituted into the statements made by the *Methodist Times*, and by Dr. Lunn at the Conference, and into the evidence upon which those statements are based, and only so far as they affect the value of this evidence do we think that personal matters should be introduced. Our brethren are not sent home to bring charges against anyone, but solely to vindicate our character and work. Second, in the contingency of any further action being desirable, our representatives are requested to wait for fresh instructions before proceeding further." Now, Mr. President, you will observe that in these instructions there is no mention made of policy. It must not, however, be understood that our brethren in India object to the discussion of policy. They have always been ready to discuss policy; they have always been ready to assist in such discussions to the utmost of their power. Nor must it be taken to mean that the brethren who have sent us are of opinion that it is not necessary at the present stage to discuss policy. We think we truly represent the opinions of the brethren in India, when we say that they are almost unanimously of opinion that it is extremely desirable that certain questions of policy should be fully and freely discussed, such for example as the education policy, the question of lay-agency, and the whole financial management of the Society. And they are willing that we should assist in such discussions. But what I would point out to the Committee is this—that in so far as we may be privileged to assist this Committee in considering such questions, we shall do so not as representatives, but as private individuals; we shall then speak each in his own personal capacity. Our words will carry no weight that is not given to them by our own experience, or judgment, or character. We do not, on questions of policy, represent our brethren abroad. But this Committee knows very well that it was not on a question of policy that the Indian brethren were asked to send two representatives to England. There is a prior and more important issue than any mere question of policy. According to the words of our instructions, we are commissioned to "vindicate the life and character of missionaries." And in this we *are* representatives. While in everything else we speak, each of us, only with his own voice, in this matter we claim that our voice is the voice of all our brethren in the East. The one word in our instructions that is to be emphasised, is the word "vindicate"—vindicate against what? Against a certain description of us which, in the statement that we adopted at the Bangalore Conference, we declare to be false—declare to be a caricature of our life and spirit. We there say that we should regard missionaries such as we have been described to be, as base in the extreme; unfaithful to their calling; unworthy of the confidence of their church. And where are these statements to be found? They are to be found in the second article by "A Friend of Missions," published under the title of "The Evils of a False Position," as that article is supplemented, enlarged, and expounded in subsequent notes in the *Methodist Times*. It is true that since we came to this country another pamphlet has been put into our hands. It was put into our hands last Saturday, and the gentleman (a member of this Committee) who spoke a few minutes ago, expressed a desire that our attention should be confined to this pamphlet. We cannot confine our attention to this pamphlet. (Hear, hear.) The statements against which we object are not in this pamphlet. We think we can reply with ease to everything that this pamphlet says, but what is to us infinitely more important than anything in the pamphlet is the description of our life and spirit, which the pamphlet does not contain. I need not enter into the article I refer to with any minuteness of detail, and yet I cannot summarise its statements. They are almost incapable of being summarised. I cannot classify them, for the description given of us hangs together in all its parts. But, in brief, we are described as living in a state of luxury to which the best-paid preachers in our Connexion at home cannot aspire. We are described as submitting to social entanglements which are inimical to the interests of the mission—which mar our work. We are stated to have imbibed, with one or two exceptions, a spirit of lordly separation from those whom we have been sent out to evangelise. We are represented as giving a welcome to conveniences, elegancies—not to say luxuries—that we should be better without, and that are unbecoming missionaries of the Cross. All this is stated explicitly, and by implication we are further accused of have acquiesced in all this, of having submitted to it silently, though the evil of it is so plain that a young man who has been only a year in the country could detect it, and the remedy so patent that that young man can suggest it. Now we say that such a description of us, if it is true, condemns us. We were amazed, we were astounded, to find that Mr. Hughes should base on such a description a demand for nothing more sweeping that a new policy. New policy, forsooth! If the half of what he says is true it is not a new policy that you want; it is new men: and if that article can be substantiated before this Committee, then we ask you to recall us, and to send men abroad that are not tainted with this spirit of self indulgence; to send men abroad who can retain upon them the freshness of their vows for more than a year; to send men abroad whom you can trust. (Hear, hear.) I have spoken strongly. When I rose this morning I resolved to follow Mr. Hughes's advice as far as I could to avoid adjectives. But the adjectives I have used are very much the adjectives that the whole world has used. We are not singular in our interpretation. It is but fair to Mr. Hughes to remember that he has said again and again that the articles which he published and which derive all their force from his sponsorship were not, in his opinion, an impeachment of men, but of policy. We cannot follow Mr. Hughes in this. We cannot understand it. We simply take his word for it. We have said that we acquit Mr. Hughes gladly of any intent to attack us personally, but that is all we can do. We cannot be bound by any private and personal interpretation of Mr. Hughes. We must take the plain meaning of the English language; we must take the interpretation which all the world has put upon these articles; the interpretation which is put upon them by the secular and religious Press throughout the world; the interpretation that was put upon them by us in India when first we read them; the interpretation that was put upon them by this Committee and by the last Conference. It is wholly unnecessary that I should defend that interpretation; but I should like, if the Committee will permit me, to read to it one or two short extracts from an entirely independent Anglo-Indian paper as illustrative of views which were taken in Anglo-Indian circles. That paper is the *Times of India*. There is evidence that the articles from which I am about to read were not inspired by a Missionary or by a Methodist, because Mr. Hughes is described as a young Welsh Congregational revivalist, and because it supports Mr. Hughes in his education policy. When the *Times of India* read the first article by "A Friend of Missions" it approved of it. When it read the second article it expressed itself as follows: "The whole gist of the matter is that when men come out here as missionaries they get £300 a year and a bungalow, buy a dress-coat, get presented to the Viceroy, set up a phaeton, keep an 'establishment,' go into society (with a large S), and—then! away goes all missionary enthusiasm like chaff before the winds! And if this is the drift of the article it is a cruel libel on an earnest, sincere, and hard-working body of men who have exchanged home and kindred for disease, and perhaps death, in order to evangelise a race which has lain for thousands of years in the lap of crudest superstition. The charge is ridiculous as well as unjust. The assault on the mission, which we took at first to be a helpful criticism of the system, turns out to be a covert attack on the missionaries, who are alleged to have been lured from their sacred trust by £300 a year, a bungalow, and 'Society!' And the outcome is that 'men who left the London Docks with the simplest ideas of life and duty, full of lofty purposes of self-denial and devotion, have scarcely trodden Indian soil a twelvemonth before they find themselves settled down to a mode and fashion of living from which a year ago they would have shrunk back in dismay.' The position of a missionary in India, according to the *Methodist Times*, is nearly equal to that of a bishop at home, but 'no one would dream,' fatuously exclaims the writer, 'of attempting the evangelisation of England by bishops only!' And he adds, 'the effect of this mode of living is inevitably to separate the missionary from the people, instead of bringing him into close contact with them. It is almost impossible for any man to occupy for years the position of a feudal lord without developing the feudal spirit. Men do successfully fight against it here and there, but it is not in human nature generally to yield almost to absolute power, and receive abject reverence without losing sight, more or less, of the great Christian principle of the brotherhood of all men.' In short, if the *Methodist Times* is to be believed, the missionary in India is a despicable fraud, drawing money for work he does not do, occupying a position calculated to draw down upon him the contempt of every honest man, and false alike to himself, to his employers, and to his God. It seems to us that the *Methodist Times* has allowed itself to be made the medium of private spite, for it is almost incredible that an honest man, with an honest desire to render aid in a difficult problem, could frame in cold blood an indictment such as this. We know very little about the *Methodist Times*—except that it has always had the reputation of being a well-conducted journal—but it certainly has a higher mission than stabbing its friends in the back under pretence of helping them out of the mire." Subsequently, when Mr. Hughes had had time indignantly to deny that anything in the articles of a Friend of Missions were intended to be construed as charges against missionaries, the *Times of India* returned to the attack, and said: "The most serious of the English criticisms are those of Mr. Olver, who is guilty of what the Friend of Missions amusingly calls the 'innuendo' that the writer has 'made accusations against the brethren in India,' and of the Rev. R. Stephenson, who accuses him of dogmatism and audacity. To the former the writer replies with singular calmness that he repudiates the innuendo, and that he 'stated clearly that the responsibility for the existing state of affairs does not rest upon the present generation of missionaries at all.' Is it necessary to remind this disingenuous writer that his charges against the 'present generation of missionaries' have been recorded in cold type in the columns of his own journal, and that no amount of verbal shuffling will extricate him from their responsibility? What he said, as distinctly as the Queen's English would allow him to, was: The 'present generation of missionaries' forsook their trust, were false to themselves, their employers, and their God, and that, for the sake of 'Society,' an establishment, a phaeton, and a dress-coat, they allowed their efforts to wane and their ministrations to die of moral atrophy. If these are not 'accusations against brethren in India,' language has evidently for the 'Friend of Missions' ceased to have any meaning whatever." I submit these extracts as a fair example of the meaning that was attached to these articles by independent outside critics, and therefore I say, on behalf of my brethren in India, we demand an inquiry into their truth. If these things are true, they can be proved to be true. If they cannot be proved to be true, let them fall to the ground, and give us once more the confidence which throughout an influential minority at least of our Church we have lost. (Hear, hear.) Now, Sir, I have been asked, if we hold such strong views, why have we been silent so long? I cannot tell you how often that question has been put to me since I came here. What I have had said to me by prominent Methodists is this: "Why have you been silent so long? It is more than a year since these things were printed; you have never denied them. We believed that you were innocent, but our confidence has been rudely shaken, for we find that after a certain amount of virtuous bluster you allowed the matter to drop. If you can disprove these statements, do so, and we shall be delighted, but if you don't disprove them, you must not be surprised if we as business men come to the conclusion that these statements are substantially true." Now, Sir, why has our reply been almost exclusively confined to the columns of a magazine published in India—viz., the *Harvest Field*? Because in England our replies have been used to fill the editorial waste-paper basket. On this point I am bound to speak strongly for I feel strongly. I say—and I say it having in my hands the means of proving my statement to the letter, that the mode of elucidating the truth adopted by the *Methodist Times* has consisted chiefly in deliberate suppression of everything on the opposite side. No, Sir, we could not answer untruths in the journal in which those untruths have been published to the world. We could not follow the insinuations into the circles to which those insinuations were sent, and therefore we were compelled to appeal to this Committee and to Conference to reopen the question which, by the by, was never properly closed. We say, Let the question be reopened; let every statement that has been made be examined; let it be inspected; let the inspection be ruthless, searching, complete, merciless, and then, if it is true that we are as we have been represented, let us bear our shame; let us be dishonoured if we deserve dishonour; but let us not be beaten openly and uncondemned. (Hear, hear.) We wish facilities for a complete, a thorough, and an impartial investigation, and we are prepared to do everything in our power to promote and assist such investigation. We only had a fortnight between receiving the notice to come here and the day of our sailing from Madras. We were not able in a fortnight to do everything that we wished to have done, but we did a good deal. We endeavoured to collect evidence that we shall submit to this Committee. We endeavoured to collect it first from missionaries of wide experience. We do not, Sir, put any peculiar value upon the first impressions of young men. We know what our own first impressions were, and we know how they vanished away as wisdom came with years. We believe that first impressions are always unsafe and generally foolish; and therefore we have not taken the trouble to collect the impressions of young men of one year's service in India, but we have gone to men who have proved their devotion to India by giving their lives to the work. We have asked them to give us the results of their experience. We have got many such testimonies of various sorts. Then, as it happens, very fortunately for this inquiry, several Churches have quite recently been looking into the very question which we are now about to look into. We have got official statements of various sorts from Secretaries and from Deputies, statements of the results of their investigations and of the policy which they are advocating on the basis of the inspection. We have also obtained from missionaries and Christian laymen of long experience in India and of public repute, testimony on such questions as the comparison between life in India and life in England. Then we have turned to our own missionaries, and, Sir, I blush to lay upon the table the circular which Mr. Findlay and I sent to every one of our own men in India. I blush because this circular is an inquisitorial investigation into private matters which most men guard with jealous care. It may be said that we had no need to do this; that the humiliation of answering such a circular is a humiliation that we put upon ourselves. Be it so. We did not know what arguments might be adduced by those who have assailed us, and we wished to be prepared with an answer to any question that might be put to us. We did not expect that many of our brethren would answer this circular; but, in justice to them, let me say that almost every one has answered it. They have answered it with a meekness that is beyond all praise. For the love of the Church which they wish to serve, for the love of the truth, and to facilitate inquiry, they have shown themselves ready to unveil to the prying gaze of friends, if not of foes, those secret facts of their life which every man is justified in keeping secret. We wish to add to that evidence some more that I trust we shall have shortly, and I think perhaps it is in order for me now at this point to request this Committee to assist us in the collection of it. While in India Dr. Lunn wrote a journal. That journal is of great value, and of great interest. I was privileged to read certain parts of it.

I ask you, Mr. President, to request Dr. Lunn to put before the Committee the whole of his Indian journal. I have heard incidentally, also, that Dr. Lunn has been in correspondence with ministers of other Churches. I think we ought to have that correspondence. (Hear, hear.) I have received statements from Mr. Hughes and Dr. Lunn in which certain letters appear. I have looked to see whether we have there a letter from Professor Lindsay, of Glasgow. I know that Dr. Lunn wrote to Dr. Lindsay, but Dr. Lindsay's answer has not appeared. We on our side are prepared to put in anything that Mr. Hughes may call for, and to submit the whole of our evidence to him.

Mr H. P. Hughes: Dr. Lunn will submit all the evidence. (Hear, hear.)

Mr. Patterson: Very well. Dr. Lunn will be anxious to tear our evidence in shreds if possible. He must have the fullest opportunity of doing so, and we also must have the opportunity of treating his evidence in a similar manner. Now, Sir, it is not for me to suggest anything to the Committee this morning as to the mode in which this inquiry should be carried out. It is for the Committee to decide that. There is only one thing that I should like to say, and it is this: The inquiry will of necessity be a prolonged one. We must ask with all the urgency in our power that nothing be passed over as of no moment; that nothing be put on one side as irrelevant—unless, of course, it really be irrelevant; that the points raised be gone into one by one, patiently, impartially, fearlessly; and that the verdict which is reached on the basis of evidence shall be given to the Church, together with the evidence on which it rests. When this has been so done, and when the air has been cleared of much that at present obscures vision and perverts judgment, then we can go on to the question of policy. When a distinct answer has been given to questions of character, and when the whole Church accepts that answer, then only will it be possible for questions of policy to be calmly and fairly discussed. When that time comes we shall be ready to give the Committee every assistance in our power.

Address by the Rev. W. H. Findlay.

The Rev. W. H. Findlay said: I desire, first of all to express the great relief and satisfaction, and the devout thankfulness to God which is felt by your missionaries in India who have made us their spokesmen, that they at last have the opportunity of free utterance before so large and representative an assembly of their ministerial and lay brethren, and, through you, before the public of Methodism. A year ago to-day we received in India the first of the articles on "A New Missionary Policy," and until this anniversary we have suffered under what we have felt to be the cruellest and most injurious blow that could have been inflicted on the work of God through us; and the worst of our trial has been that we have found ourselves all but helpless to undo the harm which has been done; for while our critics have been in absolutely the most advantageous situation possible for winning and keeping the ear of the public and ensuring its confidence, we have been in the most disadvantageous situation possible for replying to their impeachment. From a position of commanding influence, won by high character, surpassing ability, and splendid service to Methodism, Mr. Hughes has assailed us; and he has had other subsidiary, but by no means unimportant, advantages—in living in London, conducting an influential journal, and being able to control other journalistic springs, as well as to reach the private ear of many of our most influential people. We, on the other hand, are personally unknown, most of us even to our ministerial brethren at home, much more to the general public, and we are scattered through the length and breadth of the continent called India, with slow and scanty means of communication with each other. Thousands of miles from England, we can receive but meagre, intermittent, and belated information of what is passing here; and our voice, when we have succeeded in articulating utterance, has in its turn arrived here too late for the occasion. We have struggled helplessly, with little to maintain us but the conviction that the truth must finally prevail, and that God would defend His cause; knowing, meanwhile, that our motives and desires, no less than our circumstances, were being—unintentionally, no doubt, but, unceasingly—misrepresented at home; that through all available journalistic channels the public ear was being filled with those reiterated assertions which to the careless multitude are the equivalent of proof; and that in the narrower circles of thoughtful men, statements and arguments of tenor unknown to us were being industriously disseminated to our injury. I refer to these operations of our critics not to condemn methods which they doubtless thought it fair to employ; but to remind the Committee at the outset of what has been the embarrassment of our position, so that if, as we know has happened, some members of it have been inclined to prejudge us, they may realise how long and how utterly we have been incapacitated from laying before them the truth of our case. Face to face at last, after a very heavy nightmare of helplessness, with you and the Methodist public, we have this first request to make, that you will not prejudge us, that no one of you will, even in his thoughts, and whatever he may have heard, condemn us until he has heard also all that we have to tell. Our satisfaction then, in standing here, is that the whole truth may be known. We have come to tell all that is to be told about the life and spirit and circumstances of your missionaries. We have nothing to keep back and nothing to disguise; on the contrary, we wish, we are even strongly anxious, that you and all who desire it shall have the fullest possible information on this whole question. There are reasons—two main reasons—why, in a normal state of public opinion, we should regard it as equally our wisdom and our right to withhold the arrangements and circumstances of our life from the inquisition of curiosity or suspicion. We should hold it, ordinarily, to be wise to do so, because there are necessarily circumstances connected with life in a foreign country and among a foreign people which cannot be rightly appreciated except by the help of experience. The conditions of the preservation of health and prosecution of work in a tropical climate, and the proprieties of intercourse with people of an alien race are matters that no measure of description and explanation, but only prolonged experience, will qualify you fully to understand. There are sure to be features about the life of an Indian missionary, and equally about the life of a Chinese, African, Fijian missionary, the propriety and necessity of which cannot be brought home to people who have never left England or Europe, as certainly as there are features of Christian life in England that cannot be explained to the satisfaction of the native of India, whether Hindu or Christian. The Church cannot in regard to its missionaries in any land or at any period escape the duty of trusting them. Do you imagine that by accepting what Mr. Hughes tells you about missionaries and following the policy he prescribes, you would have attained a solid and complete understanding of Indian affairs, and a reasoned and final wisdom in your Indian administration? He has not furnished you, and no one can furnish you, with all the considerations that would be necessary to enable you wisely to apply your judgment to the questions in detail; and as for the particular house of cards that he would raise, what is to save it from the touch of the next assailant, who, one year or ten years hence, should bring to you his facts and figures and illustrations in favour of some " Newer Missionary Policy," in favour perhaps, of the German " Via," or the Salvation Army " Via?" I make bold to assert that in matters such as are now in dispute you cannot rationally or rightly use any other guide than the collective experience and judgment of the men whom you have chosen and sent forth, checked by the accumulated wisdom of the generations of those of the same race who have lived in the same land. However, a section of the Church has been led to attempt to apply its judgment to these matters too distant for it; and, lending its ear for the purpose, it has heard only what arouses its suspicion. It asks for more; and we feel that to withhold information now, on the ground that an English public is not a fit judge of these matters would only increase the suspicion. We are, therefore, ready to tell you everything; but at the same time we assert that, in an inquiry into such matters as these, whether you acquit or condemn us, you will have had in perfect materials for your verdict; and that if you are to carry on God's work among the heathen, you will ultimately have to come back to this—you must send out men whom you can trust, and trust them. The second main reason why, in a normal state of the public mind, we should have declined to yield you much of the information which we come to-day prepared to grant, is that we claim the right as much as any minister or layman in England, to hold our private affairs sacred from the intruding criticism of any man on earth. Mr. Hughes does not presume to enquire, or to announce in his paper how many courses his English brethren have at dinner, or whether they travel first, second, or third class on the railway; in regard to all such things he would say of any one of them, "To his own conscience he standeth or falleth." We claim the same right to be left in all these things to the arbitrament of our own conscience. Stipends of English ministers are not determined by a scrupulous calculation of the necessities of food and clothing, of charities and boots; they are decided by a general estimation of what it is suitable for the Church to give, and suitable for its ministers to receive. The Church's solicitude is that none should have too little; if any has too much, his own conscience is trusted to direct him how to use the surplus for the glory of God. We know no reason why ministers abroad should be otherwise dealt with. Mr. Hughes, however, has chosen—with the best of motives, doubtless—but he has chosen—to open the door of our private lives and invite all the public in. How are we to meet such action? To close the door, as we have full right to do, in the face alike of Mr. Hughes and his public. But in the circumstances we fear that that would increase the suspicions of us which have been already improperly engendered. Therefore, for the sake of God's work in our hands, the primal necessity of which is that we should have your confidence, we throw wide the door. You would take stock of our meals? Come, watch us as we buy and cook and eat them; you would finger our clothing to guess what it costs, and how long it would wear; there it is in the press—take it. Count our servants, measure our rooms, search for our savings'-bank book. We have borne other things for our work's sake, and though we did not expect to have to bear this humiliation at the hands our friends, yet we can bear it. Only we would make one protest—Let not our yielding to this inquisition be made a precedent for brethren that are to come after us, that their lives should be subjected to, and their stipends regulated by, such treatment as that to which we are submitting ourselves. And I cannot but add that of all men whom I have known and honoured, Mr. Hughes is among the last whom I should have expected to find leader in such an enterprise as this! We have resolved then, in spite of the considerations I have referred to, which might have justified an opposite course, to hold nothing back from your knowledge or from the knowledge of any who care to read. We are anxious that you should know whatever you wish to know, whatever there is to be known about your missionaries as a class, their circumstances and their behaviour. And we are equally anxious, as we showed by our desire that this inquiry should be fully reported, that what you learn from us should be communicated to all whose interest is centred upon the controversy. If any man speaks henceforth of there being something concealed, something kept in the dark about the life of your missionaries, he will have himself or his friend to blame. The door is open now for you to search wherever you please. Let me say a word as to the spirit in which it is desirable that this inquiry shall be conducted. Mr. Hughes has expressed a strong hope, which has been echoed from many quarters, that in the further discussion of the questions raised in the *Methodist Times* " personalities should cease." I presume that by personalities he means the attributing unchristian feelings, motives, designs to individuals. If this be so, I would point out to him and to the Committee that on our side personalities have long ago ceased, and that at Bangalore we distinctly and formally abjured them. In the manifesto of the Bangalore Conference, in response to which this inquiry has been instituted, your Indian missionaries have declared their hearty acceptance of Messrs. Hughes's and Lunn's disclaimer of intentional moral imputation. However hard we may have found it, in our first indigation, to dissociate statements so false and injurious from fault in the authors of them, we have now deliberately and sincerely debarred ourselves from charging Mr. Hughes or Dr. Lunn with any intention to defame our character. We accept them as having discharged what they conceived to be a Christian duty in publishing the statements that for a year past have burdened our life. Personalities, therefore, are already banished from the controversy so far as we are concerned; and it only remains that Mr. Hughes should follow our example and acquit us, as he has not yet done, of improper motives in our prosecution of the controversy. With the conciliatory statement of the Bangalore Conference before him, he still accused us of implacable temper, and he has not yet, so far as I know, ceased to assume and to declare that our insistance in defending our character is due to anger, bitterness, and other feelings unworthy of Christian ministers. I call upon Mr. Hughes, if he would have a discussion free from personalities, to renounce such utterances and such belief. I call upon him to admit, and to believe, that in the action the Indian missionaries have taken and are taking they are as little actuated by unchristian feelings, and as much by high and worthy motives, as he believes himself to be. I claim this for two reasons, first, in the name of Him who has said, "Judge not, that ye be not judged," and as the due of a minister to his brother ministers; and, secondly, because so long as he and those who agree with him continue to believe that we are actuated by these unchristian feelings, their eyes must inevitably be blinded to the facts and arguments we have to allege. If he finds it difficult to understand, except by the supposition of bitterness and personal animosity, how it is that we persist in regarding the second of his four articles as defamatory, though he did not intend it to be so, I would assure him that we found at least equal difficulty in understanding how he could have published such an article without intending and recognising it to be injurious to our character. We have surmounted this difficulty on our side, and with sincere goodwill accept Mr. Hughes expression of friendship and confidence. May I not entreat him then to show us a similar charity, and to believe that though we cannot for a moment regard the second article as anything but a most serious attack upon us, yet we attribute to him no ill intention, and bear him no ill-will in connection with it? I am persuaded that the first step toward the peaceful solution of this most unfortunate controversy must be the recognition by Mr. Hughes and those who agree with him that Indian missionaries in their part in it are actuated by no desire for revenge, no jealousy, no animosity, but by a calm but immovable sense that the work of God in India will suffer irreparable injury unless the statements made in the *Methodist Times* are proved to all the world to be false. Let him judge that our head is wrong, as long as he can; but let him acquit our heart. And when, as I confidently trust will be the case to-day, Mr. Hughes withdraws these accusations of animosity, and accepts, as he has never done yet, the purity and righteousness of our motives, personalities will have ceased from the controversy, never, I trust, to be revived. I unhesitatingly agree with my colleague that the object of this inquiry, as we conceive it, and as those who have sent us from India conceive it, is to ascertain the truth or untruth of a number of assertions published in the *Methodist Times*, which form when taken together a description of the life of Indian missionaries —your missionaries among others. We have been sent from India for this, and nothing but this. What is the genesis of the investigation which you are this morning commencing? A request made by the Bangalore Conference and laid before you on the 12th of February last, and this request accompanied by a full statement of the subjects calling for inquiry, and the reasons which made it imperative. Read that statement from beginning to end, and you will find that it calls attention to nothing, it criticises nothing but certain definite and indicated assertions, describing present missionary life and character. If your inquiry to-day is granted at the request of the missionaries assembled at Bangalore, then it is an inquiry into the truth of certain definite statements made in the *Methodist Times*, or it is a mockery of your missionaries. Mr. Hughes has reiterated, and others have echoed it, that he intended to raise, and raised, only questions of policy, and that it is only policy that this Committee has to consider. Let me explain the mistake that lies here. We do not deny that Mr. Hughes has raised questions of policy—that the proposal of a "new missionary policy" was the real object and business of the articles called by that name. Mr Hughes has the right to propose a new policy, and to ask the Committee and the missionaries to consider it. His proposals exist, and will, perhaps, in due course, deserve the consideration of our missionary authorities. And it is possible that Mr. Hughes's new stipend-policy might have been proposed in such a way and on such grounds as to raise no question of present fact, though I may point out that even a pure proposal of policy does commonly imply assertions as to the existing state of things, and may involve a slur upon character as distinct as the most categorical insult. If, for instance, I were to propose that the class-meeting system be introduced into the London Mission, I should not have to wait long to be told that I had uttered, by implication, a damaging untruth. But without pausing to discuss whether Mr. Hughes's policy, taken by itself, does or does not involve aspersions upon missionaries, I go on to remark that in the articles called by the common name "A New Missionary Policy" there was more than proposals of policy. The first article contained a proposal in regard to missionary educational work, but the proposal was preceded by what professed to be a historical account of its origin and progress, and a description of its effects. The second and third articles developed the new stipend-policy; but here again the proposals in the third article were preceded, in the second, by a description of the present scale and style and spirit of living of missionaries, and a statement as to how they had become established. The bill had, in fact, a preamble which professed to deal, as a preamble should, with matters of fact. The second article was headed, "The Evils of a False Position," and professed to describe the existing evils of an existing false position. The title leads us to expect a description of what is—not a suggestion of what should be—assertions, not proposals; and the article corresponds with the title; from beginning to end it consists of assertions. I grant that it may have held a subordinate place in Mr. Hughes's mind and intention; that it is only the introduction to the third article; that it is merely the preamble of a bill. But it is there; the assertions are made; and though Mr. Hughes may wish to go on to the bill itself, and have his proposals discussed, yet we, on our part, finding this preamble startling and flatly untrue, decline to pass it by. That is the situation as it presents itself to me. The policy is there, but the description also is there, and as it professes to be a description of us, among others, and as we hold it to be most seriously defamatory, we claim to have it investigated, and we are here to-day that it may be investigated. Let me briefly consider two or three reasons which Mr. Hughes has at various times put forward why it is not necessary or not advisable to conduct this investigation. This article, he contended, and other passages in the *Methodist Times* in harmony with it, were not intended to be defamatory, and do not appear to him to be so. He has assured us that his love and confidence towards us are unaffected by the opinion expressed in his journal. We accept the assurance and are glad of it. But it affords us only a new, though a somewhat remarkable instance of the often observed psychological fact that opinions and convictions properly exclusive of each other may co-exist in the same mind. Mr. Hughes has been too long accustomed to regard his brethren in the ministry, abroad as well as at home, with the confidence of a faithful and generous brother, to have that conviction disturbed by recent and hearsay information, however firmly credited, or by facts imagined to suit a policy; and Dr. Lunn has too recent and intimate memories of missionaries as they are, to be able to think of them, however he may write of them, as bad men. It is not hard, therefore, to believe that the authors of these statements do not find their confidence in us appreciably disturbed by the statements they have made, and do not consider their assertions injurious to our character. But it is surely not usual to decide whether or not a description is defamatory by the opinion of the author of it, or even by his admitted intention. It is surely a commonplace of experience that a man may libel others most seriously without understanding that he has done so, or meaning to do so. We confidently assert that, to those who judge as the world commonly judges men, to those who are ready—as, alas! we are all too ready—to believe and infer evil when it is possible, to those who are not, as Mr. Hughes is, absorbed in policies, and so occupied with the future as to spare only a careless glance for the present, to those who have not Dr. Lunn's experience of the actual character of missionaries—for the real character of your Indian missionaries is the one subject upon which Dr. Lunn's Indian career qualified him in some measure to speak—and to those who have not Mr. Hughes's habit of confidence in his brethren—to all these, that is to say, to the general readers of these articles, they must, I have no hesitation in saying, appear to affect our character most intimately, and to be, if true, utterly condemnatory of us; if not true, grossly defamatory. Mr. Hughes has further tried to avoid the challenge and investigation of his description of missionary life by declaring that words and phrases have been misunderstood. But our complaint is not of words and phrases. The libel upon us, the slander of us is woven into the texture of the article; and I venture to say that Mr. Hughes's retraction of words and confession that unsuitable language had been used, did not alter the impression produced by the original in the minds of the people. Along with his resignation of particular words and phrases Mr. Hughes reasserted that his opinions, that is to say the substance and matter of the article in question, had remained unchanged; and it is the opinions expressed, and not the language in which they are expressed, that we complain of. So far from Mr. Hughes withdrawing anything material, so far, from his attempting to erase or change the image of us which he has engraved on the public mind, I find that the pamphlet which was put into our hands four days ago is stated to be in support of the original publication—that is to say, of the second article as well as the rest. Hence the article of which we complain still stands, and the impression it has created still exists, and the necessity for investigation still remains. Mr. Hughes has further argued that it is undesirable, even if it were not unnecessary, to discuss the truth or falsehood of this article, because it cannot be done without bitterness. He says that when we make such a serious matter of a few paragraphs in the *Methodist Times*, when we declare them to be defamatory of missionary character, we are making the question a personal one, and insuring a bitter wrangle in place of a dignified and profitable discussion. I should like to consider for a moment in what sense we can be said to be raising a personal question, when we require investigation into the statements made in the *Methodist Times*, on the ground that they assail our reputation? If we came here to contend that these statements were directed against individuals—that, openly or under a cloak, they were intended to expose the character and life of particular men—A, B, and C—we should be raising what would properly be called a personal question, and one, the discussion of which, would probably be unfruitful and possibly bitter. But we make no such contention. Although the " Friend of Missions " professes to write from experience, and we know the individuals among whom his experience was gained, we are quite certain that his statements were not intended to apply solely or mainly to them; and the missionaries in question, of whom we are two, have not the slightest sense of being implicated more than any others in the charges made. We admit that the *Methodist Times* wrote of missionaries not as individuals, but as a class—as missionaries; and we are sent home to vindicate not individuals, but the class. The question is not, therefore, in any right sense of the word a personal one; and there is no necessary danger in its discussion of that high feeling which is often generated in discussions regarding individuals. But while the *Methodist Times* wrote generally and of a class, it wrote not of a class of abstractions, but of a class of persons; of the position, habits and behaviour of persons; and by inference immediately attending its statements, if not by the statements themselves, of the character of persons. The question we have to press upon the Committee, a question raised, we contend, not by us, but by the *Methodist Times*, is not a personal question, but it is a question of character. This fact it is that gives the question its seriousness and urgency; but it need not give it bitterness. I confess that it is not a pleasant thing to have one's character assailed, even though it be not as an individual but only as a member of a class. I confess that there have been moments of indignation since this day last year, when some of us have not restrained ourselves from bitterness of spirit, and perhaps of speech, that our own, our familar friends in whom we trusted, should thus have lifted up their heel against us. But a year has now passed, and men cannot be missionaries without becoming somewhat case-hardened to what is thought of them, even by their friends; and in the fear of God, I assure Mr. Hughes and the Committee that we are prepared to discuss this general question of missionary character without a trace of bitterness or personal animosity. We are impelled to its discussion solely for the sake of the work of God, and we declare our desire and, God helping us, our determination to deal with it as dispassionately as with any question whatever affecting God's work in our hands. Mr. Hughes attributes to bitterness even our contention that the question is a question of character, and one that must be investigated. I have endeavoured to show him earlier in my speech that such an assumption as to our motives is unworthy of him and unjust to us. Let him give up this *à priori* condemnation of us, and I will undertake that he shall not in the course of this inquiry have cause to resume it. I have dealt with the reasons adduced by Mr. Hughes why this inquiry should not be of the nature required by your Bangalore missionaries —viz., an investigation into the truth or falsehood of the article on "The Evils of a False Position," and other statements in the *Methodist Times*. I have shown that Mr. Hughes's innocence of intention to injure us, and his opinion that he has not done so, do not by any means settle the question; that his professions of correcting his statements have left them substantially as they were; and that the question not being in any correct sense a personal one, we may hope to be able to discuss it calmly and judicially. I must now ask your further patience while I refer to positive reasons why the inquiry into the truth or untruth of the *Methodist Times*' assertions should and must be granted. The great and sufficient reason is that the question at stake is the question of the character of your missionaries. It is this fact that rightfully gives it precedence of all questions of policy; it is this that forbids us in India to give you any rest until you have investigated and decided it. If anyone had prophesied to us eleven months ago that it would ever be necessary to argue in a company of Englishmen the question whether or not the article on "The Evils of a False Position" reflects on the character of the class described in it, we should have ridiculed the prediction. We should have declared that whatever Mr. Hughes might in the future have to say or unsay about that article, he would never venture to assert to anyone able to read plain and vigorous English that it did not touch our character. Yet it is necessary to argue this question to-day, and I must ask you to bear with me while I enter into some detail on a matter which cannot but seem self-evident to most of you. It will not be denied, I trust, by Mr. Hughes that the article contains, and largely consists of assertions respecting the position, surroundings, habits, and behaviour of missionaries. And, when the habits and behaviour of men are described, it is a commonplace that inferences as to their character are inevitable, and follow as closely as the shadow follows the man. Which of us can hear an account of the habits and behaviour of a man, or a class of men, without involuntarily passing judgment on their character? Do we not indeed, commonly, when we wish to describe a man's character, tell what his actions and habits are, knowing that that is quite equivalent to an enumeration of his qualities? "By their fruits ye shall know them." Further, the particular habits and behaviour described in this article were such as were plainly out of harmony with, even contradictory of, the previously received conception of missionaries, were such as to destroy belief in those very qualities which it is most essential that missionaries should possess. And, therefore, I say that readers who believed these statements must inevitably derive from them views, and adverse views of missionary character. Further, I maintain that the writer himself knew that what he was writing practically concerned character and condemned missionaries. Not only does he introduce himself twice over in the first paragraph as bringing a "charge" against missionaries, but he takes elaborate pains in the closing paragraphs to exculpate them. What from, if not from the imputations of their character conveyed in the preceding assertion? If it is true that *qui s'excuse s'accuse*, it is generally true also that he who excuses another accuses him; and where is the occasion, I should like to know, for the Friend of Missions to asseverate that we are self-sacrificing and are not responsible for the state of things he describes, if that description is not, taken by itself, such as would condemn us, and if the article does not concern our character at all? Nothing is plainer than that the writer himself understood that his assertions, unless qualified and corrected, would form a serious charge against missionaries. The only possible defence, then, for Mr. Hughes, against the assertion that this article is destructive to our character, lies in the contention that one part of the article undoes the mischief which the other part does; that though the poison is there, the antidote is there with it; that although we are accused, we are also abundantly excused. Readers are cautioned, it may be said, against drawing inferences injurious to missionaries from the assertions made, though those assertions would naturally lead to such inferences; they are definitely told that such inferences are not correct. Let us look at this defence for a moment—though I must again apologise for occupying the attention of the Committee with proof of what I cannot but believe is a self-evident thesis. The article declares, even reiterates, that we missionaries have a self-sacrificing spirit; and the author of it, I doubt not, believed the declaration. Would such a declaration undo the mischief? Is it anything more than the declaration that, "Brutus is an honourable man?" That declaration is often repeated in the famous speech; but does it weigh a straw against the graphic and detailed description of actions and behaviour in the midst of which it occurs? And suppose that Anthony had sincerely believed that Brutus was an honourable man, do you think that, the rest of his speech remaining what it was, his belief in Brutus would have availed a jot to undo the effect of his vivid words? They drive in fashionable vehicles called phaetons; but missionaries are self-sacrificing men! They live in a way that would cost £1,000 a-year in London; but they are self-sacrificing men! They regulate their dress by the necessity of appearance at Court; but they are self-sacrificing men! When Mr. Hughes described the habits and actions of missionaries and so gave his readers materials for forming their own judgment of missionary character, he had no right to expect that they would refrain from doing so, and accept his judgment instead. They may follow him in many things, but they will not follow him in bestowing their love and confidence on the strength of his mere assertion, and where their knowledge (as they fancy) leads them only to distrust and condemnation. But Mr. Hughes may say that the article not only declares that missionaries are self-sacrificing men, but gives evidence of it. Let us look at these evidences. The first consists in the enumeration of a few missionaries who, for once, actually gave back to the society some small portion of their stipends! Did Mr. Hughes really think that the *Methodist Times* had readers whom this evidence would convince when they had been told in the paragraphs before that missionaries were every year receiving at least twice as much as they needed? Another argument in excuse of missionaries is found in the opening sentence of the article, and repeated at its close. It is, that the present style and scale of missionary living were adopted because of the necessities of educational work among the aristocratic classes. This excuse for us, however, has, singularly, never been referred to again by Mr. Hughes in any of his many attempts to exculpate us from his own charges. The audacity that invented it has not proved equal to maintaining it in face of the incontrovertible fact that the present scale and style of missionary living were in vogue scores of years before educational work was thought of. There remains only one excuse for missionaries by which the article attempts to relieve them from its own injurious imputations, and that is, that they have to submit to a system, for the maintenance of which they are not responsible any more than for its introduction. This excuse is the one that Mr. Hughes still puts forward when he tries to acquit us of blame in leading the life he attributes to us. Now, Mr. Hughes could not have shown his ignorance, both of the conditions and of the facts of missionary life in India, more completely than by professing that, in matters such as these, we are or can be bound by any system. The bondage of system belongs to large societies, to countries where the conditions and circumstances of life are constant, and where there is an accumulated force of tradition and usage. System, as a bondage, we may almost literally say, does not exist for missionaries in India, living in isolation or in small groups eager and restless to try every means that can be devised that can help them in the stupendous work committed to their hands. "Bound by system!" Why, I venture to say, Sir, that there is not one of our missionaries in India who cannot to-morrow, if he pleases, adopt the "Via Media" without let or hindrance; and at the very time when this critic, with vigorous voice, stood waving us to the "Via Media" that he called "untrodden," he might have known, if he had looked about him, that there were at least two of our own men returning, broken in body and in heart, along that very road, which they had trodden to their life-long cost. And if he had inquired at all into the past of our history, as we might have expected him to do, he would have found that not only this, but a dozen other experiments in missionary life and bearing, had been tried by one and another of your missionaries before now. "Bound by system," forsooth, when our thoughts and longings, and our experiments are being continually directed to the discovery of new methods for the advancement of our work. No! gentlemen of the Committee, if it be true that your missionaries are living in luxury, and if this is the best defence that can be made for them, you will not be far wrong if you write them down knaves. It may be that ordinary people whom the *Methodist Times'* description of us has reached, have not knowledge enough to appreciate the flimsiness of these excuses; but they have an instinct which tells them that men supposed to be self-denying and zealous, and living in the way described, are beyond all excuse; and, I warrant, they do not for a week remember, if even they trouble to read, these apologies for us that I have referred to. I should not envy the position of the missionary who should go with no better defence for himself than that which Mr. Hughes supplies, to ask for help in his work from a plain town or country Methodist. "You want money from me, do you? But I understand you are getting £300 a year when £150 would do for you well enough. What becomes of the other £150?" "Well," says our missionary, "when the Society is in very great straits, I have occasionally given part of it back to the Mission funds." "Oh! . . . And at other other times?" "As a rule I am bound to spend it on myself." "Indeed! A great trial that must be. But how does it happen that you are bound to spend it on yourself? I should be obliged if you can explain that to me." "Well, you see," Mr. Hughes's poor missionary has to say, "a long time ago missionaries foresaw that thirty years after them it would be found to be a good thing to start mission schools; and they foresaw that the pupils in these schools, being aristocratic, would wish their missionary teachers to live in good style, and so to prepare for that day they determined to start in good style themselves; and we had to keep it up ever since." "Indeed! Indeed! That needs a little thinking over, it seems to me. But are you in a mission-school teaching aristocrats?" "No, I cannot say that I am myself." "Then why need you spend £300 on yourself when £150 would do?" "Well, of course, I must do the same as the others. The system's established, and we must all go according to it." "Even if you're wanting money so badly that you're entreating the Lord and man for it with all your might, and have got plenty in your pocket all the time, you can't use it because it would be against the system, eh?" "Exactly; when the system is established, it would never do to go against it." "Well, then, my dear Sir," I think we might expect our plain Methodist friend to say, "I've got a system as well—the system of not giving my money except where it's needed; and I'm afraid I mustn't go against my system. Good morning, sir." I make bold to say that no one can have read and believed this article—no one except Mr. Hughes and those who have grown, as he has done, into a conviction that their brethren are untrustworthy—and not entertain a feeling of, at least, coldness and suspicion towards Indian missionaries. I do not say that all who are so affected by it will realise that the change is due to the article. Some, no doubt, imagine at present that their changed attitude to us is due to our "bitterness" and "persecution" in connection with this controversy; others, it may be, conceive that their loss of interest in Indian missions is due to disagreement with us on questions of policy. But this much is certain, that wherever this article has come and been believed, there warmth has changed to coldness, and confidence to suspicion; and a sufficient explanation of the change is to be found in the fact that the article is utterly destructive of our character. I have said that the question before us, if it be one of character, rightly claims precedence of all questions of policy; for this reason, that the Church's confidence in its missionaries depends on what it believes of their character, and this confidence is the vital breath of missionary operations. Questions of policy may be large, intricate, long-lasting, and a question of character may be temporary, accidental, easy to be settled. But the question of character, when it does arise, and while it

E

lasts, has an importance, an urgency surpassing that of any question of policy; for discussing policy is only discussing which of many paths our society is to walk in: discussing character involves the question whether or not the Society shall be left with any breath to breathe. When we out yonder feel that the confidence of our Church is passing from us—when we realise, we can scarcely tell how, that the interest, the sympathy, the prayers, the gifts of our people are not with us as they used to be—we begin to feel as the diver at the bottom of the ocean would feel if the tube on which depended his breath and life were closed or severed. The tide of our battle begins to waver, we know not how, when the hands of the Church are, for any cause, not lifted up on our behalf as aforetime. There are those who tell us, however, that confidence has not been seriously disturbed by the allegations we complain of; that they have been here, there, up and down the land; and everywhere our people still trust us, and scout the misrepresentations of us that have been circulated. Thank God for those who do so trust us! But we are told by others, especially by those whom duty carries into circles where their own choice would not carry them, of individuals, of households, of societies, and of congregations, whose mouths are filled with the stories circulated by our critics, and in whose affections our Indian Missions no longer hold a place. Those, too, whose finger is on the pulse of public opinion, tell us that by now, owing to the reiterations of our critics and our enforced silence, the general public verdict is wholly against us. And we in India scarcely need to come home to learn whether or not the Church's confidence in us is waning, for we are not only, as I said a moment ago, seriously, even fatally, affected by the withdrawal of its confidence, but we are quick and sensitive to detect, in ways that it is not easy to analyse, the symptoms of diminished confidence. It is the builders on the walls who soonest discover disturbance of the foundations, and measure best the seriousness of the disaster; and though some of you looking on, tell us that all is right, and that we should go on building as if nothing were the matter, we cannot do it; we must come down and have the foundation examined on which our building stands. And we feel at the same time, and feel very strongly, that our duty in this matter does not depend on what you or we can discern as to the extent to which the representations of the *Methodist Times* have actually won credence and disturbed confidence. It does not depend on a counting of heads on one side or the other. The fact that we have been seriously maligned in a public journal in our own land, by an eminent minister of our own Church, is sufficient to impose on us the painful duty that we have undertaken. There is, for the self-respecting man, an instinct in regard to the preservation of his character corresponding to the instinct of physical self-preservation. And if there is, even among men of the world, a jealousy in regard to personal honour, which recognises that a public and serious defamation of their character must on no account be ignored, how much greater jealousy of our reputation should there be among us, when not only our personal repute among men, but the very prosecution of God's work under our hands depends upon the estimation in which we are held by the Church that has sent us forth? Whether up to the present moment, the disturbance or confidence in us has been wide or narrow, severe or trifling, it is not to be doubted that should these allegations of the *Methodist Times* stand as they are, should we allow them to enter the record of history unretracted, uncontradicted, unrefuted, then we should not only be leaving to whosoever chooses to take them up weapons for an assault that would then be irresistible on us or our successors at any future date, but we should be leaving in our Church seeds of distrust and disaffection that, in their growth and spreading, would ruin our Indian missions. Aye, and those very men who tell us now to be quiet and 'live it down' would be the first, when the evil had manifestly declared itself, to tell us that we had not been firm enough in dealing with its first beginnings, and that we should on this occasion have been resolute to have the evil things cast out. What is it, then, we ask for, in the name of all your Indian missionaries? It is for a thorough and searching inquiry into the truth or untruth of those statements in the *Methodist Times*, which we regard as affecting our character. And when your Indian brethren unanimously, with entreaty, with urgency, with insistence, ask for this or any other thing as essential to their prosecution of God's work, I believe, Mr. President and brethren, that you will ask, Why should we not grant it? rather than, Why should we grant it? I appeal to Mr. Hughes, I say to him, When statements that have been prominently made in your journal are flatly and publicly contradicted, are declared to be wholly false and unfounded; when a body of your own brethren declare that the interests most precious to them demand that the truth or falsehood of these statements shall be searchingly investigated; and when they undertake, as I again undertake in the presence of God and in the face of this assembly, that they are prepared to prosecute this investigation without bitterness or animosity, in the most dispassionate manner possible; when these things are so, I do not know what else the world can say, if you should persist in resisting this inquiry, than that you dare not face the issue raised. We appeal to the Committee for thorough inquiry, and for the publication of all that the inquiry reveals. We do not come to it to procure a condemnation of Messrs. Hughes and Lunn; we do not ask it to pronounce a verdict on any question in regard to which the Committee, or any section of it, stands in the position of plaintiff or defendant; we do not desire it to attempt by formal pronouncements to foreclose the questions at issue against the verdict of that ultimate tribunal to which our eyes are turned—the judgment of our Church. Our desire is that the Committee, making itself the instrument of investigation, shall be a speaking trumpet through which the truth and the whole truth shall become known to all who care to hear it, for we are confident that the day when the whole truth is known will be the day when we shall receive back in full measure that confidence which is our most precious possession. Allow me, in conclusion, again to express our devout thankfulness to God that at last we are admitted to the opportunity of free and face-to-face utterance with you and with our people; and the hope which springs up in us this day, that the cloud which has hung over us for a year past, more black and gloomy than I can tell, may yet prove to be "big with mercy" and "break in blessings on our head."

The Committee adjourned for luncheon at half-past one.

Afternoon Session.

The Committee reassembled at half-past two.

The Rev. JOSEPH POSNETT offered prayer.

The Rev. H. P. HUGHES, M.A., said he did not wish to shirk any inquiry, but the only immediate effect of the appeal that had been made to them that morning would be to go over the same ground that had already been gone over in the Committee and in the Conference, and with no other result than that which had been reached before. He thought that his brethren attached too much importance to the rhetorical and literary style used in a certain newspaper article. Now, the article alluded to was founded upon certain convictions as to matters of fact. What those facts were was not fully explained. It was an expression of opinion rather than a statement of evidence. If the Committee thought he should give the evidence upon which those opinions were founded that might lead to a happy result. But whatever that Committee might think as to the particular way in which certain conclusions were reached in that article, that would not settle the question as to whether the facts stated were facts or not. There were questions of logic, and there were questions of rhetoric, and it seemed to him that those two things were in very great danger of being confounded. He had already informed the Committee that he was unable to accept the interpretation of the real meaning of the article objected to which had been given to them that morning, but he certainly would have not have printed it in that form if he had anticipated that such an interpretation would have been given of it. Some one had said to him that a change in the structure of half-a-dozen sentences would have altered the whole effect of the article. If he could have foreseen that, he need scarcely say that he would have done his best to avoid any phrase that was likely to do injury to the work of God at home or abroad. But at that moment they were just where they were twelve months ago. He wished they could see their way to some practical dealing with the question that would enable them to reach some practical conclusion. If the Committee were to say that he and Dr. Lunn had a most mischievous way of expressing their opinions, he should, of course, be sorry for that, but that would not much effect the main issue. As a matter of fact, in his wide circle of acquaintance, he had not met with a single man or woman outside their own circle of official laymen who had put upon that particular article the extreme interpretation that his brethren from India had put upon it. On the other hand, both ministers and laymen had expressed to him their strong conviction that there was no discourtesy in the article seeing that they held the views they did. (Cries of "Oh! oh!") The very fact that some of them cried "Oh! oh!" indicated to what an extent they had reached a fore-gone conclusion. He was very willing to take part in any inquiry that might elicit the true facts of the case. The statements to which exception had been taken must be regarded as a whole. When they spoke of the Indian missionaries allowances as being equal to £300 a-year and a bungalow, every man must attach to that his own interpretation. He confessed, however, that it seemed to him the only way to reach a satisfactory solution of the question before them was that of considering the questions of fact which were raised in the Bangalore Report, and also in his own statements. (Hear, hear.) If it should turn out that their missionaries in India—although he very much objected to the limitation of the subject in that way, which gave it a personal aspect which he very much resented; but he supposed they could not avoid, there at any rate, the limitation of it to their own Society—he repeated, if it should turn out that their missionaries in India could not live in comfort and health and happiness on a smaller stipend than that which they now received, then that particular article would be entirely discredited, and, without discussing words and phrases, it would be shown that it was not justified, and must be withdrawn. In that case, he would do all he could to give publicity to the fact that those statements had been made upon misconception and error. But, unless it could be proved that their missionaries could not live on such stipends as were given to American missionaries and to the missionaries of the London Missionary Society, he was sure that the feeling outside would be that the main question had been evaded. (Hear, hear.) He could not contemplate commencing that discussion afresh with any satisfaction. He was quite unable to admit that the presence of those distinguished brethren from India had placed them in a very much better position to settle the question than they were in before. Nobody could complain that Indian interests had been unrepresented on that Committee, and therefore so far as the expression of opinion concerning the import of certain phrases was concerned, they were proposing to discuss a question that had been already discussed *ad nauseam*. At the same time he fully recognised the fact that they were very much troubled—that they believed there had been a reflection upon their character, and that they were anxious that this should be removed — and he was anxious to assist in that removal; but what he deprecated was the commencement of an interminable controversy on points which had been already fully considered, and he confessed to a strong conviction that Mr. Bond was right in the advice which he had given that morning. The heart and centre of the question was a question of fact. If it could be proved that Dr. Lunn and himself were entirely mistaken on a question of fact, then the house they had built up was a house of cards, and it must fall to pieces; but if they could not dispose of those facts, they had achieved nothing effectual. That was his position. At the same time he was anxious to assure his brethren of the love he felt for them. (Hear, hear.)

Dr. JENKINS: I do not agree with Mr. Hughes in saying that we are just now where we were twelve months ago. We are farther on than we were, and for that advancement we are very much indebted to the admirable addresses that have been delivered this morning by the brethren from Madras and the Bangalore District. Now, if it be a matter of fact, if it be a question of salary, or of financial support, and that only, or that chiefly, those brethren need not have come. (Hear, hear.) That matter could have been deliberated upon in Committee and in correspondence with India. But that is not the important matter that just now presses upon us. It is not the matter of rhetoric employed in those articles that is complained of. It is not to be explained by rhetorical exaggeration in any way. I grant, with one of the brethren who spoke this morning, that it may be difficult for us to analyse those articles; but the point to be dealt with is the defamation of missionary character

(Hear, hear.) Mr. Hughes says that it is a matter of fact. It is so. Certain statements have been made, and there must be patient inquiry as to the ground upon which those statements are based. That can be done; but I rather doubt whether it can be done in a very large Committee. I hope there will be the appointment of a competent Sub-committee, who shall go patiently through all the details which these brethren are prepared to present to us, and publish their report. (Hear, hear.)

The PRESIDENT: Has Dr. Lunn anything to say to us?

Dr. LUNN: I have nothing to say at present.

The Rev. THOMAS CHAMPNESS said he was not prepared to argue the question at full length, but he should like the facts of the case to be dealt with by that Committee as far as possible. He was in possession of a certain amount of knowledge, and the knowledge that he had led him to act on certain lines. It should be borne in mind that the question before them would be settled outside as well as inside those walls, and their people would listen to everything that was said without having the privilege of listening to the two brethren who had spoken, and they would look at the figures as they were brought before them. He was not prepared to speak to the question of how much married men should have, because he had only one married pair who were working under his direction at present. But he had certain unmarried men, and it was upon his experience concerning these that he had formed his opinion. He had discovered that two or three unmarried men living together might live in great comfort in India at a cost of £50 a year each—and that he was prepared to prove so far as figures could prove anything. He knew from his own observation that those men lived as well as young men in this country lived—barring the difficulties of Indian life as compared with English life—and better. He would not like anybody to think that he wished to bring his missionary brethren down to the same level as the men whom he employed. (Hear, hear.) He would be prepared to allow them £80 instead of £50 and £30 to keep a horse—in which case £50 would still be left unaccounted for. He might be wrong, but he had a right to express his opinions, and he would express them in that Committee first. (Hear, hear.) It should not be forgotten that he had himself been a missionary. Now, his point was this. If it was possible for an unmarried minister to live in comfort on £110 a year, they ought in all fairness to their people to save the other £50. That was his line, and he should be glad for anybody to say what he liked about it. (Hear, hear.)

Dr. RIGG: I hope, Sir, we have not got down to this level. (Hear, hear.) I confess my amazement that this should be considered an important contribution to the consideration of the grave matters that are now before us. I am surprised that Mr. Hughes should say that his main contention was that ministers could live on less than what they now receive.

Mr. HUGHES: I beg pardon. It is my main contention only on that particular issue. (Hear, hear.)

Dr. RIGG continued: Sir, I take it that this is the very least point, and it is the only point on which Mr. Hughes has specifically spoken. Then are we to understand that we have nothing to do here to-day but to decide whether we can in future save £20 or £30 each from the allowances to our missionaries? I feel humbled. I must remind this Committee also, as that is touched upon, that we must be exceedingly careful what sort of a rebound we provoke in this country. (Hear, hear.) Let our brethren come and visit the homes of those who criticise them. (Hear, hear.) As a matter of fact, it is not £300 and a bungalow that our missionaries receive, but £250 and £230. But let it always be remembered that the increase in the allowances of Indian missionaries has been far less in ratio than the increase in the allowances of ministers at home during the last thirty years. I feel ashamed that any of our home ministers, whose average allowances have been increased from £130 to £180, should speak after this manner. The largest amount I ever received in any circuit was for one year £170, and, during the three years out of the last four I travelled, my allowance was £130. Compare those allowances with what my brethren are receiving to-day! It is perfectly monstrous that we, with this great percentage of increase upon our allowances in the country—sitting still here at home—should be directing our criticism to the allowances made to our ministers abroad. (Hear, hear.) I do not say this because I am not in favour of economy. I have worked for economy. But, after all, what does this kind of talk amount to? Does it touch any really important question whatsoever? We are able to look after these things, and if Mr. Hughes had come to our Committee and brought up evidence on these subjects, he would have been listened to. (Hear, hear.) And so likewise would Dr. Lunn. But we have to consider what our brethren have said to us. They tell us that the charge against them is that their spirit has not been that which becometh Christians—that there has been a general luxury of character about their equipment—that they have been guilty of conformity to the world—for that is what it comes to—conformity to the world in its usages, and what is supposed to be fine society, which has been incompatible with the spiritual consecration of missionaries. That is what it is. Nevertheless, I so far agree with Mr. Hughes that I think we have already pronounced upon these subjects, and that upon sufficient evidence, and I think we pronounced a full acquittal. (Hear, hear.) But the missionaries say that that has not been brought sufficiently out by the English public—that their defences have been suppressed. These men have a right to feel strongly on that subject, for they say that the effect of this in India has been something terrible. It is no use quoting to us here this morning what some men in England may think of those articles, when we have articles read to us from the *Times of India*. That paper is one of enormous influence. The other day I had a paper sent to me from India by a great official, and he chose the *Times of India* as being the best paper he could send. Now, if the *Times of India* regards those articles as we are told it did regard them, do not let us be told that they did no damage—that it is altogether a mistake in which we confound rhetoric with statements of fact. It is absurd to tell us these things. Why, surely the writers in the *Times of India* understand the difference between what is called rhetoric and fact as well as Mr. Hughes. Besides, what right have Christian ministers to write rhetoric that can be so construed? It reminds me of what we read in the Bible of those who send out arrows and say, "Am I not in sport?" We cannot do with people saying "Am I not in sport?" This has been a very serious business. Thousands of pounds down in our income at home —confidence in missions shaken among English residents and among natives abroad—and the native papers catching at all this and making the very worst of it! I think we have acquitted the missionaries of the imputations cast upon them, but if the missionaries come to us and say, "We do not consider that the evidence has been sufficiently gone into; we do not consider that we have been properly heard; we have something to say to this ourselves," and demand that they shall be heard and their evidence brought forward, I do not know how we can refuse them. As for this document that Mr. Hughes has just put in, I do not think that that is our first concern. We shall understand the worth of it better after we have appointed a Committee to go into it. You have heard that some evidence which should have been brought forward was not produced.

Mr. HUGHES: It was not at hand at the time of publication.

Dr. RIGG (continued): Reference has been made to the allowances made to American missionaries. It should be known that the average allowance given to ministers in America is very much lower than the average amount given to ministers in this country. A few men in large cities have large salaries, but if you ascertain what the average allowance is, you will find that, having regard to the purchasing power of the dollar and the purchasing power of the shilling, the average is decidedly lower than in this country. But I do not think we have any right at this moment to found our conclusions upon this pamphlet that has been written, signed, and circulated by Mr. Hughes and Dr. Lunn. (Hear, hear.) I am sorry that that pamphlet does not contain such a restatement as we ask for. A clear restatement of what they intended to say is not to be found in this document. I think we have no alternative, therefore, but to concede the demands made by our brethren from India. We have heard these brethren. They are a sample of our missionaries. Are they not entitled to be treated with as much confidence as ourselves? Have we in them an average sample of Methodist ministers at home? Just ask that question. Let us put it to ourselves, are these brethren liable to be criticised as to whether their allowances shall be £230 or £250 and a bungalow, and criticised in public? God forbid that any people should take to criticising us in this manner, or these severe critics would catch it pretty well all round! Again, I ask are these brethren to be lectured by Methodist journalists as to themselves and their consecration to their work? We must be nauseated with the idea. (Hear, hear.) There are a great many things about Indian missions that need considering, no doubt, about that. If Mr. Little were here he would corroborate my own statement. When he was in this country some years ago I said: We shall have to consider how it has happened that our missions in India have, comparatively speaking, been a failure, but we shall have to consider Western Africa at the same time. We have been learning wisdom from past experience in West Africa, and so we shall have to learn wisdom from past experience in India. My own view is that it is not so much that we have done wrong as that we have not done other things besides. (Hear, hear.) If we had a broader Indian field—if we had a greater variety of work there—if we had more money to spend there, we might see far greater results. We have not had sufficient continuity of labour there. But that is no new doctrine. Some of us have been preaching that doctrine for twenty or thirty years, but the Committee have not had funds to carry that work out as it should have been carried out. The people have not " taken " to our Indian Missions as they have to other missions; they have been rather intolerant of the expense. My dear friend Dr. Jenkins many years ago proposed that we should have a mission to the native tribes on either side of the river Godavery. Why did not we? There were not the funds. That was the sole reason, and where you have not an indefinite supply of funds you have to suffer repulse (Hear, hear.) I have no doubt that there is much in regard to policy that needs to be carefully considered. I believe that some adjustments with regard to salaries may very well be made; there is a great deal that may be done in regard to India, but in order to do it we must first of all have confidence in our men. (Hear, hear.) I do not mean to say that every Indian missionary has been a consecrated man in the right and full sense of the word. I do not think so. There are men who have not stuck to their work there. There are men who have gone to the work for a time, and it has not answered. There are men who, while they were in the work, did not do it credit. But what of all this? Does this affect the character of our missionary brethren in India as a whole? Look at the list of names—what a galaxy? What can be said against our missionary abroad that may not with equal truth be said of our ministers at home? Let us trust our brethren abroad, and now that they have demanded this investigation, let us give it them, and let us give it them to the full. (Hear, hear.)

The Rev. Dr. STEPHENSON said it seemed to him that they were all of one mind as to the necessity of permitting the brethren in India a renewed examination as to the facts of the case in accordance with their demands—and he added his tribute of admiration as to the form and spirit of them. He hoped that in continuing their discussions they might avoid any unnecessary excitement of feeling. It was necessary that they should have this examination, for some things had been said without sufficient proof. He could not accept, for instance, Dr. Rigg's statement as to the comparative value of American and English minister's salaries. But he would not argue the case, as that was a point that might very well be considered by a Sub-committee. He would take the responsibility of moving: "That a small Sub-committee be appointed (he would suggest nine as the number) to examine into all the facts and statements on both sides of the controversy, and to report to this Committee." (Hear, hear.)

The Rev. G. W. OLVER, B.A., said he should be glad to second that proposal. He was thankful for the tone and temper of the whole of that morning's conversation. It showed that that whole business might be gone into thoroughly, and so gone into as thoroughly to satisfy their people on the whole question. He was sure that no other course was open to them. The secretaries were of opinion that a Committee of nine would meet the case. The only request they would make would be that no one of the officers of the Society should be among the nine; but that they should be at liberty, one or more of them from time to time, to attend for the purpose of giving any information that might be required. Of course, it should be understood that the members of that Sub-committee would be men who would command the confidence of the whole Connexion, and who would go into the matter thoroughly, and, as Mr. Patterson had said, "mercilessly." He believed that they would all rejoice together when they found that they had arrived at conclusions which would at the same time clear entirely their brethren in India, and assure their people at home that the missions of to-day were worthy of the best traditions of the missions of their forefathers. (Hear, hear.)

The Rev. John BOND suggested that the Sub-committee should be instructed to consider not only facts and figures, but also those other points which he had mentioned that morning. (Hear, hear.)

Mr. BEAUCHAMP supported the resolution. He said that the three great questions were—(1) Are our missionaries paid too much? (2) Do they separate themselves too much from the natives? (3) Do they spend too much time and money in education in comparison with evangelistic work? He thought that these were the questions for the Sub-committee to inquire into, and then let them report. (Hear, hear.)

Mr. J. W. JEPPS thought it was distinctly understood that the Sub-committee was to go into the facts and statements of the *Methodist Times* without going into the question of policy at all? (Hear, hear.)

The MAYOR of BURSLEM (Mr. Edge) hoped that they would not fetter the Sub-committee. (Hear, hear.)

Mr. T. MORGAN HARVEY wished to know what their Indian missionaries thought of the proposal.

The Rev. J. E. CLAPHAM hoped that the reference would be sufficiently wide to enable the Sub-committee to take cognisance of any new facts that might be brought before its notice. What they must have at this time was a thorough and exhaustive inquiry. He hoped it would be understood that that Sub-committee would approach the subject impartially, and that men would be appointed on the Committee who were not committed on either side. (Hear, hear.)

The Rev. H. O. RATTENBURY wished to understand what subjects were to be remitted to the Committee. If both the pamphlets were to go before it, everything went to it.

Dr. STEPHENSON hoped that the reference would not be too limited. Mr. Arthur Smith had suggested that, inasmuch as laymen would be on the Committee, it would be well to have an equal number. (Hear, hear.)

Dr. JENKINS objected to the remitting of the subject of education to the Sub-committee. (Hear, hear.)

The Rev. JOSEPH POSNETT said it was most important that they should have the minds of the Indian missionaries perfectly satisfied and at rest touching all that they described as affecting character, and all those moral qualities which fitted them to become true missionaries of the Cross. As he listened to them that morning he found an undercurrent of pain—he found that they were wounded to the quick. And why? Because their character was touched. (Hear, hear.) Now, they must have that matter put right, for nothing would be settled until that was settled. Mr. Hughes had as great a heart as any of them touching the character of those men. He believed that Mr. Hughes wished that those articles had never been written. He was as magnificent a man as there was in that room—but sometimes it was good for a big-hearted man like Mr. Hughes to make a good, large-hearted confession. ("Hear, hear," and laughter.) He (Mr. Posnett) believed that he had not been large-hearted enough in his penitence. He could not understand how it was that he had not somehow or other expressed a deeper penitential spirit. On the general question he (Mr. Posnett) deprecated a cheese-paring policy.

Mr. FLITCH hoped that they were not going to touch the question of how much their missionaries ought to have in India and elsewhere. Their Finance Committee was well able to deal with that question. If they reduced the allowances of their missionaries to the lowest minimum, they would by-and-bye come to the question of stipends at home. He held that the admission of missionaries into the *élite* society of India depended not on the question of income, but of character. (Hear, hear.) The men whom they sent out to India were known to be men who were reliable and truthful and honest gentlemen, and worthy of the best society, and that was the secret of their social position. (Hear, hear.) He deeply regretted that the articles to which too much reference had been made had ever been written. Great injury had been done by them to the Methodist Society both at home and abroad. He did not think that their missionaries were overpaid. They ought to be placed in such a position that they could show hospitality and contribute in various ways to the material advancement of the work. (Hear, hear.) He hoped the Sub-committee would do their work very thoroughly. (Hear, hear.)

Mr. QUIBELL asked whether the question of policy was to come before the Committee? If not, when would that question be raised? He thought that their people would regard that as the largest question they had before them. (Hear, hear.)

The PRESIDENT said that a great question of policy ought not to be debated in a Committee which had not been called to consider it. (Hear, hear.)

The Rev. GEORGE PATTERSON agreed with the President. He said he should object to the mixing up of two questions—(1) Because Mr. Findlay and himself were not representatives of the Educational question; and (2) Because if they combined the questions of policy and character, the former would override the latter, and put it out of sight, and that ought not to be. He agreed that the question of policy was incomparably the larger question, but it was not for that reason the most important one. He wished to say another thing—viz., that they would be perfectly contented with any Sub-committee that satisfied the General Committee and the Methodist Conference. They had nothing to do with the formation of that Committee or with the precise form in which the issues were to be presented to that Committee. (Hear, hear.)

After some other remarks on the same subject by the Revs. Silvester, Whitehead, Professor Findlay, Dr. Greeves, and Messrs. J. W. Lewis, W. O. Quibell, and W. Hedges,

The Resolution,

moved by Dr. Stephenson, and seconded by the Rev. G. W. Olver, B.A., was read as follows, viz:—" That having heard the Revs. G. Patterson and W. H. Findlay, deputed by the Indian missionaries, the Committee resolves—That in the judgment of this Committee it is necessary for the satisfaction of the Indian missionaries and the supporters of the Society that the statements made in the articles entitled "A New Mission Policy" should be thoroughly examined by an influential Sub-committee. That a Sub-committee of nine members be therefore appointed to examine into all the facts and statements bearing upon the position and character of the Indian missionaries, and to report to this Committee. The Sub-committee shall have power to request the attendance of any witnesses, either members of our own or other Churches, and to obtain evidence from documents, &c.

The resolution on being put to the vote was declared by the President to be carried *nem. con.*

The Rev. H. P. HUGHES, M.A., said he might be permitted to say that he felt as strongly as any of the brethren who had spoken in appreciation not only of the ability, but of the spirit in which their brethren from India had spoken that day. (Hear, hear.)

Mr. GEDYE suggested that the nomination of the Sub-committee should be left with the President.

This was ultimately agreed to.

It was also agreed, after some conversation, that the Sub-committee should meet on Tuesday in Whit-week, the President to occupy the chair. The Sub-committee to consist of five ministers (including the President) and four laymen. It was further agreed that an arrangement should be made for the reporting of the proceedings of the Sub-committee, similar to that which had been made for the meeting of that day—with the understanding that the report should not be sent to the newspapers until it had been before the General Committee.

The Doxology was sung, and the meeting was closed with the Benediction, at a quarter-past five o'clock.

THE
PROPOSED NEW MISSIONARY POLICY.

To the Members of the Wesleyan Missionary Committee.

Mr. President and Gentlemen,

We beg to submit the following statement in compliance with your request that we would furnish you with the facts and arguments which have led us to propose a "new missionary policy" for India. We do this the more readily in the prayerful hope that it may remove the extreme misapprehensions which are entertained and circulated respecting our views and objects.

For many years past, Mr. Price Hughes has taken a deep interest in the Wesleyan Missionary Society, and has been permitted by God to render it some services which are, perhaps, not yet completely forgotten. Ever since he was instrumental in promoting the effort by which the old debt of the society was swept away, he has striven to secure a spirited missionary policy abroad, and to awaken missionary enthusiasm at home. But he has found dissatisfaction in every part of the country. As long ago as 1885, there was a discussion in the Conference which proved how deep and widespread was the popular discontent. In that debate, Mr. Posnett called attention to the ominous fact that :—

"During the last nine years there had been a deficiency in the income from the home districts of over £12,000."

In the Conference of 1886 there was another discussion of the same sort. Mr. W. H. Stephenson

"Pointed out that the home income of the Missionary Society was only £5,000 more than it was 40 years ago, and yet since then the population had vastly increased."

The Right Hon. Henry H. Fowler, M.P., and other influential laymen spoke strongly in the same direction.

In the Conference of 1887, Mr. W. O. Quibell

"Exceedingly lamented the constant diminution of income."

This long-continued feeling of dissatisfaction found expression abroad as well as at home. In a special article published in

F

the *Methodist Times*, on January 28th, 1888, Rev. W. H. Findlay, M.A., of Negapatam, said :—

"There is undeniably something seriously amiss with our foreign missions. Since 1883 the receipts from the home districts have fallen year by year, and were lower in 1886 than they have been for fifteen years previously. To check this fall many plans have been devised and attempted; there have been declamations on platforms, discussions in committees, legislation by Conferences. Scarcely a fortnight has passed during the last year or two without letters in your columns, or those of *The Recorder*, containing prescriptions for the relief of the Society's malady. . . . The number and variety of these proposals show that there is probably a radical evil deeper than they reach."

After referring to the fact that the mission house exchequer "does not fill," although Mr. Clapham and others can get all they want "for large undertakings in city and country," Mr. Findlay adds :—

"This is accounted for, I believe, by *a widespread and perfectly justifiable feeling that the general progress of our foreign missions is not such as might fairly be looked for.*"*

Our Comparative failure in India.

There is no part of the mission field where our comparative failure is more marked than in India, where we might reasonably expect our greatest triumphs. Rev. H. Little, chairman and general superintendent of the Negapatam and Trichinopoly district, forwarded to us last year the following tabular statement of the relative position of the principal Indian missionary societies in 1881, when the last census was taken :—

NAME OF SOCIETY.	Foreign Missionaries 1881.	Native Missionaries 1881.	NATIVE CHRISTIANS.		
			1851.	1871.	1881.
Church Missionary Society ...	95	110	35,162	69,114	98,983
Gospel Propagation Society ...	41	57	22,621	45,083	80,812
American Baptist Mission ...	13	59	122	6,810	57,070
London Missionary Society ...	46	37	20,077	39,879	55,138
Gossner's Missionary Society ...	14	2	123	14,804	32,800
American Board	24	30	2,852	8,161	13,816
Leipsic Lutheran Mission ...	17	8	2,957	9,265	12,272
American Methodist Mission ...	32	17		1,835	7,054
Wesleyan Methodist Mission	38	9	440	1,011	3,591

This statement, with our society at the bottom of the list, speaks only too plainly for itself.

* The *italics* in this and other quotations are ours, and are used for the purpose of emphasising important facts.—H. P. H.—H. S. L.

In the *Harvest Field* for last November, Rev. W. H. Findlay calls attention to the fact that in 1885 the Wesleyan Missionary Society, while occupying, amongst English societies that work in India the *sixth* position in age, and the *seventh* in the number of missionaries employed, was only *fifteenth* in the number of its communicants, and *sixteenth* in the number of its adherents. Rev. H. Little, in a letter to the *Methodist Recorder*, threw a very vivid light upon the state of affairs in India. He showed that out of 316 teachers employed in our mission schools in the Madras and Negatapam districts 128 *were heathen*. It was yet more impressive to read that out of 410 members of society in his own district, only 111 were gaining an *independent livelihood*. He added

"In my District we have to day six native ministers; two of them may be regarded as the fruit of our own work. We have 21 catechists, of whom one was won by us from Romanism, and the rest were all baptised outside our mission. *With one exception they have joined us for the work and pay we give them. It is 26 years since I landed in India, and every year has deepened the impression that we are on the wrong tack.*"

Mr. Little and Mr. Findlay believe that the failure which they so emphatically record, is due to the fact that our work there has been fatally devoid of concentration, continuity, and thoroughness. We heartily agree with these distinguished missionaries in tracing failure to our policy and not to our agents. WE NEVER FOR A SINGLE MOMENT IMPUTED PERSONAL BLAME TO OUR MISSIONARY BRETHREN. We were well aware that Indian missionaries are always picked men; and we sincerely believed that the average Indian missionary was superior both in ability and in devotion to the average minister at home. It never occurred to us that anyone could misconstrue our criticisms of policy into a personal attack, and we are still of opinion that our proved love of the missionary cause ought to have protected us from such an imputation. We have the highest confidence in the integrity and devotion of our Indian brethren; and we are, therefore, quite sure that our comparative failure in India is due not to personal shortcomings, but to mistaken policy, for which our missionaries are not responsible.

The Secret of our Failure.

What is the mistake? We entirely agree with Mr. Little and Mr. Findlay that we ought to establish powerful and well-manned mission centres in India. But we think their reform does not go far enough. In addition to that, we hold that we ought to completely transform our educational policy. We believe (1) that educational agencies should be quite subordinate to the direct work of preaching the gospel; (2) that educational agents should be, as far as possible, laymen; and (3) that the advantages of education should be given mainly to our own native converts, and especially to those of them who may become catechists or ministers. No one can seriously believe that we disparage education. But we do hold that in India it has been allowed to absorb far too much of our limited resources of men and of money. Success there has been in direct proportion to the prominence which the various missionary societies have given to the evangelization of the masses. The evidence of this is overwhelmingly complete. We may quote for example the following extract from a letter written to Mr. Champness by one of the most energetic of our Indian missionaries, Rev. G. Mackenzie Cobban :—

"If you need any arguments for sending out men for evangelistic work, here are one or two :—Evangelistic Missions have won *thousands* of converts where we have only won *hundreds*, sometimes *tens*. We gained *six hundred* converts in *sixty years;* the Arcot Mission (Presbyterian) gained *six thousand* in *thirty* years. Among all the *five thousand* villages in our district there are not *six* efficient itinerating Evangelists belonging to all the Missionary Societies professing to work there. In the city of Madras there is *less preaching to the heathen than there was forty-five years ago. Eleven* Englishmen are at work in the Madras Christian College among 1,400 students. In my circuit are 1,400 villages, among them only one Scotchman."

In South India, the chief scene of our educational work, we spend £13,582 a year, and report 2,038 members. The Church Missionary Society spends in the same region £3,000 a year more than we, and reports 67,533 members. The Propagation Society spends £600 a year less than we, and reports 46,466 members and 12,617 catechumens. Whatever allowance we may make for the greater severity of our church membership test, it will not bridge over the immense chasm between 2,038 and 46,466. The Free Church of Scotland, which has carried out Dr. Duff's policy even more thoroughly than we, and is almost entirely educational, reported in 1888 in the Madras district 78 adults and 187 children as the total number of its baptized adherents. The total number received into that mission since its foundation is 622, and during that period this result has been secured by an expenditure of not less than £150,000. The cost of the educational policy is as great as its definite result is small. Now turn to the Telagu Mission of the American Baptists. They have gone to the opposite extreme. They have put no trust whatever in education as an evangelistic agency. Because they believe literally in the Day of Pentecost, the record of their mission reads like a chapter in the Acts of the Apostles. In 1867 their church at Ongole numbered eight members; ten years later it reported 3,269. In a single preaching tour one missionary and his helpers, in the course of two months, baptized no less than 1,243 persons. We read of 565 conversions in one station in a single year, and in another station the number 1,443. This mission records twice as many conversions in one year at one station as the Free Church of Scotland Mission records in the entire Presidency during the whole fifty years of its existence. Such is the difference between the well-meant but mistaken policy of the saintly Dr. Duff, and the old-fashioned policy of the apostle Paul, and our Methodist forefathers.

Repudiation of the Ethnological Explanation of our Failure.

An attempt has been made to break the tremendous force of these figures by arguing that other societies have succeeded far more than we, not because their methods were far less educational and far more evangelistic, but because we have happened to sow upon the harder soil of Hindu caste, whilst they have had to deal with the more impressionable aborigines. This ethnological excuse has been refuted from Government Blue Books, and we need do no more here than quote the emphatic testimony of Rev. W. H. Findlay in *The Harvest Field* of last November :—

"This is the apology for our condition which is regularly used by the Mission House authorities both on the platform of the Conference and in the Press, to silence such students of our statistics as are to be found at home. . . . We in India know that the case is far otherwise. We know that whilst there are a few missionary areas peopled by aborigines alone, there are none whatever peopled solely by the untractable classes. We know that in the immense majority of cases—and in all our districts without exception—tractable and untractable classes alike are within geographical reach of the missionaries. We know, for instance that in the Tanjore district, where we have a mere handful of Christians, other Christian churches have found classes tractable enough to be won over by thousands ; and that on the border of one of our districts where we have spent *seventy* years in raising a church of a *few hundreds*, the American Board of Foreign Missions has in *fifty* years reached a strength of *ten thousand* among a population closely similar to ours."

The Missionary Style of Living.

The special prominence which we desire to give to the direct evangelization of the masses of the Indian peoples, raises the question of the style of living which Committees at home should encourage missionary evangelists to adopt. If we could have foreseen the way in which this subordinate issue would excite personal feeling and divert attention from the main point, we would have said nothing about it until the main point was settled. But we were influenced partly by a desire to present a complete programme, and yet more by a desire to protect Indian missionaries from an extreme policy which was being vehemently advocated in influential quarters at the beginning of last year. Distinguished men both in Church and State were loudly contending for the ascetic method which members of the Salvation Army and some High Anglican celibates had adopted. We believe that the maintenance of a Christian Home is essential to the healthy evangelization of India. Therefore we strongly opposed the ascetic extreme, whilst paying our tribute to the saintly disinterestedness which prompted it. Seeing how apt the public when disaffected, are to run to extremes, we feared they might be led to favour the ascetic method. We therefore proposed a "Via Media," believing that it was our duty to bring our missionary evangelists as near those to whom they preach, as is consistent with health, civilization, and reasonable comfort. We felt deeply the force of the social circumstances described by the Rev. Robert Stephenson, B.A., in the following letter to Rev. Thomas Champness:

"Even at home it is often painful to the minister of a congregation in a poor part of a great town to *live away in a pleasant suburb.* He feels the danger that more than the mere distance in space should separate him from the people. *The poorer people are under restraint* in coming to a house that seems to them a mansion, and in himself he dreads the *subtle temptation* to imagine that his more pleasant surroundings are his rights, and indicate personal superiority. It was this feeling in an *intensified degree* I realized on going to India and finding myself located, like other Englishmen, IN A LARGE HOUSE SURROUNDED BY BROAD GROUNDS. I felt there was quite enough to make intercourse with the people to whom I was sent as a messenger of Christ difficult, almost impossible, in their language, their manners and customs, and modes of thought, and it seemed to me a *great aggravation* of the evil that we should live so APART FROM THEM, as the character and position of our homes implied and almost necessitated. I should have liked to live in the midst of the people, and when after a while, I had to find my own house I longed to go into the native town and take a house in a street of respectable Hindoos. But I soon found it could not be."

We believe it is not so impossible as Mr. Stephenson imagines. Christian missionaries during the last two thousand years have overcome much more serious difficulties. Be that as it may, Mr. Stephenson expresses exactly the social difficulty we wish to overcome. We never stated that English missionaries generally yielded to the temptation of their circumstances, but only that such temptation exists, and that it is the duty of the Committees at home to reduce such temptation to a minimum.

The Opinions of Native Christians.

We are bound to add that in some cases English missionaries have yielded, no doubt unconsciously, to what Mr. Stephenson rightly describes as the "subtle temptation" of their social environment. This is sufficiently proved by the pamphlet published some time ago by Mr. S. Satthianadhan, M.A., LL.B. (Cantab.), ex-Foundation Scholar of Corpus Christi College, Cambridge; Assistant to the Director of Public Instruction, Madras; Acting Professor of Logic and Moral Philosophy, Presidency College, Madras. In that pamphlet this distinguished native Christian makes the following statements :—

"The life of a missionary in India is entirely different from what it was twenty or thirty years ago. Even in the remotest corners of the country he finds the more congenial and cultured society of his countrymen and countrywomen. He moves on the most intimate terms with the Collector or Doctor, or Engineer of the station, and receives the same homage from the natives which they ungrudgingly render to the collector Sahib, and those who move in his circle. India is no more his adopted country. The strong ties which bind him to his own country, the increased facilities for visiting England, and the liberal provision made for his stay once a year in a hill station, all these prevent his identifying himself completely with the people among whom he has come to work. . . . . Many a missionary returns home with *no more knowledge of the inner life of native Christians than that learned from Catechists and Mission Agents*. House to house visitation is becoming *rarer and rarer*, and in the majority of cases where such visits are made the missionary seldom loses sight of the SOCIAL GULF which separates him from the native Christian. There are, of course, noble exceptions— men who rise above the force of circumstances, and who in spite of all their *artificial surroundings* make themselves one with the natives. But, unfortunately, this is not the case with all. An almost heroic sacrifice is needed on the part of missionaries in the present state of life in India to reach that standard set before himself by the Apostle Paul when he spoke of 'becoming all things to all men.' . . . . The following remarks of Col. Osborne demand attention, though I am not prepared to go the length he does in laying so much stress upon the absence of free social intercourse between Europeans and natives as the cause of missionary failure. 'The chief obstacle which besets the missionary is that occasioned by the peculiar relationship which exists between Englishmen and natives. The English are not merely the rulers of the country, but rulers in whose inner life as individuals the people are of no account—that is to say, the English in India form no attachments. A few among them may associate with the natives from a sense of duty, but for their mental and moral needs their own countrymen are sufficient. . . . . No greater obstacle in the way of mission work can be conceived than a state of mind such as this. It denotes the want of that touch of nature which makes the whole world kin. And yet it is a defect from which the English missionary is of necessity as little exempt as the English official. . . . . Contrast this attitude of ALOOFNESS with the feelings of the Apostle Paul towards individual members of the churches which he had founded, and we shall find little difficulty in understanding why Christianity in India does not spread and develop as in the days of Imperial Rome.'"

We may add that we have just received a letter from Mr. Satthianadhan in which he adheres fully to all the statements in the pamphlet from which we have quoted; and in which he adds, that if there is need for further corroboration, he will send us THE PERSONAL OPINIONS OF NATIVE CHRISTIANS IN ALL PARTS OF INDIA. Mr. Satthianadhan rightly maintains that those he represents have a claim to be heard on this question, and in our judgment their opinions should have special weight. He makes a further remark of great importance when he contends that what we ought to seek is the judgment of *independent* native Christians. Native ministers and native catechists who are dependent for their bread upon the favour of European missionaries cannot be accepted as unprejudiced and independent witnesses in relation to their employers.

We might add here, while speaking of different kinds of witnesses, that there is another class in India whose testimony as a class would also be of little value on this question. We refer, of course, to official Anglo-Indian Society. Many Anglo-Indians are noble exceptions. But as a class they represent a military despotism, receive " exile allowance," and are by their very relation to the natives the last persons in the world to understand either the natives themselves or those who regard the natives not as subject races, but as the redeemed and beloved of God.

We shall now proceed to give the opinion of a witness who must at any rate be allowed to be free from race prejudice, being neither English, American, Anglo-Indian, Eurasian, nor a native of India. Miss Joseph, of Benares, a Christian Jewess engaged in the Baptist Zenana Mission, and enjoying the same position, privileges, and salary as her English co-workers, writes in no hesitating terms with regard to the question of missionary separation from the natives. She says that this—

"Unchristian state of things exercises a four-fold evil influence in this land—first, it hinder's the Lord's work ; secondly, it stands in the way of natives embracing Christianity ; thirdly, it obstructs the progress of civilization ; fourthly, it mars the mind and character of Eurasians."

These quotations are taken from a printed letter addressed by her to the General Conference on Foreign Missions, held in London, June, 1888. Dealing with her second point, she says :—

"The uneducated villager and the needy dependent may appreciate the assistance and patronage of missionaries and want nothing else, but *no respectable member of society can be satisfied with the sort of treatment missionaries give natives and others.* I once met a native Civil Surgeon in the West of India, who had been educated in England and came out with his official appointment. I was informed that he had a leaning to Christianity, and that some Christians endeavoured to get him to cast in his lot with Christians, but how did the man meet their persuasions ? He invariably replied, 'If I openly embrace Christianity I and my family will be cast out of our society, and *Christians will not receive us into their society.* Can we remain separate and isolated from all ?' Such is the expression of many hearts. I cannot tell you *how many respectable natives have uttered almost the very same words in my hearing.*"

This is only one of several instances of a like nature given by Miss Joseph.

Inferior Status of Native Ministers.

It is exceedingly difficult for any Englishman in India to maintain always towards the natives that attitude of absolute brotherly equality which Jesus Christ maintained towards all men. We cannot but think that even our brethren have unwittingly and unintentionally fallen short.

In the first place, it is the custom in South India, and, we believe, in the North also, to hold two District Meetings. The first is styled the European, and the second the Native District Meeting. During the first meeting the ORDAINED native ministers who are in full connexion with the Wesleyan Conference, and whose names are printed in the minutes of the Conference in the alphabetical list of the ministers of our church, are excluded. It may be said that this meeting discusses only the policy and work of the society and its finances in so far as they affect the European brethren. This is true with regard to the finances, but it is impossible, or ought to be, to draw any hard and fast line between the work of the European missionary and that of his native helper, and the policy which should guide the efforts of both. It is useless to assert that native ministers are regarded as in any real sense the equal colleagues of the European missionary when they are excluded from half the deliberations of the annual District Meeting.

This gulf between the European and the native minister is further accentuated by the fact that, at any rate in the Negapatam and Trichinopoly District, the native ministers only dine on one day of the whole District Meeting week with their European brethren, and that is regarded by all concerned as a praiseworthy endeavour to bridge the gulf. During the whole of Dr. Lunn's twelve-months' residence in India he never, so far as his memory serves him, excepting on that one occasion, was invited to take a meal at the same table as a native Wesleyan minister.

But the Bangalore Conference itself affords the strongest proof of the fact that this gulf does exist. At this Triennial Conference of the Wesleyan Methodist Church in India, the fifth gathering of its kind, how was the spirit of brotherhood with the native ministry manifested? This Conference was not summoned for the mere purpose of replying to criticism. It was, the great triennial gathering of our church. It considered the gravest questions of church polity in which the native ministers as representatives of the Indian Methodist Church were, if possible, more interested than the English missionaries. It considered the propriety of giving a "definite constitution to the triennial meetings which have been held during the past twelve years," a subject of the gravest import to all native Christians. It debated at considerable length the question of Educational versus Evangelistic work. It considered carefully the question of handing over a part of our Indian work to the Australian Conferences, and numerous other issues momentous in their bearing on the future of Indian Methodism. Under these circumstances it might have been anticipated that English missionaries, careful to assert their full recognition of the brotherly equality of their Indian colleagues, would have secured their full representation in the *personnel* of the Conference. The facts however are far otherwise. Appendix I. in the report of the Bangalore Conference quotes a "list of ministers in connection with the Wesleyan Conference, 1889." This list contains the names of 86 ministers, who are printed in exactly the same type, without any distinguishing mark. Fifty of these ministers are English missionaries, the remaining thirty-six are Indian ministers. Twenty-four English missionaries represented their countrymen at the Bangalore Conference. *Not a single Native minister had a place in that assembly.* What would be thought in this country if the British Conference were specially summoned to discuss Welsh affairs, and from first to last not a single Welshman was present? Would that either represent or conciliate Wales? It may doubtless be said that the native ministers were not deliberately excluded at Bangalore; and we are glad to see that some provision has now been made for their representation at future Conferences. But the fact that they were totally unrepresented on such an occasion as the present indicates an unconscious attitude of mind in relation to the natives which no Englishman in India can overcome without ceaseless vigilance and effort.

The report of the Bangalore Conference contains further unconscious but impressive evidence that our brethren in India, notwithstanding their true and deep love for the natives, have not yet succeeded in making that love as irresistibly manifest as they and we desire. On page 18 of the Report, we are told that the statements in the *Methodist Times*, have not only had a "pernicious influence" amongst "the Hindu population" in India, but that they have "also affected the Christian population *both native and European*." The Report goes on to tell us that "subscriptions .... have in some places been withdrawn, and on many hands missions and missionaries are completely discredited. The effect produced in some places upon the native Christians has been even more calamitous. Confidence in the unselfish devotion and purity of purpose of those who are their spiritual fathers and guides is rudely shaken, and the conviction is widely *gaining ground* amongst them that missionaries have become such because they can thus gain a more decent and comfortable living than they could get at home." We would never assert that the bond which unites the Indian missionaries and their flock is so slight that it could be severed by such criticism as has taken place; and that Europeans who have lived long years in the East only needed the outside influence of articles published in an English religious journal to induce them to withdraw their support from Indian missions. We do not believe that the facts are as dark as our Indian brethren have painted them. An old African missionary said to us the other day, " no criticisms from outside would ever have made my people lose confidence in me. They would have been the first to rally to my defence." We believe our brethren greatly exaggerate the influence of the articles in *The Methodist Times*. But whatever amount of truth there may be in the gloomy statements we have quoted, only proves how urgently necessary it is that we should do our utmost to come into close brotherly relations with the peoples of India.

We are very sorry for any pain we may have unintentionally occasioned to devoted missionaries, but we cannot close our eyes to such evidence as we have just summarized. We cannot ignore native Christian opinion. We are compelled to consider what practical steps can be taken to bring English missionaries nearer to the natives of India. We believe that nothing will tend to this more effectually than such an extremely simple style of living as will distinguish missionaries conspicuously from Anglo-Indian society, and will make it easy for them to cultivate social intercourse with native Christians. This brings us to the question of stipends.

Actual Income of Indian Missionaries.

We have stated that the average income of an Indian missionary is £300 a year and a bungalow. As this statement is controverted, it may be well to give the exact average of all the principal English and Scotch societies. The figures of the following societies have been taken as the basis of calculation: Church Missionary Society, Society for the Propagation of the Gospel, London Missionary Society, Wesleyan Missionary Society, Baptist Missionary Society, Established Church of Scotland, Free Church of Scotland, and United Presbyterian Church. The average stipend paid by these societies to their married missionaries, including horse allowance, is £315 per annum, with allowance for bungalow, and in most special cases considerable allowances for children, both in India and in

England. Nor is the assertion wide of the mark as applied to our own Society, which pays its missionaries, including horse allowance, from £260 to £280 per annum, besides allowances for children, postage, taxes, gardener, medicine, pundit, hill allowances, furniture, and bungalow. But we may avail ourselves here of the exact and full information printed in the financial Tables of the Bangalore Conference, and reproduced as an Appendix to this statement.

What the "Via Media" does not involve.

Before we examine the figures of the Bangalore Conference Report, it may be well to re-state the scale of allowances suggested in the article entitled "The Untrodden Via Media." In doing so it is desirable to point out once more, that whilst our suggested policy encouraged a simple style of Indian missionary life, it was also a friendly protest against the extreme asceticism of the Salvation Army. The following sentences will sufficiently prove this assertion. "The Salvation Army, as the authorities themselves say in their annual report, is still on its trial in India. . . . The truth is that the Hindu Fakir can always beat the Christian pseudo Fakir on his own ground. Christianity is not an ascetic religion. Hinduism, in some of its phases, is essentially so. Unnatural asceticism is anti-Christian, and these attempts have so far proved that Christianity cannot be propagated by non-Christian methods." (New Missionary Policy, p. 9.) There were also certain very important qualifications and reservations in the suggested policy, which must be noted. In the first place it was stated that "it might certainly be desirable, under any circumstances, that THE CHAIRMEN OF DISTRICTS, whose official relations bring them constantly in contact with members of the Government, SHOULD MAINTAIN THEIR PRESENT STYLE OF LIVING." (New Missionary Policy, pp. 7 and 8.) It was also laid down very clearly in the following passage that the new policy should apply only to men who entered in the future: "If any such change as is here proposed should come within the range of practical missionary politics, it would be necessary at once to insist that such a change of life should be COMPULSORY ON NO SINGLE MISSIONARY who has entered the work under the old *régime*. (New Misionary Policy, p. 10.) It was further urged that on certain lines expenditure should be *increased* rather than diminished, as will be apparent from the following extract: "If any of the great societies should ultimately decide to adopt the policy here suggested, there are three items of expenditure which ought on no account to be reduced, but should rather be increased. The ALLOWANCES FOR CHILDREN in

England ought to be on the MOST LIBERAL SCALE. If missionaries are to spend their lives for India, they have every right to demand that the Church at home shall see to it that their children are not handicapped in the race of life as compared with the children of ministers in English work. It is hard enough for parents to be separated from their children. The Church has a sacred duty to perform in this matter, and must do it ungrudgingly. It is no part of the policy of the 'Via Media' to let the children of the missionary suffer. NOR MUST THERE BE ANY REDUCTION IN THE ALLOWANCES FOR SICKNESS. Everything must be done that can be done to keep our workers in good health, and when their health fails, the church must take care of them. THE PRESENT SANATORIA ON THE HILLS MUST BE MAINTAINED UNSPARINGLY. On these three lines of expenditure there must be no attempt at saving." (New Missionary Policy, p. 10.)

What the "Via Media" does involve.

With the special provisos thus clearly defined it was suggested that the stipend of our Indian married missionaries should in future be £150 a year WITH SPECIAL ALLOWANCES FOR CHILDREN, *leaving untouched the horse allowance, the allowances for postage, rates and taxes, medicine, furniture, pundit, and rent of bungalow.* This would mean in the case of a married missionary without children a REDUCTION ON THE PRESENT STIPEND OF £80 A YEAR in the Wesleyan mission, but in the case of a married missionary with children, the reduction would be considerably less. If, therefore, it can be shown that life can be maintained in health and reasonable comfort after reducing certain of the items given (see Appendix) in Part I., Table III., of the Bangalore Conference Report by an aggregate amount of £80, a *prima facie* case will be made out for the policy of the "Untrodden Via Media." But before we enter into these details we must be permitted to express the reluctance and distress with which we do so. Twelve months ago, Mr. Price Hughes stated at a special meeting of the Missionary Committee that he was prepared to discuss the educational question with any degree of publicity that might be desired, but that he greatly wished that questions of stipend might be reserved for confidential verbal consideration in sub-committee. From that day to this, amid constant misrepresentation and injustice, we have maintained absolute silence on these delicate details. But the action of the Bangalore Conference has now forced us to support this part of our argument with printed facts and figures.

The Cost of Food.

The first item given is food. This is set down in the six

Indian districts, for a married missionary without children, at a uniform charge of £81. It has been objected that Dr. Lunn's experience of Indian life was limited to South India, and that he knew nothing of the cost of food, &c., in other provinces. But this representative body of missionaries has here committed itself to the statement that the cost of food for a married couple is the same in every part of the Indian peninsula. This statement is not strictly correct. But it is sufficiently correct to make the cost of living at one station an approximate standard for the whole. We proceed therefore to state the cost of food at Tiruvalur in 1888. Dr. Lunn, who was stationed there, was able to buy beef from Negatapam at* 1½d. to 2d. a pound, mutton at 1d. per pound, a quarter of a small sheep for a shilling, eggs at 2d. per dozen, chickens at 2½d. to 4d. each, flour 3lbs. for 2d., bread 2d. a loaf, butter 4d. per lb., milk 1d. per pint, tea at 10d. to 14d. per lb., raw coffee 1s. per lb., bananas at 1d. a dozen to 1d. a score, pineapples 1d. and 2d. each, and other fruit and vegetables at correspondingly low rates. English jams and other preserved food could be obtained at the Madras bazaar at a reduction of from 10 to 20 % on English retail prices. The following was the style of living adopted by Dr. and Mrs. Lunn:—

6.30 a.m.—Early tea. Tea, toast, butter, jam and fruit.

9 a.m.—Breakfast. Porridge, or some similar dish, eggs and bacon, curried mutton or chicken and rice, fruit and coffee.

1 p.m.—Luncheon. Curry, sweets and fruit.

4 p.m.—Afternoon tea.

7 p.m.—Dinner. Soup, roast chicken or entrée of mutton chops, or joint of beef, curry, sweets and fruit.

This is surely *at least sufficient* for the preservation of health. This style of living cost Dr. and Mrs. Lunn jointly not more than 15s. a week or £39 a year. The Bangalore Conference Report allows £81 per year. The possible SAVING ON FOOD ALONE TO BE EFFECTED BY LIVING AS ABOVE IS £42 PER ANNUM.

The Cost of Servants.

The next item in this schedule is "Servants." Under this heading for the Madras district the sum of £49 10s. is put down; for the Negapatam district the sum of £40 10s. The following

---

* * In all these figures 1d. is used as the equivalent of one anna, a rupee (sixteen annas) being now worth about 1s. 4½d.

is the list of Dr. Lunn's servants with the wages which he paid them per annum.

		Approximately in £ s. d.
Butler	Rs. 108 per annum	7 10 0
Cook	,, 102 ,,	7 0 0
Cook's helper	,, 36 ,,	2 10 0
Sweeper	,, 36 ,,	2 10 0
Four punkah men employed six months	,, 90 ,,	6 10 0
Groom } included in horse		
Grass cutter } allowance		
Gardener—paid by Mission under heading " Rates and Taxes "		
Total :	Rs. 372 per annum	£26 0 0

This means an expenditure of about £26 per annum, and out of this sum the servants found food and clothing for themselves and their families. Few people either in England or in India would hold that seven servants in the cold weather and eleven in the hot weather were not sufficient to attend to a young married couple without children. But the adoption of such a staff of servants as Dr. Lunn employed, without attempting any further economies, would mean A SAVING for the men in the Madras District, on their own showing, OF AT LEAST £20 PER ANNUM. If this sum be added to the amount saved on food, we have already provided for a REDUCTION OF £62 PER ANNUM on the estimate of the Bangalore Conference.

The Cost of Clothing.

It is now necessary to consider the third item in this schedule—clothing. Here we find the sum of £36 per annum allowed for a Married Missionary and his Wife without children. That it would be very easy to spend this amount cannot be denied. That it is necessary for health and reasonable comfort we are obliged to deny. Dr. Lunn was exactly twelve months in India. Immediately on his arrival he bought six suits of white American drill at 5s. 3d. per suit, for summer wear. He also purchased four suits of Calicut cloth at 10s. per suit, for winter wear. His English clothes were packed away and were not used six days during his whole stay in India. These drill and Calicut clothes are now in his possession and may be submitted to the Committee if necessary. They are by no means worn out, and would certainly last another twelve months. On Sundays, and at Madras in the evenings, Dr. Lunn wore a black Cashmere suit which cost 32s. This suit would only last twelve months. The following then is Dr. Lunn's estimate for the *annual* tailor's bill of a Married Missionary in the Negapatam District:—

	£	s.	d.
Half the cost of six suits White Drill	0	15	9
Half the cost of four Calicut suits	1	0	0
One black Cashmere suit	1	12	0
	3	7	9
Incidentals	1	12	3
Total	£5	0	0

The cost of underclothing and hosiery is more difficult to determine, as men with some constitutions require so much more than men of another type. Dr. Lunn wore very little during the hot weather, and brought back this part of his outfit to England little the worse for the twelve months' wear. In his opinion £4 per annum is an ample allowance for this item of expenditure. The wear of boots and shoes is very slight in consequence of the small amount of walking that is done. Dr. Lunn purchased one pair of country boots for 10s., and one pair of country slippers for 3s. during this twelve months, and spent not more than 5s. in repairs, so that 30s. would in his opinion be an ample allowance for shoe leather. The cost of laundry is about 30s. per annum for each adult member of the household. This completes the items of expenditure under the heading for the missionary, and parallel calculations for the minister's wife would be equally fair. In her case it is customary to employ an Indian tailor, who will sit in the verandah and make any dresses of which she supplies the pattern and material, at a wage of from 6d. to 9d. per day.

The following will therefore be the expenditure for clothing in detail:—

		£	s.	d.
Missionary:	Tailor's Bill	5	0	0
	Hosiery and Underclothing	4	0	0
	Boots and Shoes	1	10	0
	Laundry	1	10	0
		12	0	0
Missionary's Wife		12	0	0
	Total	24	0	0

This calculation is based upon the necessities of life in the Negapatam District; but inasmuch as the Bangalore Conference has committed itself to the statement that clothing is equally expensive in all our Indian districts, it may be concluded that the economies suggested would equally apply all round.

The Bangalore estimates propose that our missionaries should have £23 a year to give away in charities. This is far in excess of anything allowed at home. In some of our best circuits ministers have £2 a quarter from the Poor Fund; and, if we make a similar allowance for India, it will be a generous arrangement, for the poor in India can live on two pence a day. Hence, £8 a year would go very far in the relief of the Indian poor. This effects ANOTHER REDUCTION OF £15 in our calculations.

The Bangalore Conference further asks that we should insure every missionary's life for £500, and pay him for that purpose £13 6s. 8d. We have no such custom at home. And yet our brethren in the poorer circuits are exposed to at least as great hardships and perils as our brethren in India. Our death-rate in India is not higher than that at home, because men are recalled at once if the climate does not suit them. The extra premium of the Annuitant Society is justly paid by the Missionary Society, but we cannot admit that our brethren in India have a further claim to an assurance of £500. Nevertheless, we will not press this point. Even after we have conceded that novel demand, the estimates stand as follows:—

Annual Expenditure of Married Missionary and Wife without Children.

	Estimate of the Bangalore Conference for the Madras District.			Dr. Lunn's Estimate.		
	£	s.	d.	£	s.	d.
Food	81	0	0	39	0	0
Servants	49	10	0	*29	10	0
Clothing	36	0	0	24	0	0
House Linen and Furniture	6	0	0	6	0	0
Charities	23	0	0	8	0	0
Books	8	0	0	8	0	0
Premium on £500	13	6	8	13	6	8
Income and other Taxes	6	7	6	6	7	6
Annuity Society	6	0	0	6	0	0
	£229	4	2	£140	4	2

* This is an outside estimate, being £3 10s. in excess of Dr. Lunn's outlay, in order to allow for any slight difference in the cost of servants in Madras as compared with Tiruvalar.

Thus it appears that without touching the disputed special premium on £500, we have brought the estimate £9 BELOW DR. LUNN'S SUGGESTED STIPEND. That £9 would cover sundries. We have, therefore, proved our case from the Bangalore figures. The truth is, that the cost of living is far less in India than in England, except under the following heads—(1) wine; (2) clothes manufactured in England; and (3) the education of children in England. We do not think that missionary societies need consider the item of wine. It is quite unnecessary to order clothes of English make. And we propose to provide handsomely, by a special fund, for the education of children in England.

The Wages of Artizans and Engine-Drivers.

There is one delusion, as astonishing as it is widespread, to which we ought to refer before we close this section of our statement. On page 14 of the Bangalore Report it is stated that "such classes as foremen, &c., living on £100 to £200 per annum are a figment of the writer's imagination, and that as a rule even *artizans and engine-drivers coming to this country from England receive larger stipends than missionaries of the gospel.*" THIS STATEMENT IS ENTIRELY ERRONEOUS. That the classes named are no mere figment we can abundantly demonstrate. The following extracts from letters received recently, will, however, sufficiently disprove the statement made in the report. Mr. W. S. Betts, of the South Indian Railway Company, writes from Trichinopoly, under date February 14th, 1890, to say that the "maximum pay" drawn by an engine-driver is "Rs. 200 per mensem," and further states that "*no free houses or other allowances are found by the company.*" Mr. Edward Harford, General Secretary of the Amalgamated Society of Railway Servants, 55, Colebrooke Row, London N., writes under date February 3rd, 1890, to say that "the system now adopted is to engage engine-drivers here as firemen at £10 per month, on arrival they continue as such until they have learned the roads, when they are appointed engine-men, and advanced from Rs. 10 to Rs. 20 per month yearly, if character satisfactory, *the maximum per mensem being Rs. 200.*" This statement applies to the whole of India. When it is borne in mind that the average stipend of the missionary societies mentioned above is *approximately Rs. 400 per mensem* with all kinds of allowances, the extraordinary nature of the assertion in the report will be manifest at once. In other words, the engine-driver never receives more than £170 per annum without any provision for horse, children, furniture, &c. The average European missionary receives £315 per annum, with a furnished bungalow and heavy allowances for children, and several other items, making a gross income *nearly three times as large* as that of European artizans and engine-drivers in India.

The " Via Media" an accomplished Fact.

But it may be objected that all our calculations are more or less theoretical. It may be said with perfect truth that Dr. Lunn did not live on the income of the "Untrodden Via Media" during his stay in India. And some of the Committee may naturally ask, Is there any actual illustration of successful missionary effort conducted in India on the basis of this policy? These objections would be perfectly fair and natural, but an answer is forthcoming which finally disposes of them all.

There was one great mistake in the article under consideration. That mistake consisted in the title which was given to it. The "*Untrodden* Via Media" is "untrodden" only so far as the English and Scotch Missionaries of the principal Societies are concerned. Some months after the original articles were published we learned that THE RATES OF PAY ADOPTED BY THE METHODIST EPISCOPAL CHURCH OF AMERICA WERE ACTUALLY LOWER THAN THOSE WHICH WE HAD SUGGESTED. This seemed to be such a remarkable fact, having in view the indignation with which our suggestions were received by brethren in India, that we at once wrote to Rev. Bishop Thoburn, the Methodist Episcopal Bishop for India, and to Rev. Dr. Peck, Corresponding Missionary Secretary of the Methodist Episcopal Church. We append their replies.

[COPY.]

CALCUTTA, *Dec.* 12*th*, 1889.

Rev. H. S. LUNN, M.D.,
 My dear Sir,
  In reply to your favour of November 5th, I give you the figures you ask for, but the rate of pay has varied until recently in different parts of the country. A few months ago we decided to ask the Society, in New York, to establish the following rate :—Single men for the first two years, Rs. 130 a month [at the average rate of exchange for 1889, this comes to about £105 per annum]. A married couple, Rs. 180 [about £145]. After two years, Rs. 150 for single men [about £122 per annum], and Rs. 200 for each married couple [about £167 per annum]. Rs. 20 a month is allowed for each child [£16 per annum]. A house furnished with heavy furniture is provided free of rent. *No allowance for sickness, native teacher, horse, medicine, or outfit.* A furlough is allowed after ten years' service, or at any time that a medical certificate states that it is absolutely necessary. For European missionaries engaged in this country, of whom we have quite a number, a somewhat similar allowance is made ; the salary of such men usually begins on a lower scale, but never in any case rises above the regular allowance. I may say, however, that we have several men at work who receive less than the above figures. We have quite a number of married men, now serving for

Rs. 150 a month [about £122 per annum], some of them Americans; while some single men receive Rs. 100 or less [about £80 a year or less].

Yours truly,
(*Signed*) J. M. THOBURN.

[COPY.]

Mission Rooms of the Methodist Episcopal Church,
805, BROADWAY,
NEW YORK, *Nov.* 15*th,* 1889.

Rev. HUGH PRICE HUGHES, M.A.,
The Methodist Times Office, 125, Fleet Street, London, E.C., England.
Dear Sir,
Yours of October 22nd, inquiring as to the rate of payment of Missionaries in India adopted by our Society, is at hand. In reply, I would say it is somewhat difficult to give a uniform scale of payments for our Missions in India, as they are conducted on a basis of partial self-support, certain amounts being appropriated unconditionally, and others as grants in aid. Parsonages are generally furnished to our missionaries, but where they are not, an allowance for rent is made. A very small allowance is made for medicine, but *none is made for horse hire*, that being paid from the salary of the missionary. The table on the next page gives in rupees the average payments to our missionaries in the three Conferences in India. An allowance of 100 dols. is made for children in America.

Yours very truly,
J. O. PECK.

	Salary, Married Missionary.	Each Child.	Rent.	Average. Travel.	Native. Teacher.
South India	Rs. 1,800	180	720	150	180
North India	Rs. 2,475	225	...	122	..
Bengal	Rs. 1,800	180	600	100	..

The above figures are in rupees.

[Dr. Peck's figures translated into English currency at the average rate of exchange for the last twelve months would be approximately :—

	Salary, Married Missionary.	Each Child.			Rent.			Travel.			Teacher.		
	£	£	s.	d.	£	s.	d.	£	s.	d.	£	s.	d.
South India	122	12	4	0	48	15	0	10	5	0	11	16	0
North India	168	15	5	0		......		8	5	0		......	
Bengal	122	12	4	0	40	5	0	6	15	0		......	

Mr. Price Hughes was too ill to attend the last special meeting of the Committee, but he sent a communication in which he embodied Dr. Peck's letter. He was subsequently informed that a member of the committee attempted to discount the effect of Dr. Peck's unanswerable figures by stating to the committee that the American missionaries were not paid enough to maintain them in health and comfort. As these observations would be entirely irrelevant and misleading, unless they referred to the same missionaries as those whose stipends were given by Dr. Peck, Mr. Price Hughes immediately communicated with Dr. Peck in order to discover whether he had misunderstood Dr. Peck's previous communication. The following letter is Dr. Peck's reply :—

[COPY.]

MISSION ROOMS OF THE METHODIST EPISCOPAL CHURCH,
150, FIFTH AVENUE, NEW YORK,

Rev. HENRY S. LUNN, M.D., *March 8th*, 1890.
46, Torrington Square, London, W.C., England.

My dear Sir,
Your favour of February 18th is received, containing references to the subject of my former letter on the salaries of our missionaries in India. * * * * I am astounded at the assertion ! I must believe that the gentleman has confounded others with our missionaries. Of course, he is incapable of mis-stating matters of fact as far as he has knowledge, but in this matter he must be in utter misapprehension of the facts.

There have been missionaries in South India sent out by Rev. Wm. Taylor (now Bishop Taylor, of Africa) on the *Self-Supporting Plan*. These were *not* our missionaries, though mostly Methodists; received *no salary* from us; and were not under the authority of the Missionary Society of the Methodist Episcopal Church. What they may have done or suffered I cannot say, as they had no relation to our Society. *These* men have since come over to us and receive salary. Hence, I distinctly and officially deny the truth of the assertions quoted.

We have no complaints by our missionaries that their stipends are inadequate for their health and well-being. In extraordinary emergencies or calamities they would be specially aided by the cheerful generosity of the Society.

I wish to thank you, my dear sir, and dear Mr. Hughes, for your larger faith in a daughter of British Wesleyan Methodism. You are at liberty to use this letter for the cause of truth and justice.

I am, my dear Sir,
Yours faithfully,
(*Signed*) J. O. PECK,
Cor. Sec. for India.

While this statement is passing through the press, we have received a letter from another eminent American bishop, Bishop Ninde, who recently paid an official visit to India, and whose strong testimony is therefore of such special value that we print it :—

[COPY.]

Topeka, Kansas, U.S.,
March 25th, 1890.

DEAR DR. LUNN,

Your valued favour of the 7th inst. came to hand when I reached home this morning.

I had heard of your articles in the *Methodist Times*, though I had not seen them. I am very grateful for the copy you have sent me, which I have read with keen and sympathetic interest. *I am quite in accord with your views.* I spent four months in India in 1886-7, and during that period mingled constantly with the missionaries both of your own and other boards. Our missionaries are able to live very comfortably on the amount allowed them, and I should say that any considerable increase would not be desired by the missionaries themselves. I hope nothing will deter you and Mr. Hughes from pressing your most sensible and Christian views upon the attention of the Christian public. Our missionaries in India have little to do with "society." The Anglo-Indian, as I saw him, had little sympathy with the evangelistic work of the missionaries, although there are marked and honourable exceptions. There is a "Via Media" to be pursued in India which will not decrease the real comfort of our brethren, but will give them larger influence with the natives, and will certainly increase the fruitfulness of our moderate resources

Very sincerely yours,

(*Signed*) W. X. NINDE.

The Rev. Henry S. Lunn, M.D.,
London, Eng.

The "Via Media," it thus appears, is no longer a matter of debate. It is an ACCOMPLISHED FACT. The richest and most numerous Methodist Church in the world, a Church, with a foreign missionary income of nearly a quarter of a million sterling, pays the missionaries in India SMALLER STIPENDS THAN THE LOWEST AMOUNT SUGGESTED BY DR. LUNN.

Perhaps we ought to apologise to the committee for occupying it with any other evidence than this one FACT, which is decisive and final. No amount of argument or calculation will persuade our people that the brave and devoted young men who go out to India from Richmond College, cannot live on reduced stipends which would still be a little larger than those given to their American brethren. But we did not know the American facts when we originally proposed a new policy for India. We were anxious, therefore, to prove to the Committee that we did not make our statements without prolonged and prayerful consideration.

We cannot close without calling attention to the fact that the Bangalore Report, although a transparently sincere conscientious statement, is simply the strong speculative opinion of those who live under the existing system. It contains no outside testimony. On the other hand we have relied upon the evidence of numerous authoritative and independent witnesses, and upon accomplished facts. Dr. Lunn's evidence has been limited to his actual personal experience.

We greatly regret that we have been forced to enter into all these details under circumstances anything but favourable to calm and impartial investigation. We have done nothing whatever to re-open the controversy which we had hoped was closed at the last Conference. Above all, we protest against the false accusation that we have made personal charges against our Indian brethren. We have discussed policy, and policy only; and our discussion has related to all the missionary societies, and a GREAT DEAL MORE TO SOME OF THEM THAN TO OUR OWN. Both discussion and progress will be impossible unless we are allowed to criticise policies and methods without being involved in odious personalities. We yield to none in our affection for Indian missionaries, and in our desire to co-operate with them. In the original articles we were careful to bear our testimony to the disinterested zeal and self-sacrificing spirit of our Indian brethren. But everything that has occurred only strengthens our conviction that the *sine quâ non* of the evangelization of India, is the bending of every energy and the subjection of every consideration to the supreme necessity not only of cherishing, but of exhibiting—conspicuously and unmistakably—in all our words, in all our habits, and in all our ways, the homely brotherliness of Jesus Christ.

We are,

Mr. President and Gentlemen,

Your obedient Servants,

HUGH PRICE HUGHES.
HENRY SIMPSON LUNN.

LONDON, *April,* 1890.

REPORT

OF

SPECIAL SUB-COMMITTEE OF INQUIRY.

First Day, Tuesday, 27th May, 1890.

THE President of the Conference took the Chair at 2 p.m. The proceedings of the Sub-Committee were opened with prayer by the Rev. Thos. Allen.

The only persons in addition to the members of the Sub-Committee who had permission to be present, were the Revs. Geo. Patterson, of Madras, W. H. Findlay, M.A., of Negapatam, Hugh Price Hughes, M.A., and H. S. Lunn, B.A., M.D., with the Treasurers and Secretaries of the Foreign Missionary Committee, two or more of whom were present during all the Sessions of the Committee for the purpose of giving information whenever it might be required.

At the request of the President, the Secretary read the minute of the Special Committee constituting the Sub-Committee.

Scope and Method of the Inquiry.

The PRESIDENT suggested that it would be well for them, (1) To hear the statement of the Indian missionaries, as to what they wished the Committee specially to consider; (2) To hear the reply of Mr. Hughes and Dr. Lunn; and (3) To receive evidence in favour of either or both.

MR. POPE thought that the Indian missionaries might help them if they were to indicate the exact passages to which they objected, and on which they wished them to found their judgment.

Professor PATTERSON, at the call of the President, said: We have felt that one of the most important questions to be considered would be the initial question of settling the issues and determining the procedure. We have therefore endeavoured, in concert with Mr. Hughes, to come to some definite understanding as to what the issues should be that we should request a decision upon. Mr. Findlay and myself, with considerable thought and care, drew up a series of issues, based, in the first place, upon the original articles to which objection is taken, as those articles have been modified by the "Summary Statement," and secondly, upon such passages in the "Notes and Comments" of the *Methodist Times* as have expounded and made clear the meaning of the original articles. That list of issues was submitted to Mr. Hughes. I myself had a long conversation with Mr. Hughes upon the point, and afterwards Mr. Findlay had a similar conversation, and I think we have substantially come to an agreement as to what the issues are upon which we shall jointly ask the Sub-Committee to make a definite pronouncement. And, in order to make the matter simpler and plainer to the Sub-Committee, we have taken the liberty of having these issues, as we have formulated them, printed. Perhaps it will be well if I read them to the Committee.

Mr. HUGHES: In what sense does Mr. Patterson say "jointly"? Because they have been modified since I saw them.

Professor PATTERSON: Yes, they have been modified. Some of the modifications are Mr. Hughes' own; Mr. Hughes returned the draft, which we submitted to him, with pencil marks in the margin, and we have adopted as many of Mr. Hughes' suggestions as we could. Since then we have made changes in the wording, which would have been duly submitted to Mr. Hughes had he not been in Scotland. I must express my regret that it was not possible for us to submit them to Mr. Hughes on that account. But the issues here submitted are substantially, in all points, the issues originally submitted to Mr. Hughes.

ISSUES PROPOSED FOR INVESTIGATION.

I. Is it true that the present allowances of our Indian missionaries are :—

    (*a*) Greater in real value—that is in purchasing power in the country in which they are received and expended—than those of ministers in the home work, or than similar sums would be in England?

    (*b*) Greater than are required to maintain them and their families in health and reasonable comfort?

II. Is it true that there is anything in the style of life adopted by our Indian missionaries :—

    (*a*) That is needlessly costly, or that can in any sense be called luxurious?

    (*b*) That hinders the growth of that mutual understanding and sympathy between the missionary and the native population which is essential to the effective prosecution of evangelistic work?

(c) That hinders the growth of that brotherly unity between the missionary and the native Christian which is essential to the healthy development of the Church?

III. Is it true that the rates of stipend or the style of life of missionaries have been in any way determined by their adoption of the educational policy?

Professor PATTERSON continued: I think I shall be able to point out as we go along, that if Mr. Hughes and Dr. Lunn still maintain the position that they maintained in the original Articles, and in the "New Missionary Policy," they will take the affirmative side on each of these issues; and similarly we shall take the negative side. Now, Sir, it seems also to us that that very fact goes a long way to determine the procedure of the Committee, about which also I may say we have had a good deal of conversation with Mr. Hughes. If it be true that Mr. Hughes and Dr. Lunn maintain the affirmative on each of these issues, then the *onus probandi* naturally and properly devolves upon them, and in that case it will be both convenient and in accordance with usual custom for Mr. Hughes and Dr. Lunn, and not ourselves, to open the case. We should then suggest that they be asked by the Committee to bring forward the whole of their case—the case which substantiates their position, and on the basis of which they maintain (if they do maintain) the affirmative position on each of these issues; and that when on each issue they have thus laid their whole case before the Committee, we then examine the validity and soundness of their arguments, and adduce our own on the opposite side. It seems to us that this will be very decidedly the best procedure for the Sub-Committee to take, and we think also that in this particular Mr. Hughes will agree with us.

Mr. HUGHES: First of all, before we enter upon a detailed discussion, I think I ought to make what under the circumstances will be a purely formal protest against this whole method of procedure. I have been urged by numerous friends not to take part in this inquiry at all, but for reasons which I explained to the Missionary Committee, I have not felt it to be my duty to stand aloof from the inquiry. At the same time, I feel that the issue, as presented in this form, is very unjust to Dr. Lunn and myself, for we regard this issue as quite subordinate and dependent upon a question of Policy which is the only matter in which we are concerned. And I make this protest in order that it may appear afterwards that I am not in the least degree responsible for any results that may follow. At the same time, Dr. Lunn and myself are very anxious to render to this Sub-Committee any help in our power. It must not however be assumed that I approve of this method of conducting the inquiry. But assuming that the Committee is prepared to investigate the question in this narrow and personal form—a form very different from that which I should have preferred—I am prepared to defend the opinions which I hold, and I have no substantial objection to the way which Mr. Patterson has suggested. I think that for his particular purpose these questions are well drawn up. It would be exceedingly difficult to separate them; they are so involved that it would be impossible to complete the evidence under one head without anticipating that under another (and there are many facts and documents to be produced that bear upon many of these issues). At the same time you may mentally keep them apart, and I offer no objection provided a certain amount of liberty is granted. I did offer one objection to clause (a) under Question I. "Are the present allowances to our Indian brethren greater in value than those of ministers in the Home work?" I submitted that it would be better to limit the inquiry in the first instance to the relative value in purchasing power of a given sum of money in India and in England,—for until you have done that you have no common denominator; once you have settled that it is a very simple matter of arithmetic to determine the relative value of payments either in India, or in England. If that bears upon the issue at all, I shall be prepared personally to argue that the stipends of ministers in England are not a rule for stipends of missionaries in India. We cannot lay down a common and uniform standard. But that is a matter for the Committee to consider. My only contention at this moment is that you are introducing an element of great bewilderment by drawing up Question I. (a) in that form. I therefore object to it because it leaves it vague and ambiguous. Your first object should be to ascertain whether a given sum of money in gold goes farther in England than the same amount in India. The whole question is exceedingly complicated. In our original statement our whole contention had reference to the relative cost of living in India and in England. That is the most serious objection that I have to the statement of issues as now presented to us. I find that in Question II., both under (b) and (c), our brethren have materially altered the question since I saw it. I have always felt that the responsibility of preparing these inquiries rested with them rather than with me, because the precise form of this inquiry has been determined by their pleasure rather than mine (I should have suggested a much wider scope), and therefore we wish as far as possible to defer to the opinions of our Indian brethren. But I am a little embarrassed by the fact that I have been in Scotland all the week. I came home by the night train in order to be here, and at the last moment I find that the form of the questions has been somewhat altered, whereas I have been thinking of the questions as originally suggested. I am very strongly of opinion that to institute at this stage comparisons between stipends at home and stipends abroad would only lead to confusion.

Professor PATTERSON : Perhaps it will be well if I read the paper of issues that was submitted to Mr. Hughes. It is true that we have considerably changed the form. In our original draft, Issue I. (*a*) read thus :—" Is it true that the present allowances of our Indian missionaries are greater in real value than those of ministers in the Home work?" Mr. Hughes crossed out the last seven words and substituted for them, " than similar sums would be in England." It will thus be seen that we have accepted Mr. Hughes' suggestion not as an emendation, but as an addition. We retain our own words, and add his ; our reason for that is not that we wish to bring into comparison the allowances of missionaries abroad and ministers at home. We have never wished it. Any such comparison is utterly obnoxious to us. But I must point out that it was Mr. Hughes who originally instituted that comparison, and it is that comparison, as much as anything else, that has gone to prejudice the minds of the British public. With your permission I will read two extracts—one from *The Methodist Times* of May 2nd, 1889, the other from the *The Methodist Times* of May 1st, 1890. You will observe there is a space of nearly twelve months between them.

" The youngest and most obscure married missionary in
" India receives in gold a larger stipend than the Superintendent
" of the West Central Mission ; and relatively to the value of
" gold and the cost of living, each of these young Indian mis-
" sionaries has an income at least twice as large. The worst paid
" missionaries in India are better paid than our Missionary
" Secretaries, and our best paid circuit ministers at home."

On the 1st of May, 1890, *The Methodist Times* wrote :—

" In our opinion an Indian Missionary with £150 and £30
" for horse allowance would be as well off as a minister in
" London with £250."

Now I submit that Mr. Hughes, having raised this question himself, must now be content to have it faced.

In the original draft, Issue II. read thus :—" Is it true that there is anything in the style of life adopted by our Indian missionaries :—

    (*a*) " That is needlessly costly or luxurious ?
    (*b*) That tends to separate the missionary from the natives ?

(c) That alienates the natives in sympathy from the missionary?

(d) That hinders the healthy development of the Christian Church in India?"

Under the original issue there were thus four sections, but when we came to work out these sections we found that they logically resolved themselves into three. The difference is one of form only.

Issue No. III. remains unchanged. There is one other point that I should also like to mention—a point that Mr. Hughes has brought up. He regrets the form that we have given to these issues because they are so exceedingly "personal." I submit, Sir, that they are not personal at all. We considered that point carefully. We are as anxious as Mr. Hughes can be that no personalities shall be dragged into this question that can possibly be kept out of it. Personalities have been brought into it and they cannot now be eliminated, but we will second Mr. Hughes' attempt to keep personalities out as far as possible. I submit that the issues before us are issues that deal with matters of fact, and that they are not in any sense personal questions.

The PRESIDENT: This is a matter that must be settled by members of the Committee.

Mr. FLETCHER: I should like to know what course Mr. Hughes would prefer.

Mr. HUGHES: I do not think that under existing circumstances it is in our option to take any other course.

Mr. FOWLER: I move that this matter be considered in private.

This was agreed to, and non-members of the Committee then withdrew.

On Messrs. Patterson, Findlay, Hughes, Lunn, and representatives of the Mission House being re-admitted,

The PRESIDENT addressing them said: The Committee will conduct the inquiry according to its own opinion of what is best, quite apart from the programme submitted. The first question to be asked is,

What Allowances are paid to Missionaries in India?

Perhaps Mr. Hartley will answer that question?

Rev. MARSHALL HARTLEY: The allowances to married ministers in the four districts of Madras, Negapatam, Hyderabad and Mysore are £230 with certain additions; and in the two northern districts, Calcutta and Lucknow, £250. That covers the whole field with the exception of Ceylon. As to single men in the four districts named, their allowance is £125, and in the two northern districts, £150. Children's allowance for maintenance is £14 per child all round. Education allowance £12 per child, for six years, as in England. There is a uniform allowance to all missionaries of four guineas per annum for postage and stationery; and each missionary receives an allowance varying from £27 to £28 10s. for horse allowance and circuit travelling. These are the fixed money allowances. It is to be noted that medical attendance is allowed, and of course house rent as in this country, when necessary.

Mr. FOWLER: Is the item for furniture the same as in England?

Mr. HARTLEY: The Missionary Society finds what may be called heavy furniture; but it does not provide as much in the way of furniture as do many Circuits in this country.

Sir GEO. CHUBB: Who has the control of payment?

Mr. HARTLEY: The District Meeting.

Mr. FOWLER: How are these monies paid? Are they paid in English currency or in Indian currency?

Mr. HARTLEY: The money is paid in rupees according to the current rate.

Professor PATTERSON: I should like to point out that all the items that are now being asked for are in the report of the Committee of the Bangalore Conference, pages 24 and 25.

Mr. FOWLER: What is the present current rate?

Mr. HARTLEY: Since I have been at the Mission House it has varied from 1s. 4d. to 1s. 5½d.

The PRESIDENT: Have Mr. Hughes, or Dr. Lunn, or the Indian missionaries anything to say on this question?

Mr. HUGHES: There is only one item that has been omitted, viz., there is a special allowance when there is an increase in the family.

Mr. HARTLEY: That special allowance is ten guineas.

Professor PATTERSON: That is to say that one hundred rupees is paid to the nurse.

The PRESIDENT: Let it be noted that that is not an item of additional receipt for the pocket, it is paid directly to the native nurse.

Mr. HUGHES: The Committee will notice that there is an

addition of £10* to a young man in Negapatam and Hyderabad, when he has to keep up a separate establishment.

Mr. FOWLER: What is paid in reference to travelling expenses when a missionary's child is coming to England?

Mr. HARTLEY: We pay the passage money one way, and he pays the other way.

Mr. FOWLER: As a rule, are these educational allowances paid during the six years? and do the missionaries send their children to be educated at our Connexional schools?

Mr. HARTLEY: The number that go to our Connexional schools is proportionately small. If they wish them to go to a Connexional school they make application in the same way as a minister in the Home work, and the Mission House pays the cost—£34 for boys and £40 for girls. If the children are not sent to a Connexional school, the missionary receives £14 for maintenance, and £12 for education, and provides the latter as he chooses.

Mr. FOWLER: Is it a positive gain to the Mission House when a missionary's child is not sent to a Connexional school?

Mr. HARTLEY: It is.

Mr. ALLEN: Is there much difference between the payments made to missionaries in India and missionaries in China and elsewhere?

Mr. HARTLEY: There are minor differences in small items, but they are substantially the same.

The PRESIDENT: Mr. Hughes, have you any question to ask?

Mr. HUGHES: I believe that in some districts, in Bangalore for instance, they make an allowance for conveyance to the hill stations?

Mr. HARTLEY: That item comes under the head of medical attendance, which is allowed when necessary.

Mr. BRUNYATE: But the necessity of the case is, I presume, always taken into account?

Mr. HARTLEY: Certainly.

Mr. FOWLER: What is the average number of men who are allowed to go to the hills?

Mr. HARTLEY: Every man goes in his turn.

Mr. FOWLER: How often is a man allowed to go?

Professor PATTERSON: A man and his wife about once in

---

* The increase is not £10 but £25, and rules in Madras, Negapatam, Hyderabad and Burmah District.—(*Patterson*.)

three years—sometimes once in two years. Unmarried men are not allowed to go so frequently. The usual allowance is about one-fifth of the cost.

Mr. HUGHES: I presume that the cost of living is a necessity, whether they are on the hills or at home?

The PRESIDENT: Yes, but the cost of living at the sea-side is greater than at home.

In reply to a question,

Professor PATTERSON said that the allowance for a gardener only occurs where a missionary lives on property belonging to the mission; and in such cases it is absolutely necessary to have a man to look after the mission property. That man is not in any sense a personal servant of the missionary any more than a chapel-keeper is in England. If the missionary rents a house, then the landlord of that house pays a similar amount.

Dr. LUNN: As I am responsible for naming the gardener in the allowance, I may say that in Negapatam it was the universal rule that the gardener was provided by the Mission. Now my gardener did also waterman's work, and I thereby saved the salary of a waterman.

Mr. HUGHES: Where does the money come from to pay the gardener? Does it come out of some general District fund?

Professor PATTERSON: It is paid under the head of "rent and taxes"; but I have never known a case in which a missionary has received anything for a gardener, where rent has to be paid. It very often happens that a brother going to the hills cannot get a house within the limits that the District Meeting would feel bound to impose, and in that case the ordinary sum would be given to him, which for a man and his wife is at the rate of Rs. 45 a month. Anything beyond that a man would have to pay out of his own pocket.

The PRESIDENT: The next question is—

What is the relative value of these allowances, judged by the actual cost of living in England?

Will Dr. Lunn kindly answer this question?

Dr. LUNN: My strong conviction is that the same sum of money in India will go very much farther than it will in England in obtaining the same style of living. I base that opinion first upon the fact that during the brief space of time (seventeen weeks and two days) which my wife and I spent in our own station, we found that provisions (which, of course, are the first item of expenditure) were exceedingly cheap.

Mr. FOWLER: What station were you in?

Dr. LUNN: In Tiruvalur, in the Negapatam District—the district which is represented by Mr. Findlay. In the west of London we cannot possibly provide ourselves (three of us) with food for less than from 10s. to 11s. 6d. per week each in lodgings. But in India the cost of food was very much less. In the "Summary Statement" I put down the price of mutton at 1d. per lb.—that estimate was based on the fact that I once paid 12 annas for a quarter of a sheep—but that estimate, as a regular price, is a mistaken one. According to prices obtained by Mr. Caine (See Appendix B.) the price of mutton is 2d. per lb. Saminadha Iyer, a prominent barrister at Tanjore, gives the following prices:—

"Wheat flour for one measure (a little over 3-lbs.) 2d. (two annas—sixteen annas to the rupee); European bread, 2d. per big loaf; beef, 2d. per lb.; mutton, ditto; chickens, 4d. each." (That is what we regularly paid for fat chickens ourselves,— a fat chicken being a meal for two people.) "Eggs, 2d. per dozen (the eggs being about as big as bantam's eggs); butter, 4d. per lb.; milk 9 oz. for $\frac{1}{2}$d., *i.e.*, practically, 1$\frac{1}{8}$d. per pint (20 oz.); rice, 1d. per lb.; potatoes, two-thirds of a penny per lb.; sweet potatoes 6-lbs. for a penny; plantains (bananas), 1d. per dozen; tea, 1s. 2d. per lb.; raw coffee, 10d. per lb.; sugar, 9 oz. for 2$\frac{1}{4}$d., *i.e.*, about 4d. per lb."

From these prices it will be manifest how different is the rate we had to pay in India compared with what we have to pay in England. When we were there my wife and I made our calculations, and we came to the conclusion that we could live comfortably there at the rate of 15s. per week. I am sorry that my wife did not keep her account book. With regard to the question of service, 15s. per week for two people provided us with all the service that we needed.

Mr. BRUNYATE asked whether the meat in India was of such a character as to involve a great amount of waste.

Dr. LUNN: That is not so when you are dealing with chickens, ducks, and pigeons. But with regard to meat, I admit that it is not of the same quality as English meat by any means, but there is not much waste. One shilling's worth of meat would provide a course for dinner at night for two people, and for breakfast and luncheon next day.

The PRESIDENT: What you call "mutton," is that always part of a sheep, or is it the flesh of the goat?

Dr. LUNN: Occasionally we were taken in. But I could generally tell the difference between mutton and goat's flesh by the appearance of it and the flavour of it.

Mr. FOWLER: I suppose that things that come from England are very much dearer in India than in England?

Dr. LUNN: There is a very wrong impression about that. Goods are conveyed to India at cheaper rates sometimes than they are carried from London to Horncastle. Freight from London to Madras has been 36s. a ton, when from London to Horncastle it was 40s. a ton. The railway rates are exceedingly low in India. I had my carriage conveyed packed 250 miles at a cost of something like 30s. Jams we used to buy under English rates—I mean by that, the recognised retail price. What Crosse and Blackwell would sell at 1s., we could buy for less than 12 annas. Take the case of books. Books are sold on the esplanade at Madras by certain well-known native booksellers, at 10 annas to the shilling, some of them at nine and a half annas, or at the rate of 1s. 7d. for a book that would cost in English money 2s. Up the country there would be a small charge for carriage; but any book published in London can be obtained as cheaply there as here.

Mr. FOWLER: Is there a book post in India?

Dr. LUNN: Oh yes, and the book post is as valuable there as in England. Newspapers are more expensive than they are in England, because they are so very small.

Mr. BRUNYATE: There are no libraries in India?

Dr. LUNN: That is so. The books you get there you must purchase.

The PRESIDENT: Has Mr. Patterson anything to say on these points?

Professor PATTERSON: I should like to point out that this is one small section of an argument intended to confirm one conclusion, and we should prefer to be left to deal with the argument as a whole; but I should like to say this much for myself, there is one item that Dr. Lunn has referred to this afternoon with respect to which his statement is accurate, viz., the price of books. Books can be got at nine and a half annas to the shilling, provided you give the order and are prepared to wait four months for your book. If you go to a shop where they keep a stock, you have to pay 12 annas to the shilling. In every other item, my experience, extending over fifteen years, is totally different from Dr. Lunn's. Dr. Lunn referred to English stores. The commonest thing perhaps in English stores is jam. You can buy in this country excellent jam at $2\frac{1}{2}$d. per lb.; but in India there is nothing under $5\frac{3}{4}$ annas, and that is on a level with the worst things to be had in this country. If you go to respectable shops where you can rely on the excellence of the article, you have to give

7 to 12 annas per lb. The same thing may be said, I believe, of most of Dr. Lunn's prices. But I think I need not just at this stage enter into this subject for this reason, viz., that if the Committee accepts on the one side Dr. Lunn's evidence as to prices abroad, I shall ask permission to bring forward other witnesses—ladies from the mission-field—to give evidence on the other side.

Mr. BRUNYATE: Mr. Findlay is here, and he comes from the same neighbourhood.

Mr. FINDLAY: I feel with Mr. Patterson that the question of the prices of particular articles is a question very remote from the cost of living, *i.e.*, there are a great many intermediate considerations before the two can be connected, and it will be very hard for inquirers in this country to learn the whole of the intermediate questions. The natural way of approaching the subject would appear to me to be by the experience of those who have lived the longest in India and who have the widest experience. But if this particular question is at this moment to be considered, I would say that the list of prices that Dr. Lunn has read scarcely in any particular whatever comes near my own experience. There is a variation from 25 per cent. in some cases, to 300 and 400 per cent. in others, between the prices given by Dr. Lunn and my own experience.

Mr. FLETCHER: I should like to ask whether Messrs. Patterson and Findlay dissent from the whole of this list of prices as now given?

Sir GEO. CHUBB: I understand that Dr. Lunn is not giving his own experience.

Dr. LUNN: The figures I have given are in harmony with my own experience. But in order that I might not allow the Committee to depend upon my own experience too much, I asked Mr. Caine to get me these figures from India,—so that I might have corroborative evidence. I have quoted the retail prices as given by a man who has a great public position to maintain. These prices were sent to Mr. Caine within the last two months—specially in answer to his request. But I do not wish the Committee to understand that I think these prices range all over the Indian peninsula.

Mr. FOWLER: You have told us that certain prices rule in Negapatam. I want to know whether that statement is accurate or inaccurate. What have Mr. Findlay and Mr. Patterson to say about this? I see from the Report, that the Bangalore Conference had this matter before it, and that it was discussed there.

Professor PATTERSON: Most of our stations are connected

by railways on which the cost of transit is as Dr. Lunn describes. Everybody knows that the result of that is to equalise prices, so that if we can establish prices at any one place on the trunk railway, they are practically the same at every other place on that line. We have no lady missionary from Negapatam to give evidence on these questions unless Mrs. Findlay might come. Mrs. Gostick, from Manargudi, is in London, and I hope she will come. But at any rate Mrs. Geden, who has lived in Madras, will be willing to come, and also Mrs. Whitamore.

The PRESIDENT: What ladies can be present to-morrow morning to give evidence?

Professor PATTERSON: Mrs. Geden and Mrs. Whitamore. Allow me to say that Mr. Saminadha Iyer, to whom reference has been made, is a Brahmin; that in consequence of this he never eats meat, and in consequence of that he never buys any; and so far as European stores are concerned, his evidence can only be the evidence of a man who has not been in the habit of using them. I think that that ought to be understood by the Committee.

Mr. CLAPHAM: It should also be taken into account that he being a native, can go about the work of ascertaining prices more astutely than an Englishman could.

Mr. FINDLAY: Not only so; the store-keepers have different prices for different classes of people. The Anglo-Indian will be charged one price, the missionary another price, and the native another. If I were to go down to some Chinese shop in the East-end of London and ask the prices of Chinese goods, the answer given to me would be very different from that which would be given to a Chinaman.

Mr. FOWLER: We ought to know what the current market prices of these articles are. A great deal depends upon this cash question.

The PRESIDENT: Is there any missionary from Negapatam within reach, who himself really knows the market prices of these articles and who can speak from his own knowledge as to the state of the markets?

Dr. LUNN: May I be allowed to say that I have here prices from the Madras market. Mr. Caine has supplied the list from the Assistant Editor of "*The Hindu*"; but he also is a Brahmin and his evidence therefore is open to the objection that has been urged against Mr. Saminadha Iyer.

Mr. FOWLER: A Brahmin might purchase these articles at a different rate. I should like to know what the *English* people pay for them in Tanjore. Will Dr. Lunn tell us as an actual fact that flour and jams, etc., etc., were sold to him at the prices he has already quoted?

Dr. LUNN: I do not wish the Committee to depend upon my memory, but I believe that the prices I have quoted are accurate. With regard to some of the prices I have given my own experience; with regard to others, I have given the evidence of this Brahmin.

Mr. ALLEN: I presume it is known in India among cultivated natives that Mr. Caine has been involved in missionary controversy, and I imagine that they would have a good idea as to Mr. Caine's object in obtaining this information. For my own part, I should hardly like to rely upon information obtained in that way, because I know how these things may be presented.

Mr. FINDLAY: Dr. Lunn says that he bought beef at 1½d. and 2d. per pound. . . . I may say that I should never think of buying meat at that price, except it were in the shape of bones to make soup of. The very poorest beef would be two and a half annas per lb. Beef of a fairly decent quality would be three and a half or four annas per lb. Mutton, in Negapatam, costs 2d. per lb., and poor mutton it is. I have not as yet made out a full list of the prices, because I anticipated that this question would come up in connection with the second part of the first issue. I have the details of my own housekeeping in every particular for five years, and therefore I can give exact information of what everything costs in Negapatam. I have also a letter from an English artisan in Negapatam. The letter was written by Mr. W. H. Barden, foreman, South Indian Railway Workshops, Negapatam, and is dated May 6th, 1890. In it Mr. Barden says:—

"I have read the paragraph on page 301 of the *Methodist Recorder*, under the heading 'The Cost of Food.' This is certainly very misleading to those who have never lived in India. I have lived in Negapatam 10½ years, but could never purchase provisions for the money Dr. Lunn says he purchased them for. My friends and I have to pay twice and sometimes three times as much for every article he has mentioned. I for one cannot agree with Dr. Lunn that the cost of living is cheaper in India than in England. I know it costs us three times as much or nearly so, and you know we live very simply."

Mr. CLAPHAM: But does that agree with your own experience?—(Answer: In some things, Yes; in other things, No.)

Mr. FINDLAY: I believe that tea may be bought at 1s. 2d.

per pound, but if Dr. Lunn had been house-keeping a year instead of six months, he would have found that tea at 1s. 2d. per lb. was not an article to be drunk or to be economically purchased. The tea that we use is a mixture of one quality that costs something over 1s. 8d., and of another that costs over 2s. We mix those two kinds in equal proportions, and that is the tea we use, and have used for years.

Mr. FOWLER: Is there any duty on tea in India?—(Answer: No.)

Mr. CLAPHAM: Do you buy tea yourselves, or do you get it from some dealer who has a commission on it?

Mr. FINDLAY: We buy it from the shop, and we have monthly bills. I allow my servant to take the bill to the shop for payment, and he receives a commission from the shopkeeper. I should be charged just the same if he did not take the bill. It is the universal practice for servants to be paid in that way.

Mr. FLETCHER: I take it that to-morrow morning Mr. Findlay will be able to give evidence that the cost of living is as he has represented it to be, and to explain the difference between Mr. Lunn's figures and his own.

Professor PATTERSON: We shall not be able to explain the difference between Dr. Lunn's evidence and our own, but we shall be able to justify our own statement.

Mr. FOWLER: Are there no price lists of these articles?

Dr. LUNN: There are.

Professor PATTERSON: The price lists that are published in India are solely price lists of European goods. There are no price lists of native products. I am afraid that I shall not be able to produce a price list from any firm in Madras, because I have not one with me.

Mr. FOWLER: But the Bangalore Conference went into very great detail.

Professor PATTERSON: If the inquiry be into the total cost of living, we shall be prepared to go into that exhaustively. As to the question of prices, the ladies who will appear before you to-morrow will be able to give you all necessary information.

Mr. HUGHES: I wish the suggestion of Mr. Fowler could be carried out, and that you might have some business-like and unprejudiced statement from some house of business elsewhere.

Mr. T. MORGAN HARVEY (Lay Treasurer of the Society): I think there will be no difficulty in getting a wholesale price list, but there will be great difficulty in obtaining a retail price list.

Mr. BRUNYATE: What we want to know is what it actually costs families in the purchase of articles which they must have for comfort in India. I don't think that a wholesale price list would help us.

Mr. CLAPHAM: I think that Mr. Findlay's house-keeping book will be satisfactory, because it cannot have been cooked for the occasion, and it will enable us to get at the real facts.

Mr. ALLEN: It is very evident that there is a great difference in quality, and that difference will go far to explain the difference in price.

The PRESIDENT: Will not Col. Taylor be able to give information on this point?

Professor PATTERSON: I have asked Col. Taylor to hold himself in readiness to give this Committee the benefit of his experience, and I think we shall probably be able to get him here to-morrow. I may say that there is also another gentleman who has served many years in India, Mr. Evans, late Principal of the C. V. E. S. Training Institution, Dindigul; he is in London, and I think he will be able to come.

The PRESIDENT: If Col. Taylor can come we shall be pleased to see him, and we shall attach great importance to his testimony. He has been in India many years, and he ought to be able to give us much information. Now then as to

The Cost of Servants.

Dr. LUNN: In the "Summary Statement" page 14, compared with page v. of the Appendix, the tables which I have drawn out show that without the sacrifice of comfort the cost of servants may be reduced very considerably. On page 14, I give my own list of servants, and about this list I am absolutely certain. Possibly on one occasion I may have given the cook's helper half a rupee more, but there was not more than half a rupee per month difference. From that day to the day when I dismissed my servants I never paid more than Rs. 9 a month. I paid my butler per annum £7 10s.; the cook, £7; the cook's helper, £2 10s.; the sweeper, £2 10s.; the four punkah men, for six months, £6 10s., making a total of £26. The groom or horse-keeper, the grass-cutter who cuts the horse's grass and nothing else—they are really included in the horse allowance. In the Bangalore Report these two must have been included in the estimate of cost in order to get a total of £44 10s. I exclude them.

The PRESIDENT: As a matter of fact, don't English ladies have any female servants at all?

Dr. LUNN: I never heard of them.

Mr. BRUNYATE: I am told by a lady from India that some female attendant is absolutely necessary.

Mr. FINDLAY: I have a note here from Mr. Cooling, Chairman of the Financial Committee of the Bangalore Conference, in which he says that for a married minister who has a wife and children, an ayah is absolutely necessary.

The PRESIDENT: Have you no women servants at all?

Mr. FINDLAY: We had two women servants—one is the cook's helper and the other is a sweeper.

The PRESIDENT: Where is the washing done? Is all the washing done by a man?

Mr. FINDLAY: Dr. Lunn's list of servants is correct, and it is a little in excess of what the Bangalore Conference thought necessary for the Negapatam District. If he had added the washerman and the ayah to his list, the total would have been something in excess of £40 10s., so that there is little or no difference between his statement and that of the Bangalore Conference.

Dr. LUNN: With reference to an ayah, I never heard of a missionary's wife without children having an ayah. Mr. Little was my chairman, and I never heard of him keeping an ayah, Mrs. Findlay and Mrs. Geden, who had no children, did not keep ayahs.

Professor PATTERSON: If a man has to go away from home for a week or ten days it is very necessary that he should have an ayah to assist his wife. Mr. Little lives in the neighbourhood of a large girls' orphanage; Mrs. Little manages that orphanage, and she always has one of the elder girls with her. Even in Madras it is not always easy for a married missionary to do without an ayah, for he has often to be away for days and nights together.

Mr. ALLEN: I understand that missionaries' wives take part in church work and in educational work. I have been told that one had a school containing 175 girls, and she gave that as a reason why it was necessary to spend more on servants than they otherwise would.

Dr. LUNN: Professor Patterson overlooks the fact that there are two women about the house during the day, viz., the sweeper and the cook's wife.

Mr. FINDLAY: The sweeper has charge of the sewage arrangements and can scarcely be called an attendant on the lady of the house. As to the cook's assistant, her place is in the kitchen. She helps in mechanical offices in the kitchen. She also sweeps the floors, and it is her privilege to be away from the house as much as she pleases when her work is over. The mistress could not in any way make her a personal attendant. We have not required an ayah because my work has not allowed me to go away from home for any length of time. Also we have English neighbours within a few yards of us, and the same could be said of the other instances that Dr. Lunn mentioned, excepting that of Mr. Little, where Mrs. Little had the girls, and teachers, and the matron of the Orphanage always close at hand on the premises with her. At any rate, the Bangalore Conference Committee considered the question and came to this conclusion.

Mr. FOWLER: I understand that in the lonely country districts they do have an ayah where there are no children, but in large towns, such as Madras, it is not required.

Mr. FINDLAY: In large towns also, if the husband be away from home for considerable periods, he would probably deem an ayah to be necessary. The ayah commonly would refuse to do any sewing. She would do light house-work, such as helping to make the beds. The work she would do would be housemaid's work, but she would not make it possible to dispense with any other servant on the list.

Mr. FOWLER: Then, practically, between the two lists there is a difference of £9?

Mr. FINDLAY: Yes. Mr. Cooling gives a list. He had a servant as the head-servant of the household. There is no butler. The butler is a servant who has authority over all the other servants, and holds something like the position of a steward. He would commonly get Rs. 12 or 16 a month.

The PRESIDENT: What do you call the man that Dr. Lunn would call a butler?

Mr. FINDLAY: A boy or head-servant. The chokra is an under-servant, an assistant to the maty, the house servant. He helps in the household work, in dusting the rooms, lighting the lamps, &c. The ayah, the waterman or extra gardener, the coolie boy to carry things from market—all that is additional to Dr. Lunn's list. The washerman, Dr. Lunn puts elsewhere. The night punkahmen for two-thirds of the year receive at the rate of Rs. 7 a month, and the total is Rs. 53 a month, which makes £50 11s. a year. Mr. Cooling adds that outside the city of Madras, the coolie might be dispensed with. In Madras, where the cook has to go from two to six miles to market, he refuses to do his work, unless a boy is provided to carry his goods home for him. It is so also in Bangalore.

Dr. LUNN: May I just point out one item in that list which seems unnecessary, namely, that two gardeners should be kept for an ordinary bungalow? I think it is no harsh criticism to say that an extra gardener is not necessary.

The PRESIDENT: What is the reply to that?

Professor PATTERSON: In these things missionaries are guided by the experience of past years. It must be remembered that the man who is told off as a premise servant is absolutely necessary to the keep of the mission property. One man is necessary to look after the mission property generally. It should be remembered that the gardener has a great deal to do in India which a gardener has not to do here. He has to undertake the conservancy of a compound covering perhaps four or five acres of land. He has to clean it day by day. It is essential to the health of the family living there that dead leaves should not be left to rot there. He has to sweep it morning by morning and evening by evening. If it be supposed that these two gardeners are spending their time in ornamental flower gardening it would be a very great mistake. Unfortunately there is too little of that at our mission houses. The Missionary Committee pay the expenses of this work. It is understood that in the vast majority of cases an extra man will be required, and, therefore, when the Bangalore Conference prepared their estimate of the cost of servants, they included an extra gardener, or waterman, in the list. The waterman is really equivalent to the waterworks in this country. He has to bring the water, and a large amount of water is absolutely necessary in India. He has to fill the bath-tub for every individual in the house every day. He has to carry it some 200 to 300 yards, and it is exceedingly hard work, and you cannot get men to work in that climate for as many hours and with the same vigour as in this country. To call him a second gardener is exceedingly misleading, and therefore he is entered as he is in Mr. Cooling's list.

Mr. FINDLAY: In the mission house that I lived in, the District Meeting sanctioned two gardeners for the premises. When the whole of the services of the two gardeners was not required for the premises, and when I was able to employ one of them for personal attendance, I paid from my own pocket part of the cost. The Mission House was to that extent relieved; but in every case the missionary does require the services of a waterman either in whole or in part.

Dr. LUNN: I think this is rather an important point,

because it is one of those cases in which everything depends upon the style of living. This is referred to by the Rev. R. Stephenson, B.A., in his letter to Mr. Champness, published at page 7 of the "Summary Statement"; that letter says:—"It "was this feeling, in an *intensified degree*, I realised on going "to India, and finding myself located like other Englishmen, "in a large house surrounded by broad grounds—I felt there was "quite enough to make intercourse with the people, to whom "I was sent as a messenger of Christ, difficult, almost impos- "sible, in their language, their manners and customs and modes "of thought, and it seemed to me a *great aggravation* of the "evil that we should live so apart from them, as the character "and position of our homes implied and almost necessitated. "I should have liked to live in the midst of the people, and when, "after a while, I had to find my own house, I longed to go into "the native town, and take a house in a street of respectable "Hindus, but I soon found it could not be." The whole question, it seems to me, is whether the missionary should have a compound of four acres, which makes it necessary for him to keep an extra servant, or whether he should be content with such a compound as surrounded my own bungalow—I had about one acre. With a compound of that size one gardener is sufficient, and this illustrates my point.

Mr. ALLEN: It seems to me that that raises the whole question of our church property out there.

Mr. FINDLAY: The style of house and compound that the missionary lives in makes no difference to his own necessities with regard to the carrying of water for the personal use of his family. What we are insisting on is that every missionary must have such a charge necessarily included in the cost of servants. He may use the premise servant employed for the mission, but if he does that he ought to pay proportionately for the use of such a servant.

Mr. HUGHES: Mr. President, you have now come across a point that perhaps you will not be able to discuss now. It is absolutely impossible to dissever these two issues. In a one-acre compound, one man would be sufficient. We wish specially to submit to the Committee that when you have four or five acres this makes an outlay that cannot be required, and that is not a legitimate cost of the Indian Mission.

Mr. ALLEN: But the charge of one of these is against the Mission House, and not against the missionary. That does not affect the question.

Professor PATTERSON: The four acres are not devoted to the missionary's house alone. In the Royapettah compound, for example, there is first the missionary's house in the centre;

second, there is a large girls' boarding school, with sixty boarders; third, 60 or 70 yards in front of the house is a vast mass of buildings, where 450 young men are taught. In front of them there is a native chapel, and the whole sanitary provision for such work in India makes it absolutely necessary that the area should be of that extent.

The PRESIDENT: Are we to understand that the four to five acres spoken of is ground on which the missionary's house and all those other premises are enclosed?

Professor PATTERSON: Yes.

The PRESIDENT: And these two men of whom we are speaking are employed upon the whole of this estate with reference to the entire area of the buildings?

Professor PATTERSON: They are—of the two men of whom we have been speaking, one is the premise servant, the other a waterman or extra gardener chargeable to the missionary himself. The premise servant has charge of the premises. I should say that at Royapettah it is necessary to keep two premise servants, for one man is not sufficient. There are two premise servants who keep the whole premises in order.

Mr. BRUNYATE: The fact is, it is a great public establishment.

Mr. HUGHES: That is perfectly true with respect to Royapettah and Mr. Little's establishment, but is it the case in Mr. Whitamore's premises?

Professor PATTERSON: Mr. Whitamore's premises are in Madras at the corner of two roads, and premises exposed in that way require a great deal more looking after than if they were in another part of the city. Mr. Whitamore keeps only one premise servant.

Mr. FOWLER: Who pays that premise servant?

Professor PATTERSON: The Mission House. Wherever the missionary lived, he would quite require a waterman to carry his water.

Dr. LUNN: My premise servant carried my water, and I think the whole thing is a question of the size of the compound.

Mr. FLETCHER: The servant paid by the Mission House was your waterman, so that you paid nothing?

Dr. LUNN said: In my case I had a small compound—I needed no other servant, although in my compound there was a dispensary. In the case of Mr. Gostick, of Manargudi, who had a compound of 30 acres, it was necessary to keep another servant in consequence of the size of the grounds, and this applies to several other cases. This other servant is an assistant to the missionary.

Mr. FINDLAY: I do not know whether Mr. Gostick employs the same man as his own waterman—whether he uses him wholly as waterman, or partly as waterman and partly as servant.

Mr. BRUNYATE: Are there not some extraordinary circumstances about this 30 acres of land?

Dr. JENKINS: The 30 acres of land was given to us; it is a very valuable piece of land indeed. You must not imagine, Mr. President, that that is the style of compound the missionaries have to take care of. It is a very special case, in which a very large grant was made to us by the resident authorities some 54 years ago.

Dr. LUNN: This Manargudi property is so far removed from the town that the missionary and his wife, when they go to town, have to ride; and it would have been dear if the Government had given us £100 a year to take it.

Mr. BRUNYATE: The impression has gone forth that this 30 acres of ground is for our missionary; but when it is said that it is a gift from the Government, that alters the character of it altogether.

Mr. POPE: What are the 30 acres of land used for?

Dr. JENKINS: There is a garden close round the house, the rest is a grove of trees.

Mr. FINDLAY: I believe that the Mission has not power, however, to use the fruit of the trees.

Mr. FOWLER: But I want to know the number of men employed on that mission.

Mr. FINDLAY: I have no doubt that the mission allows two premise servants for that compound, but the missionary will no doubt have to make arrangements for the supply of water for his own household use.

Dr. LUNN: The facts are, that two premise servants are paid by the mission, and, in addition to that the missionary has to pay the waterman. Now I lived in a small compound, and I had one servant, who did all the functions that these three men do.

Mr. ALLEN: This question will touch another, viz., the surroundings of the missionary tending to separate him from the natives. We shall have to discuss this later on.

Mr. FOWLER: If two premise men are allowed for four acres, how many are required for 30 acres?

Mr. FINDLAY: The thirty acres are of a very different character, the ground not requiring cultivation.

Mr. FOWLER: You have worked it out that the cost of servants in Madras is £49 10s., and in Calcutta £64 16s. What is the cause of the difference?

Mr. FINDLAY: The difference is, that a greater number of servants must be kept. I have a list by a missionary's wife, Mrs. Elliott, of the Calcutta District. The list is as follows:—

LIST OF SERVANTS.

		Rs.
1.—Khansamah	… … … …	8
2.—Bearer	… … … …	8
3.—Cook	… … … …	8
4.—Ayah	… … … …	9
5.—Do.	… … … …	6
6.—Bhistie	… … … …	5
7.—Mehtar	… … … …	4
8.—Gardener	… … … …	5
9.—Guala or Milkman (looks after the cow, runs odds and ends of errands for me)		5
10.—Tailor	… … … …	10
11.—Dhobie (Washerman)	… … …	7
		Rs. 75.

3 Punkahwalas for 7 months, at Rs. 4. each, Rs. 12.

" This list does not include our stable servants. The bhistie
" and mehtar are represented by taxes at home. Many people
" put out their washing at home, which would be balanced by
" our dhoby or washerman. The *milkman* may not be considered
" a necessity, but we find it costs very little more to keep our
" own cow than to buy our milk, and we have the advantage of
" knowing the milk is pure and good, which with children is
" most important. The *tailor* may be considered an extravagance
" by some, but, whenever I *can*, I give him a month's holiday,
" say two months in the year. He makes most of my husband's,
" children's, and my own clothes. In England, dressmakers'
" bills partly correspond to this. I think your own Indian
" experience will justify the rest. *We cannot* get a man to do
" both bearer and khansamah's work."

That is just a single list in illustration of estimates prepared by taking the average of many such lists.

Mr. ALLEN: What would be the consequence if the missionary were to make a determined effort to break the customs of their caste in regard to service?

Mr. FINDLAY said the servants would rather leave him than be set to work which was not considered proper.

Mr. ALLEN: Do the English submit to all these customs, and make no attempt to break them down?

Mr. FINDLAY: Well, after all, the customs indicate the most convenient and economical mode of managing things

Dr. LUNN: I think I have some important evidence on this question. The Rev. W. C. Kendall writes to say that £36 is quite enough for the whole list of servants in Calcutta. He is a married man without children. He is giving his opinion as against the statements of the Bangalore Conference. He says:—" I am " sorry that the Indian missionaries have committed them- " selves to the figures of the Report, for I should be greatly " surprised if they bear examination. If they do, things must " have very greatly changed during the last few years." I have other evidence that I wish to adduce. Mr. Caine writes to me, and says:—" The most comfortable home in which I stayed in " India in the Bombay Presidency was a missionary's house. " He and his wife employed two Christian servants, and did all " the work of the house. The Missionary told me that his " expenses for food and clothing for himself and his wife, and the " wives of his two servants never exceeded £100 in any year."

Mr. POPE: I think we ought to have Mr. Kendall here.

Dr. JENKINS: I think we ought to have Mr. Macdonald.

Mr. POPE: I move that they both be sent for by telegram. This was seconded by Mr. Brunyate and agreed to.

Dr. LUNN: Before we leave the Madras figures may I criticise the list a little further? I consider that the list of servants I have given in this book is sufficient for any young married couple. In that list there is a servant put down as a chokra, and my whole contention has been that this is a question of style. If a certain style is adopted it is necessary to have this number of servants, but in such a style as the English mission- ary in India enjoys I hold that this chokra is not needed. The chokra is an assistant to what I call a butler. I wish also to point out that in that list there is a market-coolie. Now the existence of that market-coolie is made necessary by the distance at which the missionaries live from the market.

Sir GEO. CHUBB: I suppose that the charges here for servants include everything, the whole cost?

Dr. LUNN: Yes.

Cost of Clothing.

Dr. LUNN: On this question I have put down the exact cost I myself went to. I purchased four calico suits which I found to be sufficient, wearing a black cashmere on Sundays. The cost of this was 31s. 6d. The black cashmere I should wear out in twelve months. Then, of course, it will be manifest that I went out fully supplied with hosiery. This is not an actual cost but simply an estimate, and the same remark applies to boots and shoes. I bought one pair of country boots whilst I was in India, for which I paid Rs. 7, and for country slippers we paid Rs. 2 or 3 per pair. Then with regard to the laundry, the regular price in Madras is Rs. 2 for each person. This at any rate I paid when I was in Madras. I paid Rs. 2 for myself, and Rs. 2 for Mrs. Lunn. That would be equal to 30s. per head. The amount might be 5s. or even 10s. too little for some districts, making a total of £12 for the missionary. With regard to the missionaries' wives, it is customary for them to employ a tailor who sits in the verandah. My experience was that the missionaries' wives had their clothes made in India. The Indian tailor can imitate any pattern made in England, so that you may put the total amount under this head at £24.

Professor PATTERSON: Dr. Lunn has given his experience of one year. I accept it as the experience of a missionary who went out fully equipped, and who gathered his experience from one year's residence. My own experience is precisely that of the Bangalore Conference. I have never, during my 15 years' life in India, succeeded in bringing my expenditure within the sum estimated by the Bangalore Conference. That is, £18 for the missionary and £18 for his wife, making a total of £36 for the two.

Mr. FLETCHER: Do the missionaries wear white cotton clothes?

Professor PATTERSON: I have found it necessary to wear tweeds. If I wore this light cotton cloth I should have rheumatism.

Dr. LUNN: Of the five missionaries in Madras, two wore white drill.

Professor PATTERSON: I believe that is true, but one of them, as a rule, wears tweed.

Mr. FINDLAY: I have worn white drill up to recent times. I have been gradually feeling the necessity, more and more, of wearing tweed clothes I have not reached the time at which I could fairly test the result of my own experience. I should ike to read a passage from a statement made by Dr. Lunn's predecessor in Tiruvalur, Mr. Boulter. He says:—" My expense for clothing was just the amount they (the Bangalore Conference) have named." The Bangalore Conference has named

£36. He points out that Dr. Lunn has said nothing about such things as riding trousers. He would scarcely go out riding in his white drill.

The PRESIDENT: You see that at most it is a very trivial affair as between £24 and £36.

Charities.

Mr. FOWLER asked what Mr. Findlay and Professor Patterson had to say about charities.

Mr. HUGHES: It is only due to Dr. Lunn to say that I am more responsible than he for stating that this calculation of £23 is excessive. In our best circuits at home we give brethren £2 a quarter for charity, and I never had anything approaching £23 given to me for the purpose of relieving the poor. I confess to a strong conviction that £8 will be quite enough, judging from my own experience.

Mr. ALLEN: The question is whether we are to limit the charge in that way. I understand that our missionaries have to take a lead in enterprise and contributions—when a new chapel is to be built in India, I am told it is customary once a month to send a book round to friends who are in sympathy with the work, and that invariably the missionary heads the subscription list. So that I think you should not limit that word "charity" to gifts to poor people.

Mr. HUGHES: I should say that anything of that kind should come out of our own pockets rather than from a distinct fund.

Mr. FOWLER: Is it a fact that the missionaries give away £23 a year?

Professor PATTERSON: I can safely say that every missionary in Madras has to give a great deal more than this. In Madras there are claims that do not fall always on men in the country. For example, every European missionary in Madras has to pay Rs. 10 per annum to the Bible Society in order to make himself eligible for the local board of management; a similar sum to the Tract Society; a similar sum to the Vernacular Education Society; and every object, charitable and religious, appeals to him, and he is expected as a missionary to do his duty in that particular, and to set an example of liberality to the natives. If he is not in a position to set this example, then he fails, at any rate in an important part of his own influence. For myself, during the fifteen years I have been in Madras, the money I have had to give away has amounted to more than £23 every year, and in some years it has amounted to £40.

Mr. FINDLAY: Mr. Hughes' argument implies that if a minister in England does not receive anything from his circuit specifically for charities, he spends nothing in charities. Mr. Hughes has referred to the special allowance from the Poor Fund. But of what an English minister spends in charities, the greater part will be spent out of his stipend. In the same way the missionary spends out of his stipend generally one-tenth.

Mr. HUGHES: What I meant to say was that in calculating the stipend of a minister in this country, we do not calculate what he will be likely to give to the poor, &c. I should like to ask whether the same calls are made upon the missionary resident in the country districts that are made in Madras.

Professor PATTERSON: In the country districts there is greater poverty than amongst the people in Madras. There are many calls upon the missionaries in the way of relieving poor Christians, so that if we compare the two there is not much difference.

Mr. BRUNYATE: In England we as ministers are in the midst of a Christian population, but in India there is no one to sustain the character of giving as we understand it, and any reflection upon the liberality of our missionaries would be serious.

Mr. FINDLAY: In a subscription for any ordinary Christian object the missionary's name must be at the head of the list.

The PRESIDENT: Then as to books, I presume that we may consider that matter as settled?

Mr. HUGHES: With respect to the premium on £500 for insurance, I am bound to say that I have not been able to understand in what serious respect our missionary differs from our ministers at home. If a man's health breaks down in India, as Dr. Lunn's did, he is recalled at once. Seeing a man is immediately removed from India, if the climate does not suit him, I do not understand where this special liability comes in, and this special grant for the insurance of his life. The Committee, of course, is aware that the Mission House does pay an extra premium on an Indian missionary's life in the Annuitant Society. Provision for the missionary, and for his widow after him, is made precisely equal to that of a minister in this country, by a special payment from the Missionary Society, I confess that I fail to see that there is any special difference between them. We never insure any minister's life in that way at home.

Mr. FLETCHER: The Mission House only pays the extra premium.

Mr. FOWLER: Do the Indian missionaries insure their lives?

Mr. FINDLAY: Three-fourths of the missionaries are not able with their present allowances to insure their lives for £500.

Mr. FOWLER: On page 29 of the Bangalore Report we read:—
"We also assumed that every brother ought to make some pro-
"vision for old age, or for his widow in case of death, other than
"the sum he or his widow would be entitled to from the Annui-
"tant and Auxiliary Funds. We have therefore entered in our
"table the annual premium of an Endowment Assurance for
"£500 in the Star Life Assurance Society, commencing at 25,
"and payable at 60 years of age. In estimating the cost of
"assurance, however, we have not added anything for extra
"premium on account of Indian residence"

Professor PATTERSON: I should like to point out one thing: Mr. Hughes says, and says truly, that in the estimate of a minister's salary at home no such thing as provision for assurance for £500 is made. At the same time it should be remembered that in estimating the allowance of ministers at home, no such thing as clothes is entered. Is it not true, however, that the ministers at home insure their lives? As to perils, what we do know is this: that the perils of India are very considerable if we are to take the estimate of the Assurance societies.

Mr. ALLEN, referring to page 16 of the "Summary Statement," remarked: Mr. Hughes says that men who break down in India come back to England to recruit. But there is a wider question: all men who suffer in that climate do not return. A man returns if he breaks down altogether, but some men live in that climate 20 or 30 years, and they suffer in constitution very severely.

Mr. FLETCHER: The Bangalore Conference does not ask that the Society pay his assurance, but that it enable the missionary himself to do it.

Mr. SMITH: The question is whether this is a reasonable thing to do; the argument is that if so, he ought to have enough to enable him to do it.

Mr. BRUNYATE: I believe that a very considerable number of ministers in England insure their lives, and I am glad that they do it, but I believe that a great number of them very largely pay the annual premium out of the extra sums derived from fees of various kinds. In India the brethren have no opportunities of increasing their income so as to make any sort of provision of that kind.

Mr. HUGHES: But is it a fact that in India none of our brethren can make anything outside their stipends?

Professor PATTERSON: I have for the last twelve years of my

life made an income varying from £80 to £130 per annum as a public examiner, but that is simply an accident of my position. I may say also that the extra expenses involved more than swallow up the extra income.

Mr. HUGHES: I hope the Committee will not think that I object in any way to that.

Mr. FINDLAY: Examination fees are the only extra fees that fall to any of our missionaries.

The PRESIDENT: Is it proper for missionaries to make this provision for themselves? If so, is it not proper that their allowances should be in accordance with it?

Professor PATTERSON: If the Committee has done with these matters of detail, may I take up a few minutes on the general question?

The PRESIDENT: No; that cannot be allowed just now.

Professor PATTERSON: Then may I lay upon the table a statement which we have drawn up? That is particularly what I want to do this evening. We have drawn up certain definite statements which I wish to present to this Committee.

Mr. FOWLER: I object to our being diverted from the path which we had marked out for ourselves.

Professor PATTERSON: We have printed these statements with the object of saving the time of the Committee, and we have done it because we base our argument upon the broad historic basis of the case—I will simply distribute these papers amongst the members of the Committee. (See Appendix A.)

Mr. HUGHES: You are probably aware that Professor Patterson asked for Dr. Lunn's journal while in India; that journal has just been published, and I should be glad for every member of the Committee to have a copy.

Professor PATTERSON: May I ask whether Dr. Lunn has laid upon the table all other documents?

Mr. HUGHES: We are requested to lay upon the table the following documents:—First, the letters from Bishop Thoburn and Dr. Peck; they are on the table. Second, copies of certain letters from Dr. Lunn to certain American brethren; we have no copies of those letters. Third, some other letters with respect to Bishop Thoburn and others; we produce all we possess. Fourth, certain letters with respect to the payment of employés of Indian Railway Companies; these letters are produced. Fifth, Dr. Lunn's complete journal; that is here. Sixth, correspondence between Dr. Lunn and Dr. Lindsey of the Free Church of Scotland. I have not been able to lay my hands upon them. I have had long conversations with Dr. Lindsey myself, and anything he said to us is found in full in the report which is to be presented to the assembly of the Free Church to-morrow.

Mr. FOWLER: Did Dr. Lunn say that he had abandoned his views on the higher education policy?

Dr. LUNN: My present attitude is that we have been spending a very great deal too much money over higher education in India, and that we ought to have devoted a great deal more to vernacular preaching, and the education of the lower castes.

In reply to a question from Mr. Brunyate,

Dr. LUNN continued: I was gradually changing my views when in June, 1888, this incident occurred: Mr. Little came to visit the schools and go carefully into the circuit finances. There had been an unpleasant incident at Nannilam. Our "middle school" was doing exceedingly well until the Christian College commotion occurred. This frightened the Brahmins, and they induced a prominent barrister from Tanjore to come over and hold a "Nationalist" meeting, and urge the people to found a National school. The result of this meeting was the establishment of such a school, and our own school was closed in consequence. We decided to carry on our school in future as a primary school for the benefit of the lower castes and Pariahs. Mr. Little expressed a very strong opinion that we were doing too much for the Brahmins and high castes, and that it would be well to let them pay for their own education more completely and manage their schools themselves, whilst we devoted our energies to educating the degraded masses. In this opinion I quite agreed with Mr. Little, and I adopted his conclusions.

The PRESIDENT announced that the Committee would now adjourn.

Second Day, Wednesday, May 28th.

The President took the chair at 11.30 a.m.

Prayer was offered by the Rev. Wesley Brunyate.

Sir GEO. CHUBB: May I direct attention to page 44 of Dr. Lunn's book, where he says that the wages of the butler, cook, sweeper, &c., are equal to £39 per annum? But this does not agree with the figures on page 14 of the " Summary Statement," which give the amount as being £26.

Dr. LUNN: The figures on page 44 are fairly accurate, but were not intended to be placed before a Commission. In this list the gardener is paid by the Mission. The groom and the grass-cutter are paid out of the horse allowance, and the washerman is put down in my estimate of underclothing as laundry expenses. The wages that I put down in the list on page 14 of the " Summary " are what is actually paid.

Professor PATTERSON: Before we proceed to the business of the Committee, I have a request to make of a general character, and that is that we, as representatives of the Indian brethren, be supplied by the Committee with the form in which it proposes to take up the issues that have been submitted to it by the General Committee, and the order in which these issues will be entertained. I think it will be seen by the Committee that as we have been sent home with a special commission, and as we are representing our brethren abroad, it is impossible for us to do our duty, either to this Committee or to those who have sent us, unless we are supplied with this information, and are thus enabled to be ready for the Committee from day to day. We did not ask for this yesterday because I confess we were a little non-plussed by the action of the Committee. We had not anticipated it as possible that, seeing this inquiry has been embarked upon at the special request of the missionaries abroad, and that its scope and nature have been clearly defined by the General Committee, and especially seeing that in the issues that we had prepared, Mr. Hughes had expressed his general agreement—we did not on these grounds regard it as probable that the Committee would leave our issues altogether out of account, or would refuse to approach the subject committed to it in the form that those by whom the investigation was initiated requested—and we felt yesterday that we needed a little more thought before we ventured to make any general statement to the Committee, or to request the Committee for any statement of the issues which it proposes to bring up. I need not now, I think, define the position which we were sent home to occupy. It has been made clear that we are representatives of our Indian brethren, who have jointly and unanimously demanded an investigation into the truth of certain statements which they regard as exceedingly injurious to them and destructive of their work. We have drawn up issues as concisely as we could, so as to take in all those points upon which the missionaries abroad have felt, and still feel, most deeply, and this Committee proposes, as we understand it, to face those same issues in a somewhat different way. In order that we may discharge our duty aright to the Committee and to those who have sent us, it is necessary that we should understand the form which the Committee gives to these issues, and the order in which it will take them up. I therefore prefer this request, that we be provided with a definite written statement of the issues which the Committee proposes to investigate, and the order in which those issues will be taken up.

The PRESIDENT: You have made objection against certain representations which are before us in print. The Committee have taken up the charge against the Indian missionaries made in the second article of the *Methodist Times*, in reference to income, purchasing power, &c. The Committee are now ascertaining, *first*, what the income is, that they may understand whether the payments are too great. They are also now, *secondly*, examining the cost of food. We are within the first page of the second article against which your chief objection was raised. The Committee itself chooses to lay down its own mode of inquiry rather than to accept the one that is printed here. That is just where we stand at this moment.

Mr. FINDLAY: I think that in any case we should be permitted to know the course the inquiry is to take in its details, if only for the sake of being prepared from day to day, and I think further that the Committee will understand that in any such complicated and large question as that which is before us, a great deal depends upon the way in which the matter is approached, and that some knowledge is necessary for guidance as to the best way of approaching it. I think we could fairly put in a claim that the matter shall be approached in the way that appears best to us.

The PRESIDENT: That is impossible. The Committee cannot receive dictation as to its course of procedure.

Mr. FINDLAY: It presents itself to me in this light: a picture of missionary life and position has been presented to the Committee and the public from one side. We have been sent home to present a picture from our own side, and, whatever other sources of information the Committee may use, we feel that at any rate and at the outset our own picture of missionary life, presented from our own point of view, might fairly be received by it. We think the form of investigation which the Committee has begun to adopt, so far, implies large assumptions as to the facts that are in question—that there is a large and serious begging of the question involved in the form of investigation begun yesterday. For instance, the form of investigation which has been begun implies that there is a seriousness and strength in the criticisms of Mr. Hughes and Dr. Lunn that we should utterly refuse to allow to them at the outset, but which the Committee appears to take for granted, and which they do allow in all their details. We, on our part, should be prepared to maintain that they are entirely flimsy and rotten if they are approached in the way to attest their true character. The course of investigation commenced yesterday also implies that the considerations that were then taken up were the best and first considerations by which such matters as cost of living and the position of missionaries in India should be tested. That position we could not for a moment admit. The considerations by which the position of missionaries should be tested, we should judge to be largely different from those which the Committee has put first. We are perfectly ready to have everything inquired into, but we think we might fairly claim some right to indicate to the Committee what we consider the prime considerations—those on which the stress of the argument must mainly depend. In our view, the points investigated yesterday are chiefly of importance as bearing upon Dr. Lunn's credibility as a witness. Also the course pursued yesterday gives Dr. Lunn a position which we cannot for a moment allow, and must altogether repudiate. We, on our part, should think that we were trifling with the Committee if we brought forward a witness of weeks', months', or a year's experience. With the Report of the Bangalore Conference before it, and the declarations of the missionaries, we cannot help feeling very strongly that a Committee sitting in England should set over against such evidence, in the way that is at present being done, such testimony as we have heard on the other side. I myself should think that the men abroad will feel, more keenly than anything else that has happened in this matter, the course the Sub-Committee apparently was yesterday beginning to take—that with their testimony as contained in their own statement as to the cost of living before it, the Committee should apparently consider that testimony of the character that we have had from Dr. Lunn should be put in the balance on the other side. We are perfectly ready to have

K

the figures of the Bangalore Conference tested in any reasonable way, and to give any explanations in regard to them, but, at any rate, if we are to follow the course the Committee has begun, we cannot do it without saying that we do not for ourselves allow for a moment Dr. Lunn's evidence to weigh against such figures. But as to the way in which the truth will be arrived at, as to the picture of missionary life that must be ultimately set before the Committee and the public, we think that we ourselves should have some claim at any rate to suggest the course the inquiry should take.

Mr. HUGHES: Professor Patterson referred to me as being to some extent in sympathy with the suggestion he made as to the course of procedure. I presume the Committee is well aware that I objected from the outset to that course of procedure, and that I simply fell in with it from a spirit of conciliation. It must not be assumed that I had the least wish to dictate to the Committee in what particular way it was to carry on these investigations, and I am bound to say that when Professor Patterson first saw me, and suggested that a particular line should be followed, I was astonished. I had no idea of the sort. It must not be assumed for a moment that I have the least sympathy with what these brethren have said now, and I much prefer that the investigations of the Committee shall be entirely independent of dictation from one side or the other.

Mr. SMITH: I think that the Indian missionaries can hardly expect this Committee to take precisely what seems to be the spirit of these documents—that is to consider itself bound by the Report of the Bangalore Conference.

Mr. FINDLAY: Certainly not. But it appeared to me that yesterday the Committee were receiving assertions without any preliminary or concurrent investigation as to the authority that might fairly attach to those assertions and without examining beforehand what claim the assertions received had to a hearing. I think the Committee did not recognise as it might have done the strength that does properly attach to the assertions of the Bangalore Conference as compared with the assertions of Dr. Lunn.

Mr. SMITH: The Committee was receiving Dr. Lunn's evidence *quantum valeat* and nothing more.

Mr. FLETCHER: It seems to me that we must, as a Committee, take the responsibility of our own course of procedure. The kind of proceeding we have adopted will show the real character and worth of Dr. Lunn's statements.

Mr. POPE: I do not think it should be taken for granted that we attach any particular value to this statement, or that we are receiving evidence, and not judging the value of it.

Mr. BRUNYATE: I think the brethren should consider the importance which they themselves have attached to Dr. Lunn's statements. This whole proceeding arises from the fact of these publications, and now to act as if we ignore to any extent the importance of these statements, is not a course which we can pursue.

Mr. FLETCHER: We should remember the importance that is attached by the outside public to these statements.

Professor PATTERSON: We think it is perfectly right and exceedingly desirable that the Committee should go into every piece of evidence that has been put before it, and a great deal more besides, but what we wish to point out is this: that the question submitted by the Special Committee is a question of character. Now I submit that the simple question, whether the missionaries do or do not receive a few pounds too much, is not a question of character, but of policy, and we claim now, as we have always claimed, that before mere questions of policy be entered into, upon which your missionaries have always been willing to assist the Committee, this question of character should be disposed of. Now my fear, after the meeting of the Committee yesterday, was this, that the questions of character were going to be lost sight of, and the questions of financial policy alone were about to be discussed. In this I may possibly have misinterpreted the intentions of the Committee, and it is for this purpose that I would now very earnestly press the Committee to give to us the statement of issues that it proposes for itself for our guidance. We certainly think that this is our right as representatives. We are here not simply as witnesses but as representatives. I think we may fairly claim what I now ask for in order that we may be prepared from day to day. I must beg that the Committee will grant us this request. If not, and we do not know how the investigation is going to be conducted, we must remain at a loss from day to day.

Mr. FLETCHER: I am very slow to admit that the question of character comes in. The seeming reflections in the articles of the *Methodist Times* were emphatically denied.

Mr. POPE: We are examining into facts and statements bearing upon the position.

Mr. BRUNYATE: We must first ascertain the facts upon which the whole argument must rest.

Mr. ALLEN: It is not an unnatural thing that Messrs. Findlay and Patterson should make this request. At the same time I think that in the statement they have made, they have anticipated certain things—they seem to have been actuated by a fear of what may be. I do not know that we have quite determined the form of procedure ourselves. Our great question yesterday was: What are the facts? We have come to no conclusion at all in regard to the facts, and it must be remembered that we are expecting witnesses to come to-day and to-morrow who may be described as independent witnesses, and we must hear their evidence before we come to a conclusion. I think Mr. Findlay and Mr. Patterson will see that we can scarcely be expected to feel—shall I say?—in regard to Dr. Lunn and his evidence, as the missionaries in India feel, because the criticism has been made upon them, and I hope these brethren will dismiss from their minds at once the idea that we have reached any conclusion whatsoever. We are simply trying to ascertain the facts, and the first question is a natural one— What are the allowances that the missionaries receive? We want to get information upon this point, but there is another question which must follow as to the relative value of these allowances judged by the cost of living in India. It seems to me that we are approaching the subject in the natural order, and shall get at the facts as we proceed.

The PRESIDENT: So far as these statements are concerned the charges of Dr. Lunn seem to have been with reference to luxury—that was the word used—and also the reference to something like caste position in regard to the missionaries. Now the object of the court is to ascertain first of all whether there is any undue amount of comfort and luxury on the one side. The next point would be to ascertain first of all whether there is anything of this caste position that tends to separate Christian missionaries from access to the natives in such a manner as is proper; and it is upon that alone so far that we have gone We are now to ascertain the money value, the purchasing power. The next step will be to receive evidence from persons in the field.

Professor PATTERSON: Are we to understand that the Committee will ultimately give a distinct answer to the questions that were included in our paper of issues? From the references that have just fallen from you, sir, it seems that the investigation of the Committee is about to run on precisely the lines that we wish it to run on, with the exception that, instead of recognising those issues at the beginning, they are left out of account till the end. If we are to understand that, then I think that any cause of anxiety may be put on one side. But we should like to press for one point, that is, a clear indication of the order of procedure of the Committee, because it will devolve upon us to arrange for witnesses, and we cannot conduct our case unless we have at least this information before us.

The PRESIDENT: You had this information yesterday.

Professor PATTERSON: There is this question also. You, sir, have divided the issues before the Committee into two. First, the issues as to luxury; second, the issues as to lordliness, rudeness, &c. Now we may wish to bring evidence on both these points. The evidence of one of the witnesses summoned yesterday had reference to finance. These witnesses will be before the Committee to-day, and we should like to ask now, if in conducting their examination-in-chief, it will be for us to cover the whole of the field, or to confine ourselves absolutely to the question of finance. There will be gentlemen here whom we should like to examine as to the charges of aloofness and lordliness and we wish to know whether we are at liberty to take up the whole field of inquiry; or whether any question wandering beyond finance will be ruled out of order.

The PRESIDENT: That is a fair question. I shall be glad to have the mind of the Committee upon it.

Mr. FLETCHER: It seems to me that if the questions be kept distinct, the witnesses might be examined on both issues.

Mr. ALLEN: It is desirable that this investigation should be as thorough and exhaustive as possible.

The PRESIDENT: That is agreed to. Now we are ready to hear the first witness.

Mr. Evans gives Evidence.

Mr. Evans, of Dindigul, was introduced to the Committee. Prof. Patterson said that Mr. Evans had been for a number of years in India as Principal of the Christian Vernacular Education Society's Training College at Dindigul, a district of Southern India bordering on the Tinnevelly District, and situated on the South Indian Railway, and therefore in direct communication with Negapatam on the one side and Madras on the other.

In reply to questions put to him by Prof. Patterson,

Mr. EVANS said: I have lived nearly 10½ years at Dindigul. As to the cost of living, I could live in England on £250 with greater comfort than I could in India on £350. The items of ordinary cost which I consider specially dear in India are the items of servants; transport of articles from place to place; clothing, &c. It took nearly all my salary, £350 a year, to make ends meet. I had a wife and four children, and from six to twelve servants; we had a head-boy, a boy to look after the children, a horse-keeper, two men to carry water, which had to be carried a long way, a cook and cook's boy, a sweeper and a bath-room attendant. The head-boy is called the butler. These servants cost me on the average Rs. 65 a month, including Rs. 4 a month for two punkahmen. With regard to clothing, one suit of clothing costs very little, but you need to change pretty often. I do not think that upon the whole clothes cost more in India than in England. It is not difficult to dress on the same money in India; perhaps, on the whole, India is cheaper than England in that respect. I have been in the habit of using a large amount of English stores, such as flour and biscuits, but no bacon. These things I find to be much dearer in India—flour costs about 3d. per lb. The difference in the cost of living in India as compared with England is not to be found altogether in the item of servants. There are many other things to be considered; what I have given are the bare necessities of life, but when we want to get any little thing out of the ordinary run we have to give about double price. We were practically teetotalers, and I do not smoke. My wife had an ayah. I had eight months' experience in India before we had any children; we had no ayah during that time. My duties did not call me away from my own house, but we had to go to the hills now and then. We paid no house-rent. The Society paid my income-tax twice and the house-taxes, but I paid the horse-tax myself. In order to keep up the standard of health in India, we have to live slightly better than we do in England. It is because missionaries frequently refuse to do that that they suffer in health. You have to take a little richer food in India and an extra meal. Your breakfast must consist of meat or something of that sort.

The PRESIDENT: Would you suppose that a man receiving £300 would be able to live in undue comfort?

Mr. EVANS: He could live comfortably, but not in any style inconsistent with the ordinary style of an English clergyman. That would be impossible. I could save something out of a salary of £400, but out of £300 I could not.

Mr. SMITH asked what were Mr. Evans' medical expenses.

Mr. EVANS replied: We lived so well as to avoid that expense; we believed that prevention was better than cure.

Mr. BRUNYATE: Are the articles of food considerably lower in price in India than in England?

Mr. EVANS: Mrs. Evans knows better than I do, but I should think mutton, for example, is 3d. per lb. We only get beef about three times a year.

Mr. ALLEN: What is your opinion as to the quality of beef and mutton?

Mr. EVANS: The beef we can hardly touch, and the mutton is weak.

Mr. Evans said, in answer to questions put by the President: I frequently came in contact with Wesleyan missionaries, and spent some of my holidays with them. The missionaries live like Europeans. If they lived as the natives do, I do not think that they would be better thought of. As to their demeanour, it is that of men who wish to acquire the friendship of the natives. It is not patronising in an offensive sense at all, nor is it in any case likely to do them an injustice. I have seen nothing of haughtiness whatever in any missionaries I have known.

In reply to Professor Patterson,

Mr. EVANS said: I think that missionaries are separated from the natives by the style of the houses in which they live, but I do not see any help for it. Brahmins would not come into our houses unless they wanted a special favour, because it would mean that they would have to perform their ablutions a second time, but the low caste natives do not object to come. The same objection would be felt if the houses were smaller. I have been acquainted with missionaries of the Church Missionary Society, the American Mission, the London Mission, and the Wesleyan Mission. I cannot recall any instance of lordliness or aloofness toward the natives. I have known cases of abruptness which were, however, more owing to manner than anything else. But I have seen nothing of this sort to speak of.

Mr. BRUNYATE: Does Mr. Evans think it impracticable on social and sanitary grounds for European missionaries to live in any close contact as to residence with the Hindus?

Mr. EVANS: I should say that for sanitary reasons the missionary could not. The drainage is so bad, I take it, he would soon have the fever. The houses too are badly ventilated.

In answer to questions by Mr. Findlay,

Mr. EVANS continued: I have some acquaintance with the Civil Service in India. The allowance begins at Rs. 500 a month, though it looks less on paper. It amounts to about £400 sterling a year. I would not like to say that is the lowest on paper, but with the little extras it would come to £400.

Mr. ALLEN: May I ask a question as to the native Christians? If you were to invite the lower castes to come to your table, and take a meal with you, would they come?

Mr. EVANS: I do not think they would come to a meal. They might come to have a little coffee and biscuits. Their objection would arise from the fact that they do not know how to use either spoon or fork. They use their fingers.

In answer to questions by Dr. Lunn,

Mr. EVANS said: I consider that we need a great deal more attendance in India than we do in England. When we are at table, we need at least one person to wait upon us. In that respect the service in India has an advantage over England. Our bread was made of flour obtained sometimes from Australia, and sometimes from America. The Indian flour is not free from grit. The bread we had generally was made of flour at 3d. per lb.; chickens were 2½d. each; a chicken was enough for one course but not for a meal. When I wished to write a letter home, I had to use paper that cost me twice as much as in England. I was never able to purchase ordinary writing paper at 10½d. per quire. As to the cost of transport, it was about at the rate of 4s. per cwt. As to the size of the bungalows used by the missionaries in Negapatam and Manargudi, smaller bungalows would not be consistent with health.

Dr. LUNN: You said that native Christians would not come to dinner. Would you apply that remark to men like Mr. Thomas, the master in the Manargudi school?

Mr. EVANS: A relative I believe of Mr. Thomas has been at my table, but he was uncomfortable the whole time, and I would not press him to take more than a cup of coffee and a biscuit. My impression is, that men of that class generally will not come.

In reply to Mr. Hughes,

Mr. EVANS said: The place I lived in was a town with 13,000 inhabitants. I do not know the worth of all the various items of food. I know that milk was very dear, but we kept our own cows. Tea was about 1s. 4d. per lb. We used to buy coffee in large quantities at a time. The necessaries of life are generally cheaper in India than in England, but flour is very dear. I do not like the native bread, for we could not get the ground flour. The missionaries do break down in health, and I have always put that circumstance down to insufficient food. I have seen Salvation Army men and women down at our place. They tried to live without a bungalow of the ordinary missionary type, and without the dress of the ordinary missionary. I watched very carefully the result, and out of six or seven men who were appointed, I saw five break down and leave at the point of death (so I thought), and two of them actually did die. Coming between missionaries and the Salvation Army officers, I may mention the Lutherans, who live very much nearer the native style than the Wesleyan missionaries, but the death-rate with them is much higher. I have met four of them who have worked in my Presidency—two of them, I believe, were removed by death or illness. Of the other two one is a bachelor. The other is a man of 55 years of age, who lives in a large town in a nice little house. The Lutherans are paid very poorly.

In reply to Mr. Allen,

Mr. EVANS said: It is necessary in missionaries' houses to have the rooms very lofty and extensive. A small room shut up for hours becomes unendurable.

In reply to Mr. Hughes,

Mr. EVANS continued: The American houses are, on the whole, much larger than Wesleyan houses, with the exception of the houses at Trichinopoly. The American Mission is more successful because the men are more pushing, they live better. They contrive to have a good square meal, and being in better health, they do more work. They are paid Rs. 225 a month. The Presbyterian Board of Missions have also an allowance for going to the hills. They have carriage allowance and an allowance for children. My authority for speaking as I have done of the natives of India, rests upon the experience of $10\frac{1}{2}$ years. I have not heard the natives themselves object to the style of living adopted by our missionaries. On the contrary, I have heard that missionaries who lived in a different way from the ordinary missionary were reflected upon. I am referring now to the Salvation Army and the Lutheran missionaries.

In reply to Mr. Fletcher,

Mr. EVANS said: The intelligent native recognises the necessity of such a style of living as our missionaries adopt.

In reply to Mr. Smith,

Mr. EVANS said that the Lutheran missionaries had met with little success in the towns, their greatest successes were in the villages.

In reply to Mr. Fowler,

Mr. EVANS said: The Roman Catholic missionaries live very much like the people; as for their successes I cannot speak, for they kept all their statistics very quiet.

Mr. Evans then retired.

Mr. FOWLER: I want to know what number of single and married missionaries we have in India, and the gross annual cost during the last three years, including all payments or allowances, except furniture, for married men. I want the same information for American ministers.

Evidence given by Col. Taylor.

Colonel TAYLOR was next introduced to the Committee, and in reply to Professor Patterson he said he had lived in India for 30 years. Four generations of his family had served there—chiefly in the Mysore territory—their combined experience extending over 150 years. He had himself at various times resided from within sight of the Himalayan ranges down to Cape Comorin. He had seen all parts of India except Bombay. He had met and worked with the Baptists and Wesleyans in Calcutta, Dinapore, Benares, Bangalore, and Madras. He had some acquaintance with agents of the Church Missionary Society, the Society for the Propagation of the Gospel, the Presbyterians, the Salvation Army, the Papists; and in the Central Provinces, the missionaries of the Methodist Episcopal Church. He had not observed in the missionaries anything that might be described as a spirit of lordliness, aloofness, and want of sympathy. On the contrary, he believed the natives almost worshipped the missionaries. At any rate, they were on the most perfect terms of love and friendship, lending them carts, &c. One missionary whom he had met in the jungle and ridden home with, was saluted by a Brahmin in a way that excited his (Col. Taylor's) astonishment and admiration. The Brahmin, when near the missionary, touched the ground with his hand and then his forehead (a mark of the very highest respect) which he had never seen shewn to any military officer, or even to the Governor-General of India. And this was true of all the missionaries with whom he had come into personal contact. He did not remember the case of any missionary (except a Roman Catholic priest—a Jesuit) who had been complained of by his people. As to their style of living, he did not think that they would secure more respect from the natives by living in poverty. He had known all the Lutheran missionaries who went out to Chutia Nagpore intending to live a life of faith. One was a carpenter, another was a shoe-maker, a third a mason. They had each learnt a trade; they lived on charity, and had one common pot. Very often it was a case of starvation for them. Their work was a failure; the parent society in Germany would not support them; they had to throw themselves on the S. P. G., and they were at the present moment under the control of the Bishop of Calcutta. He had said to these missionaries: "How is it that none of your sons have come out into the work in India, when you all wish them to do so?" One of them answered: "If you can read German, look at that letter which I have received from my son." This son was a doctor, employed in Germany, and this is what he said: "I have felt the separation from my parents so keenly, that nothing would induce me to submit my children to the same painful ordeal that I have gone through." With regard to the Bauldwin Schools at Bangalore, a man who went there, called Richards, went away to America after three years. His successor died after three or four months. The next man left. Every one of Mr. Carter's children died, and he left. As to the Salvation Army, not one of the first party who went out there was there now, except Miss A———, who had left the Army. With regard to Commissioner Tucker, he did not believe that a year had passed without his coming to England. He was diseased and suffered from chronic dysentery When he (Colonel Taylor) saw him in Madras, he knew that they were very anxious about him and afraid that he would die. The number of deaths in the Salvation Army arising from bad food and exposure was a matter well known in India. The Lutheran missionaries did not live on quite so low a scale as did the agents of the Salvation Army, but they had to endure great hardships. He (Col. Taylor) paid the travelling expenses of one missionary to the hills, or he would have died. He knew another missionary (since dead) in the jungle. That man had been selling the produce of his own garden in order to make both ends meet. He belonged to the S. P. G., whose agents as a rule were fairly well paid.* He did not believe that the missionaries got a farthing too much. If the object of the missionaries who lived in a poorer style was to bring themselves into closer contact and sympathy with the natives, he did not believe that their object was gained by it. There was not a body of people in India who were more respected than were educated and godly missionaries. In a public speech delivered before the Lieut. Governor of Bengal, the Metropolitan of Calcutta, and the *élite* of Indian Society, the late Baboo Keshub Chunder Sen said:—"It is not the British Army that deserves honour for holding India. If unto any army appertains the honour of holding India for England, that army is the army of Christian missionaries, headed by their invincible captain, Jesus Christ." He (Col. Taylor) quite concurred with the Baboo's views. As to the cost of living in India, he did not believe that anything under Rs. 250 per month would enable a man to live there in health and comfort. He was neither a drinker nor a smoker; he lived as abstemiously as any man could live in India, and his

---

* A Baptist Missionary who had some cows given to him, sold milk and butter, and from this source of income kept some of his native workers alive.

personal expenses amounted to Rs. 250 per month. His wife said that they could live comfortably on Rs. 300 per month. It should be remembered that a missionary had a great many calls made upon him. He had been in a missionary's house when a persecuted Christian native family was brought in, and the missionary had to keep them for months! The Rs. 300 per month included food and clothing (no rent), and food for two horses. That was equivalent to Rs. 3,600 a year for two persons. With respect to the list of prices, as given by Dr. Lunn, he was very much amused by it. Dr. Lunn, for instance, mentioned bacon, amongst other things. That seemed to him almost an abomination. The only bacon that he would like to touch in India was that which was sold in tins—an extremely costly article. The ordinary bacon was nothing better than garbage—which only the very lowest and poorest of the people would eat.

Mr. FOWLER: Am I to understand that there is little or no difference, so far as monetary cost is concerned, between living in India and living in England?

Colonel TAYLOR: The difference in actual £. s. d. is very small, but there is not a man in India who would not rather have £240 in England, than Rs. 300 per month in India. There is not much difference of opinion about that. One thought had struck him. He had not come to that Committee with any party feeling, and if he spoke strongly they would forgive him. When he was in India he heard one of the wealthiest natives in Madras say of Commissioner Tucker that if he were to come to him he would fall down at his feet and worship him, because he (Commissioner Tucker) gave up a grand position in the interests of strong religious conviction, and had gone out there as a poor man to do God's work. Now that was very true; but he (Col. Taylor) held that that was true of every missionary in India. There was not a missionary in India who could not earn three times his income in secular work.

In answer to questions put to him by Mr. Hughes,

Colonel TAYLOR said: He had not known a Wesleyan missionary at Benares of the name of Solomon. It was now seven years since he was at Benares. He did not know what were the stipends of the Lutheran ministers at Chutia Nagpore, the mission had collapsed, the entire party joined the S. P. G. Society; when he was there a change had taken place. New missionaries were sent from Germany, and on better terms.

Mr. HUGHES: You have given us some account of very extreme ascetic missionaries; but have you, Colonel Taylor, had any experience of missionaries living in an intermediate state between these two, or have you known of any one?

Colonel TAYLOR: Yes, the Methodist Episcopal Church missionaries lived first on self-support, then on a salary of Rs. 120 per month, but it was found to be insufficient, and has been raised to Rs. 180. I think it is very likely they will find that to be insufficient too.

The PRESIDENT: Bishop Taylor's work in India has ended, the men have either left or the work is absorbed.

Colonel TAYLOR: Six or seven years ago the Methodist Episcopal Church lived on what they called self-supporting lines. I will give you an idea of what those lines were. Mr. Baker was at Nagpore; he received from his flock Rs. 70 or Rs. 80 per month. Dr. Lock, the Deputy Surgeon-General of the District, materially helped Mr. Baker and his wife. He provided them with a carriage, and with punkah men, and often sent food to them. He admired the man and his work so much that he did all this for him voluntarily. Put all these things together, and you will find that self-support costs something. The Conference afterwards decided that there should be a fixed income of Rs. 120 monthly, and this allowance has since been increased to Rs. 180.

In reply to further questions by Mr. Hughes,

Colonel TAYLOR said that for some time he resided in a place where they did not see a European face for three months together, so that he was not put to much expense in the way of affording entertainment to visitors. . . The following items would throw light on the cost of living: 66 measures of rice could be had for a rupee; Rs. 4 or 5 would purchase a sheep, weighing about 40 lbs., or 15 lbs. when skinned. As to beef, they never got that in India, except in towns. Milk was cheap; tea was a fabulous price, because they had to pay for the journey overland.

Mr. HUGHES: As to the minor question of bacon: did Colonel Taylor say that bacon cost 8s. per tin of 2 lbs.?

Colonel TAYLOR: I have bought dozens of these tins: some are sold at Rs. 4 and others at Rs. 8.

Dr. LUNN: I bought tins of bacon at the stores at 14 pence per lb.

Mr. BRUNYATE: Can Colonel Taylor tell us whether the general cost of living in India is very different now from what it was fifty years ago?

Colonel TAYLOR: I can tell you that thirty years ago I did buy 120 measures of grain for one rupee, but now you can't get 16 measures for that money. I could buy a cow in those days for Rs. 6; I could not get one for Rs. 60 now. I could buy a pony then for Rs 30.; you cannot get one for Rs. 200 now. I could buy a hide for 4 annas; I cannot get one now for less than Rs. 8.

Mr. FOWLER: Has the pay in the Civil Service or Military Service increased?*—(Answer: No, not in the senior grades; but there are a great many places where a man may get 50 per cent. or 80 per cent. better pay.)

Mr. HUGHES: Does Colonel Taylor mean that the cost of living varies very much in different districts in India?—(Answer: Yes.)

Mr. SMITH: How much per cent. higher is it now as compared with thirty years ago?—(Answer: About cent. per cent.)

Dr. LUNN, in reply to the President, said he had no further question to ask.

Professor PATTERSON: Colonel Taylor has spoken of the Mission of Bishop Taylor in India. He has told us that the South Indian Conference, that now practically represents Bishop Taylor's work, gives to its agents a salary of Rs. 180. I suppose that Colonel Taylor speaks from knowledge that was acquired more than 12 months ago. Does he know that since then that rate of salary has been condemned, and that it has been increased?

The PRESIDENT: I think that Colonel Taylor said enough to intimate that the rise he mentioned was not the final rise.

Professor PATTERSON: Colonel Taylor has referred to a rise in prices of cent. per cent. I should like to ask Colonel Taylor if he thinks that the rise in the *general* cost of English living is as great as that?

Colonel TAYLOR: The increase is much greater in some things and less in others. If you take one thing with another, including coffee and tobacco, you will find that my estimate is about correct. Here let me mention another thing. I have heard people complaining of our Zenana Mission, and of missionaries' wives travelling first-class. It should be known that the Government gives every warrant-officer a first-class ticket, and a first-class ticket for his family. I don't know

---

* In 1865, by abolishing the rank of ensign and doing away with single Batta stations, *every* subaltern's pay per mensem was raised from Rs. 160 to Rs. 256; in the Department Public Works, by abolishing 3rd and 4th grade engineers and accepting all comers as engineers 2nd grade, the Government practically raised the salaries of young engineers by Rs. 100 a month. The police forces were also re-modelled and their condition improved.

whether you would like your wives to travel with drunken soldiers in a train. Even native soldiers get second-class tickets; sometimes very unpleasant scenes arise on these journeys.

Dr. LUNN: Colonel Taylor said that he lived on Rs. 300 per month, and that he kept two horses and yet he could live comfortably on £250 a year in England. Are we to infer that he could live in India on £250 a year with the same comfort as in England?

Colonel TAYLOR: Oh! no, not with the same comfort, there is the climate to deal with.

Dr. LUNN: I am not referring to climate, but to expenditure.

Colonel TAYLOR: The two countries cannot be compared.

The PRESIDENT thanked Colonel Taylor for his presence and evidence.

Before leaving the Committee, Colonel Taylor wished to speak a word or two about the Zenana work in India to show how our women were covertly insulted, and with what grace they bear up. The ladies were received in the Zenana in the most courteous manner, but not in private rooms. The room entered by our English girls was regarded by the natives as polluted, and as needing to be cleansed and purified; this was done by sweeping and by the sprinkling of holy water. This was an illustration of the difficulties attending their work. There was another point. He thought it would be of enormous value to their work, if the Government were to recognise missionaries more than it did.

Mrs. Whitamore's Evidence.

Mrs. WHITAMORE said: I have lived in India seven years, $4\frac{1}{2}$ years in Calcutta and $2\frac{1}{2}$ years in Madras. *Living* in Calcutta is a little more expensive than in Madras. The average yearly cost, with two young children, for food, fuel and light was £82 15s. 0d.—that was the average of the $2\frac{1}{2}$ years in Madras without extras. The expenses of servants amounted to £59 17s. 0d. per year. The servants necessary to be kept were:—

        Boy, who received Rs. 10 per month.
        Maty   ,,   7 ,,
        Cook   ,,   9 ,,
        Coolie   ,,   3 ,,
        Tannicatchy ,,   3 ,,
        Sweeper ,, $3\frac{1}{2}$,,

Waterman, who received Rs. 3 per month.
Ayah   ,,   10   ,,
Dhobie   ,,   8   ,,
Punkah Coolies   ,,   12   ,,

The waterman is the gardener really, whom the Mission pays, but we give him Rs. 3 for carrying water. His total wages would be Rs. 8 a month—the remaining Rs. 5 being paid by the Mission. Our experience with regard to *clothing* was that, taking the whole family together, it cost as nearly as possible £50 a year. We endeavoured to reduce the expenditure. First of all we tried to do without the maty, and then without a cook, but I got so weak that I could not do without these servants. I tried repeatedly, but could not manage without them. It is not that there is too much work to do, but each servant has his own work, which means that I had to help a great deal more. Our family consists of two children. We have an ayah, and I should have tried to retain her services, even if I had had no children, as a sort of medium between myself and the men-servants. The cost of milk, bread and butter was £20 10s. 0d. per year. The bazaar cost £39 a year; this includes meat, vegetables, fish and fuel. European stores cost, with light, £23 5s. 0d. annually. This includes the necessaries we must have, such as vinegar, salt, pepper, jams and biscuits, and sometimes a little bacon. As to the relative cost of English stores in India and in England, I may say that in India biscuits for example cost 1s. per lb., jams 7d. per lb., oatmeal 5d. per lb. These prices I give from my account book. For mutton we give 3d. per lb.

In reply to a question by Mr. Smith,

Mrs. WHITAMORE said that one lb. of English meat is worth three lbs. of Indian meat.

In reply to Dr. Lunn,

Mrs. WHITAMORE said that the cost for food, £82 15s. 0d., included milk for four persons.

Dr. LUNN said he thought Mrs. Whitamore had some very pronounced opinions as to the class of society she mixed with in Yorkshire, as compared with that in Calcutta. Would she state those opinions?

Mrs. WHITAMORE : Of course, there is a vast difference—in Yorkshire they are Yorkshire people—in Calcutta they are East Indians, and Europeans.

Dr. LUNN : Does not Mrs. Whitamore think that she mixed with a very superior class of society in Calcutta?

The PRESIDENT: You can find a great difference in the classes of society in the different English circuits.

Mr. BRUNYATE: I do not think we ought to ask Mrs. Whitamore to define such differences.

Mr. HUGHES: So far as Mrs. Whitamore's experience goes, do our missionaries in Calcutta move in a different class of society from that they move in at home—that is, with persons in a different social position?

The PRESIDENT: The same thing would apply to any garrison station in England.

Mr. HUGHES: I should like to ask whether Mr. Whitamore preached to Hindus or to an English congregation?

Mrs. WHITAMORE: To an English congregation.

Mr. FLETCHER: Did your access to European society interfere with your access to the natives?

Mrs. WHITAMORE: Decidedly not. All Europeans in India are educated.

Mr. CLAPHAM: All the Europeans in Yorkshire are *not* educated. (Laughter.)

Evidence of Mr. Chas. Eales.

Mr. EALES next gave evidence. He said, in answer to questions put by Mr. Findlay, that he had lived in India about 40 years, chiefly in Bengal. He had not been largely acquainted with Wesleyan missionaries, but he had seen much of the Nonconformist missionaries. He was a Churchman himself, but his sympathies were largely with the Wesleyans and their work. He had known the Wesleyan missionaries, Mr. Richards and others, in Calcutta ever since the first chapel was built there. But he had been most acquainted with the American Baptists in Burmah and Calcutta. He was amazed to hear that charges of extravagance had been made against the missionaries. He had never come across a more self-denying body of men anywhere. He had attended many levees, but never met a Wesleyan missionary there or heard of one being present.

The PRESIDENT: Knowing Indian society, do you think it would be inconsistent for missionaries to attend levees?

Mr. EALES replied that he did not think it would be at all inconsistent. He had never heard the question of the presence of missionaries in social gatherings raised.

Mr. FINDLAY asked if he had had opportunity of observing the style of living of missionaries?

Mr. EALES: Certainly. I have been personally acquainted with them, and I have not found any reason to suppose they were living in an extravagant or unbecoming manner. In India it was absolutely necessary for a man to have a horse, or conveyance of some kind. A missionary could not live in a small house without risk to health, and it was essential that he should get away to the sea or plains, now and then to the hills. He had not heard any opinion in India that there was want of sympathy on the part of the missionaries, or that there was aloofness in their attitude toward the natives. No one treated the natives with more respect than the missionaries did, and the missionaries had done a vast amount of good in checking the evils that abound in India. Mr. Eales said the cost of living depended of course upon the size of the family; a man might live on Rs. 3 a day if he had no children. His own house cost him Rs. 125 a month, and he lived very quietly.

Mr. FINDLAY: What sum do you think would enable a man to live in India, corresponding with £250 in England?

Mr. EALES replied that what would be regarded as luxuries in England were necessaries in India. There, a coachman must be kept, and £250 would not be an extravagant sum, certainly.

Dr. LUNN: Do you think that £200 in India would enable you to live in equal style with those who receive £250 in England?

Mr. EALES: No.

Mr. CLAPHAM: Then you consider it is more expensive to live in India than in England?

Mr. EALES: Certainly; or else why do Government servants get more there than in England? It is an absolute necessity.

Mr. CLAPHAM: What do civil servants get in India?

Mr. EALES: I have two sons in the Civil Service. At first they got Rs. 400 a month, that is deducting the amount necessary to meet their pensions. That would be about £400 a year. They advance according to the length of service. When a young man has served the Government ten years, he gets fifty per cent. more. Ordinarily speaking he would get from £600 to £700 a year.

Mr. Eales then retired.

Mrs. Geden's Evidence.

Mrs. GEDEN stated that she had kept house in India for 15 months. The cost of food, fuel, and lighting for herself and

Mr. Geden for one clear year was about £75. They paid Rs. 40 a month for servants. They did not employ a punkah-man, as in the first year this is not so much needed. The total expenditure given was exclusive of the cost of punkah-men. The total for servants per annum was £36.

Head boy received Rs.	10	per month.
Cook ,,	8	,,
Chokra ,,	4	,,
Tannicatchy, or cook's helper	3½	,,
Sweeper received	3	,,
Waterman ,,	4½	,,
Dhobie ,,	6	,,

The waterman carried all the water for the baths, and pulled the punkah during meals. The four gardeners were paid by the landlord, and the amount was included in the rent. With regard to clothes, Mrs. Geden said she was afraid she could not give any information. They took clothes with them from England. Mrs. Geden never kept an ayah; she was in good health, and was never left alone for long, or such a servant would have been necessary. As to the cost of milk, bread, ordinary bazaar account, &c., Mrs. Geden said she paid 3 annas per lb. for beef, and 3 annas for mutton; she did not purchase any bacon, thinking it too expensive. On the whole, living in India was dearer than in England. As to the style in which they lived, Mrs. Geden said they had not many courses. They had tea and toast and butter at 7 a.m.; breakfast consisting of some kind of porridge or curry, and a second dish consisting of meat or eggs, and coffee at 9, and for tiffin, curry and bread, or something of that kind. Dinner in the evening consisted of soup and curry, and meat and pudding. This style of living cost them on the whole £75 per year. Mrs. Geden said that the record of her experience was that for the first six months, they lived in a style that six months' longer experience taught them was not sufficient to keep them in health and strength.

Mr. CLAPHAM: Is the cost of living in India higher than in England?

Mrs. GEDEN: We have found it more expensive living in India than in England.

Mr. HUGHES: Could Mrs. Geden tell us what particular items of expenditure are more expensive?

Mrs. GEDEN: The articles are poorer in quality, so that more is required, and that makes a difference. There is more waste, and at the same time we need more variety, and we have to buy in small quantities.

Sir GEO. CHUBB: We have two very different statements as to the price of flour.

Mrs. GEDEN: We cannot get good flour under 3d. per lb.

Sir GEO. CHUBB: Dr. Lunn spoke of native flour; he said it was wheat flour.

Dr. LUNN: I was referring then to English bread made from Indian flour.

Mr. HUGHES: What we want to know is the actual experience of missionaries, but we will present the whole of this printed evidence if you like.

Dr. LUNN: I should like to ask, if Mrs. Geden would kindly tell me, what was the expenditure on food in the month of April, 1888? This has to do with the statement made in the document that was laid on the table last night that Mrs. Lunn and myself had never lived on 15s. a week.

Mrs. GEDEN said that during that month, she had an exact account of the cook's bill. It came to Rs.120, but that did not include everything.

Dr. LUNN: I should be glad if Mrs. Geden would give an estimate to the Committee as to the probable expenditure.

Mr. BRUNYATE: Dr. Lunn was Mrs. Geden's guest during the month in question.

Dr. LUNN: I was boarding with Mr. Geden at the usual rate of Rs. 90 per month.

Mr. HUGHES: Dr. Lunn was under the impression that Mrs. Geden herself stated that the entire cost of the establishment during that month was Rs.120.

Mrs. GEDEN said: My statement was made in a conversation in the house. The European stores for the year amounted to about £25.

Mr. HUGHES: May I ask on what ground Mrs. Geden calculates this £25?

Mrs. GEDEN: I have the account for other months of the same year.

Evidence of Rev. F. W. Gostick.

Rev. F. W. GOSTICK said: I lived in the Trichinopoly district for nine years, for three years as a single man. I have had six years' experience of married life in India. My ordinary expenses in house-keeping have amounted to Rs. 75 per month for myself and Mrs. Gostick. This equals £67 10s. per annum. The amount covers meat, bread, eggs, potatoes, vegetables, rice, sugar, tea, coffee, oatmeal, tinned stores, curry stuffs, oil, fuel, and other household requisites for two persons. With reference to prices of food stuff in India, I have thought it well to lay before the Committee these three actual bills. The first is a grocer's bill dated December 19th, 1889. In it you will see the prices actually paid for such articles as bacon, jams, &c. The second bill is a meat bill from Tanjore, and the Committee will note that this is the same town from which Dr. Lunn has received quotations of prices. The third bill is for vegetables.

The bills were handed round to the members of the Committee.

Mr. BRUNYATE: Real bills like these we can rely upon. Is the cost of vegetables as given here higher or lower than vegetables in this country?

Mr. GOSTICK: Much higher. As to servants, these cost me Rs. 510, or about £38 10s. sterling per year. The list is:—

Boy	Rs. 108	per year.
Cook	108	,,
Cook's helper...	36	,,
Sweeper	36	,,
Two punkahmen	42	for ½ year.
Washerman	60	1 ,,
Ayah	120	1 ,,

Before we had children we lived at Karur, in the immediate neighbourhood of a large orphanage. With respect to clothing, it is a difficult matter to put down the cost in a yearly account, because it is purchased so irregularly. I paid for white suits about £3 3s. a year, coloured cotton suit about £1, black clothes £2, boots and shoes £2, underclothing £4, hats Rs. 15. For hill clothing, that is clothing for wear on the hills, which must be thicker, £16. The cost of clothing for Mrs. Gostick would be more than that.

Mr. CLAPHAM: What is the comparative cost of living between India and England?

Mr. GOSTICK: I have had no experience of English life. I should think that in England it will be cheaper, because the meat in India is not so nutritious. One course of meat in England is equal to two or three courses in India.

The PRESIDENT: You have seen ministers' houses in England and Indian missionaries' houses. Is there any such difference between the two as to justify the statement that the style of living in India is luxurious as compared with that of English ministers?

Mr. GOSTICK: My uncle was a minister in England, and his house was much more comfortable than mine in India.

The PRESIDENT: Observing Indian missionaries' houses and modes of life, is there anything to interfere with the good understanding between the missionaries and the native brethren? Is there anything in the style of living that would tend to alienate the native brethren from the European missionary?

Mr. GOSTICK: This is a wide question, but I answer "No" to it.

Mr. CLAPHAM: Is the relation between the missionaries and the natives cordial?

Mr. GOSTICK: Certainly. I myself have been very near to my native brethren. I love them quite as much as my English brethren. Understand, though, that there are many things in their customs and manners that make it impossible for us to draw very near to them at present. It will be a work of time, but it is being accomplished, though perhaps slowly. For instance, whilst I was in Manargudi we had as head master of the high school a native Christian who was a M.A. of the Madras University, and perhaps one of the cleverest natives of South India. He frequently came up to the mission house to tea, and we did our best to make him feel at home in conforming to our customs, but it seemed always a positive pain to him to be at the table. His customs were so entirely different that it was almost impossible for us to meet him in that way. This illustrates the difficulties we have to meet with.

The PRESIDENT: Is there anything in the mode of life of the Indian missionaries that causes the native population to think the Indian missionaries consider themselves upon a higher platform than the natives? Without standing aloof from them, is there anything in the style of living of the missionaries to justify what has been said on that point—anything to break down sympathy, brotherly feeling, and so forth?

Mr. GOSTICK: For myself, I have not met with any such suspicion.

Mr. FOWLER: Is there any social intercourse between the natives and the missionaries.

Mr. GOSTICK: Yes. On two or three occasions I have attempted to bring in some such custom as our Christian tea-parties, and have gathered our native Christians together. I have always found, however, that it was very difficult to do this, on account of their caste. There is still in India, even amongst

Christians, a very strong under-current of feeling against the mixture of classes, and I was obliged to give up the idea of getting them together for eating and drinking. Mere social gatherings, without eating or drinking, are not uncommon. Mr. Findlay has one in his circuit every Tuesday night, and I have often been present. There is no difficulty in getting them to meet thus. The caste feeling goes to this extent, that if a family has come out from among the Shudras they will not intermingle either in marriage or at meals with Pariahs or those much lower. I know of no case where it has been done.

Mr. FOWLER: How does it work in the case of the native ministers?

Mr. GOSTICK: We make it compulsory. There was a catechist on one of our stations some time since who came to us from the S. P. G. It was known that this young man was backward in going with the other catechists when they had to stay over-night, and so make a meal necessary. The matter was discussed, and the Superintendent was told to inform him quietly and kindly that it was necessary he should meet with the others. He did so after that; but this is an instance of some of the troubles we have in these matters.

Mr. FOWLER: Is there perfect equality between native Christians and yourselves?

Mr. GOSTICK: We wish, on our part, for perfect equality, but, as I have shown, at present it is impossible, and will be of slow growth.

Mr. FOWLER: Have you separate tables at your District Meetings for the Europeans and the natives?

Mr. GOSTICK: There is certainly no separate table, but our District Meetings are generally held in the houses, and we could not accommodate them all.

Mr. CLAPHAM: I wish to know whether, at ordinary meetings of the Church, European and native ministers meet in the same room and take counsel together?

Mr. GOSTICK: Certainly. There are certain questions that have always been discussed in the first session of the district when the European brethren meet. After that the native and European brethren meet together. We all meet in the same room and at the same table, and discuss the same questions. The native brethren have just the same right that any of us have, not only to be present, but to take part in the conversations. But they do not use that right. They sit in silence to a great extent, for the reason that they do not understand English thoroughly, but they have a vote.

Mr. FOWLER: Will you tell us what business was done at the sessions of the District Meeting when only English ministers were present, and what was done when European and native ministers were present?

Mr. GOSTICK: In the European session the questions considered are of finance, and have reference to the division of the grant. The money comes from home, and I think that is the reason why the European brethren have divided the work of the session. The question of the character of the European brethren comes up also in the European session.

Professor PATTERSON: Mr. Gostick makes a mistake there. The order of procedure of the Indian District Meetings, both in the European and general sessions, may be found in the Calcutta Conference Report.

Mr. FOWLER: Is the bulk of the business done in the first or second meeting?

Professor PATTERSON: The greater part of the business is done in the second meeting. Native ministers have the same rights as the Europeans; the same right of appeal and so forth.

Mr. FOWLER: Then the only business that is done apart from the natives has reference to the questions of finance?

Professor PATTERSON: Yes.

Mr. BRUNYATE: Do native ministers administer the Holy Sacrament side by side with European ministers?

Mr. GOSTICK: Sometimes I have celebrated with the native minister, and sometimes I have let him do it to his own people —I being present.

Mr. HUGHES: I cannot understand the apparent difference between Mr. Patterson and Mr. Gostick on this point. I want to know why Mr. Gostick was not aware of his mistake?

Mr. GOSTICK: The reason is, that in the absence of any case of discipline in our district, I had not particularly noticed this point.

Mr. HUGHES: Is it a fact that the European and native ministers dine together every day?

Mr. GOSTICK: They dine together occasionally, but not always. The native brethren themselves do not dine together. They are generally lodged out in private houses. They prefer this plan a great deal, and to have dinner alone, as the Hindu always does.

Mr. FOWLER: Do the native ministers attend the Conference in any numbers?

Mr. GOSTICK: I have only been to one Conference. The native brethren were not there. It was called to consider a special subject, and was more like a committee than a Conference.

Mr. HUGHES: On that point we have the Report of the Bangalore Conference in our hands, and you will find the questions discussed at the Bangalore Conference were questions in which native ministers were as much interested as European, and I should like to ask why it was that no single native ordained minister attended that Conference?

Mr. GOSTICK replied: The Conference in question was a special one, met for the special purpose of inquiring into accusations from home against us, and would not have met but for those accusations. When the brethren met together and found themselves in conference, they naturally discussed other questions, but you will find that all the questions more or less stood related to this present discussion.

Mr. HUGHES: I deliberately assert that when this question came before the Missionary Committee, this view of the Bangalore Conference was never put before us. We were distinctly told that this was the Triennial Conference that was overdue, and, as a matter of fact, it was the Triennial Conference; and a vote of £500 was passed to cover expenses. They discussed a number of questions affecting general policy. They considered the propriety, for example, of giving a definite constitution to the Triennial Conference in the future, so that I really must say, as a member of the Missionary Committee, that the view which Mr. Gostick has now given of the Conference is not the view that was given then. I submit that they discussed a great many questions of importance, and I want to know why it was that when all these questions were discussed the native ministers were not present?

Mr. HARTLEY: Mr. Hughes is entirely wrong in his assumption.

Dr. RIGG: It was repeatedly said in the Committee that this question was to be considered by that Conference when it met in general committee. I speak from personal knowledge.

Mr. ALLEN: It is very unfortunate that Mr. Hughes should have made such a mistake.

Mr. HARTLEY read the minutes of the Committee, dated September 20th, 1889, which runs:—" The General Committee " consented to the holding of a Conference of Indian mission- " aries at Bangalore, in September next, the cost of the " Conference not to exceed £250." The mistake on Mr. Hughes' part is, first, that he assumed there was a regular meeting, and second, that it was open to native ministers. It was a meeting of "Indian missionaries" and that phrase does not include native ministers.

Mr. FOWLER read from the Report of the Bangalore Conference the minute which provides that "one of the representatives from each district shall be an Indian Minister," and asked why the native ministers were not admitted to this Triennal Conference?

Professor PATTERSON said: Mr. Gostick does not remember these Conferences. I remember them all. I was present at the first. Every one of the Triennal Conferences has had native ministers sitting side by side with their European brethren. The only reason why natives are not found in this particular Conference is that it was called to consider a question peculiarly relating to European character.

Mr. HUGHES: Might I ask, further, what is the basis of representation of Indian missionaries?

Mr. ALLEN: That is a question of policy.

Mr. BRUNYATE: I was going to ask Mr. Gostick this: It is stated here that ministers in Calcutta are presented at Court. It is further said that they attended drawing-rooms. I should like to ask if that attendance at drawing-rooms necessitates an extra amount of expense, and whether Mr. Gostick has had any experience of being presented at Court?

Mr. GOSTICK: I have never attended a drawing-room, nor have I been presented at Court. Apart from our own mission circle, I have not dined out more than twice or thrice during my nine years' service in the district, and this was with the Collector of Tanjore, who has been a good friend to me and helped me very considerably in my work.

Mr. BRUNYATE: Mr. Gostick lives in the house that has 30 acres of land. What does that 30 acres of land mean?

Mr. GOSTICK: It is a special case. About 30 years ago there was a Christian collector in Manargudi who had much influence in the district. There was a small bungalow on this ground which belongs to the temple, and the collector got the temple authorities to hand it over to the mission, on a kind of perpetual lease, for Rs. 12 per year. It is covered with oil nut trees. But the mission have no right to the fruit of the trees. On this one condition they were to have it practically freehold.

Mr. POPE: How far from the centre of the missionaries' work is this house?

Mr. GOSTICK: About a quarter of an hour's walk.

Mr. FLETCHER: Are there many missionaries in India who would refuse to shake hands with the natives?

Mr. GOSTICK: I never met with one, or heard of one excepting in Dr. Lunn's statement.

Mr. FINDLAY: I think the Committee should understand that Manargudi is in the same district as Tiruvalur, and is only 17 miles from Dr. Lunn's station.

Mr. GOSTICK: I may say that it is no uncommon thing for the natives to refuse to shake hands with us. And now I should like to ask Dr. Lunn one or two questions, if I may be allowed. We had a school in Tiruvalur circuit, a good middle-class school. It is now closed—I ask Dr. Lunn by whose instrumentality it was closed?

Dr. LUNN: I think that question is fully answered in my journal at pages 106—107.

Mr. GOSTICK proceeded to read the following extract:—
" We have had rather an unpleasant incident at Nannilam.
" We had a very good middle school there which was doing
" exceedingly well, and promised to pay its way until this
" Christian College commotion occurred. This frightened the
" Brahmins, and they induced a prominent barrister from
" Tanjore, named Saminadha Iyer, to come over and hold a
" 'Nationalist' meeting and give an account of the National
" Congress and urge the people to found a National school,
" instead of being dependent on the Christian missionaries for
" their education. The result of this meeting has been the
" establishment of such a school, and the emptying of our
" school a month before the Government inspection, so that
" we lose the Government grant of Rs. 200, and nobody
" benefits by our loss. We have decided to carry on our school
" for the future as a primary school for the benefit of the lower
" castes and Pariahs." This same Saminadha Iyer is Dr. Lunn's authority for the price of beef in Tanjore. It is somewhat strange that Dr. Lunn should have to go to one of our bitterest enemies for evidence against us.

Mr. GOSTICK: Does Dr. Lunn know how the Hindus make butter?

Dr. LUNN: No, I do not.

Mr. GOSTICK: They make it direct from milk and not from cream. Now Dr. Lunn says that milk is 1d. a pint, and it takes 8 to 12 quarts of milk to make a lb. of butter. And yet Dr. Lunn tells us that Hindus sell butter at 4d. a pound. Again Dr. Lunn says he gave 2½ annas each for chickens.

Mr. LUNN: We gave 4 annas for chickens for roasting.

Mr. GOSTICK: I never did. A chicken that could be purchased for $2\frac{1}{2}$ annas would be just about enough to make a baby a cup of broth. You can get no more out of it. Dr. Lunn's statements are just, if you take a few articles, potatoes, for instance, one of our most ordinary articles of diet.

Dr. LUNN: I wish the meeting would allow me to say a word with regard to the 15s. a week I put down here. In addition to my own calculation, we had another fact in the background of our experience, and that fact was, that we had stayed with Mrs. Geden and had boarded there for two months upon the ordinary tariff. The ordinary tariff is Rs. 90 a month. We knew that the total expenses of the month of April were Rs. 120, but Mrs. Geden now estimates the amount to be Rs. $147\frac{1}{2}$ = 35s. 5d. a week for four people. During that month Mrs. Lunn was confined. In consequence of her confinement there were certain additional expenses, and Mr. Geden went to Royapettah, and said he had been involved in certain expenses in consequence of our stay there. I asked, how much? He said, Rs. 20, and I at once sent him a cheque for the amount. The result is, that instead of paying 7s. 6d. a head per week, we lived during that month for 8s. 9d. per head, per week. That is only 1s. 3d. higher than the rate I fixed for my cost at Tiruvalur.

Mr. BRUNYATE: Why could not this have been stated when Mrs. Geden was present?

Mr. HUGHES: I think Mr Brunyate has misunderstood the argument.

Professor PATTERSON: If the Committee accepts Dr. Lunn's basis of calculation to the effect that he and his wife lived on 15s. a week, it might accept that fact as a proof of Mrs. Geden's economy rather than Dr. Lunn's. It means that a missionary's wife has kept house more economically than Dr. Lunn himself did.

Mr. ALLEN: You see, under this particular economy, Dr. Lunn failed and he had to come home.

Mr. GOSTICK: Dr. Lunn has made a statement, and I want to prove that it is not true. He says that he lived on the low amount of 15s. per week. I will ask Dr. Lunn whether he took any money with him to India.

Dr LUNN: Yes, £10.

Mr. GOSTICK: And the amount that he received in India was £300. I should like to know whether he left in debt?

Dr. LUNN: I took £10 in my pocket to India, and I left

with £20 in my pocket, but afterwards remitted a balance on my accounts of about £30.

Mr. GOSTICK: What did you do with the other money? I think we ought to know. Dr. Lunn says he lived on 15s. per week, and he got the same allowance that we did. He took £10 to India and he left India £30 in debt. I want to know where he put the other money. I think that is a fair question, since it is through Dr. Lunn's accusations that I am here to-day to explain my own expenditure.

Dr. LUNN: I did not keep a cash account, but before I went to India I had been spending between £150 and £200 as a single man, living in a University. When I went to India, I lived more freely than I did before, because I did not anticipate that I should break down in health. I lost money. My carriage, which I expected to have sold, is lying at Madras. I spent about £8 in presents and £8 in telegrams, and I had very long journeys indeed. I went into Madras several times.

Mr. GOSTICK: I do not think that answers the question at all. The fare to Madras is very light. Dr. Lunn went once first class, and twice second class. The fare is really nothing compared to the amount he spent somewhere. He says he lived very freely. More freely than 15s. a week?

Dr. LUNN: The fact is, I had spent money for various things, such as riding lessons, which I needed.

Mr. GOSTICK: We have been called upon for a statement how we spent our money. We have given you the statement, and I think Dr. Lunn should show how he spent his money— £30 + £10 + £300. Dr. Lunn has given us no answer.

Professor PATTERSON: As this question has been brought up, I may say that I certainly think myself that Dr. Lunn ought to be pressed for definite statements on this point. Mr. Gostick has brought it up, and he is in a better position to do this than I am. Dr. Lunn had whilst he was in India sixteen months' stipend—that is, he received for stipend and postage £303 16s. 8d., in addition to his horse allowance, rent and everything else, which we contend ought not to be reckoned in Dr. Lunn's salary. He arrived in India with £10 in his pocket. He left India £30 in debt. Adding these sums together, we get a sum total of £343 16s. 8d. as being the amount of money which Dr. Lunn spent in his own personal expenses whilst in India for one year. Now if Dr. Lunn puts forward a claim to have lived in a style of severe economy, like that described in his "Summary Statement," what did he do with his money? We simply say it is impossible he ever did live on that sum, but if Dr. Lunn maintains that it is possible, and that he did, he must be prepared to answer all subsidiary questions that arise out of it, and to tell us what he did with the large balance of his income.

Dr. LUNN: I simply know that the money is spent, and that I had a great many special expenses from illness. Mr. Gostick referred to my going to Madras; I think I went three times in the year. On one occasion I travelled first class. I went once to the National Congress by permission of my chairman, the second and third time I went in search of health. On the third journey I took my wife and my head man-servant, and I sent by road my horse and bandy, and three or four coolies to guard the caravan as it was going along. I had a great deal of luggage to take up with me to Madras. That journey cost me in one way or another Rs. 100.

Mr. GOSTICK: I took my horse and bandy in the same way, and it cost me between 6 and 7 rupees.

Professor PATTERSON said he had reason to believe that Dr. Lunn sent an article to the *Pall Mall Gazette* describing the work of the Congress at Madras. It is fair to assume that he received some remuneration for the article.

At this point Mr. FOWLER moved that the Committee be left to themselves. This was agreed to, and all, excepting the actual members of the Committee, retired.

On Messrs. Patterson, Findlay, Hughes, Lunn, and certain officers of the Mission House being re-admitted,

The PRESIDENT, addressing himself to Dr. Lunn, said he should not ask him to state what amount he received from this or that particular paper, but whether he received any payment at all?

Dr. LUNN said he received 20s. from the *Pall Mall Gazette* for his report, and two and a half guineas for an article that he wrote. With regard to the question of his income generally, he was sorry that he was not able to lay before the Committee a general cash account. He did not keep a careful cash account in India, owing to repeated attacks of illness, and he had no accounts to show.

Mr. GOSTICK: That is all we contend for. Dr. Lunn did not keep careful cash accounts, and his estimate of 15s. a week is not a careful cash account. When I came to England, I went to Dr. Lunn and warned him that I should put this question to him. He has had fully three weeks to consider the matter, and he comes to-day and says he has no account to give.

Dr. LUNN: The answer is that I had no account, and I had no wish to " cook " one.

Mr. FINDLAY: During Dr. Lunn's stay in India, he stayed a good deal with missionaries, and I think he might present us with an approximate estimate of his expenditure.

Mr. GOSTICK: Dr. Lunn says somewhere that when he was staying with missionaries his servants' expenses went on as usual. That statement is somewhat misleading, for the last time he stayed at my house he did not bring any servant with him but the ayah, and we paid for Dr. Lunn's punkah-men.

Dr. LUNN: I admit that on that occasion I did not take my boy with me (he had to be dismissed for dishonesty), but on other occasions I did take him with me.

Mr. HUGHES: I think I must have written that note myself, and the simple object of it was to show that Dr. Lunn when he stayed with missionaries did not live at their expense, and that Mr. Gostick himself admits.

The PRESIDENT: I think we see the case now.

Mr. GOSTICK: I should like to press my former question with respect to Dr. Lunn's expenses.

The PRESIDENT: Dr. Lunn has said that he kept] no account.

Professor PATTERSON: Then are we to understand that Dr. Lunn does not know what he did with the balance of £203?

Dr. LUNN: My only reply is that I led an exceptionally expensive life in India.

The PRESIDENT: But other missionaries might have exceptional expenses too. It does not follow that they could live on 15s. a week as you say you did.

Mr. HARVEY: I should like to ask Dr. Lunn, through you, Sir, whether he kept any housekeeping accounts?

Dr. LUNN: My wife kept those accounts, and unfortunately we have been hunting for the account book and cannot find it.

Professor PATTERSON: May I ask whether Dr. or Mrs. Lunn had the account book before them when they drew up their statement to the effect that they could live on 15s. a week in India? That statement was not drawn up in India, but a few weeks ago.

Dr. LUNN: I inserted in that statement facts which I had arrived at in India.

The PRESIDENT: On pages 14 and 15 of your " Summary

Statement," you give your estimates of the cost of servants' clothing, &c.—were those estimates based on accounts which you kept in India?

Dr. LUNN: The cost of servants was put down because I knew what we paid them.

Mr. FINDLAY: In other words, those estimates were drawn from memory?

Mr. HUGHES: The statement as to the cost of particular items on pages 14 and 15, is perfectly distinct from the statement at the bottom of page 13, viz., "this style of living cost Dr. and Mrs. Lunn jointly, not more than 15s. a week." I understood Dr. Lunn to say that when he was in India, he and his wife, with their account book before them, discovered that the average cost of food for them was 15s. per week. Since Dr. Lunn came to London he has been living in lodgings, and the account book has been lost.

Mr. FINDLAY: May I ask what the nature of that account book was? Was it simply a bazaar account book?

Dr. LUNN: It was the ordinary account book, in which we entered our expenses for food.

Mr. HUGHES: Let it be noted that Dr. Lunn never said that he and Mrs. Lunn lived on 15s. a week.

Mr. CLAPHAM: Am I to understand that that statement was made at the time when Dr. Lunn was living with his brethren?

Mr. HUGHES: No; when he was living in his own house in Tiruvalur.

Professor PATTERSON: I must be allowed to correct Dr. Lunn's calculations by figures that were taken from Mrs. Geden's book, and which make it clear that the cost of food for each individual was much more than Dr. Lunn supposes. It was more like 15s. per week for one individual than for two. I submit that as Mrs. Geden has borne witness here as to the cost of her housekeeping, and her evidence is that the cost for food and European stores is Rs. 147 8 annas, we must take that as the basis of our calculations.

Mr and Mrs. Parson's Evidence.

In reply to questions put by Professor Patterson,

Mr. PARSON said he had been in India more than eight years. Mrs. Parson had been there more than four years. He had lived the whole time in Lucknow, with the exception of two years spent in Cawnpore.

Mrs. PARSON said their average annual cost of living, exclusive of a good deal of entertaining, was £67 10s. This sum was calculated upon the basis of the average amounts expended when they were not entertaining visitors. Mrs. Parson had been ill for ten weeks, and during that time the extra expenses had gone up from Rs. 200 to Rs. 300. Since her marriage she had been ill four times, and a great deal of extra expense had been involved. The amount she had named was the average cost when there had not been any extraordinary expenditure. She had made very persistent attempts to be economical, both in the accounts for the table and for clothing. Mrs. Parson had ten servants, for whom she paid. This did not include the servants paid for by the mission. For seven servants during five months of the year, and ten servants for seven months of the year, the cost was £50 10s. The servants paid by the mission were servants for the horse and garden. Mrs. Parson had employed an ayah, and was convinced that such a servant should be kept by every lady in India. With regard to clothing, Mrs. Parson thought it would have been advisable if the Bangalore Conference estimate for clothing had been a little higher for missionaries in the north. They required two different kinds of clothing. During three months of the year clothing was needed as heavy as that worn in England. In summer this clothing was put away, but frequently was so much injured by insects that new clothing had to be obtained the following season. Her experience was that £36 per annum for a man and his wife was scarcely enough for clothing. Mrs. Parson had managed to do with the allowance, but it was only by that measure of economy which might be termed "pinching."

Mr. HUGHES inquired what Mrs. Parson meant in her reference to the entertainment of visitors.

Mrs. PARSON: Sometimes brother missionaries will come and spend a week or so. We are always glad to have them, and of course we do not ask for anything extra.

Mr. HUGHES: In the south of India there is a recognised tariff, but it seems there is nothing of the sort in the north.

Mrs. PARSON: In the Lucknow and Benares district, only the Chairman receives an extra allowance for entertaining other ministers. The other ministers receive nothing. Of course we are delighted to have our visitors, and would rather deny ourselves than not have them, but I only mention this to show that there is no such thing as an extra allowance under this head.

Mr. PARSON: I have nothing to add on this point. We

have often to pay extras for medicine and nursing. For instance, last year we paid Rs. 75 more than we received from the Committee.

Mrs. PARSON: This year my extras for nursing came to Rs. 160.

Mr. HUGHES: Do not our brethren in India get medical allowances? Is there no special grant for special cases?

Professor PATTERSON: It is not a fixed sum in any case, but it is universally true that missionaries never draw anything like the whole of their medical expenses. It is considered that if they have drawn half the amount they have drawn a very large proportion.

Mr. PARSON: My work has been amongst the natives the whole time.

The PRESIDENT: Is the intercourse free between the missionaries and the natives? Is there anything like aloofness on the part of the missionaries?

Mr. PARSON: I have never seen anything of the kind.

The PRESIDENT: Do the natives feel that the missionaries assume a position of superiority and patronage?

Mr. PARSON: I never heard any remark to that effect.

The PRESIDENT: You know what the income of a missionary is. Is it such an amount as to enable him to live in an intensely costly manner?

Mr. PARSON: We have to use the utmost economy in order to keep well within our income. We could live on less if we lived like labourers do in this country. I could live on a very small amount in London, if I were obliged to do it. Artisans in Lucknow whom I know personally receive Rs. 390 per month. In addition they have most of their servants free, furnished houses free, and doctors' and medical expenses free.

Mr. HUGHES: What is the position of these artisans?

Mr. PARSON: One is an engine-driver. He works the engine, but he has natives to help him. The other has charge of a department in a mill.

Mrs. PARSON: I should be glad to answer any question as to general society in India. I have lived in Lucknow two years and four months. I have never been with people who are in society out to dinner. I might have gone once, but I was from home on the hills. I can say the same for our English missionary who is there in English work. He may have been invited to dine out once or twice, but he does not go into society any more than we do. I have called upon several people in society in Lucknow, but only to collect. In America the Methodist minister associates with judges, doctors and lawyers. In England and in India these are reckoned amongst the gentry, but in America there are no such social distinctions—I am only speaking for our own district.

Mr. FINDLAY: Mr. Parson has lived in the neighbourhood of the Methodist Episcopal missionaries. Perhaps he could give us some information about them.

Mr. PARSON: On what points do you require information?

Mr. FINDLAY: As to their stipends and allowances as compared with those of our own missionaries?

Mr. PARSON: I have not seen very much difference in the outward appearance of American missionaries and our own. They have generally better houses than we have, and better premises, and their position would appear to the native higher than ours. A married man receives Rs. 206 4 annas per month. This is about £180 a year. They send money home at 45 cents to the rupee. They have their sanatorium provided in the hills, to which they nearly all go every season and spend some months. They have arrangements by which they can live more cheaply there than in the plains. With regard to ourselves, it costs us twice as much, because we have no sanatorium to go to.

Mr. CLAPHAM: Then you preach to the natives in their own language?

Mr. PARSON: Yes; I preach in two languages, and have done so for six years.

Mrs. PARSON: The American missionaries' allowance for children is greater than ours. It is Rs. 20 a month for each child, that is, £18 a year, from the birth of the child. In America, the money is paid in dollars, at 45 cents per rupee, so that the money adds on to it one-third of its value. I was in the American mission two years. I received Rs. 150 a month for myself only, and I was living with a lady doctor. She received Rs. 150 a month, so that we had Rs. 300 a month to keep house on. We were never able to save very much.

Evidence of Rev. W. Sackett, Bangalore.

Rev. W. SACKETT was introduced to the Committee, and said, in answer to questions: I have lived in Bangalore two and a half years as an unmarried man. For about two years of that time I lived alone. I made a continued attempt at economy, from the time I entered Bangalore to the time I left it. I was receiving the ordinary stipend of a young man there, namely, £125 per annum. I was at the minimum cost of living with regard to food and servants. I thought about my servants a great deal, and tried to do without one that was usually kept. At Bangalore I had a chokra; previous to that time I lived with Mr. Haigh. On returning from Mr. Haigh's house I thought I would try to do without this young servant; I tried the experiment for a few months, but I found I could not possibly do without a chokra. I tried to do so on the ground of economy, but I found it would cost me more money in another way; I had a boy, and a chokra, and a sweeper, and a tanniketch, and a gardener, and for some time a horsekeeper, but that goes into another department. As a single man I found it necessary to keep these five servants. My expenses under the head of clothes were very small, because I went out with a large stock. I have been making calculations of the cost of food and servants, and these cost me in the first year £52. The second and third years were both broken years. Of this £52, servants cost £19 11s., the rest of the money was spent in food. This calculation was made some time ago on the basis of 1s. 4d. or 1s. 5d. per rupee. I lived in India for two and a half years, and was then obliged to come home invalided.

Professor PATTERSON: You expressed a hope that if another brother went out two of you could live on the salary of one man?

Mr. SACKETT replied that his suggestion was that a young man receiving £150—which was £25 more than he was receiving himself—might share his servants, house and furniture. There would be an allowance of £38 for a horse, but he was so circumstanced that he could hire at a cheap rate. He thought that with the £150 plus the £38, for a horse, they would be able to manage. In the light of his experience, however, Mr. Sackett feared this could not have been done unless all the expenses under the head of sickness had been paid, for in his third year he had a serious illness, which caused him a great deal of personal expense.

Professor PATTERSON: Then your experience summarised is this: that provided unbroken health for two men could be secured, they could live together on £68 more than the allowance of a single man?

Mr. SACKETT: Yes, receiving £25 extra, plus £38 for horse.

Professor PATTERSON: You have been engaged all the while in English work in Bangalore, but you have seen a great deal of the native work. What are your opinions in regard to the relation of missionaries to native Christians, and particularly to native ministers?

Mr. SACKETT said he found himself at the very first amongst

the English people, but he was anxious to get into native work, and conversed with the brethren engaged in it. He saw from the beginning that the European brethren were deeply in love with the native ministers and the native people generally. He recollected several instances in which the native brethren and the English brethren came together. On one occasion the native ministers breakfasted at Mr. Haigh's house, and then they all went to the district meeting together. On another occasion Mr. Sackett called unexpectedly upon Mr. W. H. J. Picken, and found him inviting the native ministers to tea and to a social evening in the rest-house. Mr. Sackett also remembered being told by Mr. Haigh of a walking tour Mr. Haigh had once taken with the native ministers. On that occasion they must have been together several days. Mr. Haigh related how they spoke to the native people on the way, and had familiar conversations with them, and how one day they made it a point not to let any one pass without speaking to him of Jesus Christ. Mr. Sackett, when at Tumkur one Christmas, preparing for his examinations, married a couple of native Christians. Miss Parson was there and Mrs. Gulliford. Mr. Sackett went with the native people, sat down with them, partook of their refreshments in their own way, and sought to be agreeable with them.

The Committee adjourned at 7 p.m.

Third Day, Thursday, May 29th.

The Committee re-assembled at 10.0 a.m. Prayer was offered by the Rev. H. J. Pope.

Mr. ALLEN said that whilst the Committee was waiting for the witnesses to arrive, he wished, in the kindest way possible, to ask Dr. Lunn how far, in making this whole criticism, he had been influenced by the political sentiments of his own mind.

Dr. LUNN: I should say absolutely not at all.

Mr. ALLEN: Then the question arises whether unconscious influences come in. I have thought about this matter very carefully, and have had the impression—and I may say the hope—that it has been political to a considerable extent in its origin. I remember in the Sheffield Conference Dr. Lunn gave us a statement which is in his journal, but which I saw first in the *Christian World*, of date May 27th. The journal at p. 72, reads:—" This evening Subramanyam had a garden " party for native Christians, in order to bring them together, " and let them know each other. He invited a few mission- " aries who were in sympathy with the natives." I wondered whether Mr. Subramanyam referred to political or religious sympathy.

Dr. LUNN: He referred to religious sympathy, and had not politics in his mind.

Mr. FINDLAY: Dr. Lunn is aware that Mr. Subramanyam denies altogether that he spoke of "sympathy with the "natives."

Mr. HUGHES: There is considerable conflict of statement as to that matter. If necessary, I am prepared to maintain that Dr. Lunn's statement at the time is more accurate than Mr. Subramanyam's testimony to-day, but that does not affect this issue. It had no reference to any political issue. On page 72 of the journal there is a footnote, in which it is stated that Dr. Lunn is now in correspondence with Mr. Subramanyam with reference to a reporter's error on this question. In any case there was no discussion of politics whatever, and I should like to say here that, as far as I know, our missionaries n India are, like Dr. Jenkins, looking with great sympathy upon this nationalist movement. Mr. Mackenzie Cobban is actually a member of the Congress, so that Mr. Allen is mistaken in supposing that politics have entered into the subject in the slightest degree.

Mr. ALLEN: There was an article in the *Daily News* of last Tuesday, which makes the assertion that Dr. Lunn and Mr. Hughes contend that the missionaries are far too comfortable, and that they fraternise with the English garrison. I wondered whether Dr. Lunn had simply transferred his Home Rule ideas from Ireland to India. The same terms were used, and it is very evident from Dr. Lunn's journal that he is in great sympathy with the movement in question. I quite accept his statement, but I think he has unconsciously been influenced by his political sympathy. This question does not affect the style of living at all—it does affect the question of aloofness. Mr. Hughes, on this article, in his comment in the *Methodist Times*, said that it exactly interpreted his mind, and it has been a question with me whether Dr. Lunn, as an advanced politician, as he said he was in the Sheffield Conference, did not look upon the English garrison in India very much as he looks upon the Castle party in Ireland.

Dr. LUNN: I deny that altogether. I have said that if England had no other claim for a place in history, it has a claim because of its magnificent government of India. The son of Rev. W. O. Simpson introduced me to some politicians, as I said in my journal, and we had a conversation together. At that time I sent an article to the *Pall Mall Gazette*, which was published. Mr. Little held then that it would be a very good thing for me to see as much as I could of these natives from all parts of India, and, with the full approval of my chairman, I attended the congress at Madras, in order to get to know the English-speaking Brahmins. I then arranged to give a course of alternate secular and religious lectures; the list is given in the journal. The tenth lecture was on a secular subject, namely, "What are the subjects with which the National "Congress ought to deal?"

Mr. ALLEN: There is no doubt at all that political sympathy in this country is going very largely with the native peoples. There is a similar sentiment with regard to India to that in regard to Egypt a few years ago. I heard in Horncastle that Dr. Lunn said, before he went to India, "When I get there I "shall go in for the policy, 'India for the Indians.'"

Dr. LUNN: I did take a particular attitude with regard to the Irish question, but this did not influence my attitude on Indian missions.

Mr. ALLEN: I simply want to understand how far Dr. Lunn has been unconsciously influenced upon this whole question.

He is, as we all know, an intense politician, and I was going to say, in spite of what he has just told us, that I scarcely know whether he understands the process of his own mind by which he has come to the conclusion he has reached. I think he may have acted almost more than he is aware of as a politician, and possibly as a party politician. There is a wide distinction between political sympathy and religious sympathy. A man may have no political sympathy with the natives of India, and yet have intense religious sympathy with them. This applies to England as well as to India. I simply wish to elucidate my point, and if Dr. Lunn could tell us that his criticism is to a certain extent a political criticism, my mind would be relieved.

Dr. LUNN: But I do not say that.

Mr. BRUNYATE: There is no need Dr. Lunn should say that. When Dr. Lunn was in India he expressed certain views. But I should like to ask whether at any time there was a serious difference of political sympathy between Dr. Lunn and his fellow-missionaries?

Dr. LUNN: Mr. Little and I discussed political questions, but I never had any unpleasantness of any kind.

Mr. ALLEN: I should like a little further light as to the closing of the school, to which reference has been made. It was not fully explained yesterday. I should be glad if Dr. Lunn would explain to us what actually took place.

Dr. LUNN: So far as I know the facts they are these. We had a "middle school" at Nannilam, which was doing well. But the Madras Christian College disturbance occurred, and the Brahmins, who are more or less opposed to Christian education, summoned a "Nationalist" meeting, and the result of that meeting was, that so much adverse sentiment was aroused that our school had to be closed. We then had to carry it on as a low caste school. I agreed with Mr. Little in thinking that the change was not an unmixed evil, and that we were giving too much attention to the Brahmins.

Mr. HUGHES: Might I say, seeing that reference has been made to the *Daily News* article of Tuesday last, that neither Dr. Lunn nor myself knew anything about it, nor have we any idea who wrote it?

Further Evidence by Rev. W. Sackett.

Rev. W. Sackett was asked by Mr. Clapham whether he knew the Canarese language. He replied that he did know it.

Mr. CLAPHAM further said : As to your living—did you live as your brethren generally ?

Mr. SACKETT: Yes. I think there is a little misunderstanding on that point. Some have said that I lived differently from the other missionaries. I lived with the greatest economy, consistent with the needs of the body in that country. I do not think I lived in a general way strikingly different from other missionaries.

Mr. CLAPHAM: Then you do not ascribe the break-down of your health to the style of living you followed?

Mr. SACKETT: No. I am glad to have an opportunity of speaking on this point. My break-down has been attributed to the cause suggested. But the circumstances are these. I had already got sufficient work to do with my own church and the learning of the language, which I determined not to neglect. My superintendent broke down, and a special District Meeting decided that I should take the chief part of my superintendent's duties. Mr. Haigh was to assist by taking Mr. Burnett's preaching work, but the work of the military chaplaincy was assigned to me. I was involved in further work by a large building scheme in which we were engaged. Then a Young Men's Christian Association had just been opened, and a Soldiers' Home, and the whole of the accounts in connection with that enterprise, the matter of getting money for it, and the general superintending of the scheme were left to me. I had also, of course, my own pastoral work. From morning to night I was oppressed with the work, but I did not complain, because I knew nothing else could be done. I intended to have gone on a sea trip, but before I could go I broke down, and I am only now gaining the strength which I lost. Mr. Haigh broke down for nine or ten weeks, and during that time much of his work fell upon me. It is my desire to go back, but I am afraid the Committee will not send me, for some years at least.

Mr. POPE : I should like to ask Mr. Sackett a question, but I will not press for an answer. He has told us that during the first year of his residence in India he had £125 from the Missionary Society, and he expended of that amount on food and servants £52, leaving a balance of £73. I should like to know whether he kept any account of what he did with this £73, and if so whether he will give us the information ?

Mr. SACKETT replied that he should be very glad to give the information to the Committee, but would scarcely wish for its publication. The details were accordingly given for the private information of the Committee. Mr. Sackett's estimate was that the necessary expenses of an unmarried man for the first year in India amounted to £106. This, however, would leave no margin for such contingencies as sickness, losses, and so forth.

In reply to a question, Mr. Sackett said he was not put to any expense because of drawing-room presentations or anything of that kind, indeed there was no temptation in that direction.

Mr. BRUNYATE: If you were to return to the mission field, would you adopt the same style of living as that under which your health broke down?

Mr. SACKETT: I should adopt the same style of living as regards food and clothing, but I should be more particular in regard to sleeping. I did not take a holiday, and instead of sleeping in the middle of the day, as I should have done, I generally had a bath.

Mr. ALLEN: What, in your opinion, would be the effect if the native Christians were to adopt the Anglo-Indian dress and customs with regard to eating?

Mr. SACKETT: The effect would be that those who went over to Anglo-Indian customs would lose a great deal of influence. It would be regarded as foolish mimicry.

The Committee at this point adjourned for one hour, in order to enable some of its members to attend a meeting of the Committee of Privileges.

Rev. Thos. Champness's Evidence.

On re-assembling at 12.0 noon, the Rev. Thos. Champness was introduced. In reply to questions put to him by Dr. Lunn,

Mr. CHAMPNESS said: There are three of my "Joyful News" men living in the Mysore. One has been there two years. I have had opportunity of watching their course of life. They send me a monthly account of their expenditure. I have in my possession the account for April, which reached me last week. During that month the food for the three men cost Rs. 44 13 ans. = £3 4s. 6d. The three men live together. Practically they cost 15s. a week. That amount does not include fire wood or water-carrying, but simply food, that is to say, 5s. a week for each man for food. When they first get up in the morning they have coffee and fruit and bread. They then turn out to some service, after which they return and have breakfast, porridge, or curry, or chops, as the case may be. They are in most of the day. They have tea before they go out again, fruit and bread. After coming back from work they have soup, meat, pudding, etc. That is the daily course. They have two solid meals and two lighter ones. They spend over their servants, including personal attendance, washing and water man for the three men, as follows :—

The servant	12s. 10d.	per month.
Water carrying	4s. 3d.	,,
Washing	8s. 6d.	,,

a total of £15 a year for servants. The teacher or pundit is paid specially, and ought not to go down in this list. He comes in my total of £8 6s. 8d. for the month. He costs 14s. a month. As to clothing for these three men, I am hardly in a position to speak. They took an outfit with them from England. They wear out a lot of shoes, for they are boys to walk. One of the men has been out two years, two have been out one year. One man, I regret to say, was found drowned, I am afraid by his own act; he was delirious at the time.

The PRESIDENT: Had you any medical expenses to pay?

Mr. CHAMPNESS: Yes; in this monthly account there is 1s. 5d. for medicine.

Mr. BRUNYATE: What was the character of the outfit the men started with?

Mr. CHAMPNESS: Flannel suits, and I think some linen suits.

Dr. LUNN: Can you give the Committee an estimate of the cost of the annual clothing of the men?

Mr. CHAMPNESS: I do not think they cost me £7 each for clothing through the year. It will not be anything like that.

The PRESIDENT: How do you judge of that if you have no experience?

Mr. CHAMPNESS: I have paid for some clothes, so that I know it will not be a very serious item. My men have not said anything about what they give in charity. They have debited themselves with 7s. 1d. given to them this month for the three men. I have no idea where the money comes from. I think it is likely some gentleman out there gives it to them, and of course to that extent my expenses are lessened.

Mr. BRUNYATE: The money is not the result of any appeal which is made?

Mr. CHAMPNESS: It is not. The house they live in is what would be called a cottage. They pay 2s. 6d. a month for it. It does not appear in this account, in consideration that we have been repairing it. The men go out every morning and evening into the villages. They walk about four miles, or on an average six miles a day. One of the missionaries gave them a bullock carriage. They did not do very much of this bullock work. They go to villages within walking distance, and hire bullocks when necessary. I have here the Mysore Evangelists' Account, which I lay on the table. (See Appendix C.)

Mr. CHAMPNESS: We sent out a box of provisions, which does not appear in this account. The provisions are not yet exhausted.

Mr. BRUNYATE: Why did Mr. Champness send the provisions from England, rather than let the men find them in India? Is it to any extent a question of price?

Mr. CHAMPNESS: No, I do not think it is; but I am not sure whether where they are living they can get the provisions. But about this £10 I am not very clear. Simpson's total expenses amounted to £70 16s. 8d. for two years.

Dr. LUNN: Then adding to Mr. Simpson's expenses the £10 for provisions, you have a total of £80 16s. 8d. Can you tell us how much each man's outfit cost? Does it cost about £20?

Mr. CHAMPNESS: Not more than that.

Dr. LUNN: That is to say, Simpson has not cost you for the two years more than £80. But why did these men, when they stayed with missionaries, pay Rs. 35, and only spent Rs. 16 each for the same length of time when alone?

Mr. CHAMPNESS: I do not know. They paid the missionary whatever he charged. At first they paid him Rs. 20, and then the amount was increased to Rs. 33. I found that it cost them a great deal less to live by themselves.

Mr. CLAPHAM: You assert that you have maintained these men in India upon less than £50 each per year.

Mr. CHAMPNESS: Yes. It is less than £50 each. The men have gone about the country a good bit, but they have paid for their living whilst away. Any money given to them is put down to my credit, and I include that in the £50. The men are all unmarried.

Dr. LUNN: What servants had they when they were with the missionaries?

Mr. CHAMPNESS: I do not know. I am not sure whether the missionaries found the servants or not. Whilst they have been living together they have only had one servant, and that servant does all excepting the duties of the waterman and washerman.

Mr. ALLEN: Then I suppose they do a great deal themselves?

Mr. CHAMPNESS: I daresay they do, but still they do not need to do much.

Mr. BRUNYATE: Can Mr. Champness give us any idea what amount of work these men do for themselves?

Mr. CHAMPNESS: I daresay they do something for themselves, but I cannot give all the particulars. The men had very little difficulty with regard to the cost of servants, for they had only one. This servant did all excepting the duties of the waterman and washerman.

Mr. ALLEN: They did *a great deal* for themselves?

Mr. CHAMPNESS: Yes.

Dr. LUNN: You will note that Mr. Champness' servants got over all the difficulties of caste, which were said to be insurmountable.

Mr. ALLEN: It seems the work Mr. Champness' men do for themselves enables them to get rid of the difficulties of caste.

Mr. CHAMPNESS: But suppose there were *two* servants, and they were paid 24s. a month, it would not be a big job.

Mr. HUGHES: There is some difference between the amount which it costs these brethren to live when they were living in the missionaries' houses, and when they were living alone. I want to know precisely what the difference is.

Mr. CHAMPNESS: The fact is we paid more at one time than at another.

Dr. LUNN: The account in July was Rs. 105 for the three men when living with the missionary. In September the amount was Rs. 39 10 ans. 9 pies for a single man. In October it was Rs. 35 7 ans. 11 pies for food only—Rs. 9 were paid to the man-servant and Rs. 3 to the water-carrier. When this account is looked into it will be found that other expenses amounted to about Rs. 40 for the month. All this is given in detail in the Mysore Evangelists' Account.

Mr. CHAMPNESS: Do you not think it is fair to look at the general amount these men cost? They cost only £50 a year each.

Mr. HUGHES: When they are living alone they need service, and therefore we want to know what sum must be added for this item?

Dr. LUNN: The amount to be added on account of service is Rs. 18.

Mr. CHAMPNESS: You have heard what Simpson costs. Now hear what Adkin costs. The total is £33 6s. 8d., and this includes everything. I sent them a cheque for £50 to-day, but this is for two years.

The PRESIDENT: But of course the man had his outfit?

Mr. CHAMPNESS: The outfit would be about £20.

Mr. HUGHES: I should like to ask Mr. Champness whether he has any other information to give to the Committee?

Mr. CHAMPNESS: Some time ago Mr. Cooling wrote me, saying that his colleague, Mr. Goudie, wanted me to take a Mr. Maynard and his wife as "Joyful News" agents, and allow them to work in the Trivellore Circuit under him. Mr. Cooling and Mr. Goudie said the two persons would not cost any more than £60 per year. I consented to take them.

The PRESIDENT: Why did you give up Mr. Maynard?

Mr. CHAMPNESS: Because he did not seem to be the kind of man I wanted. He wished to have a house, and to have young men under him.

Mr. BRUNYATE: Then he was dissatisfied with the allowance which he had?

Mr. CHAMPNESS: I do not think he was dissatisfied.

Mr. HUGHES: Did he wish to have young men living with him in order to improve his position financially?

Mr. CHAMPNESS: No, there was nothing of that sort. The man and his wife cost me from May 1st to November 29th, a period of seven months, £53 8s. 4d. That included all he wanted for clothes, furniture, rent and food. His wife was an Englishwoman, who had been working in the Salvation Army.

Mr. FOWLER: Did the man ever complain about his pay?

Mr. CHAMPNESS: No, there was not an unpleasant word.

Mr. Champness then read the following letter from Mr. Cooling:—

WESLEYAN MISSION HOUSE,
ROYAPETTAH,
April 3, 1889.

MY DEAR MR. CHAMPNESS,

By this mail my colleague Mr. Goudie is writing to you about a Mr. Maynard, late a captain in the Salvation Army. Mr. Goudie wants you to take him and his wife as "Joyful News" agents, and allow them to work in the Trivellore Circuit under him. Mr. Goudie will give you all details about them. I write to-day to give you my own impressions of Mr. Maynard, and to say that I fully and heartily endorse the application that Mr. Goudie is making. We have had Mr. Maynard living with us for two days this week, and I have had long conversations with him about his past history, and about his present views and feelings with reference to Christian work. He is a young man of real good mental ability, gentlemanly in manners and mode of talk. He is a man of deep spirituality, and has certainly been blessed of God in his work in the Salvation Army. He does not wish to have a fixed salary allotted to him. He strongly prefers to work on "Joyful News" lines as to pay. For one thing, he does not wish his friends in the Army to say that he has bettered his temporal prospects by coming to us. He sees that on Army principles it is impossible to work in such fields as Trivellore, where there are no Europeans and no native Christians. As he frankly says, the Salvation Army does not go to such places, and in the two or three instances in which in South India it has tried such places, it has been obliged to withdraw from them.

I FANCY £60 A YEAR WILL COVER THE COST OF HIMSELF AND HIS WIFE. Mr. Goudie will tell you that he was converted under Thomas Cook, at Tunbridge Wells, and was for a short time a member with us there. His wife, too, is the daughter of a Methodist class-leader in Redruth or the neighbourhood. I do trust that you will be able to receive him and his wife as two of your Evangelists. He has a fair knowledge of Tamil for the time he has been in the country (about eighteen months), and his experience in the Army will be of use to him in his work with us. He is not bitter against the Army; far from it. He could go back any day. But, as he says, the Army in its working out here under Commissioner Tucker is very different from what it is represented in England.

Mr. Grant has gone out to Tulikan Chuttram. I am very glad that he has got away from Madras at last. We most of us think he showed a little of the "white feather" in running away from Veringumbankum. However, he will have an equally good sphere for work at Tulikan Chattram, and perhaps be a little freer to do as he wishes than he would have been at Veringumbankum. In your last you raised the hope that ere long we may see you out here. We shall be delighted to see you whenever you come.

I am, yours sincerely,
JAMES COOLING.

Professor Patterson and Mr. Champness.

Professor PATTERSON: You have told us, Mr. Champness, that you have now four men in India, three in Mysore, and one in Negapatam and Trichinopoly. One of your men, you said, died. We sorrowed over his death quite as much as anyone. Another man, namely Mr. Grant, who was in Madras, has left you. May I ask you with respect to Mr. Grant, when he went out and how long he was in your service?

Mr. CHAMPNESS: Mr. Grant went out on Nov. 14, 1888, and left about June or July, 1889.

Professor PATTERSON: Why did Mr. Grant leave you?

Mr. CHAMPNESS: Because I found fault with the way in which he wrote to myself and my wife. He also had difficulty in acquiring the language, and I said he had better come home; but the missionaries have used him as an English missionary to the soldiers.

Professor PATTERSON: Had you any fault to find with Mr. Grant with respect to his accounts?

Mr. CHAMPNESS: I had scarcely any fault to find with him, but I had a feeling that he was going to spend a good deal of money, and I only sent him £5 at a time. He was very vexed about that.

Professor PATTERSON: I should like to get at the reasons which led you to recall Mr. Grant.

Mr. CHAMPNESS: I have said that I thought he was not acquiring the language. Mr. Cooling thought so too.

Professor PATTERSON: Do you know on what ground Mr. Cooling based that opinion?

Mr. CHAMPNESS: I am not sure. Perhaps I can find the letter. It was to this effect:—

DEAR MR. CHAMPNESS,
For some time it has been in my mind to write you about Mr. Grant. There are some things that make me feel sure he has got unsettled and dissatisfied. There may be something to justify this. He is alone with only a native helper. He has a good deal of exposure, and this brings on the fever. He is completely knocked up. He has been in Madras a fortnight or more. I was afraid he would break down altogether.

Professor PATTERSON: Practically, the reason which Mr. Cooling gives is that Mr. Grant, by the general conditions of his life, sickness—loneliness, and the rest of it—was so utterly depressed that he was not willing to continue his work abroad. May I ask Mr. Champness to lay before the Committee the letter that Mr. Grant wrote? Did Mr. Grant ascribe any part of his depression of spirits or his sickness to the style of living that was imposed upon him by your financial limitations?

Mr. CHAMPNESS: I do not remember that he did.

Professor PATTERSON: I think it is in order for me now to read a statement from Mr. Grant. I may say that I had the idea, when on the way home, that it would be necessary for us to be provided with all available information upon this matter. I therefore asked Mr. Grant to put down on paper the result of his experiences as a "Joyful News" agent, and this is what he says:—

The following is a brief statement of my experience in connection with "Joyful News" Mission work in South India, and of the convictions which have grown up within me concerning work of this kind.

I.—I was first led to think of foreign mission work by a variety of influences, and my Methodist up-bringing generally helped to turn my thoughts towards this work.

II.—While employed in the "Joyful News" Mission at home, in response to a call for men by Mr. Champness for foreign mission work, I volunteered my services. This was in 1888. I was accepted and sent to India in November of that year, in company with the Rev. G. M. Cobban.

III.—Before coming, the difficulties of the work impressed me very little. I felt confident of being able to learn the language and preach to the people within six months; the customs of the people of India did not strike me as being so very far removed from those of our own country to cause me to think much upon that point, and I imagined that all I had to do was to learn the language and commence to preach, when the heathen would be overjoyed, and receive the Gospel at once. I thought of them as hungering and thirsting after the truth—yea, dying in ignorance and sin, and all because they had no one to tell them of a Saviour.

IV.—Before leaving England I was given to understand that, until such time that I had learned the language, I was to be employed in a school in Madras; but after a very short stay there, Mr. Champness desired me to get into village work. There seemed to be a very good opening for me in a village a few miles distant, a lady having presented a house and large compound, in which were two schools, to the Wesleyan Mission. I went there with the understanding that the lady was about to leave the house, in which I could then take up my abode. I had not been there many hours before she gave me to understand that she had no intention of leaving, and that the place in which I was to live was the coach-house, which I found was damp—nothing in it but my boxes, and in a state very unfit to live in. That evening I returned to Madras until some proper arrangements could be made. The Rev. James Cooling, chairman of the District, considered it unwise for me to take up my abode there until such time that the lady gave up possession of the house. I continued living with Mr. Cobban for some time, learning the language, and helping him in his work in Madras and district, until March, 1889, when I was asked to go to a village about eleven miles distant. A native house underwent some repairs and alterations, in which I took up my abode, March 27th, it being understood that I was to work in the villages surrounding, and also to open a school for boys in the house in which I was living. The rent being 7s. per month, I applied to Mr. Champness for the rent, which he refused to pay, telling me at the same time that he did not want me to have anything to do with schools, and that he would not spend a single sixpence on schools. At the same time I was convinced that by getting hold of the boys I should stand a better chance of getting at the parents, so we still kept our school, I paying 5s. for my part of the house, and the other 2s. being paid by the Wesleyan Mission. I continued working in the villages, often having to walk many miles in the heat of the day. I fell sick and could not walk long distances, and so had to leave my work in the hands of the catechists; but after a few days spent in Madras I again returned, but found I could not visit the villages unless I rested often on the way. In these straits I applied to Mr. Champness for a grant of £10 to enable me to buy some kind of a conveyance. His answer to my letter both surprised and grieved me. He says, in a letter dated May 7th, 1889, "You ask me to allow you to buy an equipage "costing £10; I do not see my way to this at present—indeed, am rather "disappointed that you should ask it; it does not look like the way a "J. N. E. should live. It is no use for you to try to imitate men with "large incomes; that cannot be done; you must be content to live frugally. "At the same time I do not wish you to run any risk of your health, and "therefore I am somewhat inclined to take time before I give you my "final answer. One thing you may be sure about—which is that if you "are to remain in India you will have to live a very frugal life. I would "much rather you came home again and worked in England, as you did "before, than you should give my enemies room to say that a J. N. E. lived "the life of a swell." This letter was a source of much unhappiness to me, and made me feel much discouraged; my discouragement was increased by some misleading reports which had been sent home by some one regarding me. I have never known what the reports were, or by whom written, and my health suffered as well as my spirits. I finally became disconnected from the "Joyful News" Mission in November, 1889.

V.—During the time in which I was engaged in "Joyful News" work, I endeavoured most carefully to live on the smallest possible sum. I was fearful of transgressing the limit imposed by Mr. Champness, which was £50 a year. I lived on cheap and insufficient food. My food account did not exceed Rs. 25 per month; munshi, rent, travelling, etc., Rs 25 more; making a total of Rs. 50 per month. I now feel certain that my health was affected by the poor quality of the food to which I had to subject myself, but there was no help for it, as I thought; therefore I strove to continue my self-denial. I say this confidently, because since I left the "Joyful News" Mission I have been living on better and more substantial food, and my health has been excellent. For the past four months I have not had a day's sickness, though from the nature of my work I am compelled to be out in the sun, visiting the soldiers in hospital and barracks

VI.—The effect of this limited and narrow allowance on me came to be depressing. I am convinced that had my allowances been more liberal I should have had more joy, and been able much more easily to maintain that enthusiasm with which I began my work. I do not think that I should have been required to live alone in an Indian village on less than Rs. 80 per month, and if that sum were guaranteed to me I would rather live in a village and preach to the Hindus than do any other work in India.

VII.—I found the state of the Hindu people totally different from what I thought while in England. In the village where I resided, instead of being anxious to receive the Gospel, they were anxious to send it away, as well as myself. In matters belonging to my Christian life and conduct, the advice of Mr. and Mrs. Champness was excellent, and always acceptable to me; but I soon found that in matters relating to missionary work they could not possibly give to me the best advice, because they knew little or nothing of the real state of India. And I am sure that no one in England who has never really lived in India, and come to know the condition of the people here, can give wise advice concerning the kind of mission work best fitted for the people.

VIII.—I should have said that my outfit provided by Mr. Champness was liberal, but it was not well suited to this part of India; for Mysore it might have done, though even for that district the clothing would have been too warm.

IX.—In conclusion, I ought to say that since there were a number of matters concerning which no definite arrangements had been made, these things added much to my uncertainty. Provision was made for serious sickness, but none for marriage, nor was there any in the event of returning to England through ill-health. Though nominally under the chairman of the District, all details of my work were submitted direct to Mr. Champness. I felt this to be unsatisfactory, since the chairman could have examined my statements or accounts better than he. Though I do not say that Mr. Champness has intended it, his arrangements and correspondence with me went rather to separate me from the missionaries than otherwise.

O. W. E. GRANT.

MADRAS,
March 7th, 1890.

Professor PATTERSON: Mr. Grant is at present in charge of our Wesleyan troops in the garrison at Bellary. He is doing, amongst the troops there, exceedingly good work. I have had Mr. Grant's deposition read to the Committee in order to illustrate this point—that the financial limit imposed by Mr. Champness on these men may sometimes work to their detriment, and that one of Mr. Champness' men believes that financial limit *has* worked to his detriment. Again, Mr. Champness, you had for some time Mr. Maynard and his wife. You tell us that Mr. Maynard was a good missionary, and yet, at the same time, you give us the reason why you broke connection with him the fact that he had ideas that he must have a number of young men under him.

Mr. CHAMPNESS: I think Mr. Maynard was ambitious to be a leader out there. I was not prepared to indulge his views, and I thought we should have trouble, and so I told him I did not intend to make him an officer, and that he would very soon increase his expense.

Professor PATTERSON: That comes to what I want to bring out. Although a good missionary, he was not prepared to be a "Joyful News" agent, because he could not submit to the financial limitations?

Mr. CHAMPNESS: The financial limitations had nothing to do with his employment of men.

Professor PATTERSON: In giving Mr. Maynard and his wife a month's notice to quit, what reason did you assign?

Mr. CHAMPNESS: That I could not afford it.

Professor PATTERSON: Still, in choosing your agents, and determining whom you shall dismiss or not dismiss, you would not put financial considerations before fitness for work?

Mr. CHAMPNESS: I should consider financial arrangements part of the fitness; for instance, I felt that Mr. Grant was going to spend a lot of money—I could not see my way to it.

Professor PATTERSON: I should like to submit a statement which Mr. Maynard has given for himself and his wife for the ten months ending February 10th, 1890. He says that his total expenditure amounted to Rs. 1,044.4.1, which would come to considerably less than £100 sterling.

Mr. BRUNYATE: Mr. Champness has said that he paid his men their charges, and that they got what they desired. But all this evidence goes to show that whether there be a limit written down on paper or not, there is a limit written down in Mr. Champness' own mind, and that limit seems to be £50 per year, and as soon as this limit is passed his men are dismissed.

Mr. CHAMPNESS: I deny that *in toto*.

Mr. FOWLER: But we have the fact that this man (Mr. Maynard) asked for £100.

Mr. CHAMPNESS: I will not dispute that.

Mr. HUGHES: I understand this is an outlay incurred as soon as he left Mr. Champness' employ.

Professor PATTERSON: No, it is the outlay incurred whilst he was in Mr. Champness' employ. The point I wish to emphasise is that out of seven men Mr. Champness has employed in India, one has died under painful circumstances, and two have either been dismissed by Mr. Champness or have had to break away from him because of the financial limit. I submit that this is a point exceedingly relevant to the present issue.

Mr. CHAMPNESS: I should like to say that I heard some things about Mr. Grant that made me fearful that he would get wrong. The habit of smoking was one of these things, and I did not like it, and I began to pay him £5 at a time.

Professor PATTERSON: I think that if Mr. Champness brings up that argument, he ought to be prepared to submit his letters to Mr. Grant and Mr. Grant's letters to him.

Mr. CHAMPNESS: Mr. Grant wrote to me very sharply, and I began to feel that I had made a mistake in sending him out.

Professor PATTERSON: There is another of your agents living at Karur, Mr. Whittome. How long has he been out?

Mr. CHAMPNESS: Since May 27th, 1889.

Professor PATTERSON: He set sail at that date, and arrived on July 2nd, 1889. I have also a statement from Mr. Whittome. He has been living with Mr. Woodward, one of our young ministers, in a small bungalow connected with the mission, and they have in every respect shared the expenses of their household. Now Mr. Whittome writes to me under date March 6th, 1890:—"I shall be glad to send you a general "statement of my accounts. The average cost of food was "Rs. 30 per month, and for servants I paid Rs. 10 (*i.e.*, Rs. 60 "per month for food, and Rs. 20 ditto for servants for two per- "sons). I pay no rent, as I live in the Mission House. As I "told Mr. Champness, my frequent visits to the Mission "House lessen my expenses; therefore, I should not like you "or anyone else to take my present rate of living as a "standard for another. Another might not be able to live as I "live."

Mr. BRUNYATE: Then Mr. Whittome's testimony is that whenever he lives with a missionary, instead of that increasing his expense it lowers it?

Professor PATTERSON: Yes. There are three of Mr.

Champness's agents of whom I have not yet spoken. Mr. Simpson, who is out in the Mysore; Mr. Adkin, and Mr. Harris, who have each of them been out less than a year. It is from the experience of these three brethren that the printed document that Mr. Champness has laid upon the table has been drawn up. Now the Mysore is not my district. It is not Mr. Findlay's district. We are not acquainted with those men. I have no doubt whatever that very much that Mr. Champness has printed here is capable of explanation; but in order that it may be explained, I must ask to be allowed to call Mr. Sackett before the Committee again, and also Mr. Gulliford, who come from the district in which these three brethren are labouring.

The PRESIDENT: Why do you wish to call Mr. Gulliford and Mr. Sackett?

Professor PATTERSON: From what I have heard I have reason to believe that these brethren have lived for very considerable periods with missionaries and paid nothing.

Mr. FOWLER: Do you mean to say that Mr. Champness' allegation—that when his men lived with missionaries they always paid—is not correct?

Professor PATTERSON: No, I do not say that. I say that I have heard that the men, whose names I have mentioned, lived with missionaries and paid nothing. That may be utterly inaccurate, or it may be accurate, but I should like to know the real facts of the case.

Mr. CHAMPNESS: It is true that they lived a short time with the missionaries without payment.

Mr. BRUNYATE: I asked Mr. Champness whether his men always paid when they lived with missionaries, and he said, Yes.

Mr. SMITH: I also asked the same question, and I received the same answer.

Mr. CHAMPNESS: When these men lived with missionaries for some months we paid for them; but when they were simply visiting we did not pay anything.

Mr. HUGHES: Does not the confusion arise from the fact that some of the men lived with the missionaries for three or four months, and some did not?

Mr. SMITH: My question was whether they *always* paid when they lived with missionaries.

Mr. CHAMPNESS: In that case I misunderstood your question.

Rev. WALTER SACKETT again appeared before the Committee, and in reply to the question, What length of time Mr. Champness' "Joyful News" agents had lived with the missionaries in the Mysore district, said: I can only speak of Bangalore, and I cannot speak at any great length about that, for this reason: I invited Mr. Simpson to my house to stay with me; I invited him as a friend. When he had been with me three days my health broke down. Mr. Simpson then went to a friend's house in Bangalore, and afterwards returned to Mr.————. His total stay was about six weeks.

Mr. CLAPHAM: Was Mr. Simpson living *free* during the whole of that time?

Mr. SACKETT: I believe he was, but I am not certain.

Mr. CHAMPNESS: There is the following item in the account:—"To the missionary for food (twelve days) Rs. 12 = 16s. 6d."

Mr. FOWLER: It is clear that somebody must have been helping to keep him, because I see that in the following month he only received the sum of £1 15s. 9d.

Rev. HENRY GULLIFORD was now introduced to the Committee, and in reply to a question put to him by Mr. Patterson, said: Mr. Simpson was in the houses of missionaries for six weeks, and he did not pay anything for his board during that time.

The PRESIDENT: Do you know of any other case?

Mr. GULLIFORD: Yes, but it is that of an evangelist who stayed for a few days only.

Mr. HUGHES: I should like to ask Mr. Champness one general question. Did any of these brethren while in his employ complain that their health was suffering because they were not sufficiently paid?

Mr. CHAMPNESS: Mr. Grant thought so, but I allowed him to have a pony when he could not walk.

Mr. HUGHES: Then the reason why you objected to let him have an equipage was because he had a pony?

Mr. CHAMPNESS: Yes; that is an important addition.

The PRESIDENT: If Mr. Champness is simply giving us his impressions on these details, we cannot accept them without having Mr. Grant's letter before us.

"Joyful News" Evangelists and the Chairman of the Mysore District.

Professor PATTERSON read to the Committee the following

Memorandum, drawn up by the Rev. Josiah Hudson, B.A., Chairman of the Mysore District :—

Memo on " Joyful News " Evangelists at Shimoga.

I cannot say what the three men spend. I should think not more th Rs. 150 a month—perhaps less. Since Mr. Robinson left they have be living by themselves. They occupy a house, the rent of which is Rs. Mr. Robinson previously charged the same amount for the room in t mission compound. So far as rent is concerned, they are favoured Shimoga; since the rendition, European houses have been let at low rates. I should not think that less than Rs. 12 would pay the owner. At Bangalore the rent would be more than that.

Mr. Simpson has visited some of the out-stations at our request, and of course we have paid his travelling expenses. Mr. Champness, however, bears all expenses connected with them. We made no contribution.

I have no doubt Mr. Champness will be able to show the expenses are very moderate, but in addition to the item of rent being exceptionally low, it must be remembered also—

1.—That three live together, and I think that three living together ought not to cost more—or much more—than two living separately. Mr. Champness wishes two always to live together, and this is a point to be remembered in calculating the expense.

2.—They were all furnished with very good outfits when they came out, and I presume the item of clothing as yet costs them scarcely anything.

3.—I doubt if they have purchased any books, except such as are needful for learning Kanarese. Mr. Champness supplies them with newspapers, and I think an occasional book.

4.—Since the last two men came there has been no sickness.

5.—At present they chiefly visit the surrounding villages, and need no conveyance.

6.—So far as I know they are not insuring or making any provision for the future.

7.—Expenses will largely increase if they marry and have children.

8.—At the inauguration of a scheme such as this, enthusiasm makes men willing to undergo more self-denial than they will when the novelty has worn away.

While however I think Mr. Champness is too sanguine with respect to the financial part of his scheme, I have faith in it, and think it well worth a trial. I was myself disappointed that the resolution of our Conference was not more hearty. So far Champness has certainly sent us good men, who to all appearance are likely to be successful, and he has allowed me all the discretion I could desire. If my views are referred to, I should like them to be given fully.

J. HUDSON.

Mr. HUGHES: Is it a fact that Mr. Champness dismissed Mr. Maynard on financial grounds?

Mr. CHAMPNESS: I dismissed him because I thought the man was ambitious, and that he would cost me more than I could afford to give, and because he had certain schemes in his mind that I could not sanction.

Mr. HUGHES: Let it be understood that this man was not dismissed on the ground of his personal cost.

After the adjournment, Sir Geo. Chubb referred to the letter from Mr. Cooling, which had been read by Mr. Champness, and asked for the following sentence to be re-read:—

"He does not wish to have a fixed salary allotted to him. He strongly prefers to work on 'Joyful News' lines as to pay. For one thing he does not wish his friends in the Army to say that he has bettered his temporal prospects by coming to us; he sees that on Army principles it is impossible to work in such fields as Trivellore, where there are no Europeans and no native Christians. As he frankly says, the Salvation Army does not go to such places, and in the two or three instances in which in South India it has tried such places, it has been obliged to withdraw from them."

The PRESIDENT: Are you, Mr. Champness, making any provisions prospectively with reference to the marriage of the men you employ?

Mr. CHAMPNESS: I intend them to marry, and I believe that I shall have no more difficulty in raising what is necessary for married men than for single men. I think if I put it before the people they will see that it is a reasonable thing that these men should marry and bring up families.

The PRESIDENT: Have you any estimate as to the additional cost?

Mr. CHAMPNESS: I have married men employed in Ceylon. They do not cost me quite £100 a year.

Mr. BRUNYATE: You reckon that keeping a wife will double the cost?

Mr. CHAMPNESS: Very nearly.

Mr. ALLEN: Do your men form churches?

Mr. CHAMPNESS: They act entirely under the Superintendent. I have no jurisdiction over them so far as telling them what their work is.

The PRESIDENT: That is to say, they are Methodist agents, under the control of the constituted Methodist authority.

Mr. BRUNYATE: Is it Mr. Champness' impression that any considerable number of his men are looking forward to anything like "orders"?

Mr. CHAMPNESS: The only time that anything has been said in that way was by one of the men, who said he would like to be accepted as a candidate, on the condition that he lives on the same lines as at present.

Mr. BRUNYATE: Considering the large number of men with whom he started, and who have now gone away, I want to know whether Mr. Champness thinks that he has a reasonable prospect of retaining his men upon anything like the present scale of expenditure?

Mr. CHAMPNESS: Oh, certainly; I am very agreeably disappointed. I believe I have very much less change and loss than you find proportionately amongst the ministers.

Mr. HUGHES: Is it not a fact that Mr. Champness actually finds that the cost grows less rather than more?

Mr. CHAMPNESS: It is so. What the three men cost is not so much now as it was when they started first—that is, the cost is not so great where there are three men living together as when they lived apart.

Dr. LUNN: I think Mr. Brunyate does not understand that four out of the seven men sent out are still in the work.

Mr. FINDLAY: We have heard from Mr. Whittome himself what was the cost of his living. We have not heard from Mr. Champness what he himself sent to Mr. Whittome. I am, however, able to inform the Committee that he receives from the Government Rs. 33. 5. 4 per month as superintendent of a school.

Mr. CHAMPNESS: Mr. Whittome is not acting exactly as a missionary. He was sent out with the understanding that he was to have Government assistance. I have sent him out a bicycle. I do not rest on this man's case so much as I do upon the others. I may say before I leave the Committee that I am more than ever convinced that I am on the right lines, and I feel that the more the thing is examined the more the Methodist people will see that I am right in all the principles I have laid down. Of course if support did not come in I should fail, but I have no fear about that.

Mr. ALLEN: I should like to ask whether the financial limit will not act on the self-respect of the men?

Mr. CHAMPNESS: They stand in the same position as lay agents do at home. They receive just what it costs them.

The Rev. J. G. Gregson.

In reply to questions put by Dr. Lunn, the Rev. J. G. GREGSON said: I went to India in 1858, in connection with the

Baptist Missionary Society. I remained there till 1866, when I came home in consequence of illness. In 1872 I went out again to India, and remained there until 1879. I then resigned my connection with the Society, and became engaged by the Government of India in connection with Temperance work in the Army, and also as pastor of the Union Church at Mussoorie. I came home in 1886 in consequence of the illness of my wife, and I am now pastor of the Zion Chapel in Bradford. Whilst in India I was presented to the Lieutenant-Governor, and I know a good many missionaries who have been similarly presented. It is a very common thing for this to be done.

Mr. CLAPHAM: Is it not a very ordinary thing, that on the reception of the Governor, etc., the ministers, Episcopalian and Nonconformist alike, are invited?

Mr. GREGSON: The ministers are not exactly invited, but their names are sent to the Commissioner of the District, and they go as a matter of course.

The PRESIDENT: Is it regarded as a token of the loyalty of the Church to which they belong, that the missionaries are so loyal to the Queen in that way?

Mr. GREGSON: It might be so represented, but I never heard it put in that way before. I went because I was a resident in the station where the Levée was held.

Mr. CLAPHAM: Do you consider that the fact of your being introduced to the Governor of the District would impair your influence with the natives?

Mr. GREGSON: The fact of my going to a Levée would show that I was identified with my fellow-countrymen in that station, but it would not be likely to lessen my influence as a minister. I do not see that the two things are identical.

Mr. CLAPHAM: Some people think that by attending these gatherings the missionaries lose influence with the native population.

Mr. GREGSON: Such attendances would form part of the missionaries' surroundings, and that involves the great question as to whether it is desirable for a missionary to live as an Anglo-Indian amongst the Europeans. If he lived amongst the natives, his influence would be greater than if he lived amongst Europeans.

Dr. LUNN: Do you mean, by living amongst the natives, living in native quarters, or living as the Salvationists did?

Mr. GREGSON: The Salvationists, of course, identify themselves entirely with the natives, and live as natives in the native parts of the city. But it would be quite possible for a European to live near the natives and be in greater touch with them, than would be possible if he lived amongst the Anglo-Indians. The reason for living amongst the Anglo-Indians is one of health, but I have known missionaries who have lived on the borders of the city and in the native quarters, and have not suffered in health.

Mr. BRUNYATE: Then, as a matter of fact, the circumstance of a missionary being presented at Court does not damage his influence?

Mr. GREGSON: I don't think it would affect his influence one way or the other.

Mr. HUGHES: Do the missionaries live in Anglo-Indian society in the neighbourhood in which they are residents?

Mr. GREGSON: They would not.

Mr. HUGHES: Does that facilitate or hinder their work amongst the natives? You have just said that you think that if the missionary lived in or near the native town, he would be more in touch with the natives. If he lived in that way would he go to Court?

Mr. GREGSON: No.

Mr. HUGHES: So that if he adopted the style of living that would be most helpful to his work, he would not be presented at Court?

Mr. GREGSON: Yes.

Mr. BRUNYATE: Is it Episcopalian missionaries who are so presented generally, or does the custom extend to Nonconformists also?

Mr. GREGSON: I should think as many Nonconformist as Episcopalian are presented.

Dr. LUNN: I will ask whether you found, when you landed in India, that you were received into that society, the members of which were being presented at Court?

Mr. GREGSON: When I first landed in India I lived at a small station where there was no chance of being presented at Court at all.

Dr. LUNN: If Mr. Gregson had been sent to Calcutta, would he immediately have found himself in that society, the members of which were being presented at Court?

Mr. GREGSON: I do not think I should, as I do not think I should have desired it. I was not so closely identified with the Europeans as to make it necessary I should be presented.

Mr. HUGHES: As a matter of fact, you know that many Nonconformist ministers have been presented at Court?

Mr. ALLEN: Mr. Gregson says if he lived outside the English quarters he would not desire to go to Court. If he lived inside the English quarters would he desire to go?

Mr. GREGSON: I think so. Because whilst in the one case there is identification with the natives, in the other case there is identification with the Europeans. If I lived as a native I should never associate with Europeans in the station, and Europeans would not desire my company. Take the case, for example, of Mr. Tucker. He was a Government official, and was received in European society, but the moment he, along with the Salvation Army, identified himself with the natives, and lived as they did, all turned their backs upon him.

Mr. ALLEN: What was Mr. Tucker before he joined the Salvationists?

Mr. GREGSON: An assistant commissioner in the Civil Service.

Mr. ALLEN: Is it Mr. Gregson's opinion that a missionary should so separate himself?

Mr. GREGSON: Yes. I think it would be to the advantage of the missionary to live as the Salvationists live, rather than amongst Europeans. The Oxford men live with the natives.

Mr. HUGHES: Does Mr. Gregson think that any man who does not live as the missionaries usually do must identify himself with the natives? Does he not think there is a *via media*?

Mr. GREGSON: Decidedly.

Mr. BRUNYATE: Will Mr. Gregson give us a definite idea of what he means by the *via media*?

Mr. GREGSON, in reply to this question, mentioned the case of some missionaries who, some years ago, went amongst the natives and lived at a cost of Rs. 50 per month.

Dr. LUNN: Do you know any instance of a minister recently going out on such lines as you suggest?

Mr. GREGSON: Yes. I was the means of getting out men only three years ago.

Mr. ALLEN: Is it true that Mr. Bowen, who lived in India until he was 70 years of age, and to whom you have made reference, although he pursued these habits for so many years, had no evidence that he had increased his influence with the natives?

Mr. GREGSON: I do not know. He never expressed himself

in that way to me. He was greatly respected by the natives. Their appearance at his funeral was very good evidence of their respect.

Mr. ALLEN: Is it the custom of the Baptist missionaries to separate themselves from their countrymen?

Mr. GREGSON: No, it is not.

Mr. ALLEN: I understand that from the English on his station the missionary often secures large contributions, by which he is helped materially in his work. Now, suppose that a missionary took the course that you have suggested, would these English people refuse to assist?

Mr. GREGSON: No, I do not think that would be the result. I have known missionaries who lived with the natives at a small cost, and help was not withdrawn from them in their work.

Mr. ALLEN: Did the men who turned their backs on Mr. Tucker contribute to his work?

Mr. GREGSON: I know there were some who did not give.

Mr. HUGHES: I gather that in India, as in England, there are Christian men who are in sympathy with Christian work, and worldly men who are not in sympathy with it.

Sir GEO. CHUBB: How soon after you landed were you presented at Court?

Mr. GREGSON: It was several years after.

Mr. SMITH: Would the mere fact of your being present at a Levée add anything to your practical expenditure?

Mr. GREGSON: Not so far as that act went; but if I had lived as the natives did, and as I might have done, the expenditure on living would have been greatly reduced.

Mr. HUGHES: Does not being presented at Court imply a general style of living that is not favourable to the work of the missionary?

Mr. GREGSON: In answer to that, I think it would be very much better to cover the whole ground by a statement like this: Being presented at Court is in itself no great expense to the person presented. But it must be remembered that a missionary who associates with Anglo-Indian society, and with his own countrymen, gets a certain social status. He lives in a very much more expensive way than he would if he gave himself up entirely to real native work. If he took this latter course his influence with the natives would be very much greater than it is at present. He cannot acquire that influence with the natives whilst he is identified with the ruling class which he could acquire by living amongst them. As to the question whether I would advocate the Salvation Army system or that followed usually by the missionaries, I have said in public and I have written it, that if I had to select between the two I should certainly prefer the Salvation Army plan to the present plan, although I believe there is a medium course that would preserve us from either extreme. I am speaking now of missionaries generally, not of any one sect or body.

Mr. ALLEN: I presume that on some stations the missionary would have to conduct services in English and preach to English people. I suppose you would not prevent him from doing pastoral work, calling to see them, and staying to have a meal with them?

Mr. GREGSON: I would open the way for two distinctive kinds of work: one in which the missionary would have charge of Europeans, preaching and ministering to them as their pastor, and the other giving himself entirely to native work.

Mr. ALLEN: But supposing that one missionary had to do two kinds of work. You would not advocate that his own countrymen should be neglected altogether, so far as religious ordinances are concerned?

Mr. GREGSON: I should not object under these circumstances to a missionary preaching to his own people, and associating with them. I think it would be better to divide the work. But this could only be done in large military stations.

Professor PATTERSON: I think it would be well to have facts upon that point. There are many towns in India that have Europeans residing in them that have no cantonment. We have Negapatam. There are no troops there, yet there is a European population to be ministered to, and there are other places where the same thing applies.

Mr. HUGHES: I understand that Mr. Gregson's position is this—that where such circumstances obtained he would be willing for the missionary to minister to the needs of his own countrymen, but that it would be preferable for him to engage in native work.

Dr. LUNN: Referring again to the question of society—is there any class of Europeans in India with an income equal to that of the ordinary missionary, namely £300 a year, who would not be admitted to Court?

Mr. GREGSON: I do not suppose that a tradesman would be presented at a Levee.

Dr. LUNN: Do those who live in Anglo-Indian society generally live on an equality with the natives?

Mr. GREGSON: There is not much intercourse between the natives and the Europeans. I do not see how there very well can be, seeing they don't eat the same food or mix in the same society.

Dr. LUNN: Do you think it would demoralise the natives if they were occasionally to eat with the missionaries?

Mr. GREGSON: The food would disagree with them physically. It would be easier for the missionary to eat the food of the natives than for the natives to eat European food.

Mr. HUGHES: Then does Mr. Gregson mean that the general style of living of the missionaries is too high for the natives?

Mr GREGSON: It is totally different in kind.

Dr. LUNN: What do you regard as necessary for life in India?

Mr. GREGSON: That would of course depend upon the individual. Some people have lived on a vegetarian diet, and have succeeded pretty well; others as they do in England.

Mr. HUGHES: Does Mr. Gregson think that a missionary, in order to keep his health, requires *meat* four times a day?

Mr. GREGSON: I should say that the less heavy meals they have the better.

Mr. CLAPHAM: Will Mr. Gregson tell the Committee how he lived in India?

Mr. GREGSON said he had a cup of coffee and a slice of toast the first thing in the morning, and at breakfast he had curry, cold meat, and eggs and porridge. He always dined about 3.0, and dinner consisted generally of some mutton or beef, soup, pastry, and fruit and curry. Then at the evening meal he had toast and butter, tea and preserves. That was about his bill of fare from year end to year end.

Dr. LUNN: Do you consider the style of living of Nonconformist missionaries in India is similar to that of Nonconformist ministers in England?

Mr. GREGSON said he lived more comfortably in India than he does in Bradford. In India Rs. 50 would go further in purchasing power than £5 in England.

Mr. FOWLER: You went out in 1858; are provisions cheaper or dearer now than then in India?

Mr. GREGSON: They are dearer now than then. It is the habit of the natives to charge you according to your income. If you go to live in the European part of the town, the first thing the native does is to ascertain your income, and he regulates his prices accordingly. A native would thus be in a position to obtain food very much cheaper than the Europeans.

Mr. FOWLER: It is so in London. If you buy in the West-end, you buy at one price; if you buy in the East-end, you buy at another price.

Mr. GREGSON said the effect of any fear of famine in India would be that the prices would go up very much. In reply to a question from Mr. Fowler, he said that an income of £300 per annum in England would be more than equivalent to Rs. 3,000 in India. An English pastor, with £300 in England, if transferred to India with that amount converted into rupees, would be able to purchase a great deal more for his family in India. Food of every description is cheaper than in England; dress is cheaper in India, and a missionary has neither house-rent nor taxes to pay.

Mr. ALLEN pointed out that a greater variety in food and in clothing would be necessary in India than in England.

Mr. GREGSON did not find it to be so; food and clothing being cheaper in India than in England.

Mr. GREGSON, in reply to questions from Dr. Lunn and Mr. Brunyate, said that a certain number of servants in a large house in India would cost more than the same number of servants in a smaller house. It was impossible for a missionary to live in the European part of the town with only two or three servants. Answering a question put by the President, Mr. Gregson further said that a missionary living at a cheap rate could do with a less number of servants than a missionary living at a higher rate. It might be right or wrong, but the fact had to be faced, that when a man associates with his own countrymen, he must keep up a certain style in connection with that society. Comparing an ordinary missionary in India with an ordinary minister in England, the former certainly moved in the higher grade of society. A missionary living amongst natives could manage with two or three servants.

Mr. ALLEN: Then I understand Mr. Gregson to mean that in the English quarters of Indian towns the missionaries are forced to live on something like an equality with the English residents?

Mr. GREGSON replied that this scarcely represented the true position, inasmuch as there was still a difference financially and socially, between many of the European residents and the missionaries.

Mr. ALLEN: But there is a great difference in the position of ministers at home. Take Dr. Maclaren, for instance, as compared with the Baptist pastor in a small place.

Mr. GREGSON: Just so; but missionaries sent out to India all go out as though they were Maclarens. That is, they are all on an equality, whether they have the mental status of a Maclaren or of an ordinary village pastor; they receive the same salary and status.

Mr. Gregson believed missionaries gave less in the shape of charities in India than in England.

Professor Patterson and Mr. Gregson.

In reply to questions put to him by Professor Patterson, Mr. GREGSON said the first place he lived in was situated on the banks of the Ganges.

Professor PATTERSON said: It is a well-known fact that Monghyr is, of all places in India, the least subject to malaria, and was on this account chosen as a cantonment for English troops. I should like to ask what your work was whilst you were at Monghyr?

Mr. GREGSON: It was that of an ordinary missionary in charge of native work. There is no cantonment at Monghyr, and soldiers have never been quartered there.

Professor PATTERSON: You have submitted to the Committee a certain hypothesis in regard to the possibilities of Indian missionary life. Did you ever attempt to put your theory into practice?

Mr. GREGSON: No.

Professor PATTERSON: Your second station was at Agra?

Mr. GREGSON: Yes. I had charge of a native church and the European church, officiating as chaplain to Nonconformist soldiers in the cantonment. From there I passed to Mussoorie, one of the favourite sanatoriums in India.

Professor PATTERSON: When you were travelling all over India, it was as the secretary of The Soldiers' Total Abstinence Association?

Mr. GREGSON: Yes.

Professor PATTERSON: With regard to "presentation at Court," did you ever hear that expression used in India?

Mr. GREGSON: Certainly not.

Professor PATTERSON: What does that formality consist of?

Mr. GREGSON: You are introduced to the Viceroy. The invitation is issued to the public, to give expression to their loyalty to the Queen, and to attend a Levée; that is not in any case called a presentation at Court.

Professor PATTERSON : In what costume did you appear?

Mr. GREGSON : It did not cost me anything to appear there. I appeared simply in evening dress—having a coat, I used it.

Professor PATTERSON : You said that living with the native population involved exclusion from European society?

Mr. GREGSON : Yes, that is what I mean. I lived amongst the natives at a cost of Rs. 50 a month when I was travelling amongst them, itinerating in the district.

Professor PATTERSON : You said you attended a Levée of the Lieutenant-Governor. Did you see natives there?

Mr. GREGSON : No, there was a native durbar for the natives in the North-West Provinces.

Professor PATTERSON : You said tradesmen were not presented, though they might be enjoying a salary of over £300 a year?

Mr. GREGSON : Of course there are exceptional men, but as a rule tradesmen do not move in that society—that is, they do not associate with civilians.

Professor PATTERSON : Then a presentation at Court is not so much a question of finance as a question of character?

Mr. GREGSON : Yes, it is a question of social position.

Mr. HUGHES observed that whilst presentation to the Lieutenant-Governor was not a question of salary, but of a certain social status involving European connections, it would tend to separate the native population from the missionary.

Professor PATTERSON : You have been engaged in native work in connection with the Baptist Missions, and you have attended a Levée. Have you found in your experience that such attendance at a Levée hindered in any measure your native work?

Mr. GREGSON : No; that forms part of the question of a missionary being identified with the natives and with Europeans.

The PRESIDENT: You have been officiating as an army chaplain. Supposing there was a change in the commanding officer, would you not call upon him, and would not that prepare the way for you to do business with him afterwards? Would it not be a proper thing for you to observe the usual social etiquette by attending his Levée?

Mr. GREGSON: Yes.

Mr. FINDLAY : Suppose a missionary did wait upon an officer in that way, would it interfere with his influence with the natives?

Mr. GREGSON: Not at all.

Mr. FINDLAY: On the stations where there is no European society, do you think the missionary would find it hard to come into touch with the natives on account of his style of living?

Mr. GREGSON: I have always found that when a missionary lives isolated from all other Europeans, he lives in a very different style from that he lives in when he is amongst Europeans. At a place 14 miles from Agra, where we had a small bungalow, our surroundings were very different from those of Anglo-Indian society in the station.

Sir GEO. CHUBB: Has Mr. Gregson any knowledge of the amount of wages paid to artisans?

Mr. GREGSON: Yes. European artisans go out to India for various kinds of work. The platelayers, for instance, have from Rs. 150 to Rs. 200 a month. Engine-drivers will get from Rs. 200 to Rs. 300 a month. Out of that they have to pay everything—house rent, etc.

Mr. Sessions.

Mr. SESSIONS, in reply to the President, said: I reside in Gloucester, and am a member of the Society of Friends and of the Foreign Missionary Society. I visited India in the first place for recreation and instruction, but I was requested by the Society to look into the question of missions, and to inform myself upon all the topics in which the Committee are interested. We have only a small Mission. The missionaries are paid in pounds sterling so much a year. A married man receives £260, with an allowance of £25 for his horse and £10 for each child. We provide a house. Nothing is paid for education, but sometimes when the children of missionaries come home the Society of Friends assists. The amounts named cover the whole of the payments, excepting when there may be a case of illness, which is considered on its own merits. We have missionary property, but ours is not an incorporated society. Our work is almost entirely among the native population, and we have church-membership among the natives. Our missionaries live in bungalows. For Zenana work, the pay to a lady who has to keep house for herself is £120 a year, with the same allowance for travelling that a married minister has. I came in contact with missionaries of other societies. My impression was that their mode of living was such as to be favourable to their influence with the natives. I was distinctly asked to ascertain whether the £260 paid to a married missionary was too much or too little. I came to the conclusion in my own mind that whilst I should not do anything to disturb the present arrangements with the old missionaries, if a new missionary were to go out I should pay him, as a single man, £120, and an additional £120 when he married. If expected to entertain travelling missionaries, which is in some missions a very serious item, or if we expected him to correspond with friends at home (my own feeling is we ought not to stint our missionaries; they give up a good deal; they have much to contend with), I think that £240 should be given, with an allowance for horse hire, and £10 each for the children. I think that is a liberal, but not an excessive amount.

The PRESIDENT: Are all your missionaries members of the Society of Friends before they go out?

Mr. SESSIONS: Yes.

The PRESIDENT: Do you expect your missionaries to make any provision for life assurance?

Mr. SESSIONS: No one has come upon us yet in that way. We have a Sustenance Fund to meet such cases. We pay all the expenses of those coming home.

Mr. BRUNYATE: I would like to ask whether you think it is more expensive living in India than in England? Is £240 in India equivalent to the same amount in England?

Mr. SESSIONS: I am not sure. Replying to Mr. Pope, he continued: I do not remember a case in point in which missionaries' children have had to come home alone. We have had missionaries in India only about 11 or 12 years. It is a comparatively young mission.

Mr. CLAPHAM: Then I understand you would recommend for young married men £240, with the additions named?

Mr. SESSIONS: Yes.

Mr. SESSIONS, in answer to Sir Geo. Chubb, said: There has been a change in the policy of our Society. I should be quite inclined to recommend the young men of our schools to go out as itinerant village missionaries, to live with the older missionaries till they married. In answer to Mr. Smith, he said: I should most distinctly object to give up our present class of missionaries, who are doing good work and are very much respected.

The PRESIDENT: Are you forming schools on your stations?

Mr. SESSIONS: We have day schools and Sunday schools on every station at present.

The PRESIDENT: Your missions are twelve years old. What are the spiritual results?

Mr. SESSIONS: I believe there is an inner circle of pronounced Christians; there is an outer circle of men who have not made confession; another section who have cast off their idol worship; and outside that yet another section of men who, like Naaman, bow down in the House of Rimmon, because of their caste. Of pronounced Christians in the inner circle we have twenty or thirty.

The PRESIDENT: Do they bear a distinctive name?

Mr. SESSIONS: They belong to the mission church of the Society of Friends.

Dr. LUNN: How many missionaries have you had on an average?

Mr. SESSIONS: Four, including the one who looks after the orphans. I believe in the concentration of labour as much as possible within a given district. We are just about to open a high school for the high caste Brahmins and for those who are going into the Civil Service. We lay great stress upon the educational branch of our mission work, but we have not been strong enough to enter upon it. Mr. Sessions added, in reply to Mr. Fletcher, that he would prefer the missionaries being paid in gold.

The PRESIDENT: Is it so that when a man and his wife are both in your service only £260 is paid?

Mr. SESSIONS: Yes, the missionaries' wives are expected to do all the mission work they can.

Rev. W C. Kendall.

Rev. W. C. KENDALL was next introduced to the Committee. He stated that he had spent five and a half years in the Calcutta district. He went out to Raniganj in 1877, married in 1880, and returned home in 1883.

In answer to questions put to him by Dr. Lunn, he said that when he was in the Calcutta district only one or two of the missionaries there preached in the vernacular. He spent more than two years in Calcutta with the English-speaking congregation; he was then appointed to Raniganj, where there were two stations for railway employees about 16 miles apart, and where he had a native girls' school and a catechist under his superintendency. At the end of five years he was set free entirely for native work; but at the end of three or four months he had to come home. The number of missionarie in the district was six or seven. He understood what was meant by what was called the native style of living, as compared with the English and the Eurasian style of living. Many of the Eurasians were better off than many of the English, and they lived quite as well. But there was a lower class of Eurasians, some of whom lived very nearly in the native style. As to attendance at Levées, he went once or twice to see the Viceroy. He believed the Chairman of the District used to go every year, as a matter of preference and duty. There were well-to-do Europeans in Calcutta who were not admitted into what was called "society";—tradespeople, for instance; but missionaries did not rank socially with tradespeople. Missionaries in India did not, because they could not, stand in exactly the same relation to their household servants as ministers did in England; they belonged to a different race, and *caste* in India was not the same in kind as *caste* in this country. That was a thing which English people did not understand. He did not think that he had ever dined *formally* with any native catechist. The catechist would sometimes come in and sit at his table, but not to take a formal meal. As to the cost of living, he thought that upon the whole it was cheaper in India than in England—at any rate he had found it easier to live within his income there than here. In his first English circuit he received £120 with the ordinary additional allowances; in his next circuit he received £137. His stipend then rose to £140, and now it was £150. The reason why his household expenditure was greater when he first came to an English circuit, than when he lived in India, was that Mrs. Kendall and himself were not accustomed to English housekeeping. They had everything to learn.

Dr. LUNN: Do you remember the carriage that was driven by the Rev. ——————?—(Answer: Yes.) Do you think there is any analogy between that and what in this country is known as a "circuit gig"?—(Answer: There is more analogy in the purpose of it than in the carriage itself.—(Laughter.) You used to drive Burmah ponies—what was their cost as compared with the cost of country ponies?—(Answer: Two or three times that of country ponies.) In reply to other questions, Mr. Kendall said: With regard to the cost of living, Mrs. Kendall and himself spent in the bazaar about 1s. 8d. per day. But outside that they had to purchase other things, such as milk, tea, jams, bread, etc. The total amount spent in food of all kinds would be about £40 or £45 a year. On looking into his account-book he found that for two years the cost of this item was £40. His servants cost him about £30 a year. As to clothing, he and all the missionaries wore white drill. The cost was very light. He thought that £15 a year would cover everything for himself and wife. Something had been said about clothes being spoiled by insects, but he did not think that he had lost much in that way. With respect to charities, he did not think that any missionary in his district gave away so much as £20 a year, unless it was Mr.————, who was liberally disposed. For a missionary to live in a large house surrounded by broad grounds was, in his opinion, detrimental to his influence —that style of living did not tend to promote a feeling of unity between natives and Europeans. At the same time he thought that there was a radical difference between the two races that would not be completely bridged over by the circumstance of a missionary going from a large house to a smaller one. He thought it would be possible to cultivate closer relations between the missionaries and the natives.

In reply to Mr. Fowler, Mr. Kendall said that the difference he had spoken of was a racial difference; a difference also such as naturally existed between a subject people and a ruling people; between the East and the West.

Mr. SMITH: I understand Mr. Kendall to estimate the cost of living to be £40 for food, £30 for servants, £15 for clothing, £10 for charities; thus making a total of £105. May I ask whether he managed to save the rest of his income?

Mr. KENDALL: No, I did not. There are many other ways in which money goes; but I am certain as to the matter of the bazaar account.

Mr. SMITH: It comes to this; we have, first of all, an estimate of total expenditure, presented to us under certain items; and then we are told that are there other sources of expenditure outside these items.

Mr. KENDALL: There are many expenses that come in, in addition to those connected with food, clothing, servants, and charities, such as postage, travelling from place to place, amusements, presents, the purchase of a piano, etc.

The PRESIDENT: I presume that you see the bearing of that statement. Now supposing that your estimate of total expenditure as given us a few minutes ago had gone forth to the world, the great unthinking part of the world would have concluded that missionaries were very much overpaid, because these other items had not been included. It is therefore a very unfair thing to suppose that the mere bazaar and other kindred expenses cover all that is involved in a missionary's outlay.

Mr. KENDALL: But surely nobody would suppose that that is what I meant?

The PRESIDENT: I am afraid that many would, and that is precisely where the danger lies. What you have just stated qualifies very greatly your previous statements, and is a very important utterance.

Mr. HUGHES: I should like to ask Mr. Kendall whether he means that the large balance that Mr. Smith has mentioned was absolutely necessary in order that he might be provided with the necessary comforts of life? It struck me that his list of etceteras includes a great many things that are not absolutely necessary to the success of a missionary's life; but it is quite clear that Mr. Kendall's estimate is a great deal lower than that of the Bangalore Conference Report.

Mr. KENDALL: I do not think that a piano is a necessity for a missionary life, and yet you would not blame a missionary for purchasing one.

Mr. ALLEN: You told us that Mr. ——— drove two ponies. Would it be a fair thing for any one to infer from that circumstance that the general body of missionaries drive about in that way?

Mr. KENDALL: I think that for seven years the amount that was spent in horses was needlessly high. But before I left in 1883 it was brought down to the very modest sum it is to-day.

Dr. LUNN: Does Mr. Kendall know as a matter of fact that those Burmah ponies were paid for out of the district funds?

Mr. KENDALL: Mr. —— gave us to understand that he had a right to charge the district for two horses, but I don't pretend to know whether he paid for those ponies out of the district funds or out of his own pocket.

Mr. ALLEN: What would be the difference in cost between a horse and two ponies?—(Answer: My horse cost Rs. 300, and the two ponies cost Rs. 800 or 400 each.)

Professor PATTERSON: I should hardly have thought it necessary to ask Mr. Kendall any questions, but for Mr. Hughes' remark just now that Mr. Kendall's estimate of the cost of food was very much below that of the Bangalore Conference Report. I take the liberty of doubting that altogether. Mr. Kendall estimates his cost of food from one item, namely, his bazaar account. The bazaar account, however, is certainly not more than one-third of the total cost of food. Mr. Kendall's bazaar account amounted to one rupee per day. My own is about the same. But if you turn to the amount stated in the Bangalore Report, at page 12, you will see that the item of food includes not only what is usually understood to come under that head, but the cost of fuel and lighting, and sundries of all kinds connected with the house. As to ponies, our experience is that it is just as cheap to keep two ponies as it is to keep one Australian horse.

The PRESIDENT: I should like to know what Mr.————'s

reputation was in Calcutta, as to his style of living, and whether his recall had anything to do with the charge of extravagance?

Mr. HARTLEY: It was because of his extravagance in horses and house rent.

Mr. SMITH: Does Mr. Kendall admit that the bazaar account is only one-third of the total cost of provisions?

Mr. KENDALL: No, I think it is about two-thirds or three-fourths.

Mr. FINDLAY: What would bread and milk cost as compared with the bazaar account?

Mr. KENDALL: My bread would cost Rs. 3 or 4 a month for the two.

Professor PATTERSON: Bread costs a rupee for 100 ounces. I should hardly think that ten ounces of bread per day would be enough for two people.

Mr. KENDALL: I am quite sure that was all I paid.

Mr. POPE: Can you remember what your allowances were when you were in Calcutta?

Mr. KENDALL: I can tell you very nearly. I had £250 stipend; £4 for postage and £30 for horse. I never saved any money. In reply to Mr. Brunyate, Mr. Kendall continued: As to the difference between living in India and England, I always consider that my five years in India have taken fifteen years from my life, and I often say to people that I would not go out again for £2,000 a year. I do not consider the figure of £15 for insurance too much, but I think it was not spent. I was not insured till I returned home.

Mr. CLAPHAM: Would you consider that life in an English country circuit is as trying to life and health as India?

Mr. KENDALL: Certainly not.

Mr. SMITH: I presume then that Mr. Kendall agrees with the following passage from page 45 of Dr. Lunn's journal, viz.:—"If in any future chapters of this journal, which I
" intend to make as faithful a representation as possible of our
" life out here, it should seem to anyone that we are having
" too festive a time, I would ask such readers to take my word
" for it that Ethel and I, at any rate, would gladly exchange
" these lovely blue skies and this delightful temperature of 80
" degrees, and all the lovely tropical vegetation and beautiful
" birds in our compound, and our very cosy little home, and
" all our retinue of servants, for a small English house in a
" dirty street, with one housemaid on £5 a year, if we could
" only be amongst our critics once more." (Answer: Yes).

Dr. LUNN: That is simply a remark intended to illustrate my love of home.

Rev. J. A. D. J. Macdonald.

Mr. MACDONALD said, in answer to questions by the President: I have been in India until recently since 1878, and am stationed in Dum Dum, North Calcutta, and preach three times to the English in one week and also to the natives. I preach in English and Bengalee.

In reply to Mr. Fletcher, Mr. Macdonald continued: I lived in a house in a bazaar that was paid for by our mission—the centre was used as a chapel, one side as my dwelling-house, the other side by the Bengalee minister. I had no proper furniture, and I found the house exceedingly injurious to health. I had to ride about on the trams at night for fresh air. I don't intend to live in that way again.

Mr. FLETCHER: Do you think that that mode of life facilitated your work among the natives?

Mr. MACDONALD: I have no reason to think so. I had been living in a house that cost Rs. 70 a month for rent. It was a great expense to the Society, and we had no hold upon the property. At the same time we were having our converts taken away from us because we had no house of our own. I determined to live in a style somewhat below what is understood as the *via media* style, in order to obtain land for the Society.

The PRESIDENT: You have seen the Bangalore Conference Report—do you accept the estimate there made of cost as correct?

Mr. MACDONALD: I refused at the Bangalore Conference to go into the question of living. I am not prepared to state what the cost might be. I have great confidence in those who drew up the Report, and have no doubt it was done in a most careful and painstaking way. I have not read the Report very carefully. Mr. Macdonald did not think the stipend of a missionary could be materially lessened without imposing real inconvenience. He was asked to take part in the revision of the Bengalee Bible. He found he could not attend that Committee for the lack of money. It would have cost him £12 a year in travelling, and he was not justified in incurring that expense. He could not have thought of asking for a grant in respect of the matter as Mr. Hughes suggested.

The PRESIDENT asked whether Mr. Macdonald thought he could have borne any reduction of stipend without suffering personal inconvenience, and whether he believed a missionary was in a position to save money to any great extent? Mr. Macdonald replied: I think not. I have saved no money whatever. I have managed to get out of the country free from debt, but I have not been able to insure my life. I blame myself for not doing it. I have used all economy, but I found calls so numerous that I could not save anything. I have twenty villages on my plan, and a great number of causes to keep going. There were nearly forty people in my household. Multitudes of little things are required. If I were to live in celibacy and seclusion, and work on as small a scale as a Jesuit priest does, I could save money; but that is not the system for us.

Mr. ALLEN: I think we have evidence that Mr. Macdonald has spent on his work a very considerable sum of money.

Mr. MACDONALD continued: With regard to Mr. Kendall's evidence, I have told him that instead of being a witness for the side which speaks for economy, his expenditure in India would have justified him in being a witness on the other side. In reply to Mr. Hughes, he said: We have found in our work that if we hire a school, as soon as we have a convert from that school the landlord turns us out. That was done in Calcutta three times. It was such circumstances that gave us to see that we must have land of our own, in order that we might not be turned out of the villages. In this way we have succeeded in planting ourselves in sixteen places in that circuit. In answer to Mr. Brunyate, he said: I must say that I have not found any difficulty in the way of free access to the natives. In our circuit we have Englishmen, Bengalees, Hindustanees, and East Indians. We all worship in the same chapel. As their minister I know no distinctions. At the Lord's supper we take one another by the hand. There is no difficulty whatever.

Sir GEO. CHUBB: Were you ever present at the Lieutenant-Governor's Levée?

Mr. MACDONALD: I once called upon the Viceroy. It was considered the right thing to do, and I did it. I made my bow at the Governor-General's house, with other new arrivals. It is necessary for missionaries to be on visiting terms with the officer commanding the station, and with the magistrate. We are continually brought into contact with them, but I have never found it necessary to cultivate their acquaintance socially. These men frequently help us greatly. Magistrates may go with us and assist us in the villages by seeing that order is kept. When the native Christians have been persecuted, when men have tried to damage our Mission House, when there have been cases of murder and robbery in the villages, a word to the magistrate has resulted in a very thorough investigation. I should be extremely sorry to go back to India and not make familiar acquaintance with the officers of the country. I have been asked to a mess dinner simply and solely to be asked about religion. In reply to Mr. Clapham, Mr. Macdonald added that such acquaintance with the officials would not make the missionary at all less esteemed by the natives. He believed that the law must prepare the way for the Gospel in India as it did in Judea.

Mr. Hughes Proposes to bring up Further Evidence.

Mr. HUGHES: I have a very important document from Mr. Caine that I wish to present to the Committee. I have also a letter from Mr. Bullman, who occupied a position for some years in India as deputy-missionary. I also want to have an opportunity of examining Mr. Patterson's criticisms of our figures in relation to the London Missionary Society; for I have seen Mr. Wardlaw Thompson, the senior Secretary of that Society, and received from him an exact statement of the average amount received by their missionaries in India; and I am prepared to show on the authority of their Secretary that Mr Patterson's estimate is larger than is actually the case. Perhaps it will be better to have it in print. It has occurred to me that to facilitate the work of the Committee I might get these documents printed, and submit them in that form. But I am obliged to present some of this evidence either written or in print. I attach very great importance to Mr. Caine's letter. I should like to have an opportunity of presenting our view of this particular matter.

Professor PATTERSON: I should like to say that Dr. Lunn is the chief witness before this Committee, and we have not yet examined Dr. Lunn upon the basis of his evidence. Our examination of Dr. Lunn was in part anticipated yesterday by Mr. Gostick, but I feel that this is decidedly the most important part of our case; it will take up some time, and I shall have to ask the Committee to bear with us with a little patience while we examine the evidence on which Dr. Lunn's case rests.

Dr. Lunn.

Professor PATTERSON: Yesterday reference was made to Dr. Lunn's salary, and the question was asked, what had he done with the surplus? Has Dr. Lunn obtained any further light on that point?—(Answer: I have no further light.) Then I should like to direct Dr. Lunn's attention to a paragraph that appeared in The *Methodist Times* on June 13th, 1889. " Dr. Lunn " declined to receive a sum of £25 to which he was entitled as "sick allowance. The rest of his stipend was spent in providing "for his wife, his child, and himself." I suppose, therefore, that Dr. Lunn could accept this as an accurate statement?—(Answer: Yes.) Then I arrive at this result—that as a simple matter of fact the whole of your sixteen months' stipend was spent in twelve months, in providing for yourself, your wife, and your child?

Dr. LUNN: Yes, that is so. Yesterday I said that I brought presents home with me, that I had spent money in riding lessons, £8 in telegrams, Rs. 250 over a carriage, etc.— generally speaking, the amount was spent over myself and family.

Professor PATTERSON: I presume that these items in their total would not exceed the amount of debt that you left behind you in India?

Dr. LUNN: That word "debt" is somewhat misleading. I did as all missionaries do in leaving India suddenly; I put all my effects, horse, carriage, etc., into the hands of my successor, the Rev. F. W. Gostick, and he advanced me what money I required. I brought away £20 in my pocket, but remitted him a balance of £30 deficiency after he had made up my accounts.

Professor PATTERSON: Dr. Lunn adduces his own expenditure as an example of what it should cost a missionary to live in India. Did he, or did he not, live in India at the rates he has himself laid down for others?

Dr. LUNN: No, I did not.

Sir GEO. CHUBB: On page 17 of the "Summary Statement" it is stated that an answer is forthcoming that will finally dispose of these objections.

Mr. HUGHES: We hold that the Methodist Episcopal Church of America *does employ* missionaries at rates actually lower than those which we had suggested in the *via media*, and that is the answer.

Professor PATTERSON: Dr. Lunn, I have received your denial on the general question of total salary. Now I wish to inquire a little more minutely into the more important items of your expenditure. Some time ago you told me that you lived at the rate of Rs. 60 when you were living at Tiruvalur. Suppose we were to take that estimate, are you prepared to abide by it? I press this question because in the whole of the "Summary Statement" it is set forth that your experience is set forth as genuine and real, and as the ground on which Missionary Societies should found their policy. It is relevant that this experience should be thoroughly sifted. But you have given me another and somewhat different statement. Are you prepared to stand by it?

Dr. LUNN: I know nothing about it.

Professor PATTERSON: I can show you your letters.

Mr. HUGHES: What does Professor Patterson mean by saying that Dr. Lunn has abandoned his former statement?

Professor PATTERSON: I do not say that Dr. Lunn has abandoned any estimate, but that he has abandoned a record of his experience. I want to know whether Dr. Lunn abides by that record of his experience that lies before us? If he does abide by it, then I think it is perfectly right that we should press him to give us some idea of how he spent the balance of his income. If his memory is at fault on one side, I submit that it may be at fault equally on the other side. I will ask Dr. Lunn whether, in all the particulars of his experience in India, he is prepared to stand by the record of that experience which is entered in the "Summary Statement?" If he is, then he should have come home with £200 in his pocket. I want Dr. Lunn to make some approximate statement to this Committee of the use he made of that money. If he can explain that, he can justify this estimate; if not, it is worthless.

Mr. BRUNYATE: If Dr. Lunn would explain that, it would greatly relieve my mind. Dr. Lunn's position is simply a mystery to me.

Dr. LUNN: I said yesterday that I had no cash account, and that I had no wish to "cook" one.

Mr. FINDLAY: Most sums of money in India are paid by cheque, perhaps the cheque-book would help you?

Dr. LUNN: I am exceedingly sorry, but I have not kept them. I have been in lodgings since my return home, and subject to much inconvenience. The result is that every paper I could possibly put out of the way has been destroyed.

Mr. BRUNYATE: How is it Dr. Lunn's memory is so retentive on such a series of facts as we find stated here, and that he has no recollection of items of a much larger amount?

Dr. LUNN: Mrs. Lunn and myself discussed the question, and we came to the conclusion that, so far as food was concerned, we could live on 15s. a week.

Mr. BRUNYATE: Is Dr. Lunn able to tell us what has become of the bank-books and cheque-books?

Dr. LUNN: I can't find them anywhere.

Mr. BRUNYATE: Have you any impression as to what has become of this class of documents?

Dr. LUNN: I remember having these documents in my possession when I arrived in this country; but I will give the Committee an idea how I was living here for a long time. For the convenience of the West London Mission I remained in lodgings, and had one room for study, dining room and drawing room. I had a side-table in my room, which had to be used for all purposes. I had a great deal of writing of various kinds, papers accumulated, and I cleared them away from time to time, never dreaming that these things would be needed again.

Mr. HUGHES: We had precisely a similar case with Mr. Kendall this morning. My conviction is that the items on these cases have been kept by a careful wife, and the others are not available because the husband has not kept an account of his expenditure.

The PRESIDENT: The account which Mr. Kendall read was from his own book.

Mr. HUGHES: There is nothing in this book to which Dr. Lunn commits himself excepting the items on which he and his wife are agreed. The other items do not in the least affect this estimate. A careful account seems to have been kept of the household expenditure, but no account was kept of other expenditure.

The PRESIDENT: Can Mrs. Lunn tell what became of the balance of £203 that ought to have remained after paying your expenses?

Dr. LUNN: Mrs. Lunn did not keep any account but her own private account. These items occur to me now:—In the first place I lost Rs. 250 on the carriage I left behind. Then I sold a horse at a sacrifice of Rs. 50; I paid Rs. 25 for riding lessons; I paid Rs. 115 for telegrams to England. I spent on my journey to Madras, when I took my wife and servants with me, Rs. 100. I spent a similar sum on the return journey. I paid Rs. 45 for half a month's rent, at Leith Castle in Madras. I paid for a *tête-à-tête* tea service Rs. 15. We spent a good deal of money over hardware and that kind of thing. It is only fair to myself to say that in the Conference Report of the Methodist Episcopal Church, to which Professor Patterson has made reference, it states the first two years of a man's residence are the most expensive, because he is settling. I know that I spent a great deal of money in Madras during these first three weeks, in buying various little things for the house. I went over twice to visit Mr. Little specially. I took another journey to Madras, which cost me Rs. 15. There were other expenses in landing in the boat. Then when I stayed in the houses of missionaries I gave presents to the different servants, and some of these were rather heavy. I think there was an idea amongst the brethren that we had more money than we had. Then I went to the American Mission, and stayed a night there. All this kind of life was very expensive; in fact, my life in India in consequence of my sickness was almost one long tour. This "journal" was a considerable item of expense. I used to send it home, and it cost Rs. 3 every month. The postage came to about Rs. 40. I spent a good deal over the paper—that would cost, perhaps, Rs. 30 or Rs. 40 more. In addition to this I carried on a voluminous correspondence, writing four or six letters every week. I ordered some wire mattresses on the advice of my Chairman, when I went to stay with him at Karur. These are some of the items of my expenditure.

Professor PATTERSON: I am quite prepared to give Dr. Lunn the fullest credit that can be derived from the answers that he has now given the Committee, but there is one thing that I desire to point out clearly, viz., that almost every one of those items are such as might easily fall upon any brother in India—they are not therefore to be regarded as being very extraordinary. But I will drop this matter now. We have gone into it sufficiently. Let me take up a matter that springs out of it. Dr. Lunn has told us that the estimate given in the "Summary Statement" is one based upon the conclusions that he and his wife arrived at while they were in India, and with the knowledge of Indian life fresh in their memories. May I ask at what period of his Indian life he gathered his experience of independent life in India?

Dr. LUNN: It was all the way through. I cannot admit that at any point of my life in India I was not learning.

Professor PATTERSON: You told us that your conclusions as to the cost of living were arrived at when you were living at Leith Castle. It follows that at that time your mind was made up as to what should be the cost of a missionary in India.

Dr. LUNN: I did not intend the Committee to understand that my conclusions were arrived at long before they were formulated.

Professor PATTERSON: I hold in my hand a postscript to a letter addressed to the General Secretaries, dated August 18th, 1888 (it is not in Dr. Lunn's journal), and in this letter Dr. Lunn gives an account of a minor District Meeting that was held at Trichinopoly, from which there went forth a distinct and definite request to the General Committee. This is your account of it:—"The meeting with my full concurrence decided " . . . . that Mr. Little should write to the Committee, " insisting upon a minimum grant of £1,000 to commence my " work at Kumbakonam; an annual grant of £100 a year, for at

" least five years, to sustain the work thus begun, besides an
" *addition to the district grant of £350 per annum to cover my*
" *allowances.*" I ask Dr. Lunn (on the basis of his own calculation) whether at the time he wrote that letter, he was of opinion that the request which he then made to the Committee was a reasonable and proper request. Dr. Lunn at that date had spent more than three-fourths of his term of residence in India; he had witnessed the style in which his brother missionaries lived, and was as well acquainted with it as he is now, and yet he consented to ask from this Committee the sum of £350 for his allowances! I again ask, did Dr. Lunn at that time think that he was making a reasonable and appropriate request?

Dr. LUNN: I mentioned that sum because it was the average sum allowed to a married man. I had not then come to the conclusion that I have since formulated.

Mr. FINDLAY: Supposing that Dr. Lunn had lived at Tiruvalur for one year in the style which he says he adopted during four months, would his expenditure for such a year have been that which is here estimated in the " Summary Statement?"

Dr. LUNN: I had not committed myself to this estimate at that time. I think I ought to say this; I had only been a few weeks at Tiruvalur before I had an attack of fever, but even then the cost of " keeping house " seemed to me to be so small, that I wrote to my chairman and said that I should like to have a chapel as well as a dispensary for the people—there was room in the compound—it could be erected at a cost of about Rs. 200, and I intended to put it up at my own expense. That is an illustration of how exceedingly comfortable I felt with regard to my finances.

Mr. FINDLAY: But supposing that another missionary had lived at Tiruvalur in the style in which Dr. Lunn lived there, does Dr. Lunn's estimate here mean that the total cost for the year for that missionary need not have been more than £140 or £150?

Dr. LUNN: My opinion is that it would have been possible for a missionary to have lived on the sum stated in " the *Via Media.*" It is quite true that during the few months of my own experience in India I did not live within that sum; nevertheless, I regarded the policy as a possible one.

The PRESIDENT: Why did you regard it as a policy to be recommended when it was not a policy to be adopted?

Dr. LUNN: I was much troubled about the social gulf between the missionaries and the natives, and if I had had my health and strength and had remained in India for any length of time, I should myself have developed a life on some such lines as I have stated. I say on page 96 of my journal, when referring to the Salvation Army:—" This Indian Salvation " Army experiment is based absolutely on the principle of self- " sacrifice, and herein lies its great strength. Our friends at " home may be kind enough to believe that our ordinary " missionaries are 'offering ourselves up,' &c., in coming out " here, but it does not present itself thus to the average native " mind. Taking all the great English Missionary Societies, " S.P.G., C.M.S., Wesleyan, London Missionary, Baptist, and " Presbyterian, the average missionary income is about £300 a " year and a house. I am sure that no one at home will think " that this is a penny too much, and from the English " standpoint it certainly is not. But how does it look " to the natives? Three hundred pounds, at the present rate " of exchange, is Rs. 4,500, and the average wages of the agri- " cultural labourer here are Rs. 4 a month. It will thus be " seen at once that our incomes bear the same relation to those " of the working classes here that the Bishop of Lincoln's " income does to that of the Lincolnshire peasant. . . . And " what is true for England is true for India." Then I go on to say: " Some of my correspondents will ask at once, ' Then " ' why don't you save the Missionary Society Rs. 4,400 per annum, and live in this fashion?' The answer is very simple, and it is just this: " That I am not so imbued with the " spirit of self-sacrifice as to be prepared to kill myself and " my wife at once," &c. I had several conversations with Mr. Simpson about the Salvationists, and we discussed the whole situation, and we felt that the Salvationists were a standing criticism upon our methods. In this passage are contained the two premises of my present position. The Salvationist method was an ascetic extreme. Our style of living separated us from the natives. My point is that at the time my ideas were in a state of flux. They were by no means formed.

Professor PATTERSON: I have only one more question to ask. Dr. Lunn has quoted his journal to us, and from that journal he has argued that, on the one hand, he condemned the asceticism of the Salvation Army, and on the other he condemned the luxury of ordinary missionary life, and therefore his approval of the *Via Media :* What was the date of that entry in his journal?

Dr. LUNN: May 18.

Professor PATTERSON: Then that would justify me in saying that in April he professes to have come to his conclusions? Now for a letter to Mr. Little. It contains this passage :— " Indeed it comes to me at the present juncture that it would "be wrong for me to stay any longer, costing as I do £30 a "month to the Society for all the time I spend here, and doing "practically nothing to repay them." Now for so great an expenditure, I should like to ask why he should continue to insist upon a style that was needless if he had come to the conclusion that he could live much more cheaply consistently with health and strength?

Dr. LUNN: The quotation had reference to this fact: The whole question then was, whether I should go home at once, or whether I should continue in a state of doubt and hesitancy doing nothing, and receiving the ordinary allowances.

Professor PATTERSON: The letter is dated "August 26th, 1888."

Dr. LUNN: It was simply dealing with the fact that I was costing the Society a great deal of money. I certainly did not write with any idea that I should institute a reform. The whole question was whether Mr. Little should keep me in suspense. It was practically certain that I should not stay, and I mentioned £30 a month because every month I was kept there meant a loss to the Society to that extent. The result was that I remained in India three months longer, at a cost to the Society of £90 more than I should have done if Mr. Little had taken my advice. If during that time I had attempted to institute a reform it would have been a most mad proceeding.

Professor PATTERSON: May I correct Dr. Lunn's statement by a reference to another quotation in his own handwriting dated August 18th:—"The meeting, with my full concurrence, "decided that, in view of the great improvement in my health "since the dispatch of my telegram, resulting from the three "weeks' stay with Rev. F. W. Gostick at Manargudi, Mr. "Little should telegraph writing, 'Lunn better.'"

Dr. LUNN: Well, just at that time I wrote:—"I have immensely improved; should have nothing to complain of if my eczema did not keep me in my easy chair."

Professor PATTERSON: I do not say that Dr. Lunn was in robust health. This passage simply shows that Dr. Lunn was at that time in the enjoyment of such a state of health as led him fully to concur with the Minor District Meeting proposing a further stay in the country. On this question of finance I do not think I have any further questions to ask Dr. Lunn, but I have many other points on which I must question him.

Mr. HUGHES asked Dr. Lunn whether at the time of the Minor District Meeting referred to he had financially reached the conclusion stated in detail in the "Summary Statement," or whether his mind was still in a state of flux?

Dr. LUNN: No; I had not at that time reached any definite conclusion.

Mr. HUGHES: Am I to understand that during the whole of that time your opinion was slowly growing in this direction, but that up to the time you left India your opinions were not so formed as they have been since?

Dr. LUNN: Yes.

Mr. HUGHES: Had you then formulated the opinion which you announce here?

Dr. LUNN: No.

Mr. HUGHES: Then it is not a fact that you went on in India deliberately receiving this larger stipend after you had reached the conclusion stated in this journal?

Dr. LUNN: My attitude was this: I was strongly convinced that something must be done to bring the missionaries nearer the natives.

The PRESIDENT: The answers that Mr. Hughes has elicited are these: that so long as you were on the mission field you thought the allowance should be so much, but that after you came home your views altered. That is to say, when you were in India yourself, you and Mrs. Lunn did not live on the allowances you recommend, but after you returned to England, and had not to live in India, you were of opinion that the missionaries who remained, and those who succeeded you, ought to have the lesser amount.

Mr. HUGHES: Did Dr. Lunn continue to believe up to the time that he left India that his income was any more than a missionary ought to receive?

Dr. LUNN: I felt that the whole style of living was open to criticism.

Mr. HUGHES: Then are we to understand this, not that your mind remained at ease, but that you were feeling your way, groping for some definite conclusion that you had not finally reached?

Dr. LUNN: Yes.

Mr. BRUNYATE: Dr. Lunn has said that his mind was in a state of agitation and flux for a good part of the time. I want to know from the Indian brethren whether they ever received from Dr. Lunn himself any indication that the stipend of missionaries ought to be reduced?

Professor PATTERSON: I can answer for myself. Dr. Lunn never mentioned any such desire or expressed any such opinion to me. I knew nothing of it at all until I saw it in print.

Dr. LUNN: Does not Mr. Findlay remember me discussing this subject with him?

Mr. FINDLAY: I remember vaguely that there were conversations with Dr. Lunn with reference to the cost and style of living of the missionaries; but I certainly never derived any impression from such conversations that Dr. Lunn seriously thought it possible that any other style of living should be adopted.

Dr. LUNN: Do you remember that I said at Negapatam that I felt we were to the natives in the position of English bishops?

Mr. FINDLAY: I remember some such remark, but I had no impression beyond this, that it was uttered as a superficial paradox.

Dr. LUNN: But this "bishop" illustration involves the whole thing.

Mr. SMITH: I do not think this conversation brings us very much nearer the subject matter we have to inquire into. It may be interesting, but it does not affect the truth or otherwise of the statement we have to inquire into. It has been openly admitted that Dr. Lunn never contemplated adopting this style of living himself, and that the figures given us in the *Via Media* are to a great extent speculative figures.

In reply to a question by Mr. Pope,

Dr. LUNN said he had not expended the sum of £200, of which he had preserved no accounts, in any way that a minister or missionary might not rightly spend money, arising from the voluntary contributions given by our people for missionary purposes. In the *Via Media* estimate he had allowed £9 per annum for these contingencies.

Mr. ALLEN: I should like to ask about this associating with the natives. Dr. Lunn seems to put the whole pressure upon stipends and style of living. I should like to ask whether it did not occur to him, in thinking upon this subject, how much was necessarily due to social customs and habits of life? So far as I understand it, Dr. Lunn has not brought out that aspect of the case in any sense whatever.

Mr. HUGHES, in reply to the question of the President, whether he had not come to the conclusion that the social status is not affected by the amount of income the missionary has, said:—My view is that if the missionaries lived in the native villages, and in a different style, it would facilitate evangelistic work amongst the poor.

Mr. ALLEN: Another point should be noted. Dr. Lunn said

that at a certain date he knew he was already wanted in the London Mission. I want to know what that means?

Mr. HUGHES: I may explain that. It was the result of a conversation between Dr. Jenkins and myself; and I now ask Dr. Lunn whether I did not in every communication I sent to him, urge him to stay in India if he could possibly, but as the medical testimony was to the effect that he could not stay there, I asked if he would come to London?

Dr. LUNN: When I went to India, I anticipated remaining there, and my conviction is that I should have remained in India for a long time, had my health remained good.

The Committee adjourned at 8.10 p.m.

Fourth Day, Friday, May 30th.

The Committee met at 10 a.m. Prayer was offered by the Rev. Jno. Rhodes.

The PRESIDENT asked Mr. Hughes if he had any documentary evidence to present.

Mr. HUGHES: I have received the following:—

Letter from Mr. W. S. Caine, M.P.

2, STOREY'S GATE, S.W.,
May 29*th*.

DEAR DR. LUNN,
In reply to your letter of 17th, I want you to understand distinctly that I do not for a moment grudge the missionary in India all the comforts, and luxuries too, that he can get, consistent with the duty devolving upon the Committees at home of administering the money entrusted to them with rigid economy.

There can be no doubt, I think, that the position of your missionaries in India, all round, is better in every way than that of your ministers at home. Any one with any knowledge of the low cost of living in India must know that. The real difficulty in India lies in the "style." It is that, and not comforts or even luxuries, that runs away with money. If missionaries were ready and willing to get among the natives socially, and find their recompense in their generous recognition of such equality as ought to be the leading feature of Christianity, which would be evoked from the natives, all this necessity for "style" would disappear. I suppose I need not point out what you have probably discovered for yourself, that many of the agents of American Missionary Societies, who undoubtedly get more into the hearts and affections of their converts than any other, live in comfort in India upon far less than the allowances and salaries paid by your Society.

I have read all you say about the cost of living in India. I am not prepared, driven as I am just now by this Compensation fight, to criticise your details very closely, as that would require more careful reference to notes taken in India than I can give; but I think I have already supplied you with sufficient evidence from different parts of South India with regard to the market prices of the necessaries and luxuries of life to justify you in the estimates you have formed. I have no hesitation in saying that a single man can get all he needs in India in as good "style" and as much comfort as he would get in England, as an unmarried minister, for £70 a year, if he boarded with a married missionary, in company with not less than three other unmarried men, the *four* could get all they want in the way of comfort, good food, clothing, &c., for £200—£50 each.

The most comfortable house in which I stayed in India was a missionary's. He and his wife employed two *Christian* servants, who did all the work of the house, a roomy and very pleasant brick bungalow. He told me that his expenses for food and clothing for himself and his wife, and the wages of his two servants and one gardener, never exceeded £100 in any year.

However, I am sure you are well posted for your discussion, which I hope will be public and reported. I have no desire to get drawn into the missionary controversy. I have said my say last year. You, Hughes, and Champness must fight the controversy out. You are doing God's work, and will have His blessing.

May He guide us by His Holy Spirit in this and all things.

Ever yours,
W. S. CAINE.

Mr. ALLEN: Is there any evidence that Mr. Caine himself went into the native quarters and studied the conditions of native life, or does the letter that has just been read convey simply the impressions that he received in driving through India, and whilst conversing here and there with friends? Another criticism is this: If we were to bind ourselves to the standard of expenditure which Mr Caine's letter indicates, we should have no freedom in working the province, for as a rule we cannot afford to have three or four men living and working together.

Mr. HUGHES: The suggestion alluded to has reference to unmarried ministers. But the main point of this letter in my judgment is the question of "style."

Mr. FINDLAY: Does Mr. Caine give the names of the American Societies to which those missionaries belonged who lived in comfort on much less than the amount given to Wesleyan missionaries?

Mr. HUGHES: He does not give the names, but I think he refers to the Methodist Episcopal Church.

Dr. LUNN read the following letter:—

Letter from A. R. Bulman, Esq.
(Late Deputy Commissioner, Bengal Civil Service.)

26, THE CRESCENT EAST,
BEECH HILL PARK, BARNET.
May 26th, 1890.

DEAR DR. LUNN,

I have read the statement you kindly sent me, and I fully concur in your opinion that the rates of stipends and allowances of missionaries in India, as given therein, are unnecessarily high. I have had no personal experience of the cost of living in any part of India except the Bengal Presidency, and indeed practically my knowledge is confined to the Punjab, where I spent all but about two of the 28 years I have lived in India as a member of the Civil Service. I have no hesitation in saying that "an average income of £300 and a bungalow," with extra allowances for children, is excessive beyond all reasonable needs which a missionary in India can have. Officers in my own service (which is regarded as a highly paid one) begin their career on no higher pay than that, and though a large number of them marry very early in their service, I do not believe that (at any rate for the first 10 or 12 years) they generally spend more than that amount on their every day expenses; the rest of their salaries as they gradually increase, is saved up to pay the cost of furloughs and of sending their children home for education. And it will be easily understood that district officials have considerable necessary expenses from which missionaries are free, *e.g.*, entertaining and keeping up a larger or smaller stable, according to the requirements of their work. Coming now to the items of expense which you have considered in detail:—

1. Cost of food.—According to prices prevailing generally in Northern India, your estimate is certainly under the mark. I have calculated the cost of a daily provision rather less liberal than that which you give on page 13, that is, I have allowed for no meat at lunch, and only one dish of meat at dinner; and I make it 21 shillings a week instead of your figure, 15 shillings.

2. Cost of servants.—Under this head my estimate is rather under yours, viz:—

	Rs.	
Cook	8	a month.
Khitmutgar	8	,,
Sweeper	5	,,
4 Punkah Coolies for 6 months ...	8	,,
	Rs. 29 = 39 shillings.	

about £24 a year.

3. Cost of clothing and house linen, &c.—I find it impossible to make any definite estimate under these heads; but, certainly, I found the cost of clothing, both for myself and my wife and children, much less in India than in England.

This is chiefly owing to the cheapness of labour in the former country. I should mention that in my list of servants I have omitted water carrier* and washerman, as I understood you to say they are provided by the Mission.

Hoping that the above may be of some use to you,

Believe me, yours truly,

A. R. BULMAN,
Bengal Civil Service (Retired).

The PRESIDENT: That letter goes to the effect that a missionary is overpaid if in the full discharge of his duties he receives as much as the lowest pay of a civil officer. I would advise you to read that letter again very carefully. It is a letter that is very strong in the other direction.

Mr. HUGHES: Then by all means put it in. But I am sure, Mr. President, that you entirely misunderstand what I have just read, as you will see when the letter is in print. Mr. Bulman argues that if a member of the Civil Service can live in the greatest comfort and luxury with all the demands made

---

* My water carrier was paid by the Mission. The laundry included under the cost of clothing.—H. S. L.

upon him on an average income of £300 and a bungalow, a missionary could do the same.

Mr. BRUNYATE: I do not accept Mr. Bulman's testimony as to allowances as complete. I think it quite misleading.

Mr. ALLEN: There is another point. The question has reference to a married man with children. Dr. Lunn proposes that the allowances for children shall be increased. But I should like to ask whether the allowances for children either in this country or in India pay the cost of children? Does Mr. Hughes spend no more upon his children than the amount he receives for them?

Mr. HUGHES: I think that living where we do it is probable that the allowances we receive for them do not cover their cost. But we suggested that that matter should be specially dealt with.

Mr. ALLEN: But if that be the fact, it is only fair that that should be taken into calculation in estimating the stipend. It has also come out in evidence that the allowance for keeping the missionary's house is not sufficient in hardly any case.

Mr. SMITH: Mr. Hughes has once or twice made use of the expression, "the greatest comfort and luxury." Are those the words made use of by Mr. Bulman?

Mr. HUGHES; No; they are my own. Mr. Bulman's words are these:—"I have no hesitation in saying that an average "income of £300 and a bungalow, with extra allowances for "children, is excessive beyond all reasonable needs which a "missionary in India can have. Officers in my own service "(which is regarded as a highly paid one) begin their career on no higher pay than that."

Professor PATTERSON: I should like to say that we might have brought (had we been desirous of doing so) any amount of evidence of a directly opposite kind, from members of the Civil Service in India. We did not do so because on page 8 of the "Summary Statement," Mr. Hughes says:—"We might add here, "while speaking of different kinds of witnesses, that there is "another class in India whose testimony as a class would also "be of little value on this question. We refer of course to official "Anglo-Indian Society." We thought the same method of disparagement might be used in reference to their testimony on any point.

Mr. HUGHES: The two cases are perfectly distinct. I have not asked Mr. Bulman to express any opinion as to the relation of English missionaries to the natives. I merely wished him, as a matter of fact, to tell me what he thought was a sufficient amount of money to enable a missionary to live in comfort, and I limited the inquiry to that point.

Mr. BRUNYATE: There are two or three questions I should like to put to Dr. Lunn :—

    1. Did he and Mrs. Lunn keep accounts of their expenditure in India?—(Answer: Mrs. Lunn kept accounts of her household expenditure.)

    2. Were those accounts brought to this country?—(Answer: They were.)

    3. Were those accounts in Dr. Lunn's hands within the last three months?—(Answer: Certainly not.)

    4. Can Dr. Lunn tell us what has become of those accounts?—(Answer: No.)

    5. Are we to understand that in the case of bank-book, cheque-book, and account-books, and settled bills, there is absolutely nothing forthcoming?

Dr. LUNN: I am exceedingly sorry, Mr. President, but all I can say is, that Mrs. Lunn has been searching for those books and papers, and cannot find them anywhere.

Mr. BRUNYATE: I presume then that we are to accept it as settled that Dr. Lunn's "Statement" was prepared entirely from memory?

Dr. LUNN: The items respecting the cost of servants are admitted to be correct. The estimated cost of clothing has never been challenged. The only point that remains is the estimate of 15s. a-week for food, and I have stated definitely that that 15s. per week was an estimate that Mrs. Lunn and I formed when we were in Tiruvalur.

Mr. ALLEN: Still the fact remains that this paper was prepared without any documentary evidence or any statement of accounts of his own?

Dr. LUNN: Precisely.

The PRESIDENT: With the memory of this estimate which you formed with Mrs. Lunn during your residence in India?

Dr. LUNN: Yes.

The PRESIDENT: Then have you no hope of placing your hands on these documents?

Dr. LUNN: Every place has been ransacked in the hope of finding some of these documents.

Mr. FLETCHER: Mrs. Geden told me yesterday that she found an error in one of her statements here. Her estimate for stores for the year was for two people. It should have been stated that for one of the months it was for four people, so that so far as her estimate for stores for April is concerned it must be doubled.

Professor PATTERSON: I am responsible for that error. It will be in the memory of the Committee that when Mrs. Geden was asked to give the cost of stores for a particular month she said she could not. I suggested she should take one-twelfth of the yearly amount. She says in a letter I will read:—"In "April, 1888, Dr. and Mrs. Lunn were living with us, so the "stores for the month for four people would be Rs. 52. This "added to the Rs. 120 for cook's book, make Rs. 172 for food "for the month. Of course the bare account of cost of food "does not represent all the extra expense involved in "entertaining visitors for weeks at a time."

Mr. ALLEN: I have tried all through this discussion to bear in mind what, in my estimation, is a very important fact, that this criticism is really a criticism of missionary policy for India, including not only our own Church, but all other Churches. Now I should like to ask Dr. Lunn whether in these references to style of living, &c., he had in mind anybody in other Churches living in a grander style than men in our own Church? I think that is only a fair thing to take into calculation. We are looking at the subject very much from a Methodist stand-point, but still we must not overlook the wider stand-point.

Dr. LUNN: I did bear in mind very distinctly that the Scotch Societies, for instance, prepared statistics some twelve years ago, and in a statement that has been submitted by the other side reference has been made to the fact that I included the London Missionary Society. A list was published entitled "Conference of Missionaries, prepared in 1878, for private use." I had this in my possession, and I went carefully through it to obtain my averages from it, so that I was not speaking purely haphazard. Some of these estimates are very much higher than my own. For instance, the Established Church of Scotland gives as high as £600 a year, and knowing the style that was possible for a Wesleyan missionary, I recognised that a still greater style was possible amongst the ministers of the Established Church of Scotland. But I have very little experience of other societies.

Mr. HUGHES: I am glad that Mr. Allen has raised this point, because we stated that our criticism had reference to other Societies rather than our own. My statements referred to all Societies, and very much more to some than to our own. With respect to the Established Church of Scotland, which I believe pays more than any other Society, I may say that I have reason to believe there have recently been great reductions of the allowances.

The PRESIDENT asked if Mr. Patterson had any further questions to ask Dr. Lunn?

Professor PATTERSON: I have one or two questions still to ask. The first has reference to a subject that I should not have felt it necessary to touch upon if Dr. Lunn had not gone out of his way to introduce it into the evidence which he has submitted to the Committee. If the Committee will turn to Dr. Lunn's printed journal, page 87, they will find that Dr. Lunn there refers to certain misconceptions that had arisen respecting an application which it had been stated that he had made to the authorities of the Christian College, Madras, for temporary employment in that College. Dr. Lunn then went on to print two private letters of his, addressed to the Rev. Arthur Hoyle in July, 1888. I wish to ask Dr. Lunn whether his reference to this subject, accompanied by the letters to Mr. Hoyle, is to be taken as a contradiction of the statement that he had applied to the Christian College?

Dr. LUNN: The reference is to the statement that I was a disappointed candidate, and my object was to disprove disappointment and chagrin.

Professor PATTERSON: Then may I call Dr. Lunn's attention to a statement which appeared in the *Methodist Times* of June 13th, 1889, when that fact was first brought before the public? viz:—

"Mr. Hartley is next reported to have said that one of the professors at the Madras Christian College having died, Dr. Lunn applied for the post, and could not get it. It was then 'a case of the fox and the grapes,' and he came home to denounce the educational system. Every part of this statement is untrue. No professor died. Dr. Lunn did not apply for the vacant post. He did not fail to get it. The real facts are as follows:—Dr. Lunn was sent to India as a medical missionary. In the small town to which he was sent there was a well-built Government Dispensary; and he could not do his work as a medical missionary unless he had a hospital, at an estimated cost of about £1,000. The Missionary Committee being in want of money at that time, was hesitating to make so large a special grant for medical purposes. Professor Patterson, of the Madras College, being aware of all the circumstances, kindly suggested to Dr. Lunn that he should act as *locum tenens* for Professor Michie Smith, the Professor of Chemistry and Physics, who was about to have a two years' furlough. That would enable Dr. Lunn to save his own allowances of £300 a year for two years, that is to say, he could save £600, which might be used to build a medical hospital for his own permanent work. Despairing of getting the money from home, Dr Lunn was inclined to look favourably at the suggestion; although if he had gone to the College for the two years, he would simply have received the stipend of an unmarried man."

I wish to ask Dr. Lunn whether or not he assumes the responsibility of that paragraph?

Dr. LUNN: I did not write it myself, but I did, later on, assume the responsibility of its substantial accuracy. The whole point at issue was that I wished to repudiate "the fox and the grapes" illustration.

Professor PATTERSON said it was not yet clear whether Dr. Lunn had intended to deny the application itself, or only the disappointment. He must press the point, for it was important. All the world had understood the statement to mean that Dr. Lunn denied the application, and the *Methodist Times*, a few weeks later, had stated categorically:—"Dr. Lunn "was never a candidate for employment in Dr. Miller's college," and had virulently attacked Dr. Miller for making the statement. He would ask Dr. Lunn to refresh his memory from one of his own letters. The letter, which he handed to Dr. Lunn, was the covering letter of his application to Dr. Miller. (The letter was handed to Dr. Lunn).

Mr. HUGHES stated at this point that Dr. Lunn was in no sense responsible for the second statement in the *Methodist Times*. That note appeared when Dr. Lunn was in Devonshire, and Dr. Lunn knew nothing about it until he saw it in print.

Mr. FOWLER said he did not see what connection all this had with the subject which the Committee was engaged in investigating.

Professor PATTERSON submitted that it shed important light upon the accuracy of Dr. Lunn's recollections of his Indian life. It had already been elicited that all Dr. Lunn's accounts of his life in India were based upon memory, entirely unsupported by any contemporary documentary evidence. That being so, and Dr. Lunn being put forward by Mr. Hughes as his chief witness, any inquiry into the accuracy of Dr. Lunn's recollections was exceedingly relevant.

Mr. FOWLER did not accept the statement that Dr. Lunn was the chief witness. The Committee would go into the matter on evidence altogether independent.

Mr. BRUNYATE did not agree with Mr. Fowler. Dr. Lunn's testimony was before the world as evidence in support of the possibility of the *Via Media*. The example of his own life was given at great length in the "Summary Statement," and therefore he thought that it was right, as Dr. Lunn's account of his life was confessedly based on memory, that this subject should be gone into fully.

Mr. ALLEN regarded the question as one of great importance, and hoped that it would be completely sifted.

Mr. HUGHES said that as Mr. Patterson had introduced this subject, he must ask the Committee to hear him at length upon it before they dismissed it.

Mr. FOWLER asked that the room might be cleared whilst the Committee considered the point.

This was accordingly done. The doors were opened again in a quarter of an hour.

The PRESIDENT asked Mr. Hughes if he had any statement to make?

Mr. HUGHES said he believed that Mr. Patterson had something to say on the matter.

Mr. PATTERSON was quite prepared to let the matter drop. He understood Dr. Lunn to state that what he intended to deny was not the fact of the application, on which his recollection was not clear, but the disappointment, and that now that he had seen his own letters, Dr. Lunn acknowledged that he had applied. If that were so, he had no more to say. He had dwelt upon the subject only to show that Dr. Lunn's memory was not to be relied upon. He did not himself draw, nor did he wish the Committee to draw, any other inference whatever.

Mr. HUGHES said that his sole object was to prove that Dr. Lunn had not been guilty of the slightest untruthfulness. He was prepared to prove the accuracy of the statements in the *Methodist Times*. But as Mr. Patterson disclaimed all moral imputation upon Dr. Lunn, he (Mr. Hughes) would not occupy the time of the Committee by discussing the incident in detail.

Inferior status of Native Ministers.

Professor PATTERSON: I have now a remark to make in reference to what appears in the "Summary Statement," page 9, where Mr. Hughes dwells upon the inferior status of native ministers in the District Meetings. I should like to ask Mr. Hughes if he made any attempt to obtain accurate information on that matter? Before stating that "native ministers are excluded from half the deliberations of the annual District Meeting," did he make any application for the real facts of the case to the Mission House?—(Answer: No.) Then on what ground did Mr. Hughes make his statement?—(Answer: I had the statement of Dr. Lunn, and other statements made in casual ways.)

Workmen's Wages.

Professor PATTERSON referred the Committee to page 17 of the "Summary Statement," where the following passage occurs:

"Mr. W. S. Betts, of the South Indian Railway Company, writes from Trichinopoly, under date February 14th, 1890, to say that the 'maximum pay' drawn by an engine-driver is 'Rs. 200 per mensem,' and further states that *no free houses or other allowances are found by the Company*." He (Professor Patterson) asked Mr. Hughes if he would kindly read Mr. Betts' letter to the Committee, or at least that portion of it which he had quoted.

Mr. HUGHES: Dr. Lunn has the letter, and will read it.

Dr. LUNN: Mr. Betts writes, "Foremen receive Rs. 350 per month. The maximum pay of engine drivers is Rs. 200 per month, together with extra allowances for overtime and night work."

Professor PATTERSON: May I ask Mr. Hughes why Mr. Betts' account of the pay of foremen, and of the increase in the pay of engine drivers on account of overtime and night work, were omitted from his testimony?

Mr. HUGHES: Because I did not think the question of overtime was important.

Professor PATTERSON: And yet these suppressed passages substantiate the statements of the Bangalore Conference which you were attacking. But did not Mr. Hughes and Dr. Lunn know that the great bulk of the engine driver's work was night work?

Dr. LUNN: No: We did not know that.

The PRESIDENT: Why did not Mr. Hughes and Dr. Lunn give us the whole of Mr. Betts' sentence, instead of giving only a part, when the latter part so greatly modified the other?

Mr. HUGHES: We only professed to give an extract in our summary statement.

The PRESIDENT: "An extract!" The extract should have contained the whole truth. All that Mr. Betts wrote on the point should have been given.

Professor PATTERSON next referred the Committee to page 18 of the "Summary Statement," where a

Letter from Bishop Thoburn

was quoted. He would ask Mr. Hughes if Bishop Thoburn did not send him in connection with that letter a copy of the Cawnpore Report, and whether a copy of that report was not in his hand at the time that quotation was made?

Dr. LUNN: No. That report was sent from Calcutta on March 7th, so that it would get to England at the beginning of April, about the time that the "Summary Statement" was published, but not before that document was in print.

Professor PATTERSON: But the "Summary Statement" was not published till the Saturday before the General Committee met, *i.e.*, Saturday, April 19th.

Professor PATTERSON informed the Committee that the rates of pay adopted by the Methodist Episcopal Church of America, as stated in Bishop Thoburn's letter, were condemned by the Cawnpore Report.

Professor PATTERSON then laid the Report of the Cawnpore Conference upon the table, and the following passage was read to the Committee :—

"Your Committee, after very deliberate examination of the "*pros* and *cons*, recommend that the scale of salaries long in "use in the North India Conference, be the scale of salaries for "all the Conferences and Missions represented in this Central "Conference. We may state in brief the reasons on which we "base this recommendation :—

"1.—Long continued observation has proved that "this scale of salaries has been barely adequate to "maintain the missionary in moderate comfort and in "efficiency. The salary is worth much less than it was "fifteen years ago. It is upon the whole cheaper to live "in the territory of the North Indian Conference than "in the territory represented by other parts of our work. "Hence the salary is not too much for any part of the "field.

"2.—We reached the conclusion that to adopt a lower "scale of salary would work to our detriment in securing "the class of recruits desirable for our entire field."

Mr. HUGHES said that he had not read that report. His object had been to print the actual facts, as officially reported to him by Bishop Thoburn and Dr. Peck.

Mr. FOWLER: Who is Dr. Peck ?—The corresponding missionary secretary of the Methodist Episcopal Church.

Professor PATTERSON stated that Bishop Thoburn's letter of July 12, 1889, showed that the figures given by Dr. Peck on pages 18, 19, of the "Summary Statement" were incorrect. Instead of £122 for a married missionary, the uniform rate according to Bishop Thoburn was £168.

Sir GEO. CHUBB asked whether Mr. Hughes admitted the truth of this statement?

Mr. HUGHES could only say that they had printed Dr. Peck's letter in the exact form in which it had been presented to them.

They understood Bishop Thoburn's letter to be a suggestion as to what the rates of payment might be—or should be.

Mr. FOWLER asked : Is it true that all the American ministers receive £168 instead of some of them receiving £122, as stated by Dr. Peck?—I do not know whether the suggested uniform rate has or has not been adopted by the Committee of Management in New York.

The London Missionary Society and the Wesleyan Methodist Missionary Society.

Professor PATTERSON asked Mr. Hughes whether at the time he published his Postscript to the "Summary Statement" in the *Methodist Times* of May 1st, 1890, he knew that the London missionaries were permitted to send home money at par?

Mr. HUGHES said that he had taken that circumstance partially into account, but not wholly, and therefore his statement should be slightly modified. But with respect to the proportion of salary remitted home at par by the missionaries of the London Missionary Society, the following figures had been supplied to him by the Rev. R. Wardlaw Thompson, General Secretary of the Society, through whose hands all remittances passed. (See Appendix D.)

Mr. FINDLAY: I should like to ask Dr. Lunn if he has taken any steps to gather the "opinions of native Christians" referred to in the Summary Statement.

Dr. LUNN : I have written to Mr. Sattianadhan, asking him to do so, and I expect that they will arrive before Conference.

Mr. FINDLAY: I asked this question because I thought that the answer might throw light upon a passage which I will read from a letter addressed to me by my native colleague at Negapatam, the Rev. J. Ponnuswami. The letter is dated March 31, 1890, and contains the following paragraph :—

"On the 18th March (Tuesday), we went for preaching as "usual. There we found three gentlemen. In appearance, "two of them look Europeans, remainder, one, is look to be a "Eurasian. They asked us 'Are you the Wesleyan men?' "We gave in reply, 'Yes.' They said 'We received letter "' from Rev. Dr. Lunn; we are going to write reply for him. "' Write your names. Hereafter your payment and batta "' will be increased. Tell all your catechists' names and give "' their signature.' Their words were very fearful. We have "not given any reply to them."

Dr. LUNN stated that he knew nothing of the incident

described, and had not written any such letter as that mentioned.

A conversation arose on the lists of prices and the value to be attached to one list as compared with another, the result of which was that the Committee decided to compare the lists for themselves, and to form their own conclusions.

Will the decision of the Committee be final?

Mr. FOWLER asked Mr. Hughes to say whether, so far as he (Mr. Hughes) was concerned, the decision of the Committee would be the final closure of the question—not as to *policy*, but as to the unfortunate controversy that had arisen with respect to matters of fact? Was that question now to be closed, or was the battle to be fought out again?

Mr. HUGHES: All I can say is this, that I never wanted this controversy to arise at all, and that I much regret it. Had I foreseen it, I should have approached the discussion of policy from a very different point of view. I am most anxious to see the close of this controversy, and whatever the decision of this Committee is, I shall loyally accept it.

In reply to the same question,

Dr. LUNN said he presumed that the Report of the Committee would be submitted to the Conference, and possibly other matters might be brought in, but if the question was settled by that Committee, he should never re-open it.

Mr. FOWLER: We should like to look at this whole question in a peaceful spirit. Will Mr. Patterson tell us whether he and Mr. Findlay also will accept our decision?

Professor PATTERSON: I must remind the Committee that we are not exactly empowered to give a categorical reply to that question. We are only representatives, and we can only answer as far as it seems to us proper. We look forward with almost a certainty of expectation to the complete ending of this affair by the Report of this Committee, and that is what our brethren in India desire too. But of course it is impossible for us to pledge our Indian brethren to the decision of this Committee.

Mr. ALLEN: I should like Messrs. Patterson and Findlay to say that in all legitimate modes their influence will be used in that direction, because we know that great importance will be attached to their opinion.

The PRESIDENT: I will point out another thing to Mr. Patterson and Mr. Findlay, viz., that this Commission of Inquiry has been appointed in consequence of the request from the Indian missionaries, and of all people they should be the persons loyally to accept the decision of the Commission if possible.

Professor PATTERSON: And I think that the Indian missionaries *will* loyally accept it. That is as far as we can go. *We* pledge ourselves loyally to accept it. All that I mean is that we have not been put into a position to reply for all our brethren.

Dr. RIGG: I think there is a question, which, being here by the direction of the General Committee, I may put. Of course I yield to no man in the desire that this Sub-Committee's Report should be universally accepted; but are we at liberty to assume that the Committee to whom this Report will be given is bound without discussion and without any option to accept the Report?

Mr. FOWLER: Certainly not.

Dr. RIGG: I hope that brethren, if conscious on both sides of some dissatisfaction, will do violence, as far as they personally are concerned, to any natural feelings that may arise, in order that if it be possible this matter may be settled by the Committee, and may not be re-opened at the Conference. It is so important for the cause of Christianity. Many of us have had to bear a great many things that were unjust, and to bear them silently, in order that the work might go on; and though I have shown, I think, my feeling that justice must be done to the Indian missionaries, and we must have confidence in them, yet as heavenly justice is not always done even through bodies of men—if they should feel like that, I hope they will not raise the question again at the Conference.

Mr. ALLEN: The question is whether we *can* prevent it coming before the Conference?

Dr. RIGG: I don't say "come" before the Conference, but *discussed* at the Conference.

The PRESIDENT: Dr. Rigg's point is a very proper one. He appeals to the party on one side to accept the decision of this Committee in such a way that *they* will not raise it in the Conference.

Sir. GEO. CHUBB: Have Mr. Hughes and Dr. Lunn any further evidence to give us?

Mr. HUGHES: We have only some printed documents to present. They will be ready very shortly.

The room was then cleared: and after some private conversation, the Committee adjourned.

SUB-COMMITTEE ON INDIAN MISSIONS.

Report.

1.—The Sub-committee nominated by the President of the Conference, pursuant to the resolution of the Missionary Committee of April 24th, 1890, consisted of the following ministers and laymen :—

    The Rev. C. H. Kelly (President of the Conference).
    The Rev. H. J. Pope (General Chapel Secretary).
    The Rev. Wesley Brunyate (Superintendent of the Wandsworth Circuit).
    The Rev. George Fletcher (Chairman of the Bristol District).
    The Rev. Thomas Allen (Chairman of the Sheffield District).
    The Right Hon. H. H. Fowler, M.P.
    Sir George H. Chubb.
    Mr. John Clapham, J.P. (of Manchester), and
    Mr. H. Arthur Smith (Barrister-at-law, Lincoln's Inn).

The Sub-committee commenced its sessions on Tuesday, May 27th, 1890, and sat *de die in diem* for the purpose of receiving evidence on the matter submitted to it until Friday, May 30th, inclusive, and held several subsequent meetings. The President of the Conference presided. Nineteen hours were devoted to the hearing of the evidence in the case, during which every member of the Sub-committee was present.

At the first meeting Mr. H. Arthur Smith was, on the proposal of the President, elected Secretary of the Sub-committee ; and the Rev. John Rhodes was requested to take shorthand notes of the proceedings, a copy of which, together with the documentary evidence submitted, accompanies this Report.

2.—The duties of the Sub-committee were defined by the Resolution of the General Committee, by virtue of which it was appointed. This Resolution is as follows :—

    (A) "That, in the judgment of this Committee, it is "necessary for the satisfaction of the Indian missionaries, "and of the supporters of the Society, that the state-"ments made in the articles, entitled 'A New Mis-"sionary Policy,' should be thoroughly examined by an "influential Sub-committee. That a Sub-committee "of nine members be, therefore, appointed to examine "into all the facts and statements bearing upon the "position and character of the Indian missionaries, and "to report to this Committee, such Sub-committee to "have the power to request the attendance of any "witnesses, whether members of our own church or "others, and to call for documents."

(B) "That the Sub-committee shall consist of four "Ministers and four Laymen, to be nominated by the "President of the Conference, with the President "himself."

3.—The Articles referred to in the Resolution are four in number and entitled respectively :—

  i. Try Democratic Methods.
  ii. The Evils of a False Position.
  iii. The Untrodden *Via Media*.
  iv. The Secret of Missionary Finance.

It is to be observed that it formed no part of the duty of the Sub-committee to consider any questions merely affecting the Missionary policy which has at any time been or is now being pursued in India, under the direction of the General Committee. This being so, the Sub-committee considered that the first and fourth of the above mentioned articles were not within the scope of its investigation. Accordingly no evidence either in support of or in opposition to the opinions set forth in those articles was considered. The attention of the Sub-committee was confined to the second and third of the said articles, and in so far as these contain statements or suggestions of fact bearing upon the character of the Indian missionaries of our Society, they have received most careful examination.

4.—In the judgment of the Sub-committee two important charges affecting the character of the Indian missionaries and of their work were contained in these articles.

(1) In the first place, it was expressly stated that "the "charge of luxury, as our English middle-class people who "support the missionary societies understand the word, is fully "justified by the facts of the case alike among Episcopalian, "Presbyterian, London Missionary Society, and Methodist "Missionaries."

In support of this statement it is alleged that "the mission-"ary in India with £300 a year and his bungalow—and this "may be taken as a fair average of all the societies—is able, "with ease and comfort, to mix in Anglo-Indian society in a "style which he could not possibly do on less than £1,000 a "in England."

(2) Secondly, it is stated that "the effect of this mode of "living is inevitably to separate the missionary from the people

"instead of bringing him into close contact with them," and that, "compelled by the customs of the social world in which "they move to live in a certain style, their usefulness is "crippled, their influence is lessened, and the societies are "financially embarrassed."

It is alleged that "every Missionary on landing in India "finds himself at once received into Society. In Calcutta, he "is presented at Court and makes his bow to the Viceroy. In "the other Presidency towns he is always welcome at the "public receptions at Government House." Again, "Persons "who go to Court must dress in a certain style, cannot go "about in the towns in any less fashionable vehicle than a "phæton, and must keep up a certain establishment." Further, "it is almost impossible for any man to occupy for years the "position of a feudal lord without developing the feudal spirit. "Men do successfully fight against it here and there, but it is "not in human nature to wield almost absolute power and "receive abject reverence without losing sight, more or less, "of the great Christian principle of the brotherhood of all "men."

The Sub-committee has carefully enquired into the justness of these descriptions of the position occupied by our missionaries in India.

5.—The examination of the first of these statements required, (A) the ascertainment of the stipends and allowances paid to our Indian Missionaries; (B) an enquiry as to the purchasing power of money in India as compared with England, in so far as this relates to the necessaries and ordinary conveniences of life. Cognizance had also to be taken of any special expenditure necessarily incident to the conditions of life in India; and further, of the consequences of the different and varying values of gold and silver currency.

A.—The stipends and allowances paid to our missionaries in India are as follows:

For married ministers:—

(1) In the Calcutta and Lucknow districts the stipend is £250. In the Madras, Negapatam, Mysore, and Hyderabad districts the stipend is £230.

(2) In all the districts the allowance for maintenance of each child is £14, and the educational allowance is for each child £12 per annum for 6 years, *i.e.*, between the ages of 9 and 15.

(3) In all the districts an allowance of four guineas per annum is made for stationery expenses.

(4) In Madras, Negapatam, Hyderabad, and Calcutta, Rs. 360 a year is allowed for horse or travelling expenses; in Mysore the corresponding allowance is

Rs. 380, and in Lucknow Rs. 350. (These are paid in Indian currency.)

(5) For medicines and medical attendance, the sums actually paid, or such portion thereof as is sanctioned by the District Meeting, are discharged by the Mission House.

(6) The missionaries are provided with houses, rent and taxes paid.

(7) A fixed sum is paid for furniture, except in the Calcutta, Lucknow, and Burmah districts, where the actual expenditure is allowed.

(8) The sums paid for receiving instruction in native languages are met by the Mission House.

For single ministers the stipends are:—

(1) In Calcutta and Lucknow, £150. In Madras, Negapatam, and Mysore, £125.

(2) The remaining items, in so far as applicable, are the same as above; except that the allowance for horse and travelling expenses is Rs. 300 in Negapatam and Rs. 350 in Mysore.

These stipends and allowances (other than for horse and travelling, rent and taxes) are paid in gold, or its equivalent in rupees at the current rate of exchange.

For the purpose, therefore, of estimating the value of these payments in Indian currency, by which means alone we can clearly appreciate their purchasing power, and effectually compare them with the amounts paid by other Missionary Societies which pay in rupees, it has been necessary to ascertain the amount of rupees which the above sums represent.

In 1855 the rate of exchange between Madras and London averaged 2/1; in 1856, 2/1⅜ per rupee. Some of the missionaries then drew their allowances at par (2/- to the rupee), thus losing by the exchange, and others at the current rate. But from 1857 to 1878 the allowances were paid at par; since then at current rate. The stipends of £250, £230, £150 and £125, instead of being calculated at Rs. 2,500, Rs. 2,300, Rs. 1,500 and Rs. 1,250 respectively must be calculated at the number of rupees which they have realized in recent years.

The official rates of exchange for the last five years are as follows:—

	s.	d.			s.	d.
In 1886 ...	1	6·254		In 1889 ...	1	4·379
„ 1887 ...	1	5·441		„ 1890 ...	1	4·556
„ 1888 ...	1	4·898				

The value of the rupee having recently risen again to 1s. 6d., the Sub-committee has, for the purposes of this enquiry, calculated the value at 1s. 6d., and at this rate the stipends are as follows :—

In Calcutta and Lucknow Rs. 3,333 and Rs. 2,000 respectively for married and single ministers; in the other districts Rs. 3,066 and Rs. 1,666 respectively. The children's allowances amount to Rs. 186, the educational allowances to Rs 160, and the allowance for postage to Rs. 56.

B.—On the question of the value in kind or purchasing power of these sums in India and England respectively, the evidence before the Sub-committee has been to some extent conflicting. Districts in India naturally differ one from another, prices fluctuate considerably, and in comparing the prices of the necessaries and conveniences of life in detail, the differences are great—sometimes in favour of the Indian resident, sometimes on the contrary. Further, in making the comparison the Sub-committee has given weight to the facts: (1.) That the quality of articles in India is, generally speaking, inferior to that of articles passing under the same designation in England. (2.) That the climate of India compels us to include some items of expenditure in the category of necessaries there, which might reasonably be classed as superfluities here. (3.) That some of the necessities of life, which in England are provided for by public works, in particular the supply of water and the removal or sewage, have in many parts of India to be provided for by household servants, and therefore constitute, in greater or less degree according to circumstances, charges on the ministerial income.

Applying these facts and considerations to the first of the charges above recited, the Sub-committee find and report :—

> (1.) That our Indian missionaries have not the means to live, and do not live in luxury, as our English middle classes understand the word.
> (2.) That the stipends paid in India are not in any sense the equivalent of the sum of £1,000 a year in England, nor do they approach thereto.
> (3.) That, on the whole, there is no substantial difference between the purchasing power of the stipends as expended in India and the same sums if expended in England.
> (4.) That, owing to the recent depreciation of the Indian currency, the remuneration of the Indian Missionaries does now exceed the stipends and allowances paid to Wesleyan Ministers in England.

6.—On the second of the charges above specified as affecting the character of the Indian missionaries and their work, the evidence cannot, from the nature of the case, be summarised in the same concrete form as in the previous question; and since all the evidence produced to the Sub-committee is herewith placed before the General Committee, it is not necessary to particularise as to its character.

As regards the assertion that the missionaries on landing are presented at Court, the Sub-committee finds that this is inaccurate and misleading. Some of the missionaries, chiefly those stationed in or near the Presidential cities, do attend occasionally the Levées of the Viceroy or of the Lieutenant-Governors. In view of their frequent official dealings with the governing authorities, the Sub-committee considers it desirable that they should do so.

It reports, however,

(1.) That such attendances, considering the body of missionaries as a whole, are comparatively rare.

(2.) That they do not necessitate, nor do they involve the missionaries in any pecuniary expense whatever.

(3.) That there is nothing in the fact of such attendances which is calculated to, or does in fact hinder the work of the missionaries, among the native population, or in any way prejudice their mutual relations one to another.

(4.) The Sub-committee, while putting out of view all questions of policy, finds that the assertion that the manner or the place of living of the Indian missionaries tends to alienate them from the native population, or hinder the success of their native work, is not sustained. In the cases in which the attempt has been made to live in native quarters and in the manner of the native population, the sacrifice of life and health has been great, and it appears to have been attended by no compensating advantage as regards the success of the labour so carried on.

The Sub-committee also is of opinion that the relations between the missionaries and the native ministers are cordial and fraternal.

7.—While thus completely exonerating the Indian missionaries of our Society from all charges made or suggested against their character or the character of their work, whether in respect of their mode of living, or of their relations with the native population, Christian and otherwise, the Sub-committee having had before it considerable information as to the degree and mode of payment of the missionaries employed in India by other Christian churches, and of various classes of English residents in India, desires to add to its Report the following statement* as to the stipends paid by some other missionary societies which work on lines similar to our own, and the following expression of its views as to some points of missionary finance arising out of the above questions :—

1.—(1.) The London Missionary Society pays as follows :—

Stipend for married ministers Rs. 2,600 per ann., income tax being paid by the Society.

Children's allowances, under 8 years, Rs. 100 per ann.
,,   ,,   from 8 to 15   ,, 150   ,,
,,   ,,   15 to 18   ,, 250   ,,

Horse and carriage hire, Rs. 240.

Such medical expenses are paid as are sanctioned by the board of directors.

Houses are provided rent free.

A sum of Rs. 180 per annum for three years is allowed for instruction in native languages.

For unmarried ministers, the stipend is Rs. 1,700 per annum.

On appointment to the mission field a grant of £50 to married, and £30 to unmarried ministers, is made towards the provision of furniture.

(2.) The Baptist Missionary Society pay as follows :—

Stipend for married ministers, Rs. 2,700 per annum.

Children's allowance up) Rs. 192 in large centres.
    to the age of 16   ...) Rs. 144 in country districts.

Houses are provided, or house rent paid to a sum not exceeding Rs. 720 per annum.

Medical expenses and the cost of instruction in native languages are allowed.

For unmarried ministers the stipend is Rs. 1,800, except in cases where an unmarried lives with a married minister.

This Society desires it to be stated that these payments are now under consideration and may shortly be modified.

(3.) The American Methodist Episcopal Mission pays as follows :—

Stipend for married ministers from Rs. 2,475 to Rs. 2,160, according to place of residence.

Children's allowance Rs. 240 for children in India, 100 dols. for those in America.

Houses are provided rent free.

---

* NOTE.—Mr. Brunyate objects to the introduction of details of the three undermentioned societies alone. If these pay somewhat less than our own society does, it is well known that there are others which pay considerably more.—W.B. The President of the Conference concurs in this. Mr. Allen declines to commit himself to the details of comparison as to payment between our own and the other societies named.

Allowances are made for furniture, medical and travelling expenses.

For single ministers the stipends are from Rs. 1,560 to Rs. 1,800, according to length of service.

In all the above cases, all payments are made in rupees; but the rupee is calculated at its *par* value, in respect of any remittances to England or America as the case may be, out of ministerial income. The London Missionary Society makes payments in England at *par* for life insurance, school bills, support of family, or personal supplies, on authority from the missionaries; provided that such payments on account of articles for personal use shall not exceed £30 per annum.

(4.) The Church Missionary Society declines to sanction the publication of its allowances.

(5.) No evidence was before the Sub-committee as to the payments made by other Missionary Societies.

2. Without expressing any opinion as to the amount of the remuneration of the Indian missionaries, the Sub-committee recommends that the stipends should be paid in the silver currency of India rather than as at present in the gold currency of England, provided that the rupee is calculated at its *par* value in respect of any remittances to England out of ministerial income.

3. It considers it desirable that the amounts of payment should be graduated according to the length of the service of the missionary in the foreign field, the remuneration being thus more closely proportioned to the presumable value of the services rendered, and an inducement supplied to a longer continuance on the ground than is at present the average.

4. It considers that a distinction in stipends between the town (particularly the Presidential cities) and country stations, proportioned to the cost of living, ought to be established.

5. In the case of any of these recommendations being favourably considered, the Sub-committee is of opinion that the allowances and provisions for the education of children in England, and for allowances directed to the preservation or restoration of the health of the missionaries and their families should be calculated on a very liberal scale.

C. H. KELLY.
H. J. POPE.
WESLEY BRUNYATE.
GEORGE FLETCHER.
THOMAS ALLEN.
H. H. FOWLER.
GEORGE HAYTER CHUBB.
JOHN CLAPHAM.
H. ARTHUR SMITH.

APPENDIX A.

SPECIAL SUB-COMMITTEE OF ENQUIRY.

ISSUE I. (A.)

Is it true that the present allowances of our Indian missionaries are greater in real value—i.e. in purchasing power in the country in which they are received and expended—than those of ministers in the home work, or than similar sums would be in England?

On this point the *Methodist Times* has made the following statements:—

(1) "The missionary in India with £300 a year and his bungalow—and this may be taken as a fair average of all the Societies—is able with ease and comfort to mix in Anglo-Indian society in a style which he could not possibly do on less than £1000 a year in England."—("A New Missionary Policy," Art. II.)

(2) "The youngest and most obscure married missionary in India receives, in gold, a larger stipend than the Superintendent of the West Central Mission; and relatively to the value of gold and the cost of living, each of these young Indian missionaries has an income at least twice as large. The worst paid missionaries in India are better paid than our missionary secretaries and our best paid circuit ministers at home."—(*Methodist Times*, May 2nd, 1889.)

(3) "In our opinion an Indian missionary with £150, and £30 for horse allowance, would be as well off as a minister in London with £250."—(*Methodist Times*, May 1st, 1890.)

(4) "The truth is that the cost of living is far less in India than in England, except under the following heads:—(1) wine; (2) clothes manufactured in England; and (3) the education of children in England."—("Summary Statement," p. 16.)

Before entering upon any detailed investigation into the truth of these assertions, it will be useful if we briefly review the history of stipends and allowances, both in India and at home. In doing this we shall deal with them only as measured in gold, leaving for the moment out of account the further question of gain or loss from variations in the value of gold, or exchange from a gold into a silver currency.

History of Stipends.

In 1819, when our Mission was formally divided into districts, the General Committee went minutely and carefully into the question of allowances, and laid down the principles upon which they should be determined. In the records of the Committee's proceedings, under date March 31, 1819, we find the following Resolutions recorded :—

1819.

"2. That a regular and proper scale of allowances should be established for the various missionaries in sundry parts of the world, so as to provide them with what is sufficient for food, clothing, &c., in those places where they reside, according to the necessary expense of living in each place. We are of opinion also that the allowances ought to be such as will render the missionaries and their families sufficiently comfortable while engaged in their great and important work.

"3. That we therefore recommend that the allowances to be granted to the missionaries in the East Indies, the West Indies, Sierra Leone, and Gibraltar for ordinary expenses shall not exceed—

For a single Missionary.................	£150
For a married Missionary	200
For each child.............................	14

The ordinary expenses include quarterage, board, servants, washing, fuel, and candles.

"4. That not having the full information which is necessary respecting the proper allowances for several of the other stations, we judge it better to postpone fixing them until such information is obtained.

"5. That it be an instruction to the different Missionary District Committees to enquire whether there are stations in a district where such allowances as are granted for ordinaries are not more than sufficient for the comfortable subsistence of the brethren there, so that, if expended, their condition would be superior to that of their brethren in other stations, and the District Committees are to report the sum which may appear to them to be sufficient. And also if the allowances for any place appear to them from particular circumstances to be insufficient, the sum which appears to the District Committee necessary properly to meet the expenses of such station shall be also reported, with the reasons on which such conclusions are founded: the principle of allowance being understood to be that the brethren employed in foreign missions shall be supplied with all things necessary for their health and comfort, but without profusion."

In accepting these recommendations, the General Committee adopted principles which all will acknowledge to be sound, and Resolutions 4 and 5 show with what care and caution these principles were put into effect. The subsequent history of Indian allowances shows this still more clearly.

On June 9, 1821, an official letter was written to the Chairman of the Madras and Jaffna District charging the brethren with "extravagance." No copy of this letter is to be found among the records at the Mission House, but from the reply to it recorded in the District Minutes it appears to have had reference both to the personal allowances of the brethren and the expenditure on mission 'plant.' The charges preferred seemed to the sensitive brethren against whom they were made so serious, that the Chairman resigned his trust, and was subsequently only with great difficulty induced to resume it; and the brethren unitedly declared that such charges, if true, involved moral guilt and disqualified them for any longer holding the office of Christian ministers. In their defence the brethren minutely review their whole expenditure and, as far as their personal allowances go, declare their inability to reduce the rates which the Committee had laid down two years before. They state that these allowances "are in many cases very inadequate, for while other missionaries have no more, it should be remembered that they are allowed to make up the deficiencies by keeping boarding and other schools." They then conclude:—
"Worn down by fatigues, as many of us now find ourselves, into premature age, we can only submit to you one proposition, that should we, at the last, find ourselves unable to meet your views in point of expenditure, others may be sent out more able to occupy

1821.

those places which we have in vain attempted to fill to your satisfaction."

The Committee was evidently surprised at the tone of this reply, and hastened to assure the brethren that they were mistaken in their interpretation of the official letter of the Committee, for on the 19th of December, 1821, it resolved:—

"4. That it never was the intention of the Committee that if the brethren in their respective districts should show that any item of the allowances was too limited, that it should not be increased, and especially that the sum for extraordinaries should not be advanced, if a clear case were made out and forwarded to the Committee; or that an annual allowance of £200 or £300 more might not be made if absolutely required, in order to the efficient carrying on of the work in Ceylon and India.

"5. That provided the brethren abide by the financial regulations which they have received, any representations in favour of extra allowances will be affectionately considered by the Committee."

The rates thus fixed in 1819 after much anxious deliberation and conscientious care with full knowledge of the facts, and due reference to the needs of the country, remained unchanged till 1852. In that year the stipend of unmarried men in the South Indian Districts was reduced from £150 to £100. The reason for this is not apparent. The record states that the minutes of the Madras District were considered at a meeting held September 15th, 1852, and

1852.

"A proposal to reduce the income of any single preacher who may hereafter be appointed to that district to £100 per annum, in lieu of board and quarterage, &c., was unanimously adopted. A similar proposal to reduce the income of the married preachers and the children's allowances stands over for further consideration."

The Committee was apparently anxious for economy; but no trace of the "further consideration" of the proposal to reduce the stipends of married missionaries can be found. The young unmarried men alone were dealt with, and the lower rates adopted in 1852 governed their allowances for the next fifteen years. There were, it is true, exceptions to the rule, young men in the more expensive places receiving an extra £25, but speaking generally the stipends of our South Indian missionaries from 1852 to 1867 were £200 per annum for married men and £100 for single men.

In the year 1866 several communications were received at the Mission House from brethren in India respecting the general rise in prices. These letters best reveal the state of things in South India. The Rev. R. Stephenson, Chairman of the Madras District, writing under date September 28, 1866, after referring to the sufferings of the people generally from want of food, says :— *1866.*

"You will not wonder that our brethren, and especially those who have families, feel the pressure of these hard times. Formerly the missionary's salary was sufficient to save him from all anxiety and care. It has ceased to be so for some years. Now we are compelled to contract as far as possible all expenses, and even thus are scarcely able to pay our way. Every Missionary Society that I know of except our own, has during the last few years considerably raised the salary of its European agents. Our Society has not yet been asked to do so, but I believe the brethren will be compelled to make the request at the approaching District Meeting, and I doubt not it will be met by you in a kind and considerate spirit. I write now to suggest that it should not be left to the District Meeting to make this request, but that a proposal to increase the salaries should come from the Mission House. I am loth to take part in reducing the means at your disposal for the extension of the work of God, but justice to my brethren and loyalty to the Mission House compel me to make this suggestion. One of the ablest and most self-denying of our missionaries writes to me from the country, 'We feel the pinch of the times ourselves. Don't you think it would be a graceful and just step on the part of our Society to raise the scale of allowances at such a time? I have felt ashamed this year at having to be behind with some of my payments, to reduce my servants, and in one important case to fall short of my promises. I don't quite see that we ought to be silent on this subject any longer. If our allowances in these times be thought sufficient, how extravagantly overpaid our predecessors must have been.'"

The Rev. T. Hodson, who had had a very long experience in India as Chairman of the Mysore District, wrote on the 21st of December, 1866, from Bangalore, as follows :—

"For several years there has been in this part of India a steady increase in the prices of nearly all articles of food, and in consequence our missionaries cannot live upon their present pecuniary allowances.

"The other Missionary Societies have upon due representation increased the salaries of their missionaries; but the Wesleyan missionaries, remembering the struggles with poverty which many of the preachers have in the circuits at home, felt reluctant to bring this matter before you. But now they are driven by sheer necessity to mention the subject, for the brethren who have no private property are compelled to go into debt without a probability of paying, unless they obtain an increased income. I write now on behalf of all the missionaries in the district, and am sorry I did not write earlier, for had I done so, we might have known your mind at our approaching District Meeting. However, I hope you will give an early reply to this letter.

"In illustration of the pecuniary difficulties of the brethren, I will mention a few facts. Twenty-five years ago we could purchase sixteen loaves of bread for one rupee, now we receive only six of the same size and quality, so that a man with a large family must pay about 14s. a week for bread alone. Mr. Sanderson can tell you exactly what he paid at Tumkur. The price of rice has risen in the same proportion. Formerly we could purchase a good sheep for half-a-crown, but now we pay sixpence a pound for mutton, and that which is left of a joint one day will (during the greater part of the year) not keep good until the next dinner time. Servants' wages and all labour rates are more than doubled, and they are steadily rising. Gram (the substitute for oats as food for horses) was formerly seventy measures for a rupee, *now* we only obtain seven or seven and a half. Hay, grass, and straw are about three-fold their former price. I need not increase the list, but only observe there has been a very considerable advance on every article of consumption. The famine in Orissa, and the scarcity of rain in Mysore this year, have helped to raise the price of some articles, but some of them were the same price, and all others nearly the same, before the famine commenced. The increase has been steady and regular for several years, and, according to the calculation of good political economists, prices are not likely to come down very much. There will probably be some decrease in gram and rice, but upon the whole living in India will be more than double the rate it was a few years ago. In the present difficulty the missionaries do not ask for any particular amount of increase; they leave that with you. But on their behalf I beg to suggest the following, which I think you will not consider unreasonable. Expenses have more than doubled, but I do not ask for twice the amount of income. I suggest the addition of about one-fourth, namely :—

"To a married man, the following extra grants per annum—

"For salary	£20,	that is	£220 instead of	£200.
„ keep of horse.......	15,	„	35 „ „	20.
„ servants (a new grant)	15,	„	15 „ „	0

£50

"To a single man—

"For salary............... £10, that is £110 instead of £100.
,, keep of horse...... 15, ,, 35 ,, ,, 20.
———
£25

"To East Indian ministers the same advance as to a single man, viz., £25.

"Some of the brethren wish me to help them out of their present difficulty by paying the extra expense they have of necessity incurred in the keep of horses this year. I do not feel at liberty to do this except *as a loan* until I hear from you. But I earnestly entreat you to let us have an answer to this letter with the least possible delay.

"I may just observe that as some of the missionaries in this district gave liberally towards the building of our new chapel in Bangalore, and very soon afterwards to the Jubilee Fund, it has been inferred that they had an abundance of rupees. This inference is not correct. They gave largely because they loved the Lord's work, and were determined to make sacrifices for it. They paid their donations by instalments, and some of these amounts will only be settled at the approaching District Meeting."

The subject was discussed in both the Madras and Mysore District Meetings. The brethren in Madras in their general letter wrote as follows:—

"16. The famine which in some parts of India has wrought such fearful havoc has been felt, though not, we are thankful, in its full severity, in South India. All the necessaries of life have reached a price unheard of before. These excessive rates will, we trust, be reduced. But, as you are aware, there had been for many years before the famine a gradual and continuous rise in prices, and this rise it is believed will to a serious extent be permanent. Hence it has been needful to increase the salaries of our catechists and schoolmasters; and now we are compelled, though reluctantly, to ask that you will allow us to draw upon you more largely on our own account.

"17. We will refer first to the sum allowed for the keep of horses or bullocks. Many years ago this was fixed at £20 a year. Since some of us came into the country the price of gram (the substitute in India for oats as food for horses) has increased eight- or ten-fold. The cost of grass and straw and of servants' wages has also risen. Hence the allowance, once ample, is now quite insufficient. Still we have not felt at liberty ourselves to increase it, but the Chairman has advanced to each brother who keeps a horse £10 as a loan, and this sum we respectfully ask you to grant towards our extra expenses for the keep of horses during the last year. You will see that we have kept our expenditure, including this sum, within the grant to the District. We have further so far ventured to anticipate your concurrence as to assign in distributing the grant for 1867, £30 instead of £20 for the keep of each horse. We trust our doing so will have your approval.

"18. The question of salary we have felt to be one of great difficulty. An increase not only involves upon you heavy additional expenditure, but the consideration of it awakens among ourselves delicate and sometimes painful comparisons. The brethren in the district leave their case with confidence in your hands, referring you to Brother Stephenson for any information you may desire as to their necessities and wishes."

In forwarding the above document, Mr. Stephenson wrote on the 31st of January, 1867, in the following terms:—

"From the general letter accompanying the minutes of our District Meeting you will learn that the brethren in the district are compelled to ask an increase of their allowances, and they refer you to me for a more definite statement.

"You are aware that throughout India prices have long been steadily rising. The cost of living is now probably double what it was twenty years ago, and there is no prospect of material improvement. During the past year in every family in the mission efforts have been made to reduce expenditure. Servants have been dismissed, sometimes at much inconvenience, and there has been a more anxious economy in the expenditure for the table and for clothes than was known among us formerly. Notwithstanding this, I believe that some of the brethren have gone beyond their means, and that they enter upon a year of continued dearness with increased anxiety. Under these circumstances I do not think it would be right for me to allow the District Minutes to go home without adding a few words on the subject.

"The English brethren are obliged, though with extreme reluctance, to ask you to increase the expenditure of the Society on their own account. They think the salary of a married missionary should be £240 a year, and that of an unmarried missionary £125, the latter sum to be raised to £150 to a missionary remaining unmarried after being received into full connexion. It may perhaps be wise to put part of the suggested increase under the head of 'servants,' or of 'firewood and oil,' but of this you can best judge."

Mr. Stephenson also asks the Committee to increase the salaries of East Indian and native ministers on the ground of the increased cost of living. The Mysore brethren in their general letter, written at the beginning of 1867, say :—

"9. Although we do it very reluctantly, we feel ourselves obliged to request the Committee to increase our allowances. We believe that we are about the last of the missionary societies in the country to bring this subject before their General Committee. The great increase during the last few years in the price of every article of consumption and of all kinds of labour, renders an increase absolutely necessary in order that we may keep out of debt and be free from anxiety, to do our work with comfort. We do not ask for more than we believe the Committee would give us if they knew our circumstances, and we leave it in their hands. Our Chairman has already brought the subject before you and given you a statement of facts by no means extreme. He has also granted to each of the brethren a loan of £10 under the head of keep of horse, to make up a part of the deficiency in that and other items of expenditure during the past year. We have to request that this amount may be allowed us, and that the subject of increase for the future may have your *earliest attention*. We refer you again to the Chairman's letter on the subject, and ask *that any amount you may be pleased to grant may be made available for the current year*."

In response to these appeals the General Committee took the question into its careful consideration, and the following record of its decision, arrived at on the 5th June, 1867, is found in the minutes :—

"The communications, including District Minutes and letters received from India on the subject of increased allowances, were read and considered at length. Ultimately, it was agreed that as the communications now read show that a general increase of prices in the necessaries of life renders some augmentation necessary, the Committee will consent to the European missionaries being paid at the rate of £125 per annum for every single man, with £10 additional for the keep of horse or cattle, and £230 for every married minister, with £10 additional for the keep of horse or cattle."

These rates have remained unaltered up to the present time. In ordinary seasons they are fairly adequate to the modest needs of missionary life, and though in times of scarcity and enhanced prices it is not always easy to keep out of debt, missionaries have felt that their claims upon the Committee should be based not upon the necessities of years of famine, but upon their ordinary expenditure in normal seasons. On two occasions since 1867 has the whole question been thoroughly discussed by the Indian Triennial Conference, first in 1877 and again in 1889. The result of the last of these investigations is before the Committee in the printed report of the Conference, but for 1877 no report was printed, and the outcome of much careful enquiry and anxious deliberation is only to be found in the manuscript records. The conclusions which were reached may, however, be gathered from the following paragraph extracted from a printed circular issued to all the districts at the close of the Conference :—

1877 and 1889.

"Though the increased cost of living in India and Ceylon renders the amount fixed some years ago as the salary of an English missionary barely sufficient in ordinary times, and though the famine now pressing upon southern India involves many of the brethren in great difficulty, yet, remembering how urgent are the claims of the country for increased missionary labour, and remembering also that there has been a falling off in the home income of the Missionary Society, the brethren resolve not to propose at present any increase of their own income. . . . They do this with the understanding that if any missionary's expenditure be of necessity greater than that of his brethren generally, either because of his official position or because of the circumstances of the station at which he lives, he is entitled to an additional allowance to be fixed by the District Meeting of which he is a member, or by its finance committee."

From this brief sketch it will be seen that the stipends of missionaries in India remain practically what they were seventy years ago. Unmarried men receive £25 less than they did in 1820, and married men £30 more. On the other hand, the stipends of ministers in the home work have advanced during the same period probably not less than 60 per cent. In 1820 the stipends of married men in English circuits varied from £80 to £150; they now vary from £120 to £250 or more. In 1820 and for some years afterwards £150 was the stipend of the General Secretaries of our Society, and it is worthy of note that with all the facts before them relative to the needs of Indian life, such men as Dr. Bunting and Richard Watson, acting on the principles laid down in

Stipends in England.

the minute of 1819, quoted above, deliberately fixed the stipends of Indian missionaries 33 per cent. higher than their own.

But it may be said—as it has frequently been said—" True, the stipends of Indian missionaries may not have increased very much if they are measured in gold, but so to measure them is fallacious. They are received and expended in rupees, **"Gain by exchange."** and as the value of the rupee has fallen from 1s. 11d. in 1820 to 1s. 5d. in 1889, the number of rupees received as the equivalent of a given sum of gold has gone up by over 35 per cent." This is perfectly true, but as it is usually stated it is exceedingly misleading. This so-called "gain by exchange" is a subject on which the most serious misapprehensions prevail. In order that we may remove these misapprehensions it is necessary that we should examine the subject with some minuteness.

First, however, we must premise that whatever this "gain by exchange" may be, it is not, as is commonly supposed, a new thing for our Indian missionaries to enjoy it. When the stipends were fixed in 1819, it was distinctly stated that **Always enjoyed.** they should be paid in gold, and accordingly from that time until 1854 they received the equivalent of their stipends at the current rate of exchange, which varied from 1s. $9\frac{1}{2}d.$ to 2s. We also find in the records of the General Committee under date December 20th, 1820, the following resolution :—

"That if the exchange should in future become unfavourable to the missionaries, a statement of this circumstance shall be taken into due consideration by the Committee."

From this it would appear that it was the wish of the Committee that missionaries should receive the "gain by exchange" on their salaries whenever there was any, but that if there was a loss the Society should bear it. It was not necessary to act on this resolution, however, until the immense discoveries of gold between 1850 and 1855 had reduced the relative value of that metal and raised the price of silver to an abnormal height. In 1855 the rate of exchange between

Madras and London averaged 2s. 1d. for thirty days' bills, and in 1856, 2s. 1⅜d. During these two years no uniform method of payment seems to have been observed. Some of the brethren in India drew their allowances at par and others at the current rate. But from 1857 onwards, in accordance with the definite instructions of the Committee, all were paid at par. This continued for twenty years, although in 1867 the rupee was below par again, and that steady decline in the gold value of silver had commenced which has continued with slight variations to the present day. It is not easy to say why, when the rupee fell below 2s., the old system of payment at the current rate was not at once restored. It would have been in complete accordance with the recorded wishes of the Committee, payment at par having been merely a temporary expedient to protect the men abroad from a loss which they could ill bear. Every District was at liberty to re-commence payments at current rates whenever it chose to do so. As a matter of historical fact, however, none did so until 1875, when the Ceylon Districts set the example—an example which two years later was followed in India. By 1877 exchange had fallen to 1s. 8½d., and consequently the stipends of Indian missionaries, measured in gold, were lower then than at any other period in the history of the Mission, Rs. 2,300—the sum received as the equivalent of £230—being the actual equivalent of £196 9s. 2d. only. The restoration of the so-called "gain by exchange" was thus merely the restoration of the old salary as measured in gold.

It is, however, perfectly true that during the last twenty years there has been a steady advance in the real value of all fixed gold salaries,

<small>Increase in the real value of all Gold Salaries.</small> owing to the increase in the purchasing power of that metal, and as the Indian missionary's salary is fixed in gold, he has benefited by this advance. It is this that is loosely spoken of as "gain by exchange," though in strict fact exchange has nothing whatever to do with it. The sovereign will exchange for more rupees now than formerly, because it will purchase more silver; but it will also purchase more of all other commodities, and the man whose gold salary is exchanged directly for consumable commodities as really gets the benefits of this increased purchasing power as the man who

has first to convert it into another currency. The former, in fact, gets these benefits unreduced, while for the latter they are reduced by all the cost of exchange. Indeed a very little thought will show that it is in the nature of the case impossible for the recipient of a gold salary in India to receive any benefit that does not equally accrue to the recipient of a similar salary in England or elsewhere. For if the sovereign which twenty years ago exchanged for only ten rupees now exchanges for fourteen, plainly one of two things must have happened —either the sovereign has risen, or the rupee has declined in value. Either cause may be sufficient to account for the change, or both may have been operative. Now surely it needs no argument to show (1) that in so far as the sovereign may have increased in value, every recipient of a fixed number of sovereigns must be benefited, and (2) that in so far as the rupee has declined in value no recipient of rupees can be benefited. Now it is an indisputable fact that the value of gold—by which of course we mean its purchasing power—has greatly increased during the last twenty years, and every recipient of a fixed gold salary has accordingly benefited. The Indian missionary can obtain for his fixed gold salary a larger number of silver rupees, and the home minister can obtain for his fixed gold salary a larger quantity of all the comforts or necessaries of life. But as rupees are a currency, and bread, beef and broadcloth are not, the gain is manifest in the one case and obscured in the other. The fact, however, is indisputable that the very causes which have in the past twenty years increased the real value of the Indian missionary's salary, have to the same—or, if we must be strictly accurate, to a considerably greater—extent increased the real value of gold salaries received and spent at home. The following figures taken from the *Report of the Gold and Silver Commission* (1887, Appendix, p. 317) and the *Journal of the Royal Statistical Society* (March 1890, p. 141), which show the decline of prices in England between 1867 and 1888, will illustrate this point :—

Group of Commodities.	Price. (Average of 25 years, 1853-77 = 100).	
	1867.	1888.
Vegetable foods	115	67
Animal foods	89	82
Sugar, tea, &c.	94	65
Minerals (coal, &c.)	87	78

Group of Commodities.	Price. (Average of 25 years, 1853-77 = 100).	
	1867.	1888.
Textiles	110	64
Sundries	100	67
Total of forty-five commodities	100	70
Price of silver	99·7	70·4

From this table it will be seen that between 1867 to 1888 the average price of commodities in England fell from 100 to 70; that is, £70 in 1888 would purchase as much as £100 in 1867. In other words the value of gold went up in twenty-one years 42·85 per cent. This is the extent to which all fixed gold salaries have appreciated in England. In India the rate of exchange at which our missionaries' stipends were paid in 1888 was 1s. 5⅛d. per rupee, which is equivalent to an increase over par of 40·14 per cent., and this—on the assumption that silver prices in India have remained constant— is the extent to which all fixed gold salaries have appreciated in India.

It is, however, very far from true that silver prices in India have remained stationary since 1867. They have, on the contrary, very greatly advanced. It is not possible on this branch of the inquiry to bring forward evidence so precise and convincing as that available on the question of English prices. We have in India nothing analogous to the investigations carried on in England by the *Economist* and the Royal Statistical Society. We are dependent upon the experience of those who have resided for considerable periods in the country —experience which, as it has not been supplemented by minute yearly records, is necessarily somewhat lacking in precision, but derives overwhelming force from its absolute unanimity.

Increase in cost of living in India.

Among the questions which we addressed to our brethren in India on the eve of our departure was the following :—

"If you have been any considerable number of years in the country, what has been your experience as to the variation of Indian prices?"

Twenty of the senior brethren answered this question, and they are unanimously of opinion that within the range of their experience prices have risen very considerably. Food stuffs and wages are the items most frequently instanced. Some of the former are asserted in certain localities to have gone up 50 per cent., while wages have similarly advanced from 10 to 20 per cent.

A similar question was addressed to a number of representative gentlemen of long residence in India, outside our comparatively narrow circle. On the whole the result of their experience bears out the statements made above. As there is considerable difference of opinion among them, it may be well to give their answers in full.

C. SOWDEN, Esq., (of Messrs. T. A. TAYLOR & Co., Madras) :—

"On the whole I do not think there is much difference in the cost of living in Madras now as compared with twelve years ago, when I first came out. Some commodities are a trifle cheaper, while others are more costly. Servants obtain higher wages, and house-rents during recent years have been advanced. If change there is, it is not in the direction of being less costly. On the other hand it is a general complaint that cost of living in the mofussil has greatly increased."

J. L. DUFFIELD, Esq., Bank of Madras :—

"Living is, I consider, dearer than when I first came out. House rent is decidedly higher."

LOUIS MOSS, Esq., Traffic Manager, Madras Railway :—

"Expenses generally have advanced quite 50 per cent. since I came to this country in 1865."

J. P. FIDDIAN, Esq., B.A., C.S., Sessions Judge, Malabar District :—

"The cost of food and wages has decidedly risen both for Europeans and natives in the last fifteen years."

Rev. S. W. ORGANE, Local Secretary, Madras Auxiliary Bible Society :—

"Articles of consumption produced in this country are certainly 50 per cent. dearer than they were twenty years ago, and in the same period servants' wages have advanced at least 30 per cent."

Rev. E. SELL, B.D., Local Secretary, C.M.S., Madras :— .

"I have been in Madras about twenty-five years, and I estimate the increased cost of living at about 15 per cent."

Rev. JARED SCUDDER, M.D., D.D., Arcot Mission:—

"Almost everything has advanced in price during the last twenty-five years; some articles of daily domestic consumption as much as 50 per cent."

Rev. M. PHILIPS, L.M.S., Madras:—

"The cost of living is fully 15 per cent. greater than it was twenty-five years ago."

Rev. J. B. COLES, L.M.S., Bangalore:—

(1) "I have not authentic records which would afford a basis for a definite statement of the percentages, but I am quite clear as to the general fact. The commodities in constant demand—for instance, bread, rice, eggs, poultry, sheep, vegetables, horse-gram—have risen in cost very greatly. The food of servants and of day-labourers is much dearer than it was when I came to India [almost fifty years ago]. This, of course, has raised the price of their labour. I am pretty safe if I say that *some* of these commodities have risen 100, 200, perhaps even 300 per cent."

(2) "Yesterday I despatched a letter in reply to yours. . . . I wish to add a few words in explanation of one part of it. In treating of the rise in the cost of living in India, I said, I think, that some articles had risen as much as 100, 200, or perhaps *even 300 per cent.* As to this last part *in italics*, I would say that I am not prepared to represent that any considerable proportion of the articles consumed by missionaries has risen to this extent. At the same time, I remember some few facts which I think would bear me out even in this. For instance, I can remember, in my early days in Bellary, horse-gram being sold at seventy measures for a rupee. . . . We have lately bought horse-gram at fifteen measures, or, I think, even less."

Such testimony might be multiplied indefinitely, and the result of it would be to convince any impartial inquirer that Indian missionaries of to-day with £230 a year are not better off than— if indeed they are so well off as—their predecessors of seventy years ago with £200. The question then remains—Were the fathers of our Society right, when they said that in respect of the ordinary necessities of life £200 a year in India was not more than £150 a year in London? Since their day the value of English incomes has increased, while the value of Indian incomes has diminished,

Comparison of England and India.

and if they were right we should not perhaps be far wrong if we said that £150 in England is now equal to £250 a year in India, thus exactly reversing Mr. Hughes' figures. We believe that such a statement would be within the mark; it will be sufficient, however, to bring Mr. Hughes' whole case to the ground if, without attempting to establish the exact ratio between cost of living in the two countries, we simply prove that the balance of cheapness is at any rate not in favour of India. For proof of this we have no need to rely on the historical argument that we have at some length adduced, though we regard that argument as of great value in showing that the relation of stipends to cost of living has been continually before the missionary authorities and the missionaries, and that from the very foundation of the Society a consistent and economical policy has been pursued in regard to it. The simple fact that living is dearer to-day in India than in England, that is to say, that for the ordinary necessities of life and for maintenance in a given degree of comfort, a larger sum is required there than at home, is one that we should call notorious, were it not that so few facts about India are notorious in England. To maintain the contrary is something like maintaining that the average temperature of India is lower than that of England. We proceed, however, to bring forward evidence that we think will suffice to establish the truth, only premising that the Committee will be able to obtain from any part of India and from any class of Europeans who have had fair experience of life in both countries, as much additional testimony as it may desire, and all of the same tenor.

All classes of Europeans in India receive very much higher rates of remuneration than they would receive in England. This fact, we imagine, hardly needs to be proved. It is notorious. But a few extracts from documents in our possession may be useful to illustrate it.

(*a*) The following is from a letter addressed to *The Methodist Times* in August last, by GRAHAM S. BRUCE, Esq., Asst. Locomotive Superintendent, South Indian Railway, but which Mr. Hughes, for obvious reasons, did not publish :—

I. (A.)

"Starting with the statement that 'in the India of to-day there are three totally distinct modes of living—the Anglo-Indian, the Eurasian, and the native,'—he (Dr. Lunn) goes on to instance the health of 'non-commissioned officers in the Army, foremen in mills and places of business, and other Europeans who live in India on an income of £100 to £200 per annum,' not being worse than that of civilians and officers in the Army. I may here conveniently refer to the wage of the day labourer 'in India,' which in his second article is placed at 2*d*. to 4*d*. a day, as upon this among other things he appears to found his conclusion that the salary of missionaries ought to be reduced from £300 to £150. My limited experience precludes my using with any degree of truthfulness the words 'in India.' I must confine myself to the country alongside 750 miles of line between Nellore and Tinnevelly. . . . I cannot remember a single instance in which I have obtained a man's labour for less than 4*d*. a day. In a department employing over 2,500 natives, exclusive of Eurasians, it would probably be under the mark to place the average at 8*d*. per day. The pay of European foremen and under-foremen varies between £200 and £280 at present rate of exchange, the average being about £262."

(*b*) LOUIS MOSS, Esq., Traffic Manager, Madras Railway, writes:—

"I have six assistants or divisional officers, and these officers are divided into three grades. The maximum pay of the first grade is £900 per annum, of the second grade £700, and of the third grade £500. When applying for officers from home, I ask invariably for single men, and I expect newly-appointed officers to remain single until they have passed out of the third grade. I do this because I do not think a married man can live on less than £600 per annum without drifting into debt or difficulty. . . . Covenanted engine drivers received with us Rs. 7 a day, and were credited with overtime allowances. We have, however, few Europeans now left, as we have trained East Indians and natives to drive locomotives. European inspectors for weighing machines and station machinery, &c., receive Rs. 300 to Rs. 400 a month [*i.e.* £255 to £340 per annum], and this is the pay too of the locomotive foremen living at up-country stations."

(*c*) CHAS. SOWDEN, Esq. (of Messrs. T. A. Taylor & Co., Madras), writes:—

"Assistants for mercantile and bank offices, whose income at home would be £120 to £150 per annum, receive on arriving in this country a monthly salary of Rs. 300 [*i.e.* £255 per annum] with small annual increments during the term of their first engagement.

After five years' service their pay on the average is about Rs. 500 a month [*i.e.* £425 per annum].

(*d*) The following is an extract from the letter of a missionary of our Society :—

"When at home in 1886 we had a furnished house in S—— for six months, and kept careful accounts of the cost of living, with the object of comparison. We found we could and *did* live better in S—— than we do here at an expenditure of from twenty-five to thirty per cent. less.

"We have in our English Church here two European engine-drivers. Only a week ago one of them (a married man with no children) told me that in England he had £2 a week, and out here in salary and over-time earnings he gets Rs. 300 a month [*i.e.* almost £5 a week], and that he was much better off financially and was able to save more in England than he can here. He is practically a total abstainer, and lives in the quiet way a good hard-working Methodist artizan would be expected to live, and he has not had more than the usual amount of sickness which Europeans have in India."

We have many other testimonies of a similar character, but it is needless to quote them. Every one who has even an elementary knowledge of India knows that Europeans in every walk of life receive there from two to three times as much as they would receive in similar positions at home. No doubt a part of this increased payment is due to what Mr. Hughes calls an "exile allowance," but a much larger part is due to the acknowledged and inevitable costliness of life in that country. In order to bring out this point we put to the gentlemen named above this question :—

"What income in India would your experience lead you to assign as the equivalent in point of general comfort and convenience of £300 a year in England?"

We chose £300 because, including children's allowances, educational allowances, taxes, medical expenses, &c., that sum may be taken as a moderate statement of the average ministerial income at home. Our question, it will be observed, excluded all reference to "exile allowance," and was directed simply to the comparative cost of living in India and England. The following are the answers which we received. After each answer we put in brackets the equivalent in pounds per annum at 1s. 5d. the rupee:—

Charles Sowden, Esq.	Rs. 500 per month	(£425).
Rowland Hill, Esq., Supt. Govt. Press, Madras...	Do.	do.
J. P. Fiddian, Esq., B.A., C.S.	Rs. 500 to 600	(£425 to £510).
Rev. S. W. Organe	Rs. 450	(£382 10s.).
J. L. Duffield, Esq.	Rs. 400	(£340).
Louis Moss, Esq.	Rs. 700	(£595).

These estimates vary—as such estimates are bound to vary—but it will be observed that there is perfect unanimity in this, that equal comforts can be obtained for a much smaller sum in England than in India. And the gentlemen who hold this opinion have all had many years experience both of Indian and English life. A similar argument might be drawn, if need were, from the furlough allowances alike of Government servants and of all missionary societies. But what we have already said is surely enough to show the utter baselessness of the contention of the *Methodist Times*. No one would venture to defend the position which it has taken up, unless fortified by the foolish confidence which ignorance sometimes begets.

Summary. Our answer then to the contention of the *Methodist Times* under Issue I. (A) is—

(i.) That the stipends of the Society's Indian missionaries were fixed at the outset on the principle of supplying only what would suffice "for their health and comfort, but without profusion," and that when they were originally so fixed, the careful enquiries then made established the fact that at that time living was at least one-third dearer in India than in England.

(ii.) That since that day a great appreciation of gold has affected gold salaries in England and India alike (though not increasing their value in India to quite the same extent as in England); but that, to set against this, there has been in India a steady rise in prices, due to local circumstances and not paralleled by any concurrent change of prices in England.

(iii.) That it is therefore obvious, unless the Society has been mistaken in its facts throughout its whole history, that living in India to-day cannot be cheaper than in England.

But that (iv.) even apart from this historical inference, the state of the case to-day is abundantly exhibited (*a*) by a comparison of the salaries paid to Europeans in all callings in that country and in this; (*b*) by the rate of furlough allowances in all callings; and (*c*) by the unanimous and overwhelming testimony of those who have had fair experience of life in both countries.

ISSUE I. (B.)

Is it true that the present allowances of our Indian missionaries are greater than are required to maintain them and their families in health and reasonable comfort?

There are three principles by which the allowances of missionaries might conceivably be determined. They might be fixed by reference to the rights of missionaries as ministers of the Church, and in correspondence with what their brother ministers at home receive; or they might be fixed by reference to the necessities of a particular social position and environment; or, in the third place, the simple standard of what is required for health and reasonable comfort in the country and in the circumstances in which they live might be taken as a guide.

Principles determining allowances of missionaries.

The issue now raised submits the allowances of your Indian missionaries to the test of the *third* of these principles; and it is in this light that they themselves prefer to have the question considered. Even if it could be proved that ministers at home were paid in excess of what this standard would require, we should not on that account press a claim to similar treatment on behalf of missionaries. Nor are there any considerations of social position or environment which we desire to put forward as grounds for fixing stipends at a higher rate than would otherwise be sufficient. Such considerations, at any rate, could only deserve attention after the re-

Principle of 'health and reasonable comfort.'

quirements of the third principle to which we have alluded above have been satisfied. Provision such as will safeguard their health, will protect them from the intellectual and moral strain attending unaccustomed discomforts, and will ensure them against excessive anxiety in regard to their present and future maintenance—in other words, whatever is necessary for their health and reasonable comfort—this, in the interests of their work, your missionaries feel bound to require of the Society; but they require no more. The elementary obligations of the Society to the men it sends abroad, as well as the intimate connection which exists in a country like India between length of service and usefulness, will, we doubt not, make it anxious to satisfy these requirements carefully and effectually, and to err, if at all, on the side of excess rather than of defect.

In examining whether it is true, as the *Methodist Times* asserts, that the present allowances are greater than this principle requires, the main question that presents itself is as to the *actual necessary cost of living in India*. This belongs to a class of questions in regard to which men commonly, and rightly, found their judgment on the teaching of experience—not the experience, however long, of a single individual, but the composite and resultant experience of a large range and a long series of individual cases. This mode of estimation is necessary in regard to questions of this class, because they involve a multitude of varying details, which it would be hard to average, and of which many might easily be overlooked in attempting an *a priori* calculation, while others, being of irregular or occasional occurrence, would not be rightly appreciated from the brief and narrow experience of a single person. Although, however, the question of the cost of European living in India is one to be decided by general experience, it ought to admit of easy settlement when Englishmen of all classes have been living there for more than a century, and especially when missionary societies have for that length of time been seeking and gaining light upon the subject.

<small>Actual cost of living in India.</small>

What the general outcome of English experience is in regard to cost of living has been sufficiently indicated in answer to the previous issue, where it has been shown that to reach a given level of comfort and follow a given style of living, it is universally considered that a much larger outlay is required in India than in England. If further evidence is desired than is afforded by this unanimous verdict of English experience in India, the direction in which the Methodist public will naturally look for it is to the united judgment of their Indian missionaries. That judgment is expressed in the most deliberate, careful, and detailed manner in Part III. of the Statement concerning Finance of the Bangalore Conference. We would remind the Committee of what that document is and how it was prepared. The Bangalore Conference consisted of twenty-three out of the forty-five missionaries belonging to the Wesleyan Missionary Society in India and Burmah. The average length of missionary experience of those present was *more than fourteen years.* The question of cost of living had been for months prominently before their minds, and they came prepared to enter into it. At the same time the subject was sufficiently distinct from the questions more directly affecting character raised in the *Methodist Times,* to admit of being considered without animus, and on its own merits. That it was so discussed will appear from the recommendations in which the enquiry ended, given on pp. 36, 37 of the Conference Report. On the first day of the Conference a Committee on Finance was appointed, consisting of two representatives from each District, except Hyderabad and Burmah (represented by their chairmen only). Mr. Cooling, Chairman of this Committee, writes regarding it:—" The Committee met the first of all the Committees, on the second morning of the Conference, adjourned from day to day, and reported to the Conference last of all. More time was spent in Committee on this subject than on any other that came before the Conference." Several members of the Committee had come prepared with statements of their household accounts, and the knowledge and experience of the ladies of the mission was also utilized. In the Report of the Committee its labours are described as follows :—

[margin note: Financial Statement of the Bangalore Conference.*]*

"The Committee obtained from the representatives of each District information as to the cost of firewood, lighting, and of each important article of food. They had before them lists of the servants necessary in each District and of the wages which must be paid to each. These lists were carefully compared and scrutinized. The kind of clothing necessary in each District, together with its cost, was enquired into, &c."

The Report of this Committee, after thorough discussion, was accepted by the Conference; and it is this Report, prepared by such men, from such materials, with such deliberation, that Mr. Hughes describes ("Summary Statement," p. 20) as "simply the strong speculative opinion" of the Indian missionaries! *Authority of the Statement.* It is difficult to believe that Mr. Hughes understands the meaning of the words he employs. The Committee and the Methodist public will know better how to appreciate the gravity and authority of the document. The investigation of which it presents the results was applied to the cost not of an imagined manner of life, but of that which those who conducted it had actually been living; and the subject-matter of the investigation, consisting of facts and figures from personal history and every-day experience, scarcely gave room for errors arising from unconscious bias. Moreover, it will be observed that the Conference recognized no necessities of expenditure on account of social position or environment, but conducted its enquiry with an avowed and cordial acceptance of the principle of "health and reasonable comfort" which the British Conference and Mr. Hughes alike approve. Hence the Report is, in sum, a deliberate and solemn declaration by your Indian missionaries, having the utmost weight that their experience and honesty can impart, that the necessary cost of living in India is such that for "health and reasonable comfort" they need practically the full allowances now given by the Society. There is only one fact that could add to the weight of this pronouncement of the Bangalore Conference, and that fact we are able to impart to the Committee. In the circular of questions which we addressed to all our brethren in India before leaving that country, and to which we received answers from all but four of those in the country at the time, one question was as follows :—" How far does your experience agree with or differ from the conclusions of the Financial Committee of the Bangalore Conference?" The replies to this question show that, while a few brethren think one item somewhat too high and another somewhat too low, and while several think that the total is too low as regards their part of India, there is not one who thinks the total too high; so that there is practically a unanimous agreement among your Indian missionaries that this Report indicates the minimum cost at which they can be at present maintained in health and efficiency. Reject the report of the Bangalore Conference, and it is not necessary for us to indicate the nature of the condemnation which you pronounce upon the whole of your Indian missionaries.

We will now examine the strength of the evidence on which you are invited by the *Methodist Times* to reject it. That evidence consists of two parts, the testimony of Dr. Lunn, and the supposed experience of certain other missionary societies whose men are declared to be living in health and reasonable comfort on considerably less than Wesleyan missionaries receive. Mr. Hughes claims to prove by this evidence that "life can be maintained in health and reasonable comfort after reducing certain of the items given in Part III., Table III., of the Bangalore Conference Report by an aggregate amount of £80" ("Summary Statement," p. 13); that is to say, that the members o the Bangalore Conference over-estimated by more than one-third the allowances necessary for the maintenance of their own health. Such a proposition scarcely looks probable on the face of it, but we will proceed to examine the proofs that are alleged for it.

<small>Mr. Hughes' arguments.</small>

I. The testimony of Dr. Lunn. Four pages of the "Summary Statement" are occupied by an account of Dr. Lunn's experience of the cost of living in India, and by suggestions founded upon it. In reading this account one question suggests itself at the outset: Did Dr. Lunn himself follow the *Via Media*, or did he not? On pages 13 and 14 he contrasts his outlay, in the most important branches of it, with that of his brother missionaries, and recommends that they should conform to his practice; from this it would be naturally inferred that he claimed to have himself used what he calls the *Via Media*. But on page 17 we read, "It may be said with perfect truth that Dr. Lunn did not live on the income of the untrodden *Via Media* during his stay in India," and in the second of the articles on "A New Missionary Policy" he describes himself as one who has "himsel enjoyed the luxury which he undertakes to prove." What does this mean? Did Dr. Lunn live in the same style as his brother missionaries or not? If he did, then how is it that his professed expenditure under such heads as food and servants comes to only half as much

<small>I. Dr. Lunn's testimony.</small>

as theirs? And if his actual style of living was such as costs less than £150 and yet was not the *Via Media*, how is it that under the *Via Media* he allows £150 as stipend? This is only one of the many incoherences which make it difficult to treat Dr. Lunn's evidence and Mr. Hughes' proposals seriously.

It can scarcely be necessary to call the attention of the Committee to the extraordinary phenomenon presented in setting up the evidence of a single missionary, drawn from a single year's experience, against evidence of the quality which we have shown to belong to the Bangalore Report. It would not be fair to lay upon Dr. Lunn himself the chief responsibility for this remarkable proceeding, since it is commonly a character- istic of the inexperienced to be unaware of the disqualifications which their inexperience imposes upon them, and to be forward rather than backward in forming judgments and offering advice. The main responsibility for the production of Dr. Lunn as a witness must rest upon Mr. Hughes. If a young man of the Indian standing of Dr. Lunn had been at the Bangalore Conference, he would as a matter of course have been excluded from the Committee on Finance, on the ground of inexperience; and we do not suppose there is a man of sense on the face of the earth who would not consider such exclusion reasonable. And if this supposed young man, when the report of the Committee was presented to the Conference, had protested against it on the ground that his one year's experience was at variance with it, he would have been advised to be quiet until his experience more nearly equalled in length that of those who had prepared the report, and rather to correct his opinions by theirs than to seek to correct theirs by his; and again we cannot doubt that every man of sense would approve of the advice. And yet the statements of such a young man, which would, with universal approval, have been rejected as evidence of no value if they had been offered in the course of an enquiry conducted in a common-sense fashion, are now put forward as of superior weight to the conclusions of the whole body of the Society's Indian missionaries; and the Methodist public has set before it side by side, "The Estimate of the Bangalore Conference," and "The Estimate of Dr. Lunn"! We cannot regard this as anything short

[margin: Dr. Lunn v. the Bangalore Conference.]

of an extreme affront offered by Mr. Hughes to the Indian missionaries, and, except on one supposition, an equal affront to the Methodist public. That supposition is that Mr. Hughes intended to impeach the honesty of the Bangalore Conference, in which case it might be justifiable to contrast with its representations the actual experience, even though brief, of a single individual. But Mr. Hughes disclaims any such intention, declaring the Bangalore Report to be a "transparently sincere and conscientious statement" ("Summary Statement," p. 20). We hold, therefore, that in seriously asking the world to accept instead of this Report the testimony of the experience of a single individual for a single year, Mr. Hughes has equally insulted the judgment of Indian missionaries and the good sense of the Methodist public.

Up to this point we have made two assumptions concerning Dr. Lunn's evidence; first, that he actually had a year's experience in regard to the matters that he speaks of with so much confidence; and, second, that his experience actually was what he states it to have been. When we show, as, with extreme regret, we shall be compelled to do, that both these assumptions are entirely contrary to fact, the course that has been followed in setting up his testimony against that of the Bangalore Conference assumes an aspect that we dare not trust ourselves to characterise. We enquire, first, what the real experience of Dr. Lunn was, in regard to the matters on which his evidence is adduced. He speaks throughout the pamphlet of a twelve months' experience, but the chronology of his year in India shows that *he was not at his station, Tiruvalur, more than six months in all, and that the time he did spend there was broken into not fewer than eight periods, ranging in length from two months to two days.* Will it be believed that this is the length and the nature of the experience on the strength of which Dr. Lunn presumes to correct the whole body of the Society's Indian missionaries on questions of housekeeping and cost of living! The six months not spent at Tiruvalur were spent at Manargudi, Madras, Negapatam, and other places, and during the whole of this period he was boarding with brother missionaries, except for a few weeks in Madras. It is to be noted that such value as Dr. Lunn's evidence may have, does not depend on his observation of the cost of living in

His actual experience.

APPENDIX A.

the houses of these brother missionaries; they are naturally better able than he can be to testify what it costs them to live. His personal testimony can have weight only in reference to the periods of his own housekeeping, and we repeat that the longest of these periods was not more than eight weeks, and that they did not amount in all to more than six months.

At the risk of needless amplification we shall remind the Committee of some of the ways in which the brief and broken nature of this experience deprives it of all value as evidence. It is a commonplace of domestic history that the young married couple during the first months of their independent life may very easily reach wildly erroneous conclusions as to the cost of housekeeping, even when they are keeping house in England. Transfer them to the stage of Indian life, where all the conditions and circumstances of housekeeping are utterly new to them; and let their experience as to the cost of living be gained in snatches of two or three weeks at a time, in *visits* to their nominal home, amounting at most to one month in two; and does it seem likely that the wisdom attained by the young couple on the subject of Indian housekeeping by the end of a year will be such as to deserve publication to the world for the guidance of Missionary Societies?

Fruits of inexperience.

One of the common mistakes of young housekeepers is to imagine that they can buy things at cheaper prices than other people, and "manage" more economically; though when they come to look back upon their early days from the height of a few years' experience they see that, in the long run and taking everything together, it cost them just about as much to live as other people. Unless they are young people of very unusual sobriety and discernment, the only public use of their views and calculations on household management at the end of a few months will be—to raise a smile.

Men of business, moreover, and housekeepers of experience know that their calculations must take into account occasional and irregular items of expenditure, such as accidental losses, outlay required for special emergencies, and the like. They understand that the difference between a prudent and an imprudent estimate is commonly not in the ordinary and recurring items, but in the extraordinary and irregular ones for which allowance can only be made by the aid of long experience. They know that a calculation which assumed that every day would be an ordinary day and every week an ordinary week, would by the end of a year prove wofully misleading; yet this is the only kind of calculation which a young couple's experience, limited to a few weeks, could qualify them to make. Expenditure in hospitality, loss upon horses and bullocks, extra expenses connected with ill health, with travelling, and with furlough, are examples of the occasional and irregular heads of outlay that influence the missionary's cost of living in India.

Further, there are many items of expenditure connected with the management of a house and provision for personal wants which, though not irregular and accidental, recur only at long intervals, and in regard to which therefore nothing but experience can be a guide. As an example of these we may take a subject to which more than a page of Dr. Lunn's evidence is devoted—the subject of clothes. The missionary and his wife when they come out to India bring with them a stock of clothes such as for several years prevents them from discovering by their own experience what the average annual cost of clothing oneself in India is likely to be; and Dr. Lunn suffered under this disqualification as much as any other missionary. But apart from this, is it to be thought that the experience of a single year, in regard to clothing of a new character, worn in a new climate, and under new conditions of life and work, will entitle even a man of the maturest age and soundest judgment to estimate what the average cost of his clothing will be during a long period? Does Dr. Lunn imagine that in the year of grace 1890 he can throw new light on the question of how long six suits of white American drill will wear in India? The experience of hundreds of people for scores of years has established that with fair regular wear in an active life they will last for about a year; and if Dr. Lunn has indeed lighted on suits that are "by no means worn out" after twelve months' wear, the phenomenon may rightly be of interest to himself and his friends, but we should hesitate to think it important enough to be obtruded on the public. The question whether he happened to purchase drill of miraculous texture, or whether the character of his Indian career was such as not to test the wearing quality of his clothes to the average extent, is one that may or may not deserve his own attention, but that certainly cannot be allowed to disturb for a moment the conclusions of long and general experience.

Another common mistake of young housekeepers is to fail to appreciate the necessity and the cost of a number of common household requisites, which are many of them trivial individually, but add substantially to the total cost of living. It is as significant an indication as any of the extreme brevity of Dr. Lunn's housekeeping experience that there is no hint in his records and estimates of any outlay upon such matters as fire-wood, cooking and other household utensils, soap, brushes, or even upon oil for lighting purposes.

There are also certain respects in which the cost of living in India commonly increases with length of residence. Especially is this the case in regard to food. The Englishman fresh from England and endowed with English vigour and elasticity, can live in a manner that becomes impossible to him after a few years in the country have diminished his energy, disordered his digestive apparatus, and destroyed his appetite. As time goes on, he is put to increasing expense to obtain food containing the maximum of nutrition, and as tempting to the appetite as possible. Of this experience Dr. Lunn could not in the nature of things know anything.

We shall invite the attention of the Committee to only one other circumstance connected with the nature of Dr. Lunn's Indian experience, and it is a circumstance which, taken alone, should logically suffice to put entirely out of court his evidence as to what is necessary for "health and reasonable comfort." Dr. Lunn professes to show from his own experience that a given method and cost of living will serve for the preservation of health in India. But he himself was in a state of ill-health during the greater part of his term, and after a year returned home on the ground of ill-health. How can he then be so much as listened to on the question of the amount that will suffice for the preservation of health? We do not assert that his failure of health was due to his style of living and to excessive economy of expenditure; we merely point out that the experience of a man whose health was not good cannot be produced as anything

Dr. Lunn's testimony invalidated by his illness.

but *negative* testimony as to the conditions sufficing for good health. To make any argument at all, Dr. Lunn has to say that such and such a style of living *would have been* sufficient for his health, if circumstances had not interfered; and the moment he does so he passes away from the region of personal evidence into that of mere hypothesis, and proffers what would not unfairly be described as a "speculative opinion."

We have dealt with Dr. Lunn's experience, and have shown that in regard to questions of cost of living, it was an experience not even of one year but only of six months, broken into periods averaging about three weeks each; and that it was an experience of sickness which is now adduced as positive evidence in regard to conditions of health. It yet remains for us however to advert to the most serious feature of Dr. Lunn's testimony, and that is the *absolute incorrectness* of the greater part of it. We approach this most mournful part of our task with extreme pain, wishing most earnestly that it could have been in any way possible to avoid exposure of the faults of one whom we once respected and esteemed; but regard for the truth and the necessity of vindicating our brethren and ourselves leave us no alternative. Dr. Lunn's assertions—what the "Summary Statement" calls his "facts and figures"—regarding his own actual living in India have naturally had very great weight with the public, and have done perhaps more than anything else to breed a conviction that missionaries in general must be living in extravagance. It is true that thoughtful and well-informed persons must have realized that the character of Dr. Lunn's experience did not entitle his statements to consideration in the presence of unanimous testimony that contradicted them; but when they were reiterated with so much emphasis, and above all when they were distributed to the world under the seal of Mr. Hughes' certification, it was inevitable that they should produce a profound impression throughout a very wide circle. Probably if a single sentence had to be selected as the one which has done most to support Mr. Hughes' case regarding missionary stipends, it would be the assertion at the foot of p. 13 of the "Summary Statement"—"This style of living [described above] cost Dr. and Mrs. Lunn

Incorrectness of Dr. Lunn's statements.

jointly not more than 15s. a week." With a full sense of the gravity of the assertion we are about to make, we declare that Dr. and Mrs. Lunn *never lived in India on* 15s. *a week*, and that it would be as impossible to live in the style described in the pamphlet on 15s. a week as on 15*d*. In giving this flat denial to Dr. Lunn's assertion, we are not resting on any difference of interpretation of the language used. It is true that the cost of food may be variously estimated. In the Bangalore Report, as any thoughtful reader of it will detect, the cost of fuel, lighting, and of various kitchen and other utensils is included along with food.* In Dr. Lunn's calculations also, it might be assumed, if there were any coherency about them at all, that all these items had been included under "Cost of Food," since there is no other heading in his estimate, any more than in that of the Bangalore Conference, under which they could with any show of suitability be embraced. But in our denial that Dr. and Mrs. Lunn ever lived on 15s. a week in India, we are not resting on this supposition. We are willing to assume, what is probably the case, that matters so important even as oil for lighting—the equivalent of gas in England—

Dr. Lunn never lived on 15s. a week.

---

* Mr. Cooling, Chairman of the Committee on Finance, makes the following remarks on this subject :—

"The item of 'Food,' on pp. 29, 30, and 31, of the Report, includes not only what is usually understood to come under that head, but the cost of fuel and lighting, and sundries of all kinds connected with the house, or for personal use. It includes—

"(1). The cook's daily bazaar account for rice, meat, vegetables, eggs, ghee, salt, limes, curry stuffs, &c.

"(2). The monthly bread and flour bill.

"(3). The monthly milk and butter bill.

"(4). European and other stores, such as tea, coffee, sugar, jams, tinned meats, cheese, bacon, oatmeal, vinegar, biscuits, &c.

"(5). Firewood purchased daily for cooking purposes.

"(6). Kerosene oil for lighting, and in some cases for burning in a cooking stove; also lamp oil for kitchen use.

"(7). Cooking utensils, such as earthenware ovens, saucepans, chatties, &c.

"(8). Extra comforts or necessaries in case of sickness—arrowroot, corn-flour, brandy, &c.

"(9). Sundries for house or personal use—soap, blacking, knife-polish, brooms, brushes, &c."

have been wholly omitted from Dr. Lunn's memory o his life in India, and to understand "Cost of Food" to include merely the price of provisions and of fuel for cooking them; and we still assert that it is wholly contrary to truth to say that Dr. and Mrs. Lunn ever lived on 15s. a week, or anything approaching it. We declare, with extreme pain, that the assertion is not misleading merely, but wholly untrue, having no sort of correspondence with fact. It is not for us to enquire into the genesis of the misstatement. Perhaps a probable account of it is that Dr. Lunn, during one of his brief periods of residence at Tiruvalur, made, for some private purpose, such as communication to a friend or friends at home, a rough and hasty calculation of what it was costing him to live, in which, partly through inexperience and partly through carelessness, half the considerations that should have been taken into account were omitted. But it is hard to conceive that even the hastiest and most careless of men should have been content to make this rough and temporary calculation the foundation-stone of a structure which was to attract the startled attention of a wide public; and that he should dare still to maintain it as positive historical fact, when it is challenged by the unanimous testimony of other Indian missionaries, and when it is shown to lead, if true, to the gravest condemnatory inferences as to their style of living. We do not attempt to measure the degree of culpability that would be involved in such carelessness of accuracy and disregard of the responsibilities attaching to possession of the public ear; nor can we attempt to prove that the misstatement which we are exposing had this particular genesis. It only concerns us to exhibit the utter impossibility, even on Dr. Lunn's own showing, that he and his wife lived for any single week, or on the average of any number of weeks, on 15s. He has made this easy for us by giving the dietary which he followed at Tiruvalur ("Summary Statement," p. 13). Before he published this dietary, there was always the possibility that he might profess to have lived in a very frugal way, and to have so kept his expenditure down to 15s. a week. But when he tells us how he lived, we are able to judge for ourselves what his style of living must have cost him, and those of us who have lived in the same neighbourhood can deny that he and his wife lived in that style at that cost, with as much confidence as we could deny that he had travelled to India in a week. To take only one item in Dr. Lunn's dietary—the bacon, which he admits that he daily had for breakfast, would cost him, at the price which has to be paid for that luxury in India, probably *four shillings out of his fifteen*. We cannot repress some feeling of indignation at the assumption calmly made at the top of p. 14 of the "Summary Statement," that Dr. Lunn's dietary, as given on the previous page, was more frugal than that of his brother missionaries in general. He says: "The possible saving on food alone, to be effected by living as above, s £42 per annum." Dr. Lunn was a welcome guest at the table of many of his brother missionaries, and must be perfectly aware that so far from their dietary being, as he practically asserts, twice as sumptuous as that which he here describes, many of them lived more frugally, and scarcely any of them less frugally, than himself. We know, for instance, of no missionary except Dr. Lunn who does not regard bacon as a luxury wholly beyond the range of regular purchase and consumption. To convey the impression, as this part of Dr. Lunn's evidence indisputably does, that missionaries in general followed a greatly more extravagant style of living than that which he himself adopted, is a perversion of fact for which we can find no excuse whatever. Among the missionaries whose dietary has been no more liberal than Dr. Lunn's, several have lived in the same part of the country as himself, and some under similar circumstances— that is to say, in a purely native town. The experience of some of these will indicate the incredibility of any such assertion as Dr. Lunn has made. One missionary, in a purely native town, finds that mere provisions and fuel for himself and his wife cost him £72 12s.* a year instead of £39. Another in a large town not far from Tiruvalur finds the expense of his table, for himself, his wife and four children, to be £103 a year. Another, living certainly more frugally than Dr. Lunn, and in a town where many articles are cheaper, has found the mere cost of provisions and fuel for himself and his wife to be £55. An unmarried missionary who, boarding with another bachelor in a purely native town, has practised the utmost possible economy, using practically *no*

Facts from the experience of other missionaries.

* Where we are instituting comparisons with Dr. Lunn's assertions as to his own experience, we take the rupee at 1s. 4½d., as he has done.

European provisions, has found that his share of the cost of food, even in that style of living, has amounted to £25 a year.

It will be observed that Dr. Lunn gives no details in proof of his assertion that he and Mrs. Lunn lived on 15*s*. a week. He gives prices of certain articles of food in India, and these prices, <small>**Prices of articles of consumption no proof of cost of living.**</small> by their apparent lowness, no doubt encourage the casual reader to believe that in such a country there would be nothing extraordinary in living on a very small sum. But a moment's thought will show that there are many intermediate questions to be asked before cost of living can be inferred from prices of articles of food. State the cost of beef, flour, eggs, &c., in an English town, and it is easy for ordinary English people to calculate how much it would cost them to live there; but similar information regarding prices in an Indian town would be only a small part of the material needed for judging of the cost of living in it. In speaking of "beef," "mutton," "chickens," "eggs," and giving his readers no hint that those terms in India denote articles very different in quality and utility from the articles called by the same names in England, Dr. Lunn is grossly misleading the public. The only information which would really throw light upon the cost of living would be information as to the amount of the weekly or monthly meat bill, bread bill, milk bill, &c., of an economical person. If Dr. Lunn had given this information, his readers would have seen that however few pence a pound of so-called mutton may cost, the Indian housekeeper, in order to provide eatable and nutritive dishes, may have to spend as much a day upon meat as she would have to spend in England. To give the mere price of commodities with familiar names is, as regards a country like India, to circulate those half truths which are worse than whole lies.

The prices of articles of food given by Dr. Lunn, however, though entirely worthless as evidence in regard to the cost of living, <small>**But even these Dr. Lunn does not give accurately.**</small> have a value to us as additional tests of Dr. Lunn's credibility. We regret to have to inform the Committee that scarcely any, if any, of his statements as to prices are in accordance with fact.

That Dr. Lunn never "was able to buy beef from Negapatam at $1\frac{1}{2}d$. to $2d$. a pound," we can absolutely certify, for one of us bought for him and sent to him at Tiruvalur all the beef that he ever had from Negapatam ; and nearly all the other prices that he gives are wrong, with errors varying from 25 per cent. to nearly 400 per cent. The statement that English stores could be obtained at the Madras bazaar "at a reduction of from 10 to 20 per cent. on English retail prices" bears its absurdity on its face. In regard to prices at Negapatam, which is only twelve miles from Tiruvalur, and connected with it by railway, the following extract from a letter by Mr. W. H. Barden, Foreman, South Indian Railway workshops, addressed to Mr. Findlay, will bear testimony :—

"I have read the paragraph on page 301 of the *Methodist Recorder* under the heading of 'The Cost of Food' [extracted from the 'Summary Statement']. This is certainly very misleading to those who have never lived in India. I have lived in Negapatam ten and a half years, but could never purchase provisions for the money Dr. Lunn says he purchased them for. My friends and I have to pay twice and sometimes three times as much for every article he has mentioned.

"I for one cannot agree with Dr. Lunn that the cost of living is cheaper in India than in England. I know it cost us three times as much or nearly so, and you know we live very simply."

As regards Tiruvalur itself, the Rev. R. S. Boulter, who lived at that station for five years, writes : " Many of his figures as regards the cost of living in Tiruvalur are absurdly wrong." We repeat that it is of no consequence in itself what the prices of articles of food are in Tiruvalur or anywhere else, since mere information of these prices leads to no inference whatever as to the cost of living; but we submit that Dr. Lunn's credibility as a witness is wholly destroyed when he cannot be relied on to bear true testimony in such elementary matters of fact as these.

Summary.

For nearly a year Mr. Hughes has been giving the public to understand that he had in his possession evidence which, if given to the world, would " prove to the hilt " that missionaries could live in health and comfort on much less than they now receive. This evidence has at last been given to the world, and an important part of it proves to be the testimony of Dr. Lunn. At the best the testimony of Dr. Lunn could have had scarcely any weight at all against that the of Bangalore Report ; but if it had been the testimony of a full year it might perhaps have been worthy of some passing attention. We discover however that it is the testimony of a broken six months instead of a year. Still, if we had been told truly the experience even of the six months we might have shown indulgence and listened to it. But when it appears that even the record of this brief period teems with misstatements, our patience is justly exhausted. Truthless assertions drawn from a worthless experience can deserve no consideration beyond that which is necessary to expose them.

II. We now come to the second line of argument adduced by Mr. Hughes, and which he apparently regards as the main defence of his position—the example of other missionary societies, especially the Methodist Episcopal Mission and the London Mission. We have no wish to minimise the importance and weight of this argument.

II. Other Missionary Societies.

We regard the action of other societies as amongst the most important of the questions that claim consideration whenever a change of policy is contemplated. Every mission may learn from every other, for the policy and administration of any society at any particular moment must be regarded as the generalized result of the whole past experience of its agents. Any man who comes forward to advocate a new missionary policy is bound to ask whether it has ever been tried and with what results, and if he can show that it has been tried and with good results, he has in that fact stronger support than any *a priori* line of reasoning could give him. The converse is also true. If the policy has been tried and failed, it thereby receives a more crushing condemnation than any mere reasoning on principles could give it. We are therefore at one with Mr. Hughes in the great value which he attaches to arguments of this nature, and we are willing to acknowledge that if the supposed "facts" behind which he entrenches himself can be substantiated, his position is practically impregnable.

It is a little remarkable that investigations of such vital importance to his argument appear to have been the last which Mr. Hughes embarked upon. Not professedly so, however. On the 9th May, 1889, the *Methodist Times* remarked: "On this point 'The Friend of Missions' was especially anxious to secure figures well within the mark, and in his calculation of £300 a year as the income of the average Protestant missionary, he includes the figures of several *American Societies who pay their missionaries much less* * than the English and Scotch societies." And in the "Summary Statement" (p. 11), we find the following passage:— **Professed examination of other societies not really made.**

"It may be well to give the exact average of all the English and Scotch societies. The figures of the following societies have been taken as the basis of calculation: Church Missionary Society, Society for the Propagation of the Gospel, *London Missionary Society*,* Wesleyan Missionary Society, Baptist Missionary Society, Established Church of Scotland, Free Church of Scotland, and United Presbyterian Church. The average stipend paid by these societies to their married missionaries, including horse allowance, is £315 per annum, with allowance for bungalow, and in most special cases considerable allowances for children both in India and in England."

Such statements certainly give to the whole an air of accuracy and patient research, but we have only to read a few pages further in the "Summary Statement" itself to find that the research professed on paper had never been really undertaken. The Methodist Episcopal Church is "the richest and most numerous Methodist Church in the world, a Church with a foreign missionary income of nearly a quarter of a million sterling" (p. 20), and surely no investigation of American societies can claim to be complete which leaves it out of account. And yet on page 17 of the same pamphlet we read:—

"*Some months after the original articles were published we learned* * that the rates of pay adopted by the Methodist Episcopal Church of America were actually lower than those which we had suggested. This seemed to be such a remarkable fact . . . that we at once wrote to Rev. Bishop Thoburn," &c.

This failure alone would be sufficient to dispose finally of all pretentions to accuracy, but unfortunately for the credit of the case

---

* The italics are ours.

it does not stand alone. It will be observed that in the passage quoted above from the "Summary Statement," the London Missionary Society is mentioned as one of those whose figures had been examined. And yet in a postscript appended to that Statement in the *Methodist Times* of May 1st, 1890, we read:—

"Since the foregoing statement was sent to members of the Missionary Committee two additional facts of importance have come to our knowledge.

. . . . . .

"The other fact to which we refer is even more interesting and important. We have obtained information with respect to the stipends paid by the London Missionary Society to their missionaries in India. Their married missionaries receive," &c.

Such confessions make it wholly unnecessary for us to occupy the time of the Committee with any examination of the "Friend of Missions'" averages. They stand self-condemned. We shall content ourselves with an investigation into the accuracy of his account of the two societies on whose example he now mainly relies.

Methodist Episcopal Mission. And first, let us take the Methodist Episcopal Mission.

It will hardly be denied that before we can wisely base an argument in favour of the reduction of Indian or any other stipends upon the example of another society we must be assured that the lower rates of that society have been found sufficiently liberal to secure health and efficiency, with reasonable freedom from financial anxiety, to those who have for a series of years been paid at such rates. But this simple postulate sweeps away at once two-thirds of the testimony on which Mr. Hughes relies. On page 18 of the "Summary Statement" the following salaries of married missionaries **Recent salaries in South India and Bengal.** of the Methodist Episcopal Church are given on the authority of Dr. Peck:—South India, Rs. 1,800; North India, Rs. 2,475; Bengal Rs. 1,800. Dr. Peck's letter is dated November 15th, 1889. But the Central Conference of the Methodist Episcopal Church in India which met at Cawnpore in July, 1889, had already condemned the salaries in South India and Bengal as too low, and asked that they might be raised to the level of those of North India. The whole question of salaries was considered by a Committee of the Conference appointed *ad hoc*, and the following was their report:—

"Your Committee, after very deliberate examination of the *pros* and *cons*, recommend that the scale of salaries long in use in the North India Conference, be the scale of salaries for all the Conferences and Missions represented in this Central Conference. We may state in brief the reasons on which we base this recommendation :— **Acknowledged to be insufficient by the Cawnpore Conference.**

"(1). Long continued observation has proved that this scale of salaries has been barely adequate to maintain the missionary in moderate comfort and in efficiency. The salary is worth much less than it was fifteen years ago. It is upon the whole cheaper to live in the territory of the North Indian Conference than in the territory represented by other parts of our work. Hence the salary is not too much for any part of the field.

"(2). We reached the conclusion that to adopt a lower scale of salary would work to our detriment in securing the class of recruits desirable for our entire field.

"(3). It is our opinion that a time element, by which the salary would be fixed lower for a term of years in the beginning, would also work detriment, inasmuch as the first two or three years are often especially expensive to the newly arrived missionary. He often comes burdened with some debt acquired in preparation for his work, and in bringing some books and appliances; and often has special expenses in setting up in the field. Hence we think the scale as mentioned should stand as it is."

This report of the Committee was adopted by the Conference, with the single exception that a "time element" was introduced, so that henceforth "of new foreign missionaries entering the field single men receive a salary of Rs. 130 a month, and married men Rs. 180 a month for the first three years of service:"*

The salaries therefore which we have to compare with those enjoyed by Wesleyan missionaries are those given by Dr. Peck for North India, as modified by the 'time element' introduced at Cawnpore. But before proceeding to this comparison it is necessary that we should point out one or two minor inaccuracies in Mr. Hughes' account, and that we should also supplement that account by supplying at least one very important source of income which has been completely lost sight of. **Inaccuracies of statement.**

* *Cawnpore Conference Report*, pp. 34, 35.

APPENDIX A.

(1) Allowances omitted.

1. Bishop Thoburn's account of the Methodist Episcopal allowances as given on p. 18 of the "Summary Statement," is in one or two points inaccurate. He remarks: "No allowance for sickness .... horse .... medicine." In the last of these items Dr. Peck's letter (quoted on the same page) corrects him. As to the first and second items Bishop Thoburn thus corrects himself in a letter to Mr. Patterson dated March 6th, 1890 :—

"The allowance for children is twenty rupees a month. A free house furnished with the heavier articles of furniture is provided. There are no other *fixed* allowances, but invalids have their expenses paid to America or on a sea voyage, or in some cases to a hill sanitarium. The income-tax was paid for several years, but was disallowed at the last meeting of the Committee in America. No provision is made for the education of children at home, but our mission being comparatively new, this question has never been fully discussed, and it will probably come to the front in due time. An allowance is made for the travelling expenses of those who go out from their stations on actual missionary tours. It is usually called an 'itinerating allowance,' and is not reckoned for the ordinary purposes of keeping a horse for private use. In several large cities, however, missionaries receive a horse allowance from local funds."

But in any comparative statement of the personal salaries of missionaries all these sundry allowances should be left out of account. In every mission they are determined by the needs of the work which the men have to do. To add the cost of the missionary's conveyance to his salary is considerably more absurd than it would be in England to add the cost of the circuit gig. If, however, we do add them, the addition will on the whole tell in our favour. For example, every missionary of the London Society in charge of a station receives Rs. 240, the usual horse allowance, and a further sum of Rs. 400 to meet travelling expenses that the smaller allowance would not cover. No such large sum is drawn in our own mission. And yet we could not honestly put this forward as an argument, for we believe every missionary receives under this head what he needs and no more. What should be remembered is that the personal income of the Methodist Episcopal missionary is no more intended to meet the extraordinary charges of travelling on mission service, or of sickness, than is the salary of the Wesleyan missionary. Under these heads both missions proceed on the principle of granting what is needful.

2. It must also be borne in mind that Methodist Episcopal salaries vary somewhat on account of location, or official position while ours do not. For example the missionary in charge of the English Church at Calcutta receives Rs. 4,200 a year instead of Rs. 2,475. We have no such variations amongst us. *(2) Variation of allowances.*

3. But the most important point, which Mr. Hughes' informants have omitted to mention, is that Methodist Episcopal missionaries have the privilege of remitting money home at 45 cents to the rupee. This is equivalent to an exchange of $1s.\ 10\frac{1}{2}d.$, or a gain of $5\frac{1}{2}d.$ in the rupee. A man who has this privilege will naturally buy all books, clothes, European stores, &c., direct from Europe or America, and it may be safely asserted that under such circumstances an unmarried man will remit home one-third of his salary, while a man who has children at home will probably remit from one-half to three-fifths. This must be taken into account in any comparison of salaries. *(3) Remittances home.*

Let us then on this basis compare the personal salaries of a Wesleyan missionary and a Methodist Episcopal missionary. For convenience' sake, we will compare them in gold, converting rupees into sovereigns at the rate of $1s.\ 6d.$ We choose this rate for two reasons—(1) It is below the average rate of the last six years and therefore tells more in favour of Mr. Hughes' argument; and (2) it is the rate of calculation adopted by the Bangalore Conference. Mr. Hughes in the "Summary Statement" adopts $1s.\ 4\frac{1}{2}d.$—not certainly because our missionaries ever received their stipends at so favourable a rate, but presumably because it helps to buttress his argument. The lowest rate at which missionaries have ever been paid is $1s.\ 5\frac{1}{8}d.$, and that was only for one year. In order to get a complete view, we must also compare the salaries at different periods of a man's life, as the allowances for children make so large a difference. We choose therefore the following four periods:— *Comparison of personal stipends.*

1. First year of service—unmarried.

2. Fifth year of service—unmarried.

3. Married—with three children, one being at home, but none on educational allowances.

4. Married—with six children, four being at home, and two on educational allowances.

We assume also that Nos. 1 and 2 send one-third of their salaries home; No. 3, one half; and No. 4, three-fifths.

W.M.S. and M.E.S.

1. An unmarried man in the first year of service.
   Methodist Episcopal Mission—
   Total salary............ Rs. 1560
   Converted—One-third at 1s. 10½d.......... £48 15 0
   Two-thirds at 1s. 6d. 78 0 0

   Total £126 15 0

   Wesleyan Mission—
   Salary, £125; Postage, £4 4s..... .... £129 4 0

   Excess of W.M. over M.E.M......... £2 9 0

2. An unmarried man in the fifth year of service.
   Methodist Episcopal Mission—
   Total salary............ Rs. 1800.
   Converted—One-third at 1s. 10½d.......... £56 5 0
   Two-thirds at 1s. 6d. 90 0 0

   Total £146 5 0

   Wesleyan Mission—
   Salary, £150; Postage, £4 4s... .... £154 4 0

   Excess of W.M. over M.E.M... ..... £7 19 0

3. A married man with three children, one of whom is at home.
   Methodist Episcopal Mission—
   Salary .... Rs. 2475
   Children 720

   Total .... Rs. 3195

   Converted—One-half at 1s. 10½d. £149 15 3¾
   One-half at 1s. 6d. 119 16 3

   Total.................. £269 11 6¾

Wesleyan Mission—

Salary	£230	0	0		
Children	42	0	0		
Postage	4	4	0		
				£276	4	0

Excess of W.M. over M.E.M..... £6 12 5¼

4. A married man with six children, four of whom are at home, and two on educational allowances.

Methodist Episcopal Mission—

Salary .... Rs. 2475
Children 1440

Total .... Rs. 3915

Converted—Three-fifths, at 1s. 10½d. ... £220 4 4½
Two-fifths at 1s. 6d. 117 19 0

Total............... £338 3 4½

Wesleyan Mission—

Salary	£230	0	0		
Children (six)	84	0	0		
Education (two)	24	0	0		
Postage	4	4	0		
				£342	4	0

Excess of W.M. over M.E.M. ... £4 0 7½

From these detailed comparisons it will be seen that the allowances of the two missions are remarkably similar. It must be remembered also that the tendency of exchange is at present upwards, and if ever it reaches 1s. 7d. the balance of advantage will be the other way. So will it be also when the Methodist Episcopal Church faces the question of education, as Dr. Thoburn anticipates it will. On the whole there is little to choose between the two rates, and if the "*Via Media*" is "an accomplished fact" in the one, equally so is it in the other. We have reason to believe—as the following extract from a letter from the Rev. J. Brown, Chairman of the Calcutta District, will show—that Bishop Thoburn himself would agree with us in this:—"I do not see (says Mr. Brown) that there is very much difference between them and us; and this is the opinion of Bishop Thoburn, with whom I have talked the matter fully over. We have no man so well paid as W——, who is now only in his third year in the country."

Turning now to the most recently discovered example of the "*Via Media*"—the London Missionary Society—we find precisely the same serious omission vitiating the comparative statement published as a postscript to the "Summary Statement" in the *Methodist Times* of May 1st, 1890. London Missionaries are permitted to send home money at par for personal supplies, or for their children, or other members of their families in England. Their rates of salary are: for an unmarried missionary, Rs. 1,700 per annum; for a married missionary, Rs. 2,600 per annum; children under eight years of age, Rs. 100 in India or £10 in England; from eight to fifteen, Rs. 150 or £15; from fifteen to eighteen, Rs. 250 or £25.

W.M.S. and L.M.S.

If we apply these rates to the four examples taken above, we get the following results:—

1. An unmarried man in the first year of service—
    London Mission, Rs. 1700.
        Converted—One-third at par £56 13 4
                Two-thirds at 1s. 6d. 85 0 0
                Total £141 13 4
        Wesleyan Mission, as above 129 4 0
        Excess of L.M. over W.M............................ £12 9 4

2. An unmarried man in the fifth year of service—
    London Mission, as above £141 13 4
    Wesleyan Mission, as above 154 4 0
    Excess of W.M. over L.M.......... .... £12 10 8

3. A married man with three children, one of whom is at home—
    London Mission—
        Salary .... Rs. 2600
        Children 350
        Total .... Rs. 2950

        Converted—One-half at par £147 10 0
                  One-half at 1s. 6d............. 110 12 6
                  Total £258 2 6
        Wesleyan Mission, as above 276 4 0
        Excess of W.M. over L.M.............................. £18 1 6

4. A married man with six children, four of whom are at home, and two on educational allowances—

London Mission—
- Salary .... Rs. 2600
- Children 1000
- Total .... Rs. 3600

Converted—Three-fifths at par	£216	0	0
Two-fifths at 1s. 6d.	108	0	0
	£324	0	0
Wesleyan Mission, as above	342	4	0
Excess of W.M. over L.M.	£18	4	0

Thus the advantage which the London Society's missionary has in the earlier years of his service as an unmarried man is lost afterwards, but the whole difference is comparatively trifling, and depends entirely on the present low rate of silver.

We trust that we have shown that when fairly and accurately calculated, no argument in favour of any new financial policy can be based on either of the examples selected by Mr. Hughes as giving practical illustrations of the feasibility of his proposals. They do not give even the semblance of support to any one of his contentions. And he will search in vain for other examples that will serve his purpose better. It may be—it doubtless is—possible for Europeans to exist in India on smaller allowances, but the fact that the cumulative wisdom of several generations of missionaries has led almost all the great English and American societies to adopt what is practically the same scale, ought surely to be taken as sufficient evidence that that scale is the wisest and best. The Methodist Episcopal Church tried a lower scale in Bengal and South India, but found it to fail, and the emphatic declaration of the Cawnpore Conference that even the scale now adopted throughout their Indian missions is "barely adequate to maintain the missionary in moderate comfort and efficiency" is the strongest possible collateral vindication of the conclusions arrived at by the Wesleyan Conference at Bangalore. Two such independent, concurrent, and weighty testimonies ought for ever to dispose of criticisms suggested by brief and ill-remembered experience, and supported by cursory and incomplete investigation.

General agreement of all societies.

ISSUE II. (A)

Is it true that there is anything in the style of life adopted by our Indian missionaries that is needlessly costly, or that can in any sense be called luxurious?

The following are among the passages in the *Methodist Times* which render the investigation of this question necessary :—

(1) "The truth leaves no choice but to say that the charge of luxury, as our English middle-class people who support the missionary societies understand the word, is fully justified by the facts of the case ... among ... Methodist missionaries." ("A New Missionary Policy," Art. II.)

(2) "Every missionary immediately on landing in India finds himself at once received into 'society.' In Calcutta he is presented at Court and makes his bow to the Viceroy. In the other Presidency towns he is always welcome at the public receptions at Government House." (*Ibid.*)

(3) "A certain expensive style of living." (*Ibid.*)

(4) "I am fully convinced that the regular missionary gains very little and loses much by his official recognition in 'society.' It places him at once in a wrong position. Most missionaries, the writer included, would have gone down grey-headed to their graves in England without ever seeing a 'Drawing-Room.'" (*Ibid.*)

(5) "This new social status entails a number of expenses following in natural sequence. Persons who go to Court must dress in a certain style, cannot go about in the towns in any less fashionable vehicle than a phaeton, and must keep up a certain establishment." (*Ibid.*)

(6) "Men who left the London docks with the simplest ideas of life and duty, full of lofty purposes of self-denial and devotion, have

scarcely trodden Indian soil a twelvemonth before they find themselves settled down to a mode and fashion of living from which a year ago they would have shrunk back in dismay." (*Ibid.*)

(7) "The missionary in India . . . is able, with ease and comfort, to mix in Anglo-Indian society in a style which he could not possibly do on less than £1,000 a year in England. Any one who has tried to live in London, keeping a one-horse brougham, mixing in society, dining late, and everything else in harmony with these features, will know that this estimate is not very wide of the mark." (*Ibid.*)

(8) "Viewed from the native standpoint, the missionary's position is yet more 'magnificent.'" (*Ibid.*)

(9) "In the India of to-day there are three totally distinct modes of living—the Anglo-Indian, the Eurasian, and the Native. The first of these is that adopted by the civilian and military classes, and by the missionaries of the great Protestant missionary societies. The second is that adopted by the large town population of mixed descent and by the Roman Catholic priesthood." ("A New Missionary Policy," Art. III.)

(10) "To adopt the second of these styles of living . . . would mean a considerable sacrifice for all concerned. . . Instead of having, as now, butler and cook, the Eurasian plan of having one servant in the dual capacity would have to be adopted. Corresponding changes would have to be made in the rest of the staff of servants. The missionary bungalows would necessarily be houses of half the rental which is now paid. . . If once the majority of our missionaries resolutely adopted a style of living of this character, many expenses of all kinds which are necessary to maintain their present social position would speedily disappear." (*Ibid.*)

(11) "The question of stipends is of importance only from the ethical point of view. It is of paramount importance that English missionaries in India should, as far as possible, be out of reach of the temptation to fraternise with Anglo-Indian society. The ideas and habits which are current in Anglo-Indian circles are fatal to missionary success." (*Methodist Times*, June 20, 1889.)

(12) "When he [Dr. Lunn] used the word luxury, he did not then nor did he now know any other word in the language which would describe the kind of living adopted by his brethren in India. The first thing in India he found was that he was to be the partaker of hospitality in one of their mission houses. He was treated with great kindness, but he was told that he should at once engage a butler to wait upon him—a man of forty-five years of age, with a wife and family. He was told that he must have this man to wait upon him during the day, to wait upon him at dinner, and to open the door of his carriage when he went out. To their English middle-class people, having a man to wait upon him in that way would convey the idea of

luxury. He was told also that he must buy a carriage and horse, and because he had some radical notions, and did not see why he should not ride in native carriages such as those used by judges and barristers, he was told he must not do so. For such ideas to exist in missionary circles was in harmony with the use of the word 'luxury.'" (Report of speech by Dr. Lunn in Conference: *Methodist Times*, August 1, 1889.)

As the author's commentary on the above passages we subjoin the following additional extract:—

(13) "We never stated that English missionaries generally yielded to the temptation of their circumstances, but only that such temptation exists." ("Summary Statement," p. 7.)

It might logically be contended that a negative verdict of the Committee on the first issue settles also that which is now proposed for enquiry. If the allowances of the Society's missionaries are not greater than conditions of health and reasonable comfort require, it is a natural, if not inevitable, inference that their style of life does not exhibit extravagance and self-indulgence. We cannot be content, however, after the array of definite and graphic assertions regarding our manner of living which we have quoted above, to rest our vindication of it upon a logical inference, knowing as we do the inefficacy of mere reasoning to obliterate from the general mind impressions once stamped upon it. Until the issue now proposed is directly faced and dealt with, the supporters of the Society, even if satisfied in regard to the investigation already concluded, will simply be left in bewilderment to wonder how it is that if missionaries have no larger stipends than they ought to have, their lives should present such an appearance of luxury and "style." The two issues indeed, though logically connected, yet examine the circumstances of missionaries on wholly different sides. The first issue approached missionary life from the side of arithmetic; the issue now proposed approaches it from the side of description. The first issue enquired what possibilities in style of living the missionary's stipend would permit; this issue enquires how he has dealt with those possibilities. The first issue challenged Messrs. Hughes and Lunn's "figures"; it remains for us similarly to challenge their "facts."

<small>Relation between first and second issues.</small>

We will introduce the subject by setting before the Committee a consideration which connects the two issues together. Mr. Hughes asserts (Extract 13 above) that though the allowances of missionaries are such as to tempt them to an extravagant style of living, he does not consider that they have in general yielded to the temptation. We do not, for the moment, enquire how far this statement agrees with the other statements we have quoted; we only ask at present, *What have the missionaries done with their money*, if they have had enough to enable them to live in unduly costly style—£80 more, in fact, than is necessary for health and comfort—and yet have not "yielded to the temptation of their circumstances"? We are able to inform the Committee what the missionaries have done with their money; and the information will be such as to deprive Mr. Hughes of the loophole through which he has sought to escape from the responsibility of having charged his brethren with yielding to the temptation of extravagant living. One of our questions addressed to them before we left India was, "Have you been able to *save* out of your ordinary allowances?" and if we were at liberty to publish in full the facts that this question has elicited, there would be not a little indignation among the supporters of the Society that they should ever have been led to suspect their missionaries of being over-paid. Dr. Lunn (we refuse to ascribe this contention to Mr. Hughes) declines to admit that missionaries ought to be in a position to insure their lives for £500. Men are to run the Indian risks of premature disablement and shortened life,[1] which Dr. Lunn

The missionaries have lived up to their income.

---

[1] On this subject we may quote the following from a letter recently received from a Doctor of Medicine of the London University:—"I have just been looking through the statement of Messrs. Hughes and Lunn, and wish to comment on one sentence (p. 16), 'Our brethren in the poorer circuits at home are exposed to at least as great hardships and perils as our brethren in India. Our death-rate in India is not higher than at home, because men are recalled at once if the climate does not suit them.' Of the inference drawn from these data I have nothing to say just here, but as a Doctor of Medicine I should like to point out the inaccuracy of the statement.

Risks to health in India.

"As to what special '*perils*' ministers in poor circuits at home are exposed to, I am completely ignorant.

"The perils to which an Englishman in India is exposed I can easily learn from the best authorities. They are cholera, enteric fever, dysentery and diarrhœa, malarial fever, heat apoplexy, hepatitis, and some other diseases. I should say that an Indian missionary is in greater peril from these diseases than a Wesleyan can now afford to speak lightly of, but which drove him home in twelve months, and yet are to make no provision beyond the scanty sums that the Connexional funds supply, for the wife and children who may at any time be left alone in the world! And the argument in support of this ruthless suggestion is that because in home circuits special allowances are not made for charities and insurance premiums, therefore home ministers are not supposed to have any outlay under these heads! Methodist common-sense and brotherly kindness may be trusted to insist that the missionary abroad shall be able to make some modest provision for those dependent upon him, if he has to give up his work, or lay down his life, at the call of duty. What then are the facts as regards the savings of the Society's missionaries, out of these allowances that are £80 too great? They are,—that more than half your men are *not able to save anything at all*, either for insurance or for any other purpose; and that most of the rest have not saved enough for an insurance of £500. "I have tried to live inexpensively, and have not been able to save in eight years Rs. 100 [£7 10s.] out of my income." "Had I been dependent on my allowances, I think with strict economy I might have managed to save a little the first few years, but not latterly. Just now we are spending *far more than our allowances*. Were it not for a little private money, either we or our children in England would have to be stinted in food and clothes, and indeed in every particular." "I saved a few hundred rupees during my first four years—but it has all been required and more since." "During the first twelve years I saved a little. I find that

minister even when in a poor circuit at home. The premium demanded by any Insurance Society from an Indian resident is a conclusive proof of this.

"But Messrs. Hughes and Lunn say that if a man finds that the climate does not suit him, he is at once recalled. Is this *true*? Is it not a fact that our Indian missionaries do not come home before their term is up, on account of health, until they have distinctly suffered from the climate, say from dysentery or fever? Every medical student knows that if a man has once received a dose of malarial poison, his health may never be so good again. To say that the death-rate amongst all missionaries and missionaries' wives who are now, *or who have been*, in India, is no higher than amongst English ministers is absurd.

"In fact it seems to me that the sentences I have quoted ought clearly not to have been written, and it is hard to see how a medical man of average intelligence could have perpetrated this unscientific statement and have signed his name to it in print afterwards."

during the last twelve years, in spite of gain by exchange, I have not made my allowances suffice. I had no exceptional expense." We confess that as we have read the replies of which these are specimens, we have felt some warmth of indignation that men unable to save anything, and working with the knowledge that the longer they stay in India the less likely they will be to have adequate support for their old age or for those whom they may leave behind them, should be told that they are living in a "certain expensive style," and that they could enjoy health and all necessary comforts on £80 less than they receive. The Society's missionaries are not saving their money. What are they doing with it? They are spending it over their "style of living"; and hence we say that if their allowances are really excessive and such as to put temptation in their way, Mr. Hughes must submit to maintain that they "yield to the temptation of their circumstances," and are living in a manner needlessly costly and self-indulgent.

When we approach the subject of missionary style of living in detail, we are confronted at the outset with another of the pitiful incoherencies with which this new missionary policy abounds. Mr. Hughes suggests reform in stipends in order to correct the style of missionary life; and he desires this correction for the furtherance of the "direct evangelization of the masses of the Indian peoples"; being assured that this, in its turn, will remedy the "failure" of missions in India. Stipends are to be reduced, not so much for the sake of economy, as for the sake of these effects on missionary life, work and progress. This being so, we should certainly expect to find—it would even seem vital to Mr. Hughes' argument to show us—that societies which have adopted the reduced stipends he advocates are reaping from that policy the fruits which he promises. He imagines himself to have discovered, at long intervals and apparently by accident, two such societies, in which "the '*Via Media*' is an ACCOMPLISHED FACT"; but we look in vain for any intimation that in the case of either of them low stipends have effected reforms in style of living or course of policy. On the contrary, we find that both the societies which in the last stage of the controversy are held up to the public, in respect of stipends, as pioneers and patterns of the "new missionary policy," are throughout the whole discussion included

Style of living in the L.M.S. and M.E.S.

under the same condemnation with all the other societies in respect of style of living and methods of work! The "charge of luxury," based upon "careful consideration," and "a thorough knowledge of the facts," is directed against "*all Protestant societies*," and is said to be "fully justified by the facts of the case, alike among Episcopalian, Presbyterian, *London Missionary Society*, and *Methodist* missionaries." We read again, in the *Methodist Times* of May 9, 1889 (p. 445): "Several correspondents have complained strongly . . . . that we should have discussed missionary policy in public, before bringing the subject before the Wesleyan Missionary Committee. There might have been some force in that argument, if this had been a Wesleyan question. But it no more concerns the Wesleyan Society than it concerns the Church Missionary Society, the *London Missionary Society*, or the Presbyterian Missionary Society." The London Missionary Society is prominently at work in the Madras Presidency; and if its missionaries were living in different style, pursuing different methods, and securing greatly superior results to those of the other Protestant societies around, Dr. Lunn. could scarcely have failed to learn it. A "thorough knowledge of the facts," however, left him with the conviction that in all these respects they were like their neighbours; and yet all the time, as he now imagines that he has discovered, they were getting "*Via Media*" stipends! It appears then that the "*Via Media*" policy, even where it is supposed to have been adopted, has proved a failure; for it has not brought about that change in style of living and behaviour for the sake of which alone it was recommended. The very illustrations by which Mr. Hughes seeks to establish the possibility of his policy, would, even if they were sound illustrations, establish at the same time, and by his own testimony, its uselessness! What more can be needed to show the haphazard and hand-to-mouth style in which these would-be reformers have gathered their views and patched together their proposals?

We proceed now to enquire what this style of living is, which, as **Dr. Lunn's description consists of categorical assertions.** it presents itself to Mr. Hughes' imagination, is so serious a hindrance to missionary work in India. In the passages quoted above, a description is given of it in considerable detail, from Dr. Lunn's observations. We shall treat this description purely as a description. We believe that inferences have been drawn from it greatly damaging to missionary character, and that it was almost inevitable that such inferences should be drawn wherever it gained credence. But at the same time we admit that Mr. Hughes and Dr. Lunn did not intend such inferences to be drawn, and indeed have endeavoured by various and repeated asseverations to guard against them.

But though we shall completely put on one side inferences and imputations arising from these passages, we must point out that the passages themselves, all of them, either are or imply categorical statements which must be fact or fiction. They are or contain assertions about missionary life as definite and verifiable as statistics or records of work. Mr. Hughes has desired to dismiss from consideration much of the matter contained in them as "rhetoric," as mere ways of illustrating the central and solely important fact that the missionary receives "£300 a year and a bungalow." What his definition of rhetoric may be we know not. But we presume that even rhetoric and illustrations have a purpose; they are meant to produce an impression, and to help the imagination to obtain a clear and complete picture. And if the impression produced and the picture painted are false, we do not see how the rhetoric and illustration are to escape the condemnation that would attach to the most literal and unvarnished utterances. We maintain that the impression regarding the actual way of life of missionaries which these passages convey, the impression that must be conveyed in whatever sense the language is interpreted, is entirely false and unwarranted by any actual circumstances of that life.

We shall examine the description in detail under the four main heads to which it alludes, viz. (i) Anglo-Indian Society, (ii) Servants, (iii) Houses, and (iv) Horses and vehicles. It is suitable to point out before doing so that Dr. Lunn has adduced no evidence whatever in support of any of the statements we are about to examine. The "Summary Statement," in which we should look for "facts upon which" this description of the way in which missionaries actually live "is based," contains not a syllable of evidence regarding it, unless three lines at the bottom of p. 7 are to be taken as such. Dr. Lunn has not,

wholly unsupported by evidence.

however, withdrawn the statements which he does not attempt to prove, and we must therefore deal with them. But until he has some further evidence to adduce for them than his own *ipse dixit*, we shall not trouble the Committee with more than the necessary explicit assertion of their untruth, followed by such information as may exhibit the real style of missionary living.

1. *Anglo-Indian Society.*—Perhaps the most prominent feature of Dr. Lunn's description of the missionaries' style of life is his representation of them as "received into," "officially recognized by," "mixing in" and "fraternizing with" English "society" in India, and so having a "new social status." He gives the distinct impression that missionaries in general, shortly after landing in India, go through some process which gives them "official recognition" in society. The process is represented as equivalent to being at a "Drawing Room," and is spoken of as being "presented at Court." As regards Calcutta, the following extract from the *Indian Witness*,—the organ of the Methodist Episcopal Church, published in that city—will be a sufficient comment:—

<blockquote>
"'In the first place every missionary landing in India finds himself received at once into "society." In Calcutta he is presented at Court and makes his bow to the Viceroy.' This is a somewhat striking piece of news to veteran missionaries who have never been 'presented at Court.' Some of us at least have been cruelly slighted. We have not so much as heard of such a thing. The only fault we have to find with such a statement is, that it is totally untrue."
</blockquote>

As regards the rest of India, we do not suppose there are half a score of our missionaries now in India, or any greater proportion of the missionaries of other societies, who have ever been at a "public reception at Government House," though it is their duty as loyal subjects of the Queen to attend, if they reside in the neighbourhood of the seat of government. The representation that admission into "society" is connected with this official recognition at Government House, in the same way that admission into society is connected with presentation at Court in England, is equally untrue. Whatever a missionary's relations with "society" may be, they are absolutely unaffected by his calling or not calling at Government House. Attendance at a levée, when a missionary does undertake it, is as little a matter of social position and as much a matter of official duty as is an address of loyalty presented by the Conference to the Queen.

Dr. Lunn gives an equally incorrect impression of the extent to which the missionary is found in the society of his fellow-countrymen. The degree and intimacy of his association with them depends on other conditions than those which fix the boundaries of social circles in England. A duke and a costermonger if sole inhabitants of a desert island would soon be intimate; and where Englishmen are few, it is natural that they should not maintain the same artificial barriers which they allow to separate them at home. The extent to which a missionary mixes with his English neighbours will be regulated for the most part by mutual congeniality, and especially by his *leisure* for social intercourse. Friendly association with his fellow-countrymen would be of advantage to his work; for it would tend to the removal of ignorance and the creation of sympathy in regard to missions, and would help to maintain among Englishmen in India that general Christian standard of life and conduct which should be one of the most powerful auxiliaries of evangelization. The fear which Mr. Hughes is fond of expressing, that missionaries, by association with their fellow-countrymen in India, whom he calls "representatives of a military despotism," will be infected with "ideas and habits current in Anglo-Indian circles" and "fatal to missionary success," involves a gross and gratuitous libel on a body of men who, as a class, are worthy in temper and spirit and behaviour of the country from which they have come, and are rendering inestimable service by their character as well as their abilities to the country to which they have gone. As to the extent to which your missionaries do actually mix in English society, outside the circle of our own English congregations, the information we have gathered from them enables us to show you how utterly false are Dr. Lunn's representations. So many of our stations are in towns, that the Society's missionaries have, on the average, each spent four-fifths of his time in India in the neighbourhood of European society; yet in answer to the question, "What social engagements, of all kinds, have you outside the circle of our own Church?" two out of every three brethren answer, "*None whatever*," and from nearly all the rest we hear only of an official visit to a representative of government, or a meal once in a few months taken at the house of another European, or an occasional game of tennis. The following are specimens of the answers :—

"Of standing engagements I have absolutely none. I call about once a year (as officially bound to do) at the British Residency. We endeavour to return visits paid to us, but these are comparatively few. Could we find leisure for it, we doubt not it would be wise in the interests of our work that we should mix more freely with European society."

"My social engagements are and have been with Hindus and Mahomedans,—Hindus chiefly—for missionary purposes. *I have no other.*"

"*None.* For fourteen years I have often wished we might have a few, but having none we are able to give ourselves to our work from 7 A.M. to 10 P.M., which represents an average day's work."

After this information the Committee will not be surprised to learn that all that Dr. Lunn says about the influence of mixing in society upon missionary style of living is ridiculously and outrageously false. He speaks of "many expenses of all kinds which are necessary to maintain their present social position," of the "new social status entailing a number of expenses following in natural sequence." He describes them as "compelled by the customs of the social world in which they move, to live in a certain style." He even goes so far as intimate that the number of the missionary's servants, the style of his dress, and the build of his vehicle are regulated by the fact that he "goes to Court." One of our senior brethren, accustomed to call a spade a spade, writes that all this is "arrant humbug"; and we acknowledge that if such language is not permissible to us, our opinion must remain unexpressed. Even if the missionary did choose to associate with his fellow-countrymen, such intercourse need not influence his style of living; for, as we have stated above, social intercourse does not require in India as in England close similarity in style and outward circumstances. And when we add to this that your missionaries do not, as a matter of fact, mix in society at all, to accuse them of shaping their life by its requirements becomes about as rational as it would be to charge them with sacrificing influence, usefulness, and economy, for the gratification of the Man in the moon!

2. *Servants.*—We have to complain in regard to this subject as we complained in regard to "Cost of Food" under Issue I. (B.), that Dr. Lunn in the "Summary Statement" (p. 14) gives the impression that he had a wholly different kind of household establishment from that adopted by his brother missionaries round about. He knows perfectly well that this was not the case, and that if there was a difference between the cost of his servants and of theirs, it was due not to his following a different system, a "*Via Media,*" but to difference of situation and conditions. He has remembered the list of his servants correctly, and his outlay upon them was a little *in excess* of the Bangalore Conference estimate for the district to which he belonged. The Bangalore Conference, for reasons which will be given immediately, included under servants the dhobie and an ayah; and if these be added to Dr. Lunn's list, and an exchange of 1s. 6d. be taken (for Dr. Lunn never paid his servants at an exchange of 1s. 4½d.), the list appears as follows:—

[marginal note: 2. Servants.]

			£	s.	d.
"Butler"	Rs. 108 per annum		8	2	0
Cook	,, 102 ,,		7	13	0
Cook's helper	,, 36 ,,		2	14	0
Sweeper	,, 36 ,,		2	14	0
Four punkah men, employed six months	,, 90 ,,		6	15	0
			£27	18	0
Add Dhobie	,, 60 ,,		4	10	0
,, Ayah	,, 120 ,,		9	0	0
Total			£41	8	0

The amount allowed by the Bangalore Report for servants in the Negapatam District is £40 10s. The differences in cost of servants due to difference of locality and in customs of service will be illustrated by the following paragraph from the memorandum already quoted, by Mr. Cooling, Chairman of the Committee on Finance of the Bangalore Conference:

3. "I regret that I did not preserve the list of servants made out for each district. The following is the list for the city of Madras:—

[marginal note: Servants in the Madras District.]

		Rs.	as.	p.
Head servant, or "Boy"..................monthly pay		10	0	0
Cook...	,,	8	0	0
Chokra or Matie............................	,,	5	0	0
Tannikatch, or Cook's assistant	,,	3	0	0
Ayah...	,,	10	0	0
Scavenger..	,,	3	0	0
Waterman, or extra Gardener.............	,,	5	0	0
Coolie boy to carry things from market	,,	2	8	0
Dhobie..	,,	5	0	0
Night punkah men for two-thirds of a year, at the rate of Rs. 7 a month.............................		4	10	8
TOTAL............................Rs.		56	2	8

Rs. 56 2as. 8p. × 12 = Rs. 674, which at 1s. 6d. per rupee is £50 11s. Outside the city of Madras the chokra or the market coolie might be dispensed with, so an average was taken and £49 10s. put down for the District.

"There is one item in this list which for a married missionary and wife *without* children is perhaps not absolutely necessary—that is, the ayah. The question was discussed in the Committee as to whether the ayah ought to be included in the servants for a man and wife only. It was stated that a number of the brethren are on lonely stations and that in the absence of the husband from home it is almost impossible to leave the wife with only male servants in the house. This weighed with the Committee, and the ayah was left in the list. I am inclined to think it would have been better to omit the ayah from the list and to have pointed out in the Report that the allowance for *children* must cover the cost of an ayah, or, where there are more than two children, two ayahs. With two exceptions all the members of the Committee were married men with children.

4. "If the ayah is omitted from the list of servants, that will reduce the expenses of a man and wife only, by £9 a year. (Rs. 10 × 12 = Rs. 120, which at 1s. 6d. = £9.)"

It is when we come to consider the duties of the servants employed and the possibilities of reduction in their number, that the incapacity of Dr. Lunn to observe and testify is again manifested. In his speech in Conference he described the duties of the servant whom he calls a butler,[1] as being "to wait upon him during the day

---

[1] The term "butler," as used in India, properly denotes a responsible servant, whose chief business is to superintend the other servants and act more or less in the capacity of steward. He would receive from Rs. 12 to Rs. 20 a month. Only in very exceptional circumstances would a missionary need, or be able to afford to keep, a "butler." Dr. Lunn never had one, though his "boy" may have called himself, or been called by other servants, a butler, honorifically.

to wait upon him at dinner, and to open the door of his carriage when he went out." There is just as much truth in this description as there would be if it were used of the maid-of-all-work in an English minister's family. Again he proposes that under the " *Via Media* " system :—" Instead of having, as now, butler and cook, the Eurasian plan of having one servant in the dual capacity would have to be adopted. Corresponding changes would have to be made in the rest of the staff of servants." On this we have to remark, first, that the whole account of a " totally distinct Eurasian mode of living " is a myth, Eurasians, just as much as Englishmen, living in all varieties of ways, according to their varieties of means ; second, that though a low class of servants might possibly be obtained who would consent to do, very imperfectly, part of the cook's work and part of the boy's, the work left undone by this individual would fall upon the mistress of the house, forming a serious tax upon her health, and effectually debarring her from mission service ; third, that there are no "corresponding changes in the rest of the staff" that could be suggested even by Dr. Lunn. An English artizan who has kept no servant in England, finds that in India the necessities of life compel him to have as many as Dr. Lunn had. To make clear a subject that has been much misunderstood, we will briefly indicate the employment of each of the servants named in Mr. Cooling's list above :—

1. The *head servant*, or "*boy*," has general charge of the house, supervises the preparation for meals, waits at table, dusts the rooms, and attends to the multitude of miscellaneous matters connected with the proper maintenance of the modest but busy household of the missionary. He is his mistress' chief helper, but absolutely indispensable, unless she is to be tied to wearing house-work, and the Society is to lose a valuable agent. Duties of servants severally.

2. The *cook* buys the daily household stores in the bazaar, and cooks them. The fact that meat will not keep from day to day greatly increases the amount of cooking that is necessary, and in the Madras Presidency the "boy," if he is qualified for his own work, neither will nor can do the work of the cook in addition.

3. The *chokra* or *matie* is needed in a large house to help the

"boy." The use throughout the house of oil-lamps in place of gas, the prevalence of insects, and many other causes, increase the amount of house-work needing to be done.

4. The *tannikatch* is a woman who helps the cook, drawing water for kitchen purposes, grinding curry, &c. Any cook would refuse to work without such an assistant.

5. The *ayah* is either a nurse for a child, or an attendant on the mistress. Under certain circumstances (see above, p. 304), the missionary's wife needs such an attendant even when she has no children.

6. The *scavenger* is the equivalent of English drain-pipes and sanitary arrangements.

7. The *waterman* is the equivalent of English water-pipes. He draws from the well and brings to the house all the water required for household use. It must be remembered that the heat of the climate necessitates a liberal use of water for all purposes.

8. The *coolie boy to carry things from market* is needed only when, as in Madras, the market is so distant that the cook refuses to carry the provisions he purchases. In such matters the employer is at the mercy of his servants, since they will rather leave him than endure burdens or undertake tasks that are not according to the customs of their particular calling.

9. The *dhobie* is the washerman, not a permanent servant, but paying a weekly visit to receive and return the household linen.

10. The *punkah men* are employed during the hot months of the year to cool the sleeping room. They correspond, *mutatis mutandis*, to fires used in winter in England.

This enumeration will, we trust, have made it clear that many of the so-called servants are merely the equivalents of privileges enjoyed through other means by all classes of people in England; and that the rest of the staff, through their own traditions and the necessities of tropical life, could not be reduced in number with any advantage either to the missionary or the Society; and that, thirdly, the master and mistress of the house are not placed in a position of any greater convenience or comfort by this apparently great array of servants, than the English family enjoys that is waited upon by one good maid-of-all-work. Missionary experience rather is that the cares and annoyances of household life are in direct ratio to the number of servants employed.

3. *Houses.*—The chief references that Dr. Lunn has made to the subject of mission houses are as follows :—" The missionary bungalows would [under a '*Via Media*' policy] necessarily be houses of half the rental which is now paid ; " and in the "Summary Statement," p. 7, he joins Mr. Hughes in the belief that the missionary might "go into a native town and take a house in a street of respectable Hindus." The first of these proposals is the kind of off-hand suggestion which it is easy to make about a matter that has not been practically examined at all. We can without much difficulty determine the essential requirements of a mission-house ; and when they are fixed, there will not remain much doubt as to what the nature and the cost of the house must be. It will be admitted, we presume, by any one who thinks, that a house to be occupied by a missionary family should have a study, a dining-room, a sitting-room (for native visitors could not, without distaste to themselves, be always received in the eating-room), and three bed-rooms[1] (with only two, a family with children will have no room for any visitor). It will also be admitted, without objection, at least by medical men, that in a tropical climate these rooms, if they are not perpetually to endanger the health of Europeans living in them, must have thicker walls and be both higher and larger in area than the corresponding rooms in an English middle-class house. Verandahs are necessary to keep out the glare of the sun and are also useful for the accommodation, while waiting, of the numerous visitors who throng the missionary. There must be also servants' quarters, a kitchen, and store-sheds (for the missionary in charge of a station has to be a jack-of-all-trades and the possessor of multifarious stores and implements), stable and carriage-shed, moreover, for even the "*Via Media*" policy leaves the missionary's horse and vehicle scrupulously untouched. These out-buildings should, for the sake of health, be at some distance from the house itself, and the premises should also be large enough to give

marginalia: 3. Houses. Requirements of a mission house.

---

[1] Each bed-room in India has to have a small room attached, called a "bath room." The necessities and arrangements of Indian life make this essential Hence, when bed-room is spoken of, bed-room with bath-room is intended.

room for storing timber or bricks on occasion, for a carpenter's shed, and for providing shelter for native agents or homeless converts. Such are the absolutely necessary conditions which the mission-house and its adjuncts must fulfil, if they are to provide fair security for the health of the missionary and his family, and to give him the means of doing his work. What becomes then of the possibility of "going into the native town and taking a house?" No native house of the kind required could be anywhere found, and the Mission has invariably either to build its own houses, or to purchase or rent houses built for the occupation of Europeans. Where the Mission has built or rented houses, it has had regard, in choice of position, to the desirability, on the one hand, of being as near as possible to the native population, and to the necessity, on the other hand, of not occupying a site that shall endanger the health of the successive residents in the house. Even in England it has often been found advisable that the missioner in charge of a poor and crowded district should live away from it, for the sake alike of the physical and the moral health of his family; and whatever reasons there can be for such a course in England are tenfold stronger in India.

In answer to one of the queries addressed to our brethren we have received information concerning the size, accommodation, and *Our present mission houses.* cost of our present mission-houses. They are, in general, houses containing about six rooms, no larger in size than are necessary for health. Where the house has greater accommodation, it is commonly occupied by two families, or by one family and an unmarried missionary or missionary lady. In some instances large houses and properties have been purchased by the Mission at a much less cost than would have been incurred in raising much smaller buildings; but in all these cases ways have easily been found of utilizing the extra accommodation. Our largest mission house—in the north of India—holds a training-school as well as two missionary families. It must not be forgotten also that the mission-house has often to be used for meetings and services, for receptions of the native church, school prize-givings, even bazaars, and other purposes demanding considerable room. It is easy to speak of "houses of half the rental which is now paid," but any sort of attempt to reduce the suggestion to practice would exhibit at once its utter shallowness and futility.

4. *Horses and vehicles.*—Dr. Lunn has created a great impression by his references to the missionary's horse and conveyance. He has said that we drive in a phaeton, that the phaeton is a "fashionable vehicle," and that we use it in preference to something more modest and cheap, under the compulsion of the "customs of the social world in which we move." In his speech at Conference he contrasts with the missionary's "carriage" as humbler and therefore more desirable equipages "native carriages such as those used by judges and barristers." In this last utterance he falls once more into the inaccuracy which he can so rarely escape; for it would be as near the truth to speak of the "carriages used by judges and barristers" in England as less pretentious and costly than an ordinary circuit gig, as it is to describe the equipages of such people in India as humbler than the "carriage and horse" of the missionary. But a sufficient answer to every word that Dr. Lunn has uttered on this subject, and a sufficient corrective, in the minds of all thoughtful men, to any impression he has made by the use of fine-sounding names for the missionary conveyance, is found in the fact, that, in their "*Via Media*" proposals, Mr. Hughes and he *leave the horse and vehicle allowance untouched*. They denounce the "fashionable phaeton," but they know perfectly well that it is a necessity of the missionary's life, for they carefully leave him money to purchase and use it. They press for "a change in style of living all round," for a "general and sweeping reduction in stipends," and they give the impression that the vehicle is one of the features of missionary life which most urgently demands reform; yet when they have to produce their proposals, they markedly and repeatedly declare that we must "leave untouched the horse allowance." This is a significant commentary not only on their coherency and consistency in regard to this particular point, but on the weight and value of the whole body of their criticisms and proposals.

We have examined in detail the chief particulars in which Dr. Lunn has criticised the style of life of missionaries, and the Committee will be able to judge whether or not there is "any other word in the language which would describe" it, than the word "luxury." It is possible that there are some luxuries connected with missionary life in India; for every condition of life in every country probably has some luxuries, few or more, *inseparably connected with the necessaries* that belong to it. English life, even in its poorest and most straitened conditions, certainly holds luxuries, to the view of the missionary remembering it from India; and it is possible that Indian life also has certain enjoyments and advantages which missionaries might fairly be expected to dispense with, *if they were not inseparable from the necessities of the situation.* There are few missionaries who would not a hundred times prefer the inseparable luxuries of English to those of Indian life, which are at best few and trifling. But it is a waste of time to investigate their nature or measure, so long as it is shown to be the case that, such as they are, they are bound up with the essentials of life. Of *separable* luxuries we claim to have shown that the present missionary style of living holds none, and that it is in general as simple and economical as the requirements of health and conditions of work will permit. In general illustration of this we may quote from a letter from the Rev. Herman Jensen, head of the Danish Mission in Madras. He writes :—

"Let it not be forgotten that the longer we stay in India, the more nourishing food do we want. When I arrived in India I used to criticize very badly. I brought with me the strength of a Norseman. I had never been ill. I did not for a couple of years distinguish between heat and cold. Sickness has done me no harm in India, but the heat has gradually sucked the nerves to such an extent that I am now more like a mimosa than a northern oak. The first two years I could walk any distance in the sun without feeling it, but now I cannot. The heat and intense glare make us so delicate. I never lived in luxury; I never loved it, and never longed for it. Luxury is to me more a burden than a comfort; therefore I cannot take a big airy house and a good big bandy to be luxury to a European in this country. An umbrella in Europe I consider a greater luxury than a good-sized carriage in India. The Indian sun is not a thing to be trifled with, and least so in reference to those who spend many years in India. A person who spends only a year or two in India is not yet initiated in the secrets of the Indian climate. The strength he brings with him from the North prevents him from understanding the secrets of the climate. During my first two years in India I lived in a ridiculously small house, which even a poor Hindu would not have envied me. I slept well in this hut. Now I cannot sleep during nine months of the year if I do not lie in an airy room where the slight night breeze can find its way; and if I do not sleep well I

[sidenote: A Danish missionary on "luxury."]

cannot work well. Three years ago, when I went to Denmark for eighteen months, I with my wife and our two children lived in a house consisting of three rooms. They were small indeed. We kept only *one* servant. But what a comfort! what a treat! The sun did not scorch us, neither did the Indian servants vex us. Carriage we never thought of. We could again get *a walk*, which we certainly prefer a thousand times to a drive in a carriage in the sun, heat, glare, and dust of Madras. A drive here is no comfort, but a walk in Denmark is a great comfort, not to say more; but a walk in Madras or in India is the most miserable thing I know of. The perspiration goes at once through our exceedingly thin garments; the red dust falls thick on the wet clothes; and when we by such a walk arrive at our destination—say at a street preaching-place—we look much more like a loafer than a decent person, to say nothing about the exhausting state we would be in. Instead of examining the comfort of an Indian missionary, I should like to see the tables turned, and we out here formed a committee to examine the comfort of ministers at home. We might take some Hindus into our committee. What would this committee, for instance, say about an Englishman's bedroom? 'Why all those feather beds?' or perhaps even eider-down beds? Our committee, I suppose, would say, 'Throw all that luxury on the fire, and give the gentleman and lady a nice cocoanut-fibre mattress and a blanket. That is what we use in India. And why all those curtains in all the windows? Down with them; we do not use them in India. Make their rooms smaller, and it will take far less coal to keep them warm.' In this way much might be said against luxury at home. But if feather beds are necessary things in Europe to keep us from cold, big houses here are no less necessary to protect us from the scorching Indian sun. Nevertheless, the life of a European missionary and Europeans in general, and of all well-to-do Hindus, has an air about it of some grandeur or what to call it. The big house with the pillars at the front looks royal rather. The number of lazy servants we have to keep is rather royal too. The servants are lazy, indifferent, slow, careless, care only for themselves; such people cannot always be treated in the still and quiet way things go on at home. These servants demand a *master*. These *masters* and these *servants* we are not at all used to see at home. And new comers to India may take all these as comforts, or perhaps as luxuries, while we, who are familiar with them, take every additional servant as an additional *trouble* and expense. . . . . 'Poor missionaries' has in India become a public phrase. At home it seems that 'luxury missionaries' is a favourite term. The fact is that from a pecuniary standpoint we have come from the pan into the fire; but at home friends seem to think we have come from the fire into the pan. It seems that Europe will never be able to understand India. As to luxury its view is wrong, and so it is in reference to missions. When schools have no converts, they are condemned, and missions praised more or less according to the *number* of converts. It seems that Europe has no time to ask if the converts are converts to Christianity or really to Christ. I have spent all my days in India for evangelistic work. But though the schools may not get one convert, and the missions get them by hundreds, I shall still hesitate to say anything decidedly about the influence of these two kinds of work. But I *think* that the schools at the present time do more for India than the missions. We are not in need of a reformation as to our bandies and houses, but I should think we are in great need of a reformation among our mission agents. Europe ought, I think, to stop all pay by and bye to native agents, and only pay their own men. And as to the rest, trust in God. If any native Christian is anxious to be heard among his own people, let his own people support him. Where there is a will there is a way. I feel that there is so much to say that the few words I here send you will go a very short distance to clear up anything. Three years ago when I visited Denmark I spoke out my mind, but good Christian people cared very little to hear the truth. They think they know better. It seemed to me that the only thing good Christian people cared for was to get converts *at once* for their expenses."

ISSUE II. (B.)

Is it true that there is anything in the style of life adopted by our Indian missionaries, that hinders the growth of that mutual understanding and sympathy between the missionary and the native population which is essential to the effective prosecution of evangelistic work?

On this subject the *Methodist Times* has used the following language:—

(1) "The effect of this mode of living is inevitably to separate the missionary from the people instead of bringing him into close contact with them. It is almost impossible for any man to occupy for years the position of a feudal lord without developing the feudal spirit. Men do successfully fight against it here and there, but it is not in human nature generally to wield almost absolute power and receive abject reverence, without losing sight, more or less, of the great Christian principle of the brotherhood of all men." ("A New Missionary Policy for India," Art. II.)

(2) "Compelled by the customs of the social world in which they move to live in a certain style, their usefulness is crippled, their influence is lessened." (*Ibid.*)

(3) "And [if the '*Via Media*' were adopted] how great would be the gain in the work amongst the heathen around! No longer would they regard the missionary, as they often do to-day, as only one member of the same family, of which other members were the collectors, the engineers, the officers of the army, and the heads of the salt and abkari departments. They would realize vividly that these men had come to India for the love of Christ and for love of

them; and such a conviction would mightily help in the work of winning India to Christ." (*Ibid.* Art. III.)

(4) "We therefore proposed a '*Via Media*,' believing that it was our duty to bring our missionary evangelists as near those to whom they preach as is consistent with health, civilization, and reasonable comfort." ("Summary Statement," p. 7.)

(5) "But everything that has occurred only strengthens our conviction that the *sine quâ non* of the evangelization of India is the bending of every energy and the subjection of every consideration to the supreme necessity not only of cherishing, but of exhibiting—conspicuously and unmistakably—in all our words, in all our habits, and in all our ways, the homely brotherliness of Jesus Christ." (*Ibid.* p. 21.)

From these passages when taken together it will be observed that the contentions of our critics are—

Summary of criticisms. (*a*) That the style of life adopted by missionaries is such as (1) to interpose a serious obstacle to the growth of sympathy and confidence between them and the native population; (2) to expose the missionaries to the temptation of lordly indifference and isolation; (3) to lead the natives frequently to misunderstand the motives which bring missionaries to India and prompt them in their work, and consequently to beget suspicion and mistrust of them.

(*b*) That this whole evil might be remedied by a change in the outward circumstances of the missionary's life which (1) would not make it necessary for him to discard that mode and fashion of life which his English birth and training have made natural and necessary to him; or (2) endanger his health, or deprive him of those reasonable comforts upon which the efficiency of his work in part depends; or (3) hinder him exhibiting to the Hindu the beauty and sweetness of a Christian home.

Now it will be seen at once that a negative conclusion on Issue I. (B.), already considered, disposes of the *suggested remedy* for the state of things here presumed to exist. If it be true, as we think we have shown, and as the unanimous experience of missionaries asserts, that a European missionary cannot live in India with that degree of comfort requisite for health and vigour, in any other style, or on any other scale, than that now adopted, then if the effects of this life were such as they are described to be, we could only lament it as one of the many overwhelming difficulties against which missionaries in India have to struggle—a difficulty which more than any other ought to appeal to the sympathy of those whose labour is carried on under easier conditions. But though the impossibility of the proposed *remedy* may be regarded as settled, the question of the *disease* itself still remains. Hence the form that we have given to the present issue.

The issue, it will be observed, is not "Is there a wide social gulf between the European and the native in India?" nor yet "Is this gulf of such a nature as to oppose very serious hindrances to the growth of perfect mutual understanding and confidence?" To both of these questions every one who has even a slight knowledge of India would give an affirmative answer. All Europeans in India feel this gulf, and many even outside missionary circles are seeking in various ways to bridge it. The missionary sees it and feels it every day. It is one of his constant hindrances and trials. He longs to come nearer to the natives, to be more thoroughly in touch with them; and how to bring himself nearer to them and to obtain this intimacy of touch is one of the many problems which his whole life is an effort to solve. The question before us however is this:— "*Is the gulf between the European missionary and the native of India one that is caused—or mainly caused—by the difference in their style of life, and which the missionary can bridge by adopting a style of life different from that which he does now adopt?*" To this question our answer must be a clear and emphatic negative.

Before we proceed to indicate the grounds on which this answer is based, we may be permitted to point out some extraordinary conclusions which would seem necessarily to follow from the assertions which we traverse. If it be true that the "social gulf" which impedes mission work is created by differences in the merely outward conditions of life, and that it may be abolished by a change in these conditions so trifling as not to involve the surrender on the part of missionaries of that mode of life which to every Englishman is at once a heritage and a necessity; and if it be further true that these facts lie so

Inevitable conclusions from criticisms.

plainly on the surface that a young man whose acquaintance with missionary life is of the most superficial character and whose knowledge of native life is *nil* can detect them, then how extraordinary it is that a long succession of Indian missionaries of all societies should have remained through whole lifetimes of service either blind to them, or if not blind, culpably silent! Was there no serious study of Indian problems till the "Friend of Missions" appeared? Or have Indian missionaries of all societies and times preferred their own comfort to the interests of their work? Then indeed has the Church fallen upon evil days! And yet serious as these conclusions are—dishonouring either to the intellect or the heart of missionaries past and present,—it seems to us that the acceptance of one or other of them is tacitly involved in any serious discussion of Mr. Hughes' proposals. If it be really so patent that a reduction of £80 in the stipends of missionaries will suffice to remove one of the great hindrances to the spread of the Gospel in India, and to open a great and effectual door for the evangelization of "the masses," and your missionaries have never suggested and now oppose this change, then plainly they must be either selfish knaves or short-sighted fools, and in neither case is it worth the Church's while to retain them in its service. It is true that Mr. Hughes refuses to go on to either of these conclusions, and we give him the fullest credit for sincerity in his professions of confidence and love. But Mr. Hughes has to deal with a public more logical than himself—a public that is not able to accept premisses and reject the conclusion that is wrapped up in them. The "Friend of Missions" seems to have felt this logical difficulty when he wrote his second article. "And to-day," said he, "there are many men at work in India, as the writer can testify from personal knowledge, who would welcome gladly and heartily a general and sweeping reduction in missionary stipends which would compel a change in the style of living all round." Where are these men, and why do they not come forward? They do not, and never did, exist. In this, as in so many other points, the "Friend of Missions" has drawn on his imagination for his "facts."

Mr. Hughes' position illogical.

Let us now proceed to ask—What is the gulf that separates the

English missionary from the Hindu? Is it such a one as Mr. Hughes supposes? Can it be bridged in the simple fashion that he suggests?

To this last question every missionary—indeed every European of any calling who has lived half a dozen years in India—will answer in the negative. The gulf that separates him from the Hindu is not a *material* but a *moral* one. It does not consist in food and dress and habitation at all, nor in anything else that can be touched and modified by any change in financial policy or style of life. It consists in an incompatibility of sentiments and feelings and modes or habits of thought, and is the net result of three thousand years of diverse development. For a hundred generations the European and the Hindu have been growing apart, and while the faith and philosophy of the West have been quickening the conscience and fostering the growth of individuality, liberty and responsibility, these have been almost destroyed in India by a subtle pantheism and a crushing ceremonial system. The result of this is that the Hindu and the Englishman view everything from different standpoints—often opposite standpoints,—and it is years before they can enter with intelligent comprehension into each other's thoughts. This is a gulf which separates more or less all alien peoples, but which is wider between the Englishman and the Hindu than between any other two races under heaven. It is so wide and so apparently impassable that it often fills the young missionary—who has known nothing of such gulfs before—with a feeling akin to despair. He may be in the midst of Hindus, associating with them on terms of equality all day long, but he feels that he only touches the outer shell of their life. He may orientalize himself outwardly, but he is still occidental in thought and feeling, and the gulf remains as wide and as impassable as ever. It may be passed, it is passed, but not in one year or in five, and not by any change in the form and fashion of outward life. · It is passed by patient study and long-continued intercourse, by ever widening sympathy and ever increasing acquaintance with Eastern conceptions, by opening the mind to every orientalizing influence, and seeking to view everything as far as may be

The gulf that separates Europeans from natives of India a moral one,

through an oriental glass. It is thus and thus only that the European missionary can bring himself into close and intimate contact with the people he seeks to win for Christ, and the process is one that

and cannot be bridged by any outward change. demands years. There is no potent spell in a turban, no insurmountable obstacle in knives and forks, no open sesame in any "*Via Media*." The outward form and fashion of life is a thing wholly apart, and to one whose knowledge of India is based upon the experience of years, a suggestion that a "simpler life" would bring the missionary "nearer to the natives," in anything but space, is the *ne plus ultra* of childishness.

But it may be said that the "Friend of Missions" did not refer to the great moral chasm, but only to the comparative absence of social intercourse and fellowship between the European missionary and the

There is no other "gulf," natives of India, and that his contention was that this was brought about by the exclusive style of life adopted by the former. But what, we must ask, does the "Friend of Missions" mean by social intercourse? Eating and drinking together? Then we acknowledge that there is an entire absence of it. But we do not regard this as an evil, and are not anxious to remedy it. The Kingdom of God is not meat and drink. It would, however, be an insult to the intelligence of the "Friend of Missions" to suppose that this is his meaning, for the veriest tyro in Indian affairs knows very well that the hindrance to this form of social intercourse is not on our side. *But beyond this there is no social gulf, no separation.* If Dr. Lunn means—and this is undoubtedly the primary and natural sense of his words—that there are circumstances in the style of the missionary's life which keep the natives at a dis-

and no "aloofness." tance from him, whether it be that his house is so far from theirs that they cannot come to see him, or that it is so grand that it frightens them away, or that the missionary himself does not encourage their visits or bid them welcome, or that his haughty spirit and bearing repels them : if these, or any of these, are the meaning which his words are intended to convey, then we assert that his words are simply untrue, and that Dr. Lunn has had sufficient experience of the life of missionaries to know that they are untrue. During his brief stay in India he lived for considerable periods in the houses of at least five of his brethren, and if he took any notice at all of what was going on he must often have been aware of an almost continuous stream of native visitors of all ranks who came to see the missionary or his wife on all conceivable errands, some to seek his sympathy in their troubles, others to share with him some new joy, but more to ask his advice and help in difficulties of every kind. He must have observed that all were welcome, that all came with fearless confidence, knowing that they never had been and never would be repelled. He must have known that the problem which the overwrought missionary had to solve was not how to attract the natives to his house, but how to find time for all who came.

But again it may be said that the "Friend of Missions" did not so much refer to the absence of social intercourse as to the nature of it. On the one hand was the "feudal spirit," on the other the "abject reverence," and there was an entire absence of "the homely brotherliness of Jesus Christ." It will be observed that here the "Friend of Missions" passes from observation to inference, and the value of his inference depends upon the truth of the premiss which he himself supplies.

Dr. Lunn misinterprets social forms.

We can well imagine that to one totally ignorant of Indian forms of etiquette many things in our social intercourse with Indians might appear strange, and if such a one was prepared to attribute to us unchristian and unbrotherly sentiments some things in our conduct might even appear to indicate such sentiments. For example, his English notions of politeness might be outraged if he saw his host, after conversing for a quarter of an hour with a native visitor, calmly rise and bid his guest good morning, thereby dismissing him. But nevertheless such a course would be in perfect accordance with Hindu codes of etiquette, and if the host refused to follow it he would greatly embarrass his visitor. We are inclined to believe that the "Friend of Missions" has been thus misled. He has jumped to conclusions without seeking for the requisite information, and has projected upon all the world his own narrow and insular ideas as to outward expressions of cordiality and brotherliness, in a way that he would hardly have done had he lived longer and travelled more. This is shown by all he has written on the subject of shaking hands. Surely Dr. Lunn must have met scores of natives who objected to that form of salutation, and not a few who positively refused it? If he has ascribed their objection to pride, he has erred as greatly in his judgment of them as he now errs in his judgment of his brethren. Dr. Lunn would hardly thank us if, meeting him in the Strand, we imprinted on his cheek a German kiss. And he will admit that it is no contradiction of "homely brotherliness" on his part, that he does not use towards his audience at Prince's Hall the holy salutation of the early Church. But such argument need not be prolonged. To attach any serious importance to such things is to fall back from the essentials of Christian brotherhood to the merest accidentals of social life. We are anxious to give every man the greeting which he most approves, and when we err it is through failure to interpret his wish and not through any spirit of aloofness. But even errors here are of little moment. Souls are not saved by forms of salutation. And we trust that, in our manifest desire to spend and be spent in their service, we exhibit to all our Hindu friends a more convincing proof of our brotherliness than the most punctilious observance of the rules of etiquette would be.

We may fitly conclude this section by the following quotation from the unpublished letter of Graham S. Bruce, Esq., to the *Methodist Times*, dated August 19, 1889. Any number of similar testimonies might easily be obtained :—

"As to his [the 'Friend of Missions'] last assertion, or rather aspersion, I count as I write at least two dozen missionaries between Madras and Tinnevelly my degree of acquaintance with whom could not fail to have revealed to me such peculiarly grave blemishes as separateness from the people and the cherishing of a feudal spirit would be in a missionary's character, could they, with any degree of truth, be charged against them. I have always seen missionaries approached by natives, even of the lowest rank, with a ready confidence that speaks for itself. I have seen Hindu boys simply haunting the missionary's bungalow in a manner rather distressing to anyone dropping in for a visit."

ISSUE II. (c.)

Is it true that there is anything in the style of life adopted by our Indian missionaries, that hinders the growth of that brotherly unity between the missionary and native Christian which is essential to the healthy development of the Church?

On this issue Mr. Hughes and Dr. Lunn have either made or adopted the following statements :—

(1) " The immense distance which now separates the English *padre* from his Indian flock would be at least diminished by one-half. His own people would realize, what a great many of them certainly do not believe to-day, that his presence amongst them was due to love for them, and not to a desire to earn a livelihood. The manifest self-sacrifice and devotion involved in such a life would react upon the whole native Church. The mercenary spirit which now, alas! animates too many of our native ministers and catechists would be rebuked in the daily life of the missionary, and the whole tone of affairs within the Church would be purified and elevated." ("A New Missionary Policy," Art. III.)

(2) "Many a missionary returns home with *no more knowledge of the inner life of native Christians than that learned from catechists and mission agents.* House-to-house visitation is becoming *rarer and rarer,* and in the majority of cases where such visits are made the missionary seldom loses sight of the SOCIAL GULF which separates him from the native Christian." (Quoted from Mr. Sattianadhan in "Summary Statement," p. 8.)

(3) "It is exceedingly difficult for any Englishman in India to maintain always towards the natives that absolute brotherly equality which Jesus Christ maintained towards all men. We cannot but

think that even our own brethren have unwittingly and unintentionally fallen short." In proof of this it is alleged that there are two District Meetings, that Dr. Lunn, " so far as his memory serves him," excepting on one occasion, "never was invited to take a meal at the same table as a native Wesleyan minister," and that in the Bangalore Conference there were no native ministers. Mr. Hughes and Dr. Lunn then say, " We are compelled to consider what practical steps can be taken to bring English missionaries nearer to the natives of India. We believe that nothing will tend to this more effectually than such an extremely simple style of living as will distinguish missionaries conspicuously from Anglo-Indian society, and will make it easy for them to cultivate social intercourse with native Christians." ("Summary Statement," pp. 9, 10, 11.)

(4) " Dr. Lunn referred to a garden party given by a well-known native gentleman, who said he was going to invite a few missionaries who were in sympathy with their native work. He received his visitors, and shook hands with them as they arrived; but the secretary of one of the great missionary societies who was present refused to shake hands with him as a native. He said that such things were to be deplored. He never said that the missionaries were cultivating such a spirit, but that the system tended to develop such a spirit." (Dr. Lunn's speech in the Wesleyan Conference as reported in the *Methodist Times*, August 1, 1889.)

(5) "If one-half of the men and the funds devoted to the education of the Brahmans had been employed in giving the same high education and training to our poor Indian converts, the native Protestant Church in South India, if not in Bengal and Bombay, would have before now taken the foremost position in the Presidency, and native Christians would have occupied half the positions of honour and emolument." (" A New Missionary Policy," Art. I.).

These extracts show that our critics profess to believe that the style of life generally adopted by European missionaries (1) separates them from the native Christians in a way that is detrimental to the healthy development of the Church; (2) keeps them in many cases ignorant of the inner life of native Christians; (3) places them in circumstances through which they are out of sympathy with work amongst native Christians, thus leading them to neglect the Christian children and sometimes even to treat native Christians with discourtesy; and (4) causes them to regard the native ministers not with "brotherly equality," but as inferiors both socially and ecclesiastically.

Summary statement of charges.

These statements have been put forward as one of the reasons

APPENDIX A. 323

which render a new financial policy desirable, and that new policy has been represented as an available and easy cure for the state of things here described. We have dealt already with the feasibility of the new policy, but that does not do away with the necessity of the present issue. If the relations between European missionaries and the native Christian population are really such as have been described, then if the remedy suggested be an impossible one, we must straightway look for another. A disease so serious, so fatal, must not be left unchecked. The native Church should be the missionary's chief care, its development his highest aim, its healthy growth his greatest glory; and if it be true that he is so separate from that Church in sympathy that he fails in his plain duty to it and lords it over God's heritage, then the cause of such failure must be patiently searched out and ruthlessly removed. The issue before us, therefore, is, "Does such separateness as has been described exist?" That there is, and perhaps ever must be, a certain measure of isolation in life, and even perhaps in sympathies, between men of different races whose whole life has been cast in different moulds, is inevitable; but that separation exists of such a nature and to such a degree as that described in the passages we have quoted, we strenuously deny. *A negative verdict on Issue I. does not dispose of present Issue.*

It may be well first to examine the evidence on which certain specific statements have been based. In addition to the general statements that have been so freely circulated there are certain so-called "facts" that happily admit of summary dismissal. *Evidence on certain specific statements.*

In Dr. Lunn's speech before Conference, there is an account of a garden party in Madras, at which he was present. As reported in the *Methodist Times*, the speech runs thus :— *The garden-party incident.*

"Dr. Lunn referred to a garden party given by a well-known native gentleman, who said he was going to invite a few missionaries who were in sympathy with their native work. He received his visitors and shook hands with them as they arrived; but the secretary of one of the great Missionary Societies, who was present, refused to shake hands with him as a native. He said that such things were to be deplored."

When Mr. N. Subramanyan, the host in question, read this report, he wrote to the editor of the *Methodist Times* as follows:—

"My attention was only recently called to a speech of Dr. Lunn's delivered before the Conference and reported in your paper. In that speech the following passage occurs:—[The above quotation is then given.]

The host's contradiction.

I have no doubt that Dr. Lunn was referring to a garden party given by me and at which he was present. That garden party was intended almost exclusively for the native Christians of the different denominations in Madras. But I made an exception in the case of those missionaries whose work, either as pastors or evangelists, or superintendents of mission work generally, brought them into contact with native Christians. I did not invite many more European missionaries who, though my personal friends, were not working amongst native Christians. When I invited Dr. Lunn as a personal friend of mine, who I was anxious should see as much of Indian life as possible, I explained to him that he would meet a few European missionaries whose work brought them into contact with native Christians. Of course I cannot say what exact words I used, but the above was the meaning I intended to convey. Dr. Lunn has either misunderstood me, or forgotten what I said. If, therefore, instead of saying 'Missionaries who were in sympathy with native work,' he had said 'Missionaries who had come in contact with native Christians,' he would have been more correct. As to the statement that the secretary of one of our great mission societies refused to shake hands with me as a native, I cannot help saying that it is absolutely without any foundation. No European missionary has, to my knowledge, ever declined to shake hands with me. And it is extremely unlikely, however proud a man may be, he would do so, especially when he had accepted my invitation. I cannot understand how Dr. Lunn was led to make the above statement. As the above statement, unless contradicted, may lead many of your readers to erroneous conclusions, I shall be glad if you will publish this."

This letter was not published, probably because by the time it arrived the whole subject was looked upon as "ancient history." It

never published.

is true that Mr. Hughes now privately states that the report in the *Methodist Times* was a false one, that Dr. Lunn never said what he is there reported to have said, and that the only correct report appeared in the *Methodist Recorder*, where the two incidents combined in the *Times* are said to have happened at different places. Then why was the error not corrected at the time? Incidents of this kind, utterly devoid of truth though they may be, do more harm than any amount of laboured argument. The charge of want of sympathy is in this particular case, however, shown to be groundless, and if we had the true explanation of the other incident we have no doubt the charge of want of courtesy would be found equally groundless. In a quotation from Dr. Lunn's journal, published in the *Methodist Times* of May 22, 1890, Dr. Jesudasen seems to have been the gentleman affronted. The high position which Dr. Jesudasen had attained, both professionally and socially, makes it impossible for us to believe that he ever was, or ever believed himself to have been, so grossly insulted. But alas! he is now dead, and so this particular misstatement can never be set right. It is, however, to say the least, a remarkable line of argument to adduce a personal affront to a gentleman of wealth and position in proof of separation from the masses.

The chief witness in support of the position maintained by Mr. Hughes, is Mr. S. Sattianadhan of Madras. Mr. Sattianadhan is a young native gentleman of undoubted ability and considerable influence. He published a few months ago a pamphlet on missionary work in India, of which free use has been made by our critics. In this pamphlet Mr. Sattianadhan makes many general statements relative to the attitude of mind maintained by the European missionary towards native Christians, but does not indicate the grounds on which his statements are based. Mr. Patterson, being aware of Mr. Sattianadhan's views, and being anxious to obtain any definite evidence in support of those views which Mr. Sattianadhan might possess, wrote to him on the subject before leaving India. We give Mr. Patterson's letter and Mr. Sattianadhan's reply:— *Mr. Sattianadhan's testimony.*

"MADRAS, *March 5th*, 1890.

"MY DEAR MR. SATTIANADHAN,

"You are no doubt aware that our Wesleyan Missionary Committee in London has appointed a Commission[1] to inquire into the statements that have recently been made respecting the life and work of Indian missionaries. I have been appointed to attend that Commission as a deputation from India, and I am anxious to be as well informed, both as to fact and opinion, as possible.

---

[1] When this letter was written, Mr. Patterson was under the impression that a Commission had been appointed.

"A few months ago I read a pamphlet of yours on Indian missions, of which however I have not now got a copy. I should be very much obliged if you could supply me with a copy, or at least tell me where I can procure one. Also if you would be good enough to answer the following questions, it would be a great favour. I ask them from no other wish than to get at *the whole truth*, and I am sure you will be as anxious as I am that misunderstandings should be removed or abuses swept away.

"In your pamphlet you say in effect (I write under correction, as I cannot refer to your words)—

"(1) That house-to-house visitation of native Christians is practically unknown amongst European missionaries. On this I should like to ask—

"(*a*) What exactly do you mean by house-to-house visitation? Do you refer to purely pastoral attention, to visits for spiritual purposes? If so, I suppose your remark is limited to those missionaries who have direct pastoral charge of native churches?

"(*b*) On what grounds does your statement rest? On direct personal observation, or on hearsay?

"(*c*) Does it apply to any Wesleyan missionary you have ever known? I ask this because the Commission is a Wesleyan one.

"(2) You also state, I think, that many missionaries go home with no knowledge of native Christians but what they have learnt from catechists. On this I would ask the questions (*b*) and (*c*) above.

"You also made sundry statements respecting the style of life of missionaries, the neglect of native Christians in education, &c. On all such subjects I invite you to lay all the *facts* in your possession fully and frankly before the Commission. Mere unsupported opinions and hearsay evidence are worthless; it is *facts* that are wanted. I promise to put all the evidence you may entrust me with before the Commission. My sole object is to elicit the *whole truth*, and by throwing off all reserve, and descending from general statements to particulars that can be investigated, we shall all best serve the interests we have at heart—the cause of truth and righteousness and the spread of Christ's kingdom.

"Believe me, yours very truly,
"GEORGE PATTERSON."

To the above letter Mr. Sattianadhan sent the following reply:—

"EGMORE, *March 19th*, 1890.

"MY DEAR MR. PATTERSON,

. . . .

"(1) As requested, I have much pleasure in sending a copy of my little book on missionary work. I have not altered my views in the least since the publication of the book.

"(2) With regard to the question as to house-to-house visitation, not only mean by the term 'house-to-house visitation' visits for spiritual purposes, but also visits of courtesy. My remarks are based on personal observation, supported by evidence of a large number of native Christians belonging to various denominations. I fully admit that native Christians, and as for that matter native non-Christians, come more in contact with missionaries than with the other class of Europeans, but at the same time I think I am justified in saying that it is possible for missionaries to be more in touch with the people. I have been in England myself, and have moved on terms of the closest intimacy with Englishmen, but I must admit there is a barrier in India between the European missionary and the native Christian —a barrier which, I think, is more the result of the reservedness and insular character of the Englishman, which are naturally more prominent in this country than at home. While I say this, I do not forget that the bond of Christianity should be such as to overcome even these artificial barriers.

"My experience of Wesleyans is very limited; but as I have just remarked, my views are based on personal observation supported by the evidence of a large number of native Christians of all grades and denominations. I may also remark in this connection that my articles on missions were written for the *Harvest Field* at the request of the editor, who particularly requested me to state my views unreservedly, and I took special pains not to write anything which I thought did not represent the views of the majority of native Christians. I have received several letters from leading native Christians throughout India expressing their approval of my views.

"Your second question is partly answered above. In spite of Mr. Cobban's refutation of the remark of mine you quote, in his paper on missions, I still hold, and I can let you have, if you give me time, the opinions of hundreds of leading native Christians throughout the country, that missionaries as a rule know very little of the inner life of the Indians. Why, it is a stock argument for the employment of an indigenous agency that the missionary being a foreigner is not able to enter into the thoughts of the natives.

"(3) In my book I never brought forward any charge of luxury against missionaries. All that I said was that there is a prevalent idea that the style of living of missionaries is a little too high, and that there is room for more economy. I believe you are aware of the controversy on the same subject which was carried on in the columns of the *Madras Mail* not long ago, in which the style of living of Protestant missionaries was compared and contrasted with that of Roman Catholics. The controversy, I think, did not represent the Protestant side fairly, but still it indicates that the opinion you refer to is a common opinion held more strongly by some Europeans than by native Christians. I do not think that there is any specific evidence needed for my views on this subject. I only ventured to suggest a more economical policy, which friends of missions like Cust, Hunter, &c., have done, and which missionary committees themselves are endeavouring in some cases honestly to carry out.

"When your letter reached me I happened to be talking to a Syrian Christian gentleman, who is now the resident apothecary of the Ophthalmic Hospital. He is a man singularly free from prejudices for or against missionaries. I put him this question, 'Do the Syrian Christians of Malabar think that the Protestant missionaries are in touch with the people?' This was his reply—'I consider that the German missionaries are more in touch with the native Christians than the Protestants. There is a general feeling that the Protestant missionaries *ought* to be more in sympathy with the people.' I asked if he could substantiate his statement. He has promised to write to the leading Syrian Christians throughout Malabar and get their opinions. I can also get the impartial testimony of the leading native Christians in other parts of the Presidency; and if your Commission care to have the opinions of native Christians, I am prepared to send them if sufficient time is allowed. The views of independent native Christian laymen are more valuable than those of clergymen, and this I trust your Commission will attempt to obtain.

"Yours very truly,
"S. SATTIANADHAN."

In estimating the value of this letter it is right that we should state that Mr. Sattianadhan was educated at Cambridge, thus passing the most important years of his life in circumstances wholly different from anything to be found in India, and acquiring a thoroughly English style of life. During the few years that have elapsed since his return to India he has been in the educational service of the State and has been stationed first and chiefly at Kumbhakonam—a town in which there is no European missionary, and subsequently in the city of Madras, where the native church is so advanced as in every case to be under the direct pastoral charge of a native minister, the particular church to which Mr. Sattianadhan belongs being ministered to by his own father. Mr. Sattianadhan's experience therefore cannot in the ordinary nature of things give much weight to his opinions. But we will not urge this point: we prefer to take his letter on its own merits without insisting that his limited experience robs it of the weight that it might otherwise have had.

Mr. Sattianadhan's experience.

And first, let it be noted that Mr. Sattianadhan's testimony does not in the slightest degree support an affirmative answer to the issue under consideration. He does not for a moment regard the distance between the missionary and the native Christian as caused by the style of life adopted by the former, but he attributes it to the fact that the missionary is a "foreigner." No alteration in style of living will remove this "barrier" between the European missionary and the native Christian. The phrase "house-to-house visitation" conveys to the ordinary English mind the idea of visits paid for evangelistic or pastoral purposes; but according to Mr. Sattianadhan's interpretation, the words are intended to include "visits of courtesy." In further elucidation of his meaning, Mr. Sattianadhan states that he has been in England and "moved on terms of the closest intimacy with Englishmen," and it is apparently in visitation of this kind that he finds missionaries do not do what he thinks is their duty. In holding this opinion Mr. Sattianadhan is a representative of a considerable and growing class of Christian young men, who have received the highest type of Western education, and have associated, many of them, on terms of intimacy with Englishmen of various ranks in India or in England. They have become thoroughly Anglicised in habits, in thought, and in part at least in feeling, and they now claim to be treated in all respects as Europeans. We cannot but regret on some accounts this approximation to English manners and modes of thought, because it almost inevitably accompanies a growing aloofness from native manners, feelings, and sympathies. Especially will it be matter for regret if the men of "light," who should also be men of "leading" in the native Christian community, should become so separate in thought, feeling, and manner of life from the general body of their fellow native Christians, as not to be qualified for the position they ought to hold as trusted guides and supports of the native Church. But, except for this regret, we are conscious of no objections on our part to associating with these Christian young men of education on terms of perfect brotherly equality. If it has appeared that we have not sought or welcomed this social intercourse to the extent these young men desire, that fact must be ascribed to the same cause that leads us to neglect our own countrymen. The truth is, we have neither time nor strength for the mere courtesies of society, whether native or European. We cannot but think that Mr. Sattianadhan's complaint as to the aloofness of missionaries is, unconsciously

Attitude of educated Christian young men.

perhaps, founded upon the apparent social neglect we have indicated; for we do not believe that among the members of our native churches generally there is any feeling whatever that the missionary neglects or is out of sympathy with his native fellow Christians. If Mr. Sattianadhan's "opinions of hundreds of leading native Christians" should ever be forthcoming, we are confident that they would mainly be found to be the opinions of gentlemen in the position we have described. We may point out that this long letter, written in reply to Mr. Patterson's direct appeal for facts and evidence, contains confident assertions and *a priori* arguments, but nothing at all that can rightly be termed evidence.

The relation of the missionary to native Christians and his general treatment of them is a subject of the highest importance. Mr. Hughes and Dr. Lunn have endeavoured to support their contention regarding it by an appeal to the statements made in the Bangalore Conference Report, to the effect that the slanders of the *Methodist Times* have had a widespread and serious influence in the native Church. We still maintain that they have had such influence. The members of our churches, in their personal acquaintance and dealings with individual missionaries, generally—we believe almost universally—feel that they are treated with Christian kindness, sympathy, and brotherliness. But it must be remembered that the European missionary is to the average native Christian a man of another race, who has appeared on his horizon a stranger from an unknown land; and when he hears that the fellow-countrymen of the missionary, those who know, as no native can do, the circumstances and possibilities of his life, those who might be expected to appreciate correctly his relations to England, and the motives which led him to enter upon, and lead him to continue, his missionary work—when the average native Christian hears that these fellow-countrymen of the missionary are decrying and accusing him, he may well think they have better means of judging than he has, and that what he has taken for self-sacrifice and brotherly sympathy and charity has been only the prosecution of a calling carried on for the sake of a comfortable livelihood. But to take a more general ground. When was the principle established that because a slander is believed, it must be

Effect of criticisms on native Christians.

true? Let slanders be circulated concerning the best known and honoured Englishmen, not in India, but in England among the people that know and honour them; let them only be reiterated loudly and emphatically enough, and there will be found plenty of people to believe them. Let mud enough be thrown, and some of it will stick. But argument would surely have reached the depth of meanness and inanity, if it were applied to show that because these slanders had gained credence, therefore they must be true. The power to hold firmly a conviction of the unselfishness and purity of motives of others is one of the latest gifts of Christian grace; and it is small wonder if our newly-gathered native churches find themselves disturbed in their confidence, when they are told that our fellow-countrymen, who know us better than they can ever hope to do, have lost confidence in us, and regard us as living in luxury and self-indulgence; for that is the common interpretation placed upon the recent criticisms by the natives of India.

The "Friend of Missions," in his first article on "A New Missionary Policy," by implication charges the missionary with neglecting the interests of the native Christian children. No proof is offered in support of this statement; and no proof can possibly be offered; for all the facts prove the contrary. It is notorious to all who are acquainted with the state of education in India, that the native Christians are the best educated of all the native communities. When it is remembered that most of the native Christians are poor and come from the lower orders of society, the high position attained by Protestant native Christians with regard to education proves what great interest the missionaries have taken in the education of the children of their flock. There is no need to dwell on this point, for every reader of our reports knows well that a large portion of the time of the missionary and his wife is occupied with the care of schools of all kinds, in which our Christian children receive a useful and liberal education; and the large number of Christian schoolmasters, catechists, native ministers and educated laymen, as well as Bible-women and other educated women, are living proofs of what has been accomplished.

The alleged neglect of Christian children.

The missionaries are further charged with not treating the native ministers with true brotherly equality. With regard to the question of dining together, we may say that there is much more of this kind of social intercourse between the missionary and his native colleagues than Dr. Lunn seems to be aware of. His inexperience prevents him from having an accurate knowledge of the facts. But the argument based on the fact of not dining together is worthless. We must ask again, "Does Christianity consist in meat and drink? By dining together will the European missionary and the native minister help forward the salvation of India?" True brotherliness consists in none of these things. We make bold to say that there exists between the missionary and the native minister a spirit of brotherly unity and hearty co-operation that is in complete harmony with the spirit of Christ.

The treatment of native ministers (1) socially.

This spirit finds its chief manifestation otherwise than in social intercourse; indeed there are reasons, which Dr. Lunn perhaps could not fairly be expected to have grasped during his brief residence in India, why such modes of manifesting our brotherliness should be avoided rather than encouraged. We Englishmen find it hard to present to the people of India a Christianity free from Western accessories and appendages; and in proportion as we connect Western habits and manners with the Gospel that we offer, we make it hard for Hindus to accept our offer. To spread the idea that becoming Christian means becoming English is to make the task of evangelizing India infinitely harder than it need be. Yet it is difficult to avoid spreading this notion. For not only do we ourselves find it hard to distinguish between the essentials of Christianity and the accidentals that our Western upbringing has connected with them, but many of our native Christians also, by a natural process, tend to become imitators of us not only in our beliefs and religious practice, but in outward things, such as dress and manner of life. In proportion as they do so, they spread among the heathen the feeling that by becoming Christians they will lose their nationality and have to give up everything that is familiar to them. To avoid this most injurious misconception, we have to withstand carefully the Anglicizing tendency that is always operating more or less powerfully in the native church; and nowhere have we to withstand it more carefully than among our native ministers, to whom and their successors we look as the chief hope of the evangelization of India. The great mission to their own people, which God lays upon them, requires that they should remain Indians of the Indians, and exhibit Christ

Danger of Anglicization.

to their fellow-countrymen not in English but in Indian speech and garb and life. This consideration has again and again to check us when we are inclined to follow our English instincts and exhibit our unity with our native brethren in forms natural to us but novel to them.

In describing the ecclesiastical position of the native minister, Mr. Hughes and Dr. Lunn have fallen into a serious error, from which they might easily have been saved, if they had taken the slightest pains to find out the constitution of an Indian District Meeting. At the Calcutta Conference held in 1885, with Dr. Jenkins in the chair, the subject was fully discussed. In the minutes of that Conference, pp. 19 and 20, the discussion is recorded as follows :— **(2) Ecclesiastically.**

"The Conference proceeded to a consideration of the subject of topic No. 2, the rights of the native ministry. The secretary read the report of the Sub-Committee on this subject. Mr. Hudson moved the following amendment, Mr. Rigg seconded :—

"'That there be two sessions of the District Meeting, at the first of which Europeans alone should be present, while the other should be attended by both Europeans and natives. That at the first session should be considered all questions referring to the European ministry, while at the other those referring to the native ministry and Church.'

"When put to the vote this amendment was lost by 11 to 6. The following report of the Sub-Committee was then put to the Conference, and carried by 11 votes to 6.

"'With a desire to strengthen the native ministry and encourage self-support in our native Churches, and for the general furtherance of the work of God, we would suggest that such steps be taken as will tend to preserve and perfect the unity of the Ministry, foreign and indigenous, and secure the fullest rights to both. With this end in view,—

"'(1) We recognise the law of Methodism that all ministers in full connexion have an equal right to vote on all subjects provided for in the ordinary business of the District Meeting;

"'(2) We recommend that the distribution of the Committee's grant for native work, and of local funds raised for that purpose, shall be considered as part of the business of the District Meeting;

"'(3) We think, however, that the finance of European ministers, their relations to the Committee, and their appointments to circuits, should be considered and voted on by European ministers only.'"

We cannot understand how a missionary who was present at a District Meeting constituted according to the above resolutions, could so far forget what actually took place in it, as to declare that the native ministers "are excluded from half the deliberations of the Annual District Meeting." The assertion affords another proof, if any more were needed, of the gross inaccuracy and inexcusable carelessness of the "Friend of Missions."

On p. 10 of the "Summary Statement," a great deal of assertion and argument is applied to prove that the missionary has "an unconscious attitude of mind in relation to the natives"—whatever that may mean—because native ministers were not present at the Bangalore Conference. The assertions made upon the subject only show that Dr. Lunn is not better able to acquaint himself with facts of recent history in India than he was able, during his residence there, to acquire facts of observation. The Bangalore Conference was *not* the "Triennial Conference of the Wesleyan Methodist Church in India" —"the great triennial gathering of our Church." The Bangalore Conference was wholly unique in its character, not summoned in the same way nor constituted in the same way, nor having the same objects as the Triennial Conferences, of which the last had been held nearly *five* years previously. The cause of its assembling, the object without which there is no reason to suppose it would have assembled when it did, if at all, was the necessity of taking action in regard to the assertions of the *Methodist Times*. Other questions considered by it were entertained because it was felt that when a body of experienced brethren were gathered at considerable expense from all parts of India, it would be wasteful and unwise to let the opportunity pass of ventilating matters that had long been in the general mind. But since the prime subject of deliberation was the recent attack upon the life and character of the European brethren, and the action required of them in consequence, no reason existed why the presence of the native brethren should be required. Had they been present, Mr. Hughes and Dr. Lunn would have been the first to discredit the proceedings of the Conference as vitiated by the presence of men against whom no charge of any kind had been made.

It must be borne in mind, moreover, that the action of the Conference on all questions except those connected with this controversy was purely consultative, and that all its resolutions were referred for consideration to the District Meetings, where the voice and vote of the native brethren would have due weight in regard

<small>Nature of the Bangalore Conference.</small>

to them. The total absence of any such spirit as Mr. Hughes and Dr. Lunn have imputed to us on the strength of this mis-description of the Bangalore Conference, is amply exhibited by a recommendation of that Conference itself, to the effect that in all regularly constituted Conferences for the general consideration of our Indian work, native ministers shall be present in due proportion; if it had not already been sufficiently exhibited in the fact that native ministers were invariably present at the regular Triennial Conferences of which the last was held in Calcutta in 1885. The consideration is ever present to our mind that the native ministers must one day be the pillars of the Church that is rising in India; and our judgment as well as our feeling prompts us to give these brethren the fullest authority, independence, and power that they are qualified to possess, in all our gatherings. We are, at any rate, sufficiently their brethren in sympathy, respect, and affection to resent with some warmth the charge which Mr. Hughes and Dr. Lunn make against these brother ministers of theirs in another land, when they say:— "Native ministers .... who are dependent for their bread upon the favour of European missionaries cannot be accepted as unprejudiced and independent witnesses in relation to their employers" ("Summary Statement," p. 8), and when they speak of "the mercenary spirit which now, alas! animates too many of our native ministers" ("A New Missionary Policy," Art. III.).

While freely admitting that there is a separation between missionaries and native Christians partly from racial peculiarities, and partly from differences in habit, yet we strongly maintain that in all things pertaining to the spiritual life of the members and the healthy growth of the Church, the missionary is in perfect sympathy and accord with them. It is true that he is seldom, if ever, the pastor of the Church, for by birth and training he is not well fitted for that office; yet he is jealous with a godly jealousy to provide for the people pastors after God's own heart. He works in hearty co-operation with his native brethren; and both strive together for the development of the native Church. That depends not on the style of life adopted by the missionary, but on supernatural means which freely operate if there is the unity of the Spirit in the bond of peace; and this we hold is the true description of the relations that exist between the missionary and the native Christian.

ISSUE III.

Is it true that the rates of stipend or the style of life of missionaries have been in any way determined by their adoption of the educational policy?

On this subject the "Friend of Missions" made the following statement:—

"The direct result of the policy of Dr. Alexander Duff has been that the men engaged in educating and training the aristocracy of India have by a natural sequence of events taken a position in Indian and Anglo-Indian society far removed from that which would naturally be occupied by the evangelist of the masses."—("A New Missionary Policy for India," Art. II.)

Our treatment of this issue may be very brief, and yet the issue tself is important. For there is nothing that would tend more **Importance of the issue.** powerfully to prejudice the public mind against educational missions than the idea that the missionaries engaged in that particular branch of work were compelled to live in a style of greater "magnificence" or comfort than their brethren. True, even this fact would not necessarily condemn educational work. To be obliged to live in greater style than his brother engaged in vernacular preaching might be one of the trials which an educational missionary ought to be willing to bear. Still, to the thoughtless and superficial, who are generally influenced more by the outward aspects of a thing than by any deep consideration of principles, a method of evangelisation in its nature inconsistent with what is vaguely spoken of as "Apostolic simplicity of life," would almost necessarily seem unworthy of support.

It may suffice to show how purely imaginary is the relation which Dr. Lunn assumes to exist between educational work and style of life, if we briefly point out the following facts :— *No relation between education and style of life.*

(1) All the great Missionary Societies had determined their scale of allowances, and the missionaries themselves had adopted the style of life in which they are found to-day long before educational work was really begun. If Dr. Lunn will for a moment cease to teach and become a learner at the feet of Carey, Marshman and Ward, he will discover how those devoted pioneers of British Protestantism in the East were led to conclusions on this subject, which were accepted by all their successors in the field, and which have been justified by three-quarters of a century of glorious success.

(2) When the higher education was entered upon, it was nowhere found needful to increase the allowances of the men who were appointed to it. We have seen that in our own Mission the salaries of young unmarried men have been once reduced, viz., in 1852. In 1851 our first high school was opened, and the first man in the Madras District to whom the reduced allowances were paid, was the brother in charge of the high school. Thus so far from the entrance upon the higher education causing an increase of allowances, it synchronized, in our Mission at least, with a reduction.

(3) No Missionary Society that we are acquainted with makes any difference between the allowances of men who are engaged in educational work and those engaged in vernacular evangelisation; and, though many of them do take into account the special needs of particular localities, it seems to have been wholly foreign to their experience that a man engaged in education needed any special consideration on that account.

But one absurdity invariably leads on to another. Dr. Lunn having determined to link together educational work and self-indulgent—or, to use his own word, let us say "magnificent" —living, must forge a chain strong enough for his purpose. This he does by asserting that we are edu- *The so-called aristocracy of India.*

cating an aristocracy and therefore move in aristocratic circles. Such a statement is as utterly misleading as anything he has ever uttered. And yet even here there is the proverbial grain of truth. In some parts of South India the Brahmans are no doubt the principal landowners; and yet their average possessions are so small that they seldom suffice to yield more than a bare livelihood. To call such men an "aristocracy" in any ordinary English sense, is as untrue as it well could be. And yet Mr. Hughes himself is so utterly misled by the term that he even illustrates the position of the educationist in India by asking whether the West Central Mission "would survive the next Conference" if the "missioners spent much of their strength in communicating secular knowledge to dukes, marquises, and earls"! Could fatuity go further? Be it known to Mr. Hughes, then, that tens of thousands of these aristocrats are beggars seeking their food from door to door; be it known to him that out of every ten youths who implore the educational missionary to take him into his school "free" on the score of abject poverty, nine are Brahmans; be it known to him that feeding "the poor Brahmans" has been an act of merit from Manu's days to these, so that no social festival, no family event is complete without this ceremony. An aristocracy they are if by that word we denote men of religious merit, of ceremonial purity, of intellectual acumen; but in no other sense whatever. If Mr. Hughes will strip the word aristocrat of every suggestion of wealth and luxury and outward splendour, then we shall not object to his using it to denote the Brahmans of India. But when he has so corrected its signification, what will have become of that "natural sequence of events" by which "the men engaged in training and educating the aristocracy of India" have been led to take a position that "fully justifies the charge of luxury" against them?

Notes on the "*Summary Statement of Facts and Arguments*" prepared by Mr. Hughes' and Dr. Lunn, by the REV. JOHN SCOTT, late Chairman of the South Ceylon District.

N.B.—These Notes were received after our answers on the various issues had been sent to press. They are so valuable that we lay them before the Sub-Committee in full.

From the statement of the Missionary Census of 1881 ("Summary Statement," p. 4) it appears that the rate of increase in the preceding ten years of native Christians was for the American Methodist and Wesleyan Methodist missions between three and four hundred per cent. The increase of only one society (the American Baptist) was greater than this. One other (Gossner's) was over two hundred per cent. The S.P.G. had an increase of about eighty per cent., the American Board of over fifty, the C.M.S., London, and Lutheran, of less than fifty per cent. So that judging by rate of increase our Society does not come out badly. The cause of our small number of native Christians should, it appears, be sought before 1871, and even before 1851. It might be well to inquire whether other societies mean the same by the term "native Christians" as we do; and it would be interesting to know to what extent the large numbers gathered in by the American Baptists would stand the tests applied to our class members.

The note by Mr. Little as to the proportion of members in mission employ would naturally apply to a district where the members are few and the need for Christian agents (as teachers) great. Where the members are comparatively numerous, as in Ceylon, the percentage so employed is small.

As to what is called "the secret of our failure" (p. 5), I agree (1) "that educational agencies should be . . . subordinate to . . . preaching," *i.e.*, I believe that without lessening our educational work we ought to have had a greater number of men employed in evangelizing the masses. Also with some reserve I agree (2) "that educational agents should be as far as possible laymen;" but I am strongly of opinion that at the head of each large institution there should be a missionary, because (*a*) in such a position he has unparalleled opportunities of teaching the truth systematically, of meeting difficulties, and dealing with individuals; (*b*) even when he is teaching secular subjects (so-called) the influence of the man, his spirit, his justice, his self-command, his diligence, are a perpetual though unconscious testimony to the pupils on behalf of Christ. Missionaries in other circumstances have with general approbation taught the natives mechanical arts: why should not we be encouraged to take advantage of the widespread determination in the East to acquire English learning? In teaching literature and science, may not the glory of God be made manifest? For these reasons I entirely dissent from the proposition (3) "that . . . education should be given mainly to converts, and especially to those who may become catechists or ministers," though of course I am impressed with the necessity of providing education for these. Some splendid ministers however (*e.g.* G. E. Goonewardene) have arisen from the ranks of those who have come to school as heathens and been converted to Christianity during or after their education.

As a practical missionary I entreat the Sub-Committee to make no recommendation that would weaken our High Schools as a department of evangelistic work.

The success of the American Baptists, p. 6. It is hardly fair to ascribe this to their believing "literally in the Day of Pentecost," as though others did not do so. Some enquiry should be made as to the principles on which the baptisms took place and the general character of the "conversions."

Neither does it seem fair that the very candid statement of Mr. R. Stephenson should be given, and his reasons why "it could not be" suppressed. The whole of his letter should be produced. Other missionaries, probably all, would like "to live in the midst of the people"; but except in rare cases Europeans could not maintain their health under such circumstances for any considerable length of time. Strong young men might do it for a while (with probably permanent subsequent injury to themselves); but men of average constitutions could not live under native conditions for more than a few months with safety—still less could women and children. *[margin: Style of living, p. 7.]*

It is significant that the pamphlet does not attempt to prove that the adoption of the "*Via Media*" would do any good. The facts it gives rather show that it is unnecessary; as the missions which have had the greatest numerical results in South India—the C.M.S. and the S.P.G.—place their missionaries in a position quite equal to that of our own.

I do not myself believe that the "*Via Media*" would do any good or practically bridge over the interval which in the nature of things must remain between the European, residing in a climate to him unnatural and without special alleviations almost insupportable, and the average Asiatic who is to the manner born. The example of the Salvation Army is not recommended in the pamphlet; therefore it is needless to dilate on the sufferings, the sacrifice of health and life, and defections from the ranks which have resulted from that system. The "*Via Media*" would, I am certain, as the result of over thirty years' experience, lead to sufferings and sacrifices, especially in the case of women and children, which the missionary society has no right to inflict. I hope to refer to "the '*Via Media*' as an accomplished fact" (p. 17) further on.

"The opinions of native Christians" should be estimated with some discrimination, especially when there has been no opportunity of cross-examination. Regard should be had rather to spirituality than academic distinctions. I do not specially refer to the gentleman quoted; but I am sure his remarks do not apply to the majority of our missionaries in Ceylon, nor I believe in India. Indeed his statement "many *[margin: "The opinions of native Christians."]*

missionary," etc., p. 8, may be literally true when the hundreds of missionaries in India are considered, but be the reverse of the truth as to the vast majority of missionaries.

As to Miss Joseph, I have no personal knowledge; but from the extracts given it is evident that she makes no reference to our missionaries. As far as I remember the letters published in India her statements were controverted by those concerned.

I do not think that "native Christian opinion" can be very easily estimated, nor that it should be taken as quite conclusive. Many Methodists in England do not think their ministers should receive larger incomes than they do themselves; but many others have not that feeling. So it may be in India. I do not think that our best Christians in Ceylon grudge their ministers living in moderate comfort; and for myself I could (and so I doubt not could many of my brethren) adopt the sentiment of the old African missionary quoted, p. 11. I believe the present style of living of our Eastern missionaries is as "simple" in general as it can be consistently with a due regard for health and freedom from entangling cares, and that it does "distinguish missionaries conspicuously from Anglo-Indian society." I believe it to be most desirable for them to cultivate social intercourse with native Christians. The hindrance is in general, in my opinion, not so much the largeness of their stipends as the littleness of their leisure.

This, I think, is a new point introduced into the controversy. In the original articles in the *Methodist Times* native ministers were, if

<small>Inferior status of native ministers.</small> I remember right, described (very unjustly) as "mercenary." In South Ceylon there have never been two district meetings (European and native), but only one in which during my experience all ministers alike have sat as in England. The Committee of European missionaries have considered only matters of their own finance and instructions specially addressed to themselves by the General Secretaries. For the last twenty-eight years (since Mr. Gogerly's death) all missionaries and native missionaries have had their meals together at the district meetings. On other occasions native brethren have always been welcome and often present at my family table; and the same might, I believe, be said by other missionaries. For myself I have always striven to raise

the status of the native ministers and to train them to take a larger share of responsibility. As to how far this was desirable may have been a subject of different views, and legitimately so. It should be borne in mind that there are great differences between different native ministers. Some are men of sounder judgment and more administrative ability than others. So too some are to a greater or less extent Europeanised (if I may use the word), and would not be out of place at any table. Others are quite native in their habits and primitive in their modes of eating. To sit and eat with English people would be felt (by these last) rather as a compliment than a comfort.

I deeply regret that the epigrammatic, but, as I think, cruel, statement that the stipend of our missionaries (with those of other societies this inquiry has nothing to do) is "£300 a year and a bungalow" has not been withdrawn. To include horse allowance is unjust, seeing that the horse is kept for mission work. *"Actual income," etc., p. 11.* Allowances for children, furniture, &c., would never be reckoned as part of the stipend of a circuit minister in England. But the word has been given, and it is extensively believed that the £300 corresponds to the £140 or £150 paid as stipend to ministers at home. As to the horse allowance, until the fall in exchange a year or two ago this never covered the cost. Under this head I have been a heavy loser every year until quite recently.

"The allowances for children in England ought to be on the most liberal scale." That is good and reasonable, and would be an immense relief to men of twelve years' standing and upwards. But is it proposed to increase the allowances for children abroad? Otherwise it would not be here that the reduction "in the case of a married missionary with children would be considerably less" than £80. *What the "Via Media" does and does not involve, pp. 11—13.* This is one of the testing points of the case, for the present children's allowance is entirely inadequate—*e.g.* when an ámah (wet nurse) has to be provided in addition to the ayah; for nourishing food for sickly children; for extra clothing, &c.; when visits to the hills or return to England are necessary; but indeed the ordinary expenses for a family quite amount to the present stipend and children's allowances. I sincerely believe that " what the *'Via Media'* does involve " would be increased suffering, sickness, and loss of life.

1. I think it misleading to reduce Indian currency at the rate of 1*s*. 4½*d*. In my time the average rate for a year was never so low as that; only quite recently was it lower than 1*s*. 6*d*.; within a few years it was 1*s*. 8*d*. The purchasing rate at the local banks is higher than their selling rate, while the stamp duties in Ceylon are high. No one can tell whether the value of the rupee may or may not soon rise again; but at least the fall seems to have been arrested. Since the stipends and allowances were fixed many years ago (allowances for children and I believe for horse have not been raised since 1830) prices for local products have enormously risen in Ceylon—cent. per cent. I should say. Since the fall in exchange, prices for English articles have risen in proportion.

<small>Cost of food.</small>

2. I certainly think that the cost of living varies in different parts of India and Ceylon. I regard the present scale as a sort of rough average. To give what is absolutely necessary in every case would require a different scale for every station and almost every family. It would seem that brethren in quiet, out-of-the-way places like Tiruvalur, can live much more cheaply than those in the great centres.

3. If the "*Via Media*" is to be enforced, missionaries ought, I think, to have the option of leaving the mission houses, which are generally spacious and airy, though often barn-like structures, and living in small houses suited to their reduced means. That would "involve" a great hindrance to the work and risk to health, but to live in a big house (though necessary in that fearful heat) on an income reduced by one-third, would soon "involve" the missionary in debt. There are expenses direct and indirect connected with a large house; there is eastern hospitality to be considered, not party-giving, nor visits of travelling ministers and others often not of our own Society (the cost of which are in some cases met by special allowance), nor even of private friends, but visits of persons who have been helpful to the mission at out-stations, or of those who come to him for counsel, or of people connected with Methodism at home. It is difficult to specify what eastern hospitality is; but a missionary, as a public man, is much exposed to it, and the burden is far greater in a large house than it would be in a small one; especially if he were known to have removed to the small one through having been cut down to something like starvation allowance.

4. I doubt whether it is possible to form a just estimate of what a missionary ought to receive by calculating details of cost of food, clothing, servants, &c., since prices vary, necessary items may be forgotten, and unforeseen contingencies are likely, nay certain, to occur. Moreover it is difficult for persons with English ideas to realize what familiar terms mean in India. For instance, "mutton, beef, and chickens," give the idea of good living. In the East they are generally poor, tough, and innutritious. "A quarter of a small sheep" (p. 13), sounds grand: how tiny and skinny is the fact! Probably Mr. H. P. Hughes does not know what the "sweeper's" work is (p. 14), and the gentlemen on the Sub-Committee will be surprised when Dr. Lunn explains it to them. I think a fairer mode of computation would be a general comparison. Thus:—(1) Official salaries in East Ceylon are very much smaller than in India. But the Ceylon Government has decided that its lowest appointments, those held by young men fresh from England and invariably unmarried, carry a minimum salary of Rs. 3,000. (2) The class with whom missionaries are on a social equality are English employés in houses of business; but such people would not marry and set up housekeeping on less than Rs. 4,000 a year, and would then have to live quietly, economically, without style or fashion, and would be looked down on by merchants and civil servants. (3) It is universally held that the higher nominal stipends only place the possessors in a position equal in comfort to what they would have had on the lower emoluments at home; *e.g.* such a family as last referred to would tell you that to them £200 in England was worth more than Rs. 4,000 in Ceylon. I submit that the united testimony of those who "know where the shoe pinches" outweighs the theories of those whose experience of Indian life is *nil* or nearly so.

5. It is absolutely necessary that the test of time should be applied to testimony as to the entire cost of living in India. I do not in the least question the facts stated by Dr. Lunn or Mr. Champness's young men, but I believe that every year's additional residence in the East would show them the inadequacy of these facts to represent the entire cost of living. Besides the illustrations already given, it would, I believe, be found that as the vigour of the newly arrived declined, and in most cases a greater or less degree of ill-health supervened, the

list of articles to be imported from England both for the table and for clothing would be materially increased. And in proportion as the rupee falls in value so does the price of imported goods rise. When the wife is ailing, the children delicate, and the man's physical energies are failing (and these are the circumstances with most English families in the tropics), there are many sources of expense.

6. In my own case, I had not the time, nor indeed the talent, to attend to domestic economy; but my sister, and afterwards my wife, were skilful managers; we lived carefully and frugally, were total abstainers, did not go into or receive society, though we often had persons in the house who came to us because we were missionaries; yet our outgoings were a constant source of anxiety, and we were thankful if we could keep within our income. Most of our missionaries could, I believe, say much the same. But some of them, I believe, had some private means.

I have not preserved materials to go into details. So far as I can test them the price of articles of food would be at least three times as much in South Ceylon as in Tiruvalur. Nor could we live so well as Dr. Lunn's *menu* would indicate (p. 12). Of the articles he mentions, flour, butter, bacon, are with us imported. For English goods one rupee in Ceylon would not go so far as one shilling in England.

Servants. Servants in Ceylon are less numerous but more expensive for each one than in India. The following is to the best of my memory an accurate list of those we employed when my family consisted of Mrs. Scott and one child, the rest being in England. (The four absent children cost me more than £30 over the allowances for them.) If Mrs. Scott had lived after her return I do not know how we could have managed.

First servant (we did not call him " butler ")	Rs. 144
Kitchen coolie	120
House boy	120
General coolie (in part)	84
Ayah	144
" Sweeper "	42
	Rs. 654

We could have managed with one, perhaps two, less if we had lived in a house of our own selection as private persons.

I can only account for Dr. Lunn's omission of an ayah by remembering his very brief period as a householder. Some married people without children save the cost of an ayah, but only when the husband is never far away. At best it is an awkward arrangement. For a missionary to leave a young wife with only men servants at hand would not be seemly.

Unable though I am to remember detailed prices, I am certain those mentioned (pp. 14, 15) are far below the current rates in Ceylon. The differences of climate in the mountains and the low country (and we have stations in both) make both thick clothing and thin necessary. I consider woollen underclothing in all cases a necessity. Dr. Lunn "wore very little," and (probably in consequence) had to return through fever. Nor do I agree with him as to the "small amount of walking." Where there are roads, horse or bullock conveyances are used; but for cross-country work, jungles, &c., the walking is rough, and in some cases there is a great deal of it. Native leather is quite unserviceable. All clothing in Ceylon has to be imported almost invariably from England.

Clothing, charities, and miscellaneous.

The paragraph (p. 15) as to "charities" appears to be based on a misconception. No claim is made for an allowance for charities, but when it is shown how the stipend is expended, one-tenth is deducted as the least which many Christians think they ought to contribute to God's poor and God's cause. In Ceylon the claims of the poor on the missionaries are constant and heavy. The missionaries also give freely to many objects connected with our mission, and are expected to aid other religious or public objects. Nor need the Committee grieve at this. No money is more wisely given for mission purposes than that contributed by missionaries. If Dr. Lunn had been in Ceylon for a few years (no doubt also in India) his eyes would have been opened on this and many other points.

I have never been able to afford to insure my life, and for many years past I have spent scarcely anything for books.

I must say I doubt the accuracy of the statement applying " to the whole of India." I know that some of our Ceylon men re-

Wages of artizans. ceiving higher wages than those here given (p. 17) took appointments in Central or North India by way of bettering themselves. Further evidence and cross-examination is needed here.

The last sentence applies here too. I am certain that the impression I derived a few years ago by conversing with some of the brethren of the "North Indian Conference" [of the

"Via Media" an accomplished fact. Methodist Episcopal Mission] was that their allowances and ours (taken on the whole) were about equal; also that they of the South Indian Conference in whose case the Eurasian style of living was adopted were in circumstances perilous to health, and that some of them were far from happy. It would be well to know whether the sums paid by the Mission are all that the missionaries receive; "*partial self-support*" (p. 18) may swell the amount. How long have these been the only sums paid? The evidence of missionaries as well as of officials would be desirable. At all events the translation into English currency at the rate given is misleading.

APPENDIX B.

List of Prices obtained by Mr. Caine from Mr. S. A. Saminada Iyer, Tanjore—the Retail Prices in Tanjore Market.

	a.	p.	English pence. s.	d.
Wheat Flour (one measure, or little over 3 lbs.)	2	0	0	2
European Bread (big loaf)	2	0	0	2
Beef	2	0	0	2
Mutton	2	0	0	2
Chickens, each	4	0	0	4
Eggs, each	0	2	0	0$\frac{1}{6}$
Butter, per lb.	4	0	0	4
Milk, one seer (9 ounces)	0	6	0	0$\frac{1}{2}$
Rice (1 measure)	3	0	0	3
Potatoes, per lb.	0	8	0	0$\frac{2}{3}$
Sweet Potatoes, per lb.	0	2	0	0$\frac{1}{6}$
Plantains, one for a pie, per doz.	1	0	0	1
Tea	14	0	1	2$\frac{1}{2}$
Coffee	10	0	0	10$\frac{1}{2}$
Sugar (one seer or 9 ounces)	2	3	0	2$\frac{1}{4}$

	Rs.	a.	p.	English Currency. s.	d.
The Wages of—					
Gardener (per mensem)	6	0	0	8	3
Coachman ,,	7	0	0	6	10$\frac{1}{2}$
Syce (Groom) ,,	5	0	0	6	10$\frac{1}{2}$
Grass-cutter ,,	4	0	0	5	6
Butler ,,	10	0	0	13	9
Mati ,,	8	9	0	11	0
Chokra ,,	6	0	0	8	3
Cook ,,	8	0	0	11	0
Waterman ,,	5	0	0	6	10$\frac{1}{2}$
Punkah-puller ,,	4	0	0	5	6
Sweeper ,,	4	0	0	5	6
Tailor ,,	12	0	0	16	6

Price-list from Crawford Market Price Current.

(*Bombay Gazette*, May 3, 1890.)

	Maximum Rate. Rs. a. p.	English Currency. s. d.
Daily prices, Beef—		
Prime pieces, first sort, per lb.	0 2 9	0 2¾
" second sort "	0 2 6	0 2½
Briskets and Round, first sort, per lb.	0 2 0	0 2
" " second sort "	0 1 6	0 1½
Beefsteak (under part), per lb.	0 5 0	0 5
" (round), per lb.	0 1 6	0 1½
Meat for soup, per lb.	0 1 3	0 1¼
Tongues (fresh), each	0 3 6	0 6½
" (salt) "	0 7 0	0 7
Sirloin, per lb.	0 3 6	0 3½
Fore Ribs, each	0 3 0	0 3

	First sort. Rs. a. p.	Second sort. Rs. a. p.	s. d.
Mutton—			
Saddle, per lb.	0 4 0	0 2 9	0 2¾
Leg, Loin, Shoulders and Neck, per lb.	0 3 6	0 2 0	0 2½
Breast (large), each	0 2 6	0 2 6	0 2½

	Maximum Rate. Rs. a. p.	English Currency. s. d.
Bread—		
Loaves, first sort, 13 ounces each	0 1 9	0 1¾
" second sort " "	0 1 6	0 1½
" Brown, each	0 2 0	0 2
Biscuits—		
Poona, per lb.	0 4 0	0 4
Bombay "	0 2 0	0 2
Poona (mixed), per lb.	0 4 0	0 4
Sugar.		
Tea—		
Hill, per lb.	0 14 0	1 2½
First sort, per lb.	0 10 0	0 10
Second sort "	0 8 0	0 8
Vegetables—		
Onions, per seer (9 ounces)	0 0 2	0 0¼
Carrots " "	0 0 6	0 0½
Celery (large), each	0 0 1	0 1
Lettuces, each	0 0 6	0 0½
Poultry—		
Geese, each	4 0 0	5 6
Turkey Cocks (very large), each	6 0 0	8 3
Turkey Hens, each	3 0 0	4 1½
Chickens (large), each	0 6 0	0 6

APPENDIX C.

Mysore Evangelists' Account, submitted by Mr. Champness.

1888.		Rs.	a.	p.	£	s.	d.
May and June.	Travelling to Shimoga, Bedding, &c. ...	120	2	0	8	5	8
June and July.	To the Missionary for food (7 weeks)	66	8	6	4	11	9
	Other expenses	51	2	2	3	16	0½
	Total	117	10	8	8	7	9½
Aug.	To the Missionary for food	40	0	0	2	15	2
	Other expenses	30	8	6	2	2	1
	Monthly Total	70	8	6	4	17	3
Sept.	To the Missionary for food	40	0	0	2	15	2
	Other expenses	36	6	0	2	8	0
	Monthly Total	76	6	0	5	3	2
Oct.	To the Missionary for food	40	0	0	2	15	2
	Other expenses	34	10	6	2	8	8½
	Monthly Total	74	10	6	5	3	10½
Nov.	To the Missionary for food	40	0	0	2	15	2
	Furniture	57	9	6	3	19	4½
	Other expenses	29	7	0	2	0	7
	Monthly Total	127	0	6	8	15	1½
Dec.	(Away from Mission House).						
	Food ...	30	0	3	2	1	4½
	Rent ...	10	0	0	0	13	9
	Other expenses	24	7	0	1	13	8
	Monthly Total	64	7	3	4	8	9½
1889.							
Jan.	Food ...	27	3	3	1	17	7
	Rent ...	10	0	0	0	13	9
	Furniture	18	2	0	1	5	2
	Other expenses	24	1	0	1	9	9
	Monthly Total	79	6	3	5	6	3

		Rs.	a.	p.	£	s	d.
Feb.	Food	28	12	1	1	19	8
	Travelling	7	7	0	0	10	3
	Mosquito curtains	6	1	0	0	8	2
	Other expenses	43	11	6	2	19	11
	Monthly Total	85	15	7	5	18	0
Mar.	Mr. Edlin's sickness and death	19	9	2	1	7	8
	Food	35	10	9	3	0	1¼
	Other expenses	26	14	0	1	17	5½
	Monthly Total	82	1	11	6	5	3
April.	Travelling in Circuit	31	2	6	2	3	0
	„ to Bangalore	26	15	9	1	17	2
	Provision case from Madras	9	15	1	0	13	9
	To the Missionary for food (12 days)	12	0	0	0	16	6½
	Food (alone)	4	3	6	0	5	9½
	Other expenses	19	1	6	1	6	4
	Monthly Total	103	6	4	7	2	7
May.	In Bangalore	26	3	3	1	15	9
June.	Travelling from Bangalore	27	8	0	1	18	2
	New men from Harihar	35	8	0	2	8	2
	Food	22	10	10	1	11	5
	Other expenses	15	11	0	1	1	9
	Monthly Total	101	5	10	6	19	6
July.	To the Missionary for food	105	0	0	7	4	9½
	Rent	6	0	0	0	8	3
	Other expenses	21	6	0	1	9	6
	Monthly total	132	6	0	9	2	6½
Aug.	To the Missionary for food (half month)	52	8	0	3	11	8½
	Food (other half month)	28	11	1	1	19	7
	Travelling	33	10	8	2	6	7
	Rent	6	0	0	0	8	3
	Other expenses	47	2	0	3	5	6
	Monthly Total	167	15	9	11	11	7½
Sept.	Food	39	10	9	2	14	9
	Rent	6	0	0	0	8	3
	Travelling	9	9	6	0	13	7
	Other expenses	40	1	6	2	15	4
	Monthly Total	95	5	9	6	11	11

			Rs.	a.	p.	£	s.	d.
Oct.	Food		35	7	11	2	8	3
	Rent		6	0	0	0	8	3
	Other expenses		37	14	3	2	12	9
		Monthly Total	79	6	2	5	9	3
Nov.	Food		34	13	6	2	7	4
	Rent		6	0	0	0	8	3
	Other expenses		34	12	6	2	7	3
		Monthly Total	75	10	0	5	2	10
Oct. to Nov.	Mr. Adkin, in Bangalore		28	9	0	1	19	5
	Total from May, 1888, to Nov., 1889		1,708	9	3	118	6	7

To this add £10 for the value of a box of Provisions sent from England
The Clothing they brought from England is not yet worn out, but, of course, will soon have to be renewed.

"Other Expenses" include Servant, Washing, Teacher, Postage, Class-money, Boot Repairing, and other small items, which are all entered in our Monthly Account.

Mr. Simpson says, "There were two of us for ten months ; I was alone for two months ; there have been three of us for five months."

APPENDIX D.

Proportion of salary remitted home at par by the missionaries of the London Missionary Society, submitted by Dr. Lunn.

The following figures have been supplied by Rev. R. Wardlaw Thompson, General Secretary of the Society, through whose hands all remittances pass :—

Case I.—Unmarried missionary average remittance home, Rs. 250.

In the following comparisons of salaries, cases 1, 3, and 4, of Messrs. Patterson and Findlay's statement, page 25, "Issue I. (B)" have been taken as the basis of calculation :—

Case III.—Married Missionary with three children—

	Rs.	English Currency. £
For education of one child at home	400	40
Average insurance	150	15
Remitted home to friends	100	10
*Remitted home for stores	300	30
Total	950	95

* This is the maximum amount which may be remitted home for stores.

Case IV.—Married Missionary with six children—

	Rs.	English Currency. £
Education of four children at home	1,500	150
Average Insurance	150	15
†Remitted home for stores	300	30
Total	1,950	195

† This is the maximum amount which may be remitted home for stores.

A Comparison of the Income of a Missionary of the London Missionary Society with that of a Missionary of the Wesleyan Missionary Society, submitted by Mr. Hughes and Dr. Lunn.

London Missionary Society.	£	s.	d.	Wesleyan Missionary Society.	£	s.	d.
1. Converted Rs. 250 at par	25	0	0		129	4	0
Rs. 1,450	101	10	0	Horse	6	0	0
					135	4	0
	£126	10	0		126	10	0
Excess of income of Wesleyan Missionary					£8	14	0

	£	s.	d.		£	s.	d.
2. Converted Rs. 950 at par	95	0	0	Madras stipend	230	0	0
*Rs. 2,000	140	0	0	Postage	4	4	0
				Three children Education	42	0	0
					12	0	0
				(3) Horse	12	0	0
				Medicine	5	0	0
				(1) Furniture	5	10	0
				(1) New Furniture	7	10	0
				(2) Confinements	2	10	0
					320	4	0
	£235	0	0		235	0	0
Excess of income of Wesleyan Missionary					£85	4	0

* In the above calculations the amounts paid in Indian currency are calculated at one shilling and fourpence four-fifths to the rupee, being about the average rate of exchange for 1888-89.

APPENDIX D. 355

	£	s.	d.		£	s.	d.
4. Converted Rs. 1,950 at				Madras stipend ...	230	0	0
par	195	0	0	Postage	4	4	0
*Rs. 1650	115	10	0	Six Children	84	0	0
				Education (3 children)	36	0	0
				(3) Horse	12	0	0
				Medicine	5	0	0
				(1) Furniture	7	0	0
				(2) New furniture ...	5	10	0
				(3) Confinements ...	2	10	0
					386	4	0
	£310	10	0		310	10	0

Excess of income of Wesleyan Missionary £75 14 0

(1) One-tenth of total grant; London Missionary Society make no grant.

(2) One-third of grant for each confinement; London Missionary Society make no grant.

(3) The horse allowance of the Wesleyan Missionary Society is Rs. 120 more than that of the London Missionary Society.

A Comparison of the Income of a missionary of the Methodist Episcopal Mission, with that of a missionary of the Wesleyan Missionary Society, submitted by Mr. Hughes and Dr. Lunn.

Methodist Episcopal Missionary Society.	£	s.	d.	Wesleyan Missionary Society.	£	s.	d.
1. Converted Rs. 250 at				Stipend—Madras ...	125	0	0
1s. 10½d.	23	10	0	Postage	4	4	0
*Rs. 1,310	92	0	0	Horse	30	0	0
					159	4	0
	£115	10	0		115	10	0

Excess of Income of unmarried Missionary £43 14 0

* In the above calculations the amounts paid in Indian currency are calculated at one shilling and fourpence four-fifths to the rupee, being about the average rate of exchange for 1888-89.

	£	s.	d.		£	s.	d.
3. Converted Rs. 950 at 1s. 10½d.	89	0	0	Madras stipend	230	0	0
*Rs. 2,245	157	10	0	Postage	4	4	0
				Three children	42	0	0
				Education (one child)	12	0	0
				Horse allowance	36	0	0
				Medicine	5	0	0
					329	4	0
£246	10	0			246	10	0

Excess of income of married Wesleyan Missionary with three children, one being educated at home ... £82 14 0

	£	s.	d.		£	s.	d.
4. Converted Rs. 1,950 at 1s. 10½d.	183	0	0	Madras stipend	230	0	0
*Rs. 1,965	137	10	0	Six children	84	0	0
				Postage	4	4	0
				Education (3 children)	36	0	0
				Horse allowance	36	0	0
				Medicine	5	0	0
					395	4	0
£320	10	0			320	10	0

Excess of income of married Wesleyan Missionary with six children, three being educated at home ... £74 14 3

*In the above calculations the amounts paid in Indian currency are calculated at one shilling and four pence four-fifths to the rupee, being about the average rate of exchange for 1888-1889.

Notes on the "Joyful News" Mission Evangelists' Account by Rev. H. Gulliford, of Mysore, submitted by Mr. Patterson.

26, PEMBERTON GARDENS,
LONDON, N.,
June 3rd, 1890.

MY DEAR MR. PATTERSON,
The "Mysore Evangelists' Account," put in as evidence by Mr. Champness, requires a few words of explanation. Mr. Robinson, who alone could satisfactorily give evidence on this question, is too ill to attend or even to write a detailed account of his experience. I have, however, received a letter from him and a longer letter from Mrs. Robinson. These letters were not written for the Committee, and therefore I have felt it necessary to write a short statement, gathered chiefly from the facts supplied by Mr. and Mrs. Robinson.

1. The experience of the "Joyful News" men in the Madras and Negapatam districts is not given by Mr. Champness. In fairness this ought to be presented, so that all the facts might be in the hands of the Committee. The details supplied by the Mysore men alone are put

forward, as they apparently substantiate Mr. Champness' contention. Whether the experience of his other men does this, I am not able to say. If the "Joyful News" men in Mysore live more economically than the evangelists in other parts of India, the fact is due to the training they received under Mr. Robinson. They were from the first accustomed to a very simple and plain style of living. The principle adopted by Mr. Robinson is thus laid down :—" When I found Hindu life impossible, I tried to live upon as little as possible. The result was—

6. 0 a.m.		Bread, water, plantains.
9.45	„	Ragi, meat alternating with vegetable curry.
2.45 p.m.		Bread and water.
7.30	„	Soup, meat and vegetables, and milk pudding."

It is evident that simplicity in diet could not be carried much further than this. It contrasts very strikingly with another dietary table published elsewhere. To prevent any misconception, I must in justice add that this style of living was not adopted for the purpose of saving money for personal purposes, but to obtain more funds for use in the circuit, for Mr Robinson "gave away all he did not use." He would not like this to be generally known. If Mr. Champness' men in Mysore are economical, they owe it to the training they received at the missionary's table.

2.—It will be seen from the figures in Mr. Champness' statement, that the missionary charged more for food in July, 1889, than during 1888. It is only fair that the explanation should be laid before the Committee. At the end of 1888, Mr. Robinson married. With reference to the change in cost, Mrs. Robinson writes :—" When the three men were with us in July, " we charged Rs. 100 for the three, including Rs. 9 for servant for them. " . . . . The reason we charged more was simply because Mr. R. did not " charge sufficient to cover expenses, and before he was married he gave " away all he did not use. Afterwards we were unable to give that sub- " scription to Mr. Champness in the way of food, &c., which Mr. R. had " given before his marriage, for you will know Rs. 20 would by no means " cover expenses. Then again I must tell you how we lived when the " three men were with us. In no other way could we have kept them for " the price.

6.30.	Dry bread and tea.
10.30.	Ragi, and meat of some kind with potatoes, and plantains. Every alternate day rice and vegetable curry took the place of meat.
2.30.	Dry bread and tea. Occasionally some preserve which I made from mangoes out of our compound.
6.30, 7 or 8.	Dinner. Soup, meat or fowl, which we could get (of course one was too small), and plain pudding of some kind, rice, sago, or such like.

" I am quite sure this was not sufficiently nourishing food to keep up " the strength needed to work as Mr. R. did, and battle against the effects " of the climate. It is not enough even if one takes it easy. We see the " result of this as well as other things in Mr. R. now. I am only sorry my " husband ever tried it, and when we go back we shall act differently." She further adds that her husband is convinced that " to maintain " strength sufficient for a missionary's work it is necessary to live as the " brethren generally live, and thinks that if he had kept up the style of " living of the———— he would not have been in his present position." It is but right that the missionary who has done so much for Mr Champness' men should have the opportunity of making this statement.

A A

APPENDIX D.

3 (*a*).—Mr. Champness' figures require to be rightly interpreted. At the bottom of the statement it is stated:—" Mr. Simpson says, ' There " were two of us for ten months ; I was alone for two months ; there have " been three of us for five months.' " From this we are to conclude that Mr. Champness supported—

```
2 men for 10 months = 1 man for 20 months
1 man  „    2   „   = 1   „       2   „
3 men  „    5   „   = 1   „      15   „
                                  ——
                                  37   „
```

or 1 man for 37 months for £128 6s. 7d., including the box of provisions. At this rate of calculation the cost of one man for a year would be £41 12s. 5d. But, though Mr. Simpson's statement is quite accurate, yet these men were not chargeable to Mr. Champness for the whole of that time. When Mr. Simpson and Mr. Adkin were in Bangalore, the missionaries there and others, being anxious to help Mr. Champness, were pleased to entertain these evangelists for nothing. The missionaries in the Mysore have ever looked upon Mr. Champness' work with sympathy, and in many ways have shown their appreciation of it. No mention would be made of this small matter of entertaining were it not that Mr. Champness wishes to demonstrate that his men—and, therefore all men—can live in India on much less than most men do at present. The true figures are—

```
2 men from June 14 to end of March, 9½ months = 1 man for 19 months.
1 man for April and part of June, or   ...   ...   ...   1½   „
3 men from July to September, 3 months = 1 man for  ...   9   „
2   „   for October and Nov.,   2   „   = 1   „    ...   4   „
                                                         ———
                                                         33¼   „
```

During May and part of June Mr. Simpson was in Bangalore, and during October and November Mr. Adkin was in Bangalore, during which period nothing was charged to Mr. Champness for food. The total length of service is equal to that of one man for 33¼ months.

(*b*). Mr. Champness has converted the rupee into English currency at the rate of 1s. 4⅝d. Money has never been available at that low rate for any length of time. The fairer rate would be 1s. 6d. At that rate, the cost would be £128 2s.

(*c*). To this must be added the £10 for box of provisions, and a certain sum for clothing. The outfit of the five men sent to the Mysore must have been considerable, and if we put down £40 it will not be an extravagant sum. This will make the total cost, leaving out the gift of a coach by a missionary, £178 2s. The cost per year is therefore £63 16s. It will thus be seen that Mr. Champness' men cost more in India than they do at home.

4.—It must further be borne in mind that the experience of Mr. Champness' men is very limited. The figures only relate to the first 17 months of their service, and living as they did, these would undoubtedly be the cheapest. The experience of Mr. and Mrs. Robinson must also be borne in mind. In addition to what I have already quoted, Mrs. Robinson writes:—" As I look back now, the conviction I had in India that our diet " was not sufficiently nourishing is confirmed. Every kind of meat in " Shimoga is very poor, and I am certain that butter and eggs and a

APPENDIX D. 359

" greater variety in food as well as in puddings and such things as those
" are absolutely necessary to maintain the strength needed for work.
" Good milk cannot be bought there, and butter we never saw but what
" was unfit for use." Mr. Robinson also says :—" I am convinced now that
" this [the diet given above] is insufficient to maintain strength enough to
" withstand the climate while doing the work of a *missionary*. If the
" 'Joyful News' men live as I taught them to live, my conviction is that
" they will do less work than I, or break down."

Taking into consideration the limited experience of Mr. Champness' men, remembering that the missionary who tried to live in a very frugal style completely broke down, and bearing in mind the emphatic testimony of Mr. and Mrs. Robinson quoted above, it is evident that no weight can be given to the printed statement and the conclusions sought to be drawn from it.

I shall be glad if you will bring these facts before the Committee.

Yours very sincerely,
H. GULLIFORD.

OFFICIAL MISSIONARY STATISTICS

RELATING TO THE

AMERICAN METHODIST EPISCOPAL CHURCHES.

The following official statistics were communicated to the Rev. David J. Waller, the Secretary of the Conference.

IN the controversy on Indian Missions reference has been frequently made to the amount of salary paid by the Methodist Episcopal Church of America to its missionaries. It has been assumed that the rate of payment by the American Board of Missions is at the rate of about £150 a-year, with *no allowance* for horse-hire.

The conclusion arrived at has been that if the richest and most numerous Methodist Church in the world—a Church with a missionary income of nearly a quarter-of-a-million—pays the missionaries in South India and Bengal an *average* of Rs. 1,800 per annum, a sum equivalent to about £122, reckoning the rupee at the recent average rate of exchange, and in North India an *average* of Rs. 2,475 per annum, a sum equal to £168, the payments to the missionaries of our own Society ought therefore to be greatly reduced.

The Secretary of the Conference during his visit to the United States made it his business to obtain complete and accurate information on this subject. By the courtesy of Bishop Andrews, of New York, and Dr. Baldwin, the Missionary Record Secretary, every facility was afforded him and the fullest information supplied. They not only showed him the estimates for the several mission-fields, but also furnished copies of the estimates for the three Indian Conferences. In China, Japan, Mexico, and nearly every other part of the mission-field, except India, *the American Board of Missions pays in dollars*, and a married missionary receives at the rate of 1,200 dollars, or £240 sterling. In addition he has a house provided, or a sum for rent in lieu of it, and also children's allowances and travelling expenses. With regard to India, however, the salaries have in recent years been paid in rupees.

NORTH INDIA CONFERENCE.

Estimates for 1890.

MISSIONARIES' SALARIES.

Kumaon District :—
- T. Craven ... ... Rupees 3,375
- F. W. Foote 2,975
- S. S. Dease 2,700
- J. T. McMahon 3,375
- J. H. Messmore 2,475
- Pastor Nynee Tal Church 1,800

Oudh District :—
- B. H. Badley ... ... Rupees 3,600
- J. H. Schiveley 2,925
- A. J. Maxwell 2,700
- S. Knowles 3,150
- J. C. Lawson 3,150
- H. Mansell 2,475
- A. T. Leonard 2,040
- N. L. Rockey 2,925
- T. S. Johnson 2,475
- J. W. Waugh 3,150
- W. H. Mansell 1,560
- G. F. Hopkins 2,475

Rohilcund District :—
- T. J. Scott ... ... Rupees 2,925
- F. S. Neeld 2,700
- P. T. Wilson 2,700
- R. Hoskins 2,975
- C. L. Bare 3,150
- J. C. Butcher 2,700
- J. E. Scott 2,700
- C. M. Simmons 2,700
- W. R. Clancey 3,150
- E. W. Parker 2,475
- Three new missionaries 7,050
- Passages of missionaries 6,000

SOUTH INDIA CONFERENCE.

Estimates for 1890.

MISSIONARIES' SALARIES.

	Salary.	Rent.
Bombay District—		
E. F. Frease	Rupees 1,980	420
C. E. Delamater	1,200	720
A. W. Prautch	1,800	720
W. E. Robbins	2,580	720
D. O. Fox	2,400	720
W. H. Stephens	2,280	264
W. W. Bruere	2,280	
Principal Poona High School	1,800	
J. E. Robinson	3,300	840
Madras District—		
A. H. Baker	Rupees 2,280	
J. H. Garden	2,100	840
W. L. King	2,280	
D. O. Ernsberger	1,680	
J. Lyon	3,120	900
Missionary at Tandur	1,200	
B. Peters	900	240
A. W. Rudisill	1,800	

BENGAL CONFERENCE.

Estimates for 1890.

MISSIONARIES' SALARIES.

		Grants in aid. Rupees.	Uncon- ditional. Rupees.	Total. Rupees.
Ajmere District—				
C. P. Hard, P.E.,	Salary	—	2,940	
,,	Rent	—	600	
,,	Travelling	—	300	
,,	Furniture	—	500	
				4,340
A. Gilruth,	Salary	1,170		
,,	Rent	—	480	
				1,650

	Grants in aid. Rupees.	Unconditional. Rupees.	Total. Rupees.
Burhanpore—			
A. S. E. Vardon, Salary ...	—	2,340	
,, Itinerating ...	—	100	
			2,440
Khandiva and Harda—			
T. E. F. Morton, Salary ...	—	1,800	
,, Itinerating ...	—	60	
			1,860
Burmah District—			
P. Elder's Salary	—	2,580	
,, Rent	—	900	
			3,480
Burmese Work.			
Rangoon—			
H. Gershom	—	1,200	
,, Rent	—	600	
			1,800
Tamil Work.			
Ezra Peters	—	600	
,, Rent	—	360	
			960
Calcutta District—			
S. N. Dass	—	720	
,, Rent	—	240	
,, Itinerating ...	—	60	
			1,020
Presiding Elder's Salary ...	—	2,900	
,, Travelling ...	—	68	
			2,968
Muzaffurpore—			
H. Jackson, Salary ...	—	2,760	
,, Rent	—	900	
,, Itinerating ...	—	150	
			3,810
Asansol—			
W. P. Byers, Salary	—	1,800	
,, Rent	—	500	
,, Itinerating ...	—	60	
			2,360
Pakur—			
J. P. Meik, Salary	—	1,800	
			1,800
N. Madsen, Salary	—	1,020	
,, Rent	—	600	
			1,620

	Grants in aid. Rupees.	Unconditional. Rupees.	Total. Rupees.
Muzaffurnagar—			
J. D. Webb, Salary	—	1,980	
,, Rent	—	360	
			2,340
Roorkee—			
C. N. D'Souza, Salary	900	—	
,, Rent	—	600	
,, Itinerating	—	100	
			1,600
Lahore—			
C. H. Plomer, Salary	—	1,620	
,, Rent	—	360	
,, Itinerating	—	100	
			2,080
E. S. Busby, Salary	900	—	
,, Rent	240	—	
			1,140
Mussoorie and Rajpore—			
P. M. Buck, Salary	—	3,120	
			3,120
F. J. Blewitt, Salary	—	1,500	
			1,500
Mussoorie District—			
D. Osborne, P.E., Salary	—	3,120	
,, Rent	—	750	
,, Travelling	—	250	
			4,120

In reference to the above statistics it is important to observe:—

(1) "That parsonages are generally furnished for the missionaries; but when they are not, an allowance for rent is made."

(2) "That it is difficult to give a uniform scale of payment for missions in India, as they are conducted on the basis of partial self-support, certain amounts being appropriated unconditionally, and others as grants in aid." (See Dr. Peck's letter.)

(3) That another very important fact to be taken into consideration is that although the present value of the rupee is very low—only about 33 cents—the American Board of Missions in all remittances from its missionaries counts the rupee at 45 cents—that is to say, instead of reckoning it at about 1s. 4½d., it is taken at 1s. 10½d.

Reckoning 45 cents to the rupee, and assuming that *one-third* of the income is remitted home at 1s. 10½d. to the rupee, and *two-thirds* expended in India at 1s. 6d. to the rupee, the sterling values of typical incomes are given below:—

Rs. 2,475	=	£201	1	10
2,800	=	227	10	0
3,000	=	223	15	0
3,100	=	251	17	6
3,300	=	268	2	6
3,600	=	292	10	6

It is of course understood that a portion of the salary is raised on the mission field, and that in this portion the rupee is reckoned at the rate of currency.

In instituting a comparison between the *average* salaries paid by the American Board of Missions to its missionaries in India, and the allowances made by our Missionary Committee to its missionaries, it should be borne in mind that the American Mission includes a number of agents who have not been sent out from the United States, but who have been engaged in India.

BOARD OF MISSIONS METHODIST EPISCOPAL CHURCH, SOUTH.

Report of the Committee on Estimates for 1890-1.

BRAZIL MISSION CONFERENCE.

	Salary.
Rio de Janeiro District—	
J. W. Tarboux (including 3 children) ... Dollars	1,800
J. M. Lander (including 2 children) ...	1,400
J. S. Mattison (including 1 child)	1,300
J. W. Wolling, P.E.	1,200
One new missionary	1,200
Sao Paulo District—	
J. L. Kennedy	1,300
M. Dickie	1,200
One new Missionary as teacher in Boys' School, Piracicaba	1,200
One new missionary	1,200

CHINA MISSION CONFERENCE.

Shanghai District:— Salary.
  Young J. Allen (including 2 children) ...Dollars 1,400
  C. F. Reid (including 4 children) 1,600
  G. R. Loehr (including 3 children) ... 1,500
  W. B. Bonnell (including 6 children) ... 1,800
  M. B. Hill (including 1 child) 1,300
  W. B. Burke 1,200
  H. L. Gray 750
Suchow District:—
  A. P. Parker 1,200
  J. L. Hendry (including 1 child) 1,300
  W. H. Park (including 1 child) 1,300
  D. L. Anderson (including 4 children) ... 1,600
Bishop Wilson's Call:—
  Three single missionaries 2,250
  One married missionary 1,200

JAPAN MISSION CONFERENCE.
                                                        Salary.
J. W. Lambuth ... ...Dollars 1,200
O. A. Dukes (including 2 children) ... 1,400
W. R. Lambuth (including 3 children) ... 1,500
B. W. Waters 1,200
J. C. C. Newton (including 1 child) ... 1,300
S. H. Wainright 1,200
W. C. Towson (including 1 child)... ... 1,300

CENTRAL MEXICAN MISSION CONFERENCE.
Mexico District:— Salary.
  J. M. Weems (including 1 child) ... ...Dollars 1,300
  D. F. Watkins (including 1 child)... ... 1,300
  D. W. Carter (including 3 children) ... 1,500
San Luis Potosi District:—
  J. W. Grimes (including 5 children) ... 1,500
  G. B. Winton 1,200

MEXICAN BORDER MISSION CONFERENCE.

	Salary.
Monterey District:—	
A. H. Sutherland (including 3 children) ... Dollars	1,600
Durango District:—	
S. G. Kilgore (including 2 children) ...	1,200
J. D. Scoggins (including 3 children) ...	1,300
Sonora District:—	
John F. Corbin (including 3 children) ...	1,300

The American Methodist Episcopal Church, South, has no mission in India, but it will be seen from the above that it has missions in Brazil, China, Japan, Mexico and elsewhere. The scale of allowances is the same as that of the Methodist Episcopal Church, being, for married missionaries, 1,200 dollars, which is equal to £240 sterling, exclusive of the usual allowances for children, house, travelling, and other expenses.

DAVID J. WALLER,

WESTMINSTER COLLEGE,   *Secretary of the Conference.*
July 4, 1890.

ADJOURNED MEETING OF THE GENERAL COMMITTEE.

THIS important Committee re-assembled in the saloon of Centenary Hall on Tuesday, July 1, at 11 a.m. There was a large attendance. The President of the Conference was in the chair. The meeting having been opened with prayer by Dr. Jenkins, the minutes of the Special Committee, which met on April 24, were read by the Rev. Marshall Hartley, who also presented a printed copy of the Sub-committee's Report, which, after a few verbal corrections, was taken as read.

Dr. RIGG said that he rose to move a resolution in regard to the Report of the Sub-committee, because his object was to minimise discussion as far as possible. Of course that matter had been a source of great anxiety to all of them, but at the present stage he wished to abstain from everything beyond the barest statements. Those who had read the Report which had been forwarded to them would find that it falls naturally into two parts. The first part ended with page 7, which might be spoken of as the Report proper. Pages 8 to 10 consisted of what he might speak of as a sort of appendix of suggestions —suggestions arising out of the information which came into their hands. But they had to distinguish between those suggestions which related to policy and the Report proper— which had no concern with policy. The resolution which he was about to move was in three parts, and perhaps it would be advantageous if he read the resolution first and then offered some observations upon it. The resolution was as follows :—

1. That this Committee adopts the unanimous findings and judgment of the Sub-committee of Investigation, contained in the first seven pages of the document now presented to the Committee as the Report of the Sub-committee, which findings and judgment are, to use the language of the Sub-committee (page 8), a "complete exoneration of the Indian missionaries of our Society from all charges made or suggested against their character or the character of their work, whether in respect of their mode of living or of their relations with the native population, Christian and otherwise."

2. That this Committee receives and reserves for its special consideration at the earliest opportunity the important and

valuable suggestions at the close of the Report (pp. 9, 10) bearing upon the financial policy of the Committee in the future—suggestions, it is satisfactory to find, that are in close harmony with the resolutions on the same subject which were adopted by the last Conference on the recommendation of this Committee, but which the necessity for carrying out the investigation now completed has prevented the Committee from embodying during the year in detailed plans and instructions as to financial arrangements in India.

3. That the warmest thanks of the Committee are due and are hereby presented to the members of the Sub-committee, and especially to its lay members, who, at the request of the President of the Conference, have served upon the Sub-committee, for the invaluable service which, at the cost of so much labour and care to themselves, they have rendered to the Committee and the Society, and the cause of Christ at home and abroad.

In regard to these resolutions, the first referred to the unanimous findings and judgment of the Sub-committee of Investigation on pp. 1-7. So far as pp. 8 and 9 were concerned the statement therein contained was not unanimously endorsed by the Committee. The President, Mr. Brunyate, and Mr. Allen had committed themselves to expressing their want of agreement with the statement there concerned. But he apprehended that there was no want of unanimity so far as the suggestions at the close were concerned. He wished to refer to the findings and judgment of the Committee contained on the first seven pages. The General Committee defined the work which the Sub-committee of Investigation was to do—they were "appointed to examine into all the facts and statements bearing upon the position and character of the Indian missionaries." The interpretation which the Sub-committee put upon that direction was to be found on page 4, beginning: "The articles referred to in the resolution are four in number, and entitled respectively: 1. Try Democratic Methods; 2. The Evils of a false Position; 3. The Untrodden 'Via Media'; 4. The Secret of Missionary Finance." As to the first and last of these articles, the Sub-committee said that they had nothing to do with them; the articles which it was their business to investigate were the second and third In the judgment of the Sub-committee two important charges affecting the character of the Indian missionaries were contained in those articles—viz., the charge of living in luxury, and that involved in the statement that the effect of this mode of living was inevitably to separate the missionary from the people, &c. On those two charges the Committee gave express findings. That was the whole of their work as given distinctly in answer to the reference of that Committee, and the whole of that work was disposed of by the replies which they gave to those charges. Those replies were to be found on pp. 6 and 7. He had heard it said that the Report of the Sub-committee was in its language and phraseology and tone a disappointing result. To him it was nothing of the kind. He did not expect from that Committee anything but a dispassionate statement of conclusions forced upon them by evidence. He no more expected any touch of sentiment within their findings than in the findings of a jury. The series of conclusions given in their report was as cold as steel, and on that account he thought it was all the more decisive and impressive, and therefore he did not share the feeling of those who thought that there should have been some show of sympathy, so far as the Indian missionaries were concerned, in the findings and judgment of that Committee. But further, that Sub-committee, having had so much evidence before them, felt that they were in possession of information that might well lead them to make certain suggestions in regard to payments to be made in the future which it would not be right for them to withhold from the Missionary Committee and the Connexion, and they were much obliged to them for the suggestions which they had given. It was not possible, however, for the Committee to effect the transition from the Report proper to those "suggestions" without a sort of linking paragraph, and in that paragraph (their functions as a jury being at an end) they had gone farther towards giving some colour to their conclusions than they had in any other part of the document. On page 8 the report read, "While thus completely exonerating the Indian missionaries of our Society from all charges made or suggested against their character, or the character of their work, whether in respect of their mode of living, or of their relations with the native population, Christian and otherwise, the Sub-committee having had before it considerable information as to the degree and mode of payment of the missionaries employed in India by other Christian Churches and of various classes of English residents in India, desires to add to its Report the following statement as to the stipends paid by other missionary societies," &c. It was in regard to that statistical statement that there was an interruption of unanimity on the part of the Committee of Investigation. Mr. Brunyate intimated that there was no statement in regard to the Presbyterian Society that was parallel to their own; and the Church Missionary Society had declined to give any evidence. He (Dr. Rigg) wished to state in general in regard to the particulars that might be given of this kind that it was absolutely essential that they should know what was the meaning of "Averages." There were missionaries in the foreign field employed by societies who were not Englishmen, and who had not been trained in England

These were not paid at the same rate; nevertheless they were amongst the agents employed. That was the case with several of the Missionary Societies here referred to—he rather thought with all of them. It was important to know whether the comparison rested upon the same level—whether it referred to missionaries trained for mission work at home and sent out with such training, or whether it referred to those who might be found in India, and who might have been something else before they were ministers and of a different nationality. He mentioned these things simply as samples of what might arise in statistics of that sort, so that it was impossible to give statistics that would not be misleading unless it was clearly proved that the comparison of details was equal on all sides. He thought that these were quite sufficient reasons for feeling that those statistics rested upon an entirely different footing from the Report proper. The suggestions that followed this statement were an addition to the Report, and they were in close harmony with the findings of the General Committee itself twelve months ago, and with the resolutions of the last Conference. If they turned to the " Minutes " of the Conference for 1889, pp. 213, 214, they would read as follows:—

Allowances to Missionaries in India.—(1.) The Conference is of opinion that the principles on which the allowances to missionaries should be calculated are—

> (*a*) That missionaries should continue to be placed in a financial position fairly corresponding to that of ministers in comfortable circumstances at home.
>
> (*b*) That adequate allowances should be made to them for all special costs arising out of the peculiarities of climate, and of residence out of England, *e.g.*, the larger premiums for life insurance, the greater cost of education, the expenses incident to the occasional separation of families, with other matters necessarily involved in the career of a missionary.

(2.) The Conference is further of opinion that alterations may with advantage be made in the present scale of payment, so that the claims of missionaries of varying ministerial status, and living under varying climatic and social conditions, may be more equitably dealt with. The Conference hopes that by this means considerable economies may be effected.

(3.) The Missionary Committee is instructed to consider and report upon the details of a plan in accordance with the foregoing resolution, and to include in its report a recommendation as to the re-adjustment of the gain by exchange.

After reading those resolutions it would be seen that the suggestions at the end of the document which he held in his hand were in close harmony with the conclusions already provisionally adopted, and that they would strengthen the hands of the Missionary Committee in carrying out the policy which in outline had been suggested. He hoped, therefore, they might be able to agree unanimously upon the resolution which he had submitted. He had avoided, as far as possible, matter which could by any possibility have a personal bearing. He wished to say, before he sat down, that when the London Missionary Society's and the Baptist Missionary Society's payments to their missionaries were considered, they could not lose sight of the payments of the London Missionary Society and the Baptist Missionary Society at home and the payments of their own ministers at home. He moved that the Committee adopt the resolution which he had read. He was sure the Committee would desire to emphasize their expression of thanks "especially to the lay members" of the Sub-committee. (Hear, hear.)

Mr. T. MORGAN HARVEY said: I think it is desirable that this resolution should be seconded by a layman. I do not rise simply on the ground that I am a layman, but, occupying the position of Lay Treasurer to the Society, I think it is my duty to second this resolution. I am glad to believe that this is a day in which the fulfilment of some prophecies I ventured to utter is taking place. It is also a day of promise. I believe that the irritating and annoying correspondence that has been carried on on both sides will from this day cease. The suggestion made as to the financial part of the business of this Missionary Committee is very valuable indeed. I confess that for a long time I have been opposed to the system which has obtained in reference to payments in India, especially in reference to gains on exchange. We shall now have time to devote to these very serious and important considerations in reference to the future of our work in India. I do not think it is necessary to trouble the Committee with statements in addition to those which have been made by Dr. Rigg. Personally, I am greatly indebted to the gentlemen who have given so much time and attention to this work. Perhaps I may say that, in view of these proceedings, when the question was first mooted I objected to the calling of missionaries from India. I objected on the ground of expense, because I foresaw that a very large sum of money would have to be paid by some one. This has been fully realised, because the bill of costs will be very large. I ventured to suggest in Committee that, although in the first instance these expenses must be paid by the Missionary Committee, the damages should follow the verdict, whatever that verdict might be. I say that seriously. We have to do with large sums of money that have been contributed by our people through the length

B B

and breadth of the land, and we should hesitate before the question, By whom should these large sums be paid? I second the resolution.

Dr. JENKINS said: I wish I could share the hopeful spirit with which the Treasurers have spoken this morning. I believe it is their very sincere desire, and certainly it is mine, that this unhappy business should close as speedily as possible. Will you allow me to speak with freedom this morning, and to speak what is in my heart? I suppose the Sub-committee did not consider it part of the task assigned them to express any opinion as to the character of the attack which has been made upon the Missionary Committee. If so, that duty, in my opinion, devolves upon this Committee. (Hear, hear.) Dr. Rigg is reported to have said he hopes the question may not be discussed at the Conference. Let me assure the Committee that if we do nothing more this morning than pass the resolution before us, we shall have to discuss it. I think, however, we have another duty, besides that of passing this resolution, and it is far better that the discussion should be here than at the Conference. At any rate it is far better that we should face the whole question of this attack from beginning to end, so far as we can do it, here. Otherwise there will be another scene in the Conference, which I cannot contemplate myself without uneasiness. Let me express in the first place my satisfaction at the impartial and exhaustive manner in which the evidence has been collected. Everyone of us I have no doubt, has conscientiously read it. I am thankful for that evidence. It has unmasked one of the grossest impositions ever attempted on the public credulity. The fabric raised has been penetrated by an impartial and masterly examination, and it has collapsed, and its ruins and fragments are spread before us this morning. We shall never have such another fabric, in my opinion. Now, Sir, I do not condemn the attack because of certain charges preferred against the missionaries abroad. I do not condemn charges. I can conceive that a man may feel it to be on his conscience to make certain allegations against a man, a society, or a policy. Nor do I condemn the attack because it has not been sustained by facts, because I can quite understand that an attack may be made conscientiously by a man who has not gone through the entire range of the subjects he has examined, and, as we are all fallible, even he may err in his judgment. I neither condemn the charges themselves nor on account of the fact that they are not sustained. But I do condemn the manner and spirit in which the attack has been made. (Hear, hear.) Perhaps it is uncharitable for me to say I condemn the spirit: I condemn the manner. In my judgment it has not been conscientious. It was a great responsibility, in the first place, to undertake an accusation of this kind and not to do it in Committee, where it ought to have been done in the first instance. (Hear, hear.) If it had been done there, we should not this morning have witnessed this *fiasco*. I consider that an attack of this gravity ought only to have been made after examination, after a competent experience, after a keen sense of self-distrust, after being corrected by counsel with others who are older and more experienced. Now, Sir, what have we before us? We have not a business that can be concluded by this Committee, or, I am afraid, by the Conference. There has been, to my certain knowledge, and the knowledge of every gentleman here, a profound and operating uneasiness throughout the entire Connexion, the result of which we have found already in a reduced income to the amount of some £9,000. That I do not think so much about. There are fluctuations of income; it may rise or fall. But there is an effect produced by this attack upon honest, cordial, and hearty Methodist people, partially informed, who take their opinions from public journals, and who cannot make the reservations in their minds that the journalists do when they write—(hear, hear)—who take an accusation or an implication *simpliciter*. That attack has been the means of producing a revolution in missionary opinion and enthusiasm of which I hope I may live to see the end. I believe I shall. But, nevertheless, I cannot acquit those who are the authors of this attack; at any rate I must express my regret, and I think that the regret of the Committee should find expression in some resolution passed this morning. I do not wish to perpetuate personalities. I do not wish to introduce any bitterness whatever into this discussion. But I do wish that the feeling of the Connexion should be satisfied by the expression which this Committee will give to our sense of the injustness of this accusation, our sense of the groundlessness of the most serious of these accusations. It is true that in this report the Committee has exploded the second charge, and the most serious one by far—I mean that the brethren are living in luxury, and also that that kind of living separates them from the natives, imperils their work, and brings an embarrassing expense upon the Committee—for that is the charge which is before us. I believe that if those who have made these charges had been a little more cautious in the beginning, had made inquiries, had had a variety of consultations, and had been—I do not use the word reflecting in any way on their morality—thoroughly honest, these articles would never have been written—at least those parts of them which refer to the character of our brethren. I approve of the contempt which has expressed itself in the silence of the great Missionary Societies, who are charged with ourselves, and I did wish in the first instance that that same contempt would have characterised the reply of our own brethren abroad. But I feel for our brethren there, who have had this exceedingly painful baptism of suffering to go through, and I rejoice they have been able to send men who have so thoroughly discharged the painful duty entrusted to them. They have done it admirably. I beg pardon for saying so much.

Mr. ARTHUR said: I should have liked to second that final resolution of thanks to the gentlemen of the Sub-committee, and I should have felt disposed to make even stronger than in the original wording the thanks to the lay members of that Committee. There is one thing in which Methodism has been miserably poor, and in which to me it seems likely to continue so—that is, in men of leisure. If we had a number of laymen of leisure it would be no great surprise if they gave so much time and effort as these gentlemen have given. But we had four laymen on the Sub-committee—two of them professional, two mercantile, none retired—and for them to give such work as they have given is no small thing. But, Sir, anyone who was here twelve months ago will remember that I said at once to the Committee that, as to the charges of luxury, they were not worth a snap of the finger. The real charges were the charges of alienation from the people, those were the charges that ought to be gone into. I said: You must go into the financial question, and, as I said also in Conference, you must take plenty of time to do it. Now, two things are on the face of this Report. Firstly, that the Committee felt themselves pressed for time. They were bound to wind up in a few days. Even you, Sir, were unable, as I understand, to stay throughout the proceedings.

The PRESIDENT: I stayed until the findings on pp. 6, 7 were adopted. I was not present when the statistics of the London Missionary Society, the American Society, and the Baptist Missionary Society were considered, because I was in the Irish Conference. But I was present from first to last at the meetings at which evidence was taken.

Mr. ARTHUR: I am glad to hear that, but that does not alter the fact that the Committee had not much time. To my mind it should have been a matter of weeks. I should have wanted them to have plenty of time to go into the matter. But, being pressed, I do think they have done a wonderful amount of work, with remarkable skill and ability. That is the impression made upon me by the Report. But one effect of the pressure is this, that all the facts and statements committed to them affected two points—the position of our ministers, and the character of our missionaries. For myself, the question of position had very little weight, the question of character was vital. Now, what a leisurely committee would have done, would have been this: Instead of reducing themselves to two charges, which was done with great ability and insight, they would have taken all the articles and drawn out from them all the propositions contained in them, and a tremendous array of propositions it would be. Anything more destructive of the character of a body of men professing to preach the Gospel of Christ I do not know. Of these propositions, had they been so drawn out, how many have been attempted to be sustained? As that Report stands, these propositions divide themselves into propositions overlooked, propositions dropped, and propositions attempted to be sustained. I am sorry to say I cannot find one proposition retracted, and I am certain I do not find one sustained. (Hear, hear.) First, as to the proposition that "the missionary in India with £300 a-year and his bungalow . . . . is able, with ease and comfort, to mix in Anglo-Indian society in a style which he could not possibly do on less than £1,000 a-year in England"—Was any attempt made to sustain that in Committee? I cannot find it in your Report. Secondly, as to the proposition that "the youngest and the most obscure married missionary in India receives in gold a larger stipend than the superintendent of the West-Central Mission"—Was any attempt made to sustain that statement? Then as to the proposition that "the truth leaves no choice but to say that the charge of luxury . . . is fully justified by the facts of the case"—We have been told that this is not a personality. If I brought a charge of telling lies against John Walton, that would be personal; but it would be honest and open. But, if I brought a charge of telling lies against every Methodist preacher in England, that would not be personal, it would be general. Unless, however, it was true equally of everyone, the proposition itself would be falsehood. When you make a universal statement it is false unless every part in it is true. You cannot get out of it. Well, then, "the truth leaves no choice but to say that the charge of luxury . . . is fully justified by the facts of the case"—There were attempts made in the Committee to do something like sustaining that charge; how they ended the Committee has shown. Here is another proposition: "Every minister immediately on landing in India finds himself at once received into 'society.'" Now, the *Indian Witness*, the organ of the Methodist Episcopal Church of India, says, "The only fault we have to find with such a statement is that it is totally untrue." When I quoted to this Committee the language of Dr. Miller last year, calling in question the truthfulness of an Indian missionary, I said I believed that was the first time that the name of a Methodist missionary had been subject to that, but it is a very serious thing to have the organ of the Methodist Episcopal Church in Calcutta saying of the words of a Methodist preacher that they are "totally untrue." Was an attempt made to establish that proposition? Then, Sir, here is another, "This new social status entails a number of expenses following in natural sequence. Persons who go to Court must dress in a certain style." Was any attempt made to sustain those statements? Were they retracted? (Hear, hear.) I find no attempt to sustain them in the Report; I find no attempt, I am sorry to say, to retract them. I might take several others of them, but now come to the matter of the spirit and character of our men. These other propositions have referred to their position. "It is almost impossible," we are told, "for any man to occupy for years the position of a feudal lord without developing the feudal spirit." And I heard from the lips of Mr. Hughes, before the Methodist Conference, that he had never charged our men with yielding to that temptation. "Men do successfully fight against it here and there; but it is not in human nature generally to wield almost absolute power, to receive abject reverence, without losing sight, more or less, of the great Christian principle of the brotherhood of all men." Will the Committee tell us what proof was given that a missionary in India "wields almost absolute power?" Will they tell us what attempt was made to sustain or to give anything like the colour of decency to a statement of that kind? I cannot find a trace of it. "Absolute power!" Could Dr. Lunn, while in India, command a policeman? Could he command the services of a coolie without the consent of that coolie? Could he get a letter sent for less postage than any other man in India? "Absolute power!" A man who could write that, and an editor who could take it in, are certainly men to be looked at. These are very grave charges. (Hear, hear.) The articles are announced with a flourish. "They will go to the root of the matter." They have gone to the root of good men's hearts. They have gone to the root of your character as a truth-speaking people. "Compelled by the customs of the social world in which they move to live in a certain style, their usefulness is crippled, their influence is lessened." Whoever compelled Daniel Sanderson to live in other way than he had lived? I lived just in the style that I found prevailing there, and a very good style it was. The doctors always said it was necessary for health. There was no compulsion of any kind. As to the charge about men who are presented at Court having to dress in a different way from other people, the amount of ignorance displayed in the making and circulating of it is to me beyond ridicule. Here is another proposition, introduced with great solemnity, as a means of setting right historical considerations: "The direct result of the policy of Dr. Alexander Duff has been that the men engaged in educating and training the aristocracy of India have by a natural sequence of events taken a position . . . far removed from that which would naturally be occupied by the evangelists of the masses." Was any attempt made to sustain that historical fact, which would be cardinal, if it were known? It shows an intensity of ignorance difficult to illustrate to the English mind. It is as great as if the writer were to say: "The direct result of the policy of the Nottingham Conference in adopting Lay Representation was that amongst the Methodists the laymen began to preach, and now their names appear on the circuit plan." (Laughter.) This is precisely the same sort of information that the readers of these articles get. I am an old man, and in old age one feels at times very thoughtful. When I read these papers first, I was away on the shores of the Mediterranean and I said "It is some ship doctor who has written these articles." That was my opinion, but I was wrong. I have been through these documents. I have analysed them carefully. I say that the number of propositions that were attempted to be sustained in the Committee were few. There was evidence brought before the Committee, and that evidence divides itself into evidence adduced, evidence cited, evidence suppressed, and evidence misquoted. There was evidence adduced. There was, first, Mr. Gregson. Did he confirm that which was the *crux* of all the charges, about position? Did he agree with Dr. Lunn with regard to style of living? No. Did he confirm Dr. Lunn's testimony about going to Court? "With regard to 'presentation at Court,' Professor Patterson asked, 'Did you ever hear that expression used in India?'" Mr. Gregson replied, "Certainly not." That is the evidence that Mr. Hughes calls in support of Dr. Lunn! Does Mr. Kendall support that charge? He gives an estimate that a man's expenses may be covered by £105. Mr. Smith asks whether he managed to save the rest of his income? He replies, "No, I did not. There are many other ways in which money goes." Then there is evidence cited. There is a note from Mr. Bulman, and a very curious note it is. I do not know whether Mr. Bulman belongs to one or other of three classes in India—those who know missionary work and are in sympathy with it, those who oppose it, or those who are indifferent to it; but he says, "I have no hesitation in saying than 'an average income of £300 and a bungalow,' with extra allowances for children, is excessive. . . . Officers in my own service (which is regarded as a highly paid one) begin their career on no higher pay than that." From that statement what did Mr. Hughes say to the Committee? That Mr. Bulman had said that the officers in the Civil Service on the average lived in more luxury and comfort than the missionary on £300 a year. But that is not correct. Mr. Bulman makes the simple statement that they *begin* on £300 a year. My impression is that Mr. Evans is correct when he says that it is £400 a year. Does he sustain the scale of prices? Oh, no, because for a lighter diet he gives a heavier scale of prices. Then, Sir, with regard to the note from Mr. Caine. He says, " I have no hesitation in saying that a single man can get all he needs in India . . . . in company with not less than three other unmarried men . . . . for £200—£50 each." I think that is about one of the worst of all the proposals made. Then he speaks about living in a missionary's house where the missionary kept only one servant and a gardener, whose cost was only £100 a year. Now, if I had the man here, I have no doubt I should find that he too would admit that there are many other ways in which the money goes. Where, then, is this sustained? There is one thing that Mr. Caine is sure about. "I am sure (speaking of Mr. Hughes) you are well posted up for your discussion." (Laughter.) You and the Committee can judge of that. Now, Sir, you will remark that there has been very little attempt to produce evidence in support of such a tremendous indictment as the world has never seen before. God grant that our Connexion may never see it again! On the other side, I find that you have three witnesses before you —Mr. Evans, who has been ten and a-half years in India; Colonel Taylor, who has been thirty years; and Mr. Eales, who has been there forty years. Now that is a very different kind of testimony from that which is given in the note of Mr. Bulman and from that contained in Mr. Caine's letter. Do they sustain any one of the allegations? They do not. You also had suppressed testimony. You had the testimony of Mr. Betts, and I am sorry to say that you had that testimony misquoted. Here it is. " Professor Patterson: May I ask Mr. Hughes why Mr. Betts' account of the pay of foremen, and of the increase in the pay of engine-drivers on account of overtime and night work were omitted from his testimony? Mr. Hughes: Because I did not think the question of overtime was important. Professor Patterson: And yet these suppressed passages substantiate the statements of the Bangalore Conference which you were attacking!' But did not Mr. Hughes and Dr. Lunn know that the great bulk of the engine-drivers' work was night work? Dr. Lunn: No; we did not know that." Imagine a man who had been twelve months in the streets of London being asked whether he did not know that the bulk of the work of the omnibus men was done in the day time, and saying "No, I did not know that," and then suppressing the fact! There are many such propositions which would have appeared at once in a clear light to a man like Colonel Taylor, or Mr. Eales, or Mr. Evans, that appear in a very dim light to a man who never lived out of England. I entirely concur with the sentiment of Dr. Rigg that the Committee were profoundly right in expressing no sympathy with missionaries in India. I concur entirely with the sentiment that their deliverance ought to be as colourless as that of a jury. But the duty of a jury in giving a colourless deliverance is to mark the justice of the case. When a libel is simply untrue, and is not frivolous and vexatious, they say it is simply untrue; but when it is both untrue and frivolous and vexatious it is the duty of a jury to say it is untrue, frivolous and vexatious. (Hear, hear.)

Dr. RIGG: I think it will occur to many that the resolution which I have proposed is one which might be considered entirely apart from certain considerations that have been brought before us, yet, if this Committee thinks good *after* adopting these resolutions to bring forth any other resolution it would be in order to do so.

The resolution was then put to the meeting, and carried; one member of the Committee only declining to vote.

Dr. JENKINS gave notice of a resolution which he would move after dinner.

Mr. WALLER said that if it were in order he should be very glad to bring certain facts before the Committee as to the salaries paid to American missionaries.

Dr. STEPHENSON said that he thought that Mr. Waller's information would be most valuable to them, but suggested that it might be reserved for future consideration.

Mr. RATTENBURY thought that Mr. Waller's statement ought to be heard and embodied in their report.

Mr. HUGHES said that if Mr. Waller brought before the Committee some additional evidence, he should like to mention that the Rev. C. P. Hard, of the Methodist Episcopal Church in India, and who was second in official position to Bishop Thoburn, was in London, and that it might be well for him to be sent for to give evidence on the other side.

Mr. OLVER said that for all practical purposes it would be sufficient to say that the Secretary of the Conference had informed the Committee that he had very important communications to make, based upon documents which had been officially submitted to him during the year.

Mr. WALLER: In all these matters we require facts, and I think I ought to state what I know to be facts. I have not the slightest objection to Mr. Hard being summoned before this Committee, but I am going to submit to you certain official documents which have been put into my possession in order that we may correct what I am assured is an entire misapprehension on this side of the Atlantic as to what salaries are paid to American missionaries. I think the Committee ought to know what are the facts of the case.

Dr. STEPHENSON submitted that if they were to have any further resolutions bearing upon the personal question, it would be desirable that those resolutions should be taken before they embarked upon the very wide question which Mr. Hughes' remarks showed would have to be gone into very thoroughly indeed.

Dr. JENKINS said it was really very important that a resolution of the kind he wished to move should be prepared with great care, and in the midst of the excitement pervading that large Committee, it was impossible for him to satisfy himself as to the diction of the resolution which he should like to put before the Committee. If the Committee would wait a few minutes he would do his best to draw it up.

Mr. FOWLER: I would ask Dr. Jenkins, in the interests of peace and in the interests of the Missionary Society and in the interests of our work, which I think the Sub-committee regarded as paramount during the whole of their inquiry, not to press any resolution of a personal character. Dr. Rigg has done justice to the Sub-committee, and I think no more than justice, in saying that we endeavoured to discharge this very painful duty in a judicial manner, and we have come practically to a unanimous conclusion. Dr. Rigg will recollect that before we closed our deliberations we asked the combatants in this dispute if they would be content to accept the verdict of this Committee and close this unhappy controversy, and I am bound to say that on both sides that appeal was candidly and honourably responded to, and we have drawn up our report influenced by the belief that we were bringing to an end a very unhappy controversy which it is not in the interests of the Missionary Society of Methodism to prolong. Take our verdict for whatever it is worth. I am not going to say what it amounts to or what it does not amount to, but I do not think that anyone can find fault with it as being partial or vindictive or prejudiced. We have endeavoured to do what is right and fair. Now, I think if we had one resolution based on the two preceding paragraphs, couched in wise, statesmanlike words, and reflecting the judicial character of this Committee, and if we let it go before the Connexion, it will have weight with our people, and I believe it will tend to allay this storm. But as a practical man of the world I say if you attempt now, after the controversy so to speak has been judicially closed, to re-open it, to criticise the report, to amend so much on this side and so much on that, if you put us into the position of explaining and defending our report, it would have been better if you had not referred this matter to us at all. I entreat this Committee to have no more resolutions on this question. Close the matter. Undertake any inquiry which is necessary to be undertaken; get all the information you can from Mr. Waller and from everybody else—that question must be dealt with upon its own merits, and I have no doubt that the Missionary Committee, when it proceeds to deal with that question, will come to a just conclusion upon it—but so far as this public controversy is concerned it will end in the best manner if you let the resolution which has been passed unanimously go forth to the Connexion and to the world as the findings of this Committee. (Hear, hear.)

Mr. ARTHUR made a remark to the effect that he quite concurred with Mr. Fowler's view.

Dr. GREEVES said that his whole judgment was in accordance with Mr. Fowler's deliverance. He thought that if that Committee now began to discuss further questions it would be very unwise and would very likely lead to a divided vote which would not impress the Connexion with their unanimity. At the same time he felt bound to say that he could not hold himself pledged not to bring this matter before the Pastoral Conference. They stood committed to the fact that some of their brethren had dealt shabbily with truthfulness. The doctrine seemed to be allowed that statements need not be accurately made so long as they were bold—that it was right sometimes to tell part of the truth if that would strengthen a case—that they might give an extract from evidence, when if they gave the whole the result would be quite the opposite of that which they wished to produce, that if these misdoings were brought home to them they were not bound honestly to retract them, but to aver that if they had made by accident impressions which were false impressions, they were not bound to correct those impressions. Now, these things went against his conscience, they went against the doctrine which he had taught his children and his people, and he did not think they could without debate allow the Conference to seem to be committed to them. He could quite believe that there might be a good deal to say about journalists and their responsibilities; but that he did not believe in—he was prepared to trample it down. He wanted his brethren to understand that, whilst he did not think it came within the province of that Committee to deal with ministerial character, he should not feel that his conscience was discharged unless he reserved to himself the right of saying in the Conference that, in his judgment, the documents before him gave evidence of a great breach of the Saviour's command. (Hear, hear.)

Mr. ALLEN said he sympathised to a great extent with Dr. Greeves' remarks, but he was inclined to think on reflection that it would be a mistake if they were to pass a strongly worded resolution condemning that whole business. He thought it would be a calamity if they were to do anything to prolong what might be called a party discussion of that whole question. At the same time he felt that they could not rest just where they were, and he was disposed at that moment to make a suggestion to Mr. Hughes if he would accept it. At the last meeting of that Committee he (Mr. Hughes) made a statement to this effect: "If these articles are proved to be without foundation, of course they must be withdrawn." Well, it seemed to him that if he were in Mr. Hughes' position he would withdraw the articles—he would do so candidly and honourably; and he thought that if Mr. Hughes did that it would relieve the difficulty. (Hear, hear.) He was sure that it would save Mr. Hughes from a very painful position, for when party newspapers got hold of that document they would discuss it, and they would say very strong things. Now, nothing would tend to check a discussion of that kind more than a candid withdrawal of the articles by Mr. Hughes. (Hear, hear.)

Dr. JENKINS said that, in the interests of what was more valuable than anything else, he would not press his resolution. He was glad for the conversation that had taken place, and he thought it would do good service. As for what Mr. Allen had said, he attached great weight to the request he had made to a man whom he had always highly respected and deeply loved. (Hear, hear.) He thought that in former years his (Dr. Jenkins') words would have had some weight with him. He would now affectionately ask him to contribute something towards the peace which they all longed for. He could do that more effectually than could any other brother, and he thought that what he knew to be groundless in the accusations he should retract, and those who knew him would not misinterpret that act. It would not diminish in any sense that very high reputation for honourable conduct which had always distinguished him. This was a great crisis in their Connexion, and no one could do more than their dear brother Hughes towards settling that dispute, and what he asked was that what he knew to be groundless he should withdraw. (Hear, hear.)

Mr. HUGHES: I do not need any appeal from Mr. Jenkins to withdraw anything that I feel to be groundless. All that I can do I am prepared to do. There is one point on which I think a great mistake has been made, and that is the one to which Mr. Arthur has referred—viz., the omission of a statement from the letter affecting Indian Railway employés wages with respect to overtime. I confess that I had not any idea at the time that overtime and night-work were an important item in the account. I can only assure the Committee that that was not suppressed in any way designedly, and I am prepared, publicly, to state that I very much regret what was purely accidental and unintentional. I believe that there was also a minor error with respect to the stipends of the London Society's missionaries. We did not take into account the whole of the benefit that they obtained by sending money to this country at par. That also I shall be very happy to correct. I, of course, accept the verdict of the Sub-committee; but I do not know by what process, mental or moral, I can compel myself to believe everything that members of this Committee wish me to believe. I accept the decisions of the Sub-committee, and am prepared to act upon them, I do not know what more I can do. You cannot force a man's convictions. I can only say with respect to Dr. Greeves' charge of personal dishonesty that I appeal from Dr. Greeves to God. It is the most painful statement that was ever made respecting me since I was born. I cannot believe that even yesterday God would have blessed me as He did if I were the dishonest man Dr. Greeves asserts I am. I am quite prepared to admit that if it is a fact (as stated by the Sub-committee under head No. 3 on page 6) that on the whole there is no substantial difference between the purchasing power of money in India and in England, that in that case the original statements in the article on the "Via Media" were extravagantly absurd, and they must all fall to the ground. I am prepared to treat them as such. I believe that the decision of the Sub-committee is inconsistent with the accuracy of the second article. As to what our private opinion may be, I am unable to coerce my own judgment, but I am prepared to accept the decision of the Committee, to act upon it, and in all future discussions to assume their statements as axiomatic. I am bound to add, however, that it seems to me that the verdict which the Sub-committee give is not consistent with the financial suggestions which they make at the end of their Report. I hold that the Indian missionaries are entitled to the full benefit of the verdict in their favour. After accepting this verdict, I should strenuously resist the reduction of any Indian missionary's stipend by a single sixpence.

Mr. SMITH: I rise to order. The Sub-committee did not wish to express any opinion on the subject of stipends.

Mr. HUGHES continued: No man who knows the state of our finances would venture to say that it is possible to propose in this Committee that the nominal stipend should be raised from £230 to £307, which is what must be done if the Indian missionaries are to be paid in a depreciated silver currency, without suffering a reduction of salary. I say that practically that recommendation means a very serious reduction of stipends —a reduction of about £60 a year. I merely mention it here to show how logically and fully I accept the decision of the Committee. As to the statement that our missionaries are "living in luxury," I am prepared to base all my future public utterances with respect to this issue on the Sub-committee Report. Controversies of this kind must be brought to a close. I entirely repudiate the construction which members of this Committee have put upon the original articles. It must not be forgotten that more than twelve months ago I entirely repudiated that construction. I voted for the resolution that has just been passed. We deeply regret any pain that we have unintentionally caused any of our Indian missionaries. I speak for Dr. Lunn as well as myself. I hope Dr. Lunn will have full credit for that. There is something in Dr. Lunn's manner when he is nervous which causes much misconception and injustice. I have always said that what we wanted to do was to discuss policy, and nothing that in the least degree affected character. I believe now, as I have always believed, that the first part of Dr. Rigg's resolution is perfectly true. I have always done what I could for the Missionary Society, which I greatly love.

Mr. FOWLER made a remark to the effect that Mr. Hughes had put an incorrect construction upon the finding of the Sub-committee; the point of his explanation was that notwithstanding the reduction of the gold value of the rupee on exchange between India and England the purchasing power of the rupee in India had not been depreciated; and that, therefore, any addition to the number of rupees paid in India was a corresponding addition to the stipends. He specially called the attention of the Committee to the letter which appeared in *The Methodist Recorder* from Mr. Isaac Hoyle, M.P., in confirmation and explanation of his assertion.

The PRESIDENT: I wish Mr. Hughes would make a distinct declaration to this effect: That seeing the Committee had found so and so, he retracts the statements which this Committee has found to be incorrect.

Mr. HUGHES: It is most hateful to me to appear to hesitate to do frankly what the President and others request me to do. I am prepared to say publicly that I accept the decision of this Committee. I do not know what more I can do consistently. In the sense in which you understand the articles I did withdraw them, as soon as I found that any one put such a construction on them. Moreover, I very much regret that they were written in a form which admitted of that construction. Now that we have had a prolonged and bitter controversy, I am in a very different position from that which I occupied originally. I also have to complain of much injustice, and while I am prepared to repudiate the construction that was put upon the articles, and to accept the decision of this Committee *ex animo*, I do not know what more I can do.

Mr. ALLEN: May I point out where I consider the weakness of Mr. Hughes lies? In many of the statements made he has exaggerated to an enormous extent, and, if he will allow me to say so, that is a characteristic of the man. He has so much force that whenever he expresses himself he goes miles farther than he ought to go. Now, I am afraid lest by a note in his paper he should say, "Well, I accept the decision of the Committee, but I have my own convictions still."

Mr. HUGHES: I am prepared to accept the decision of this Committee, and to say that in future everyone must accept that decision as the basis of discussion. (Hear, hear.)

Mr. FLETCHER hoped that no further pressure would be brought to bear on Mr. Hughes. (Hear, hear.)

Mr. OLVER said it would entirely depend upon the course which Mr. Hughes and Dr. Lunn took in the *Methodist Times* as to whether that business were to close or whether they were to go on with one of the most terrific contests that had ever wrought mischief in Methodism within the last thirty years. Before the Committee closed its session he thought that it should express its great satisfaction that their missionaries in India had been so completely exonerated. He begged to move that.

Mr. HEDGES appealed as a layman to Mr. Hughes to retract the articles to which reference had been made, and to make his retraction as public as the articles themselves. He seconded Mr. Olver's resolution.

Dr. RIGG hoped the Committee would adopt the resolution. He congratulated his brethren from India that they had come out of the ordeal as they had, and as he had always expected they would. He hoped that the admirable illustration of the history and condition of their Indian Missions contributed by Mr. Patterson and Mr. Findlay would be read by all their people. (Hear, hear.) If the literature on this subject were widely diffused and read by all who were interested in Methodist Missions he thought the Society would surmount its present difficulties and that confidence would be restored. (Hear, hear.)

Dr. STEPHENSON said he believed that Mr. Hughes would endeavour not only in word, but also in spirit, to act up to what he had said in that Committee. As for the resolution it did not exactly meet his view. He thought they ought not to separate without assuring their Indian brethren of their sympathy with them in the circumstances in which they were found. He suggested that some expression of their sympathy should be embodied in the resolution.

Mr. OLVER did not think that his brethren from India desired any expression of sympathy. Sympathy whilst they were in the midst of the fight helped to sustain them, but now the fight was over, and they thanked God that he had vindicated their righteousness.

Messrs. POSNETT, GARRETT, and ARTHUR supported the resolution.

Mr. CANDLER objected to any further resolution.

The PRESIDENT: The resolution reads as follows :—

"That this Committee expresses its great satisfaction that its missionaries in India have been thus so completely exonerated, and records its profound regret that charges so grave and so unsustained should ever have been brought against them." Those in favour show hands.

The result of the vote was that all with one exception voted in favour of it.

www.ingramcontent.com/pod-product-compliance
Lightning Source LLC
Chambersburg PA
CBHW031415230426
43668CB00007B/315